To Die In Chicago

Confederate Prisoners

at Camp Douglas

1862—1865

BY

George Levy

Evanston Publishing, Inc.
Evanston, Illinois 60201

Evanston Publishing, Inc.
1571 Sherman Avenue, Annex C
Evanston, IL 60201

Printed in the U.S.A.

10 9 8 7 6 5 4 3 2 1

Library or Congress Number: 94-070759

ISBN: 1-879260-20-4

ACKNOWLEDGMENTS

The staffs of following archives and libraries graciously made their material available.

Interlibrary Loan, Roosevelt University
Library of Congress–Prints & Photos-Manuscripts
U. S. Army Military History Institute
Chicago Historical Society
Newberry Library, Chicago
Chicago Park District
Chicago Public Library
Louisiana State University, Middleton Library
American Philatelic Society
Duke University, Perkins Library
St. James Catholic Church
Museum of the Confederacy
Rush Presbyterian-St. Luke's Medical Center
Moody Bible Institute
University of Kentucky Library
North Carolina State Archives
Tennessee State Archives
Illinois State Historical Library
The Filson Club, Louisville

A number of persons willingly assisted me in my requests for information and documents.

Eileen Flanagan–Chicago Historical Society
Sara Schwartz–Illinois Regional Archives Depository
Soubretta Skyles—Oak Woods Cemetery
Charlotte Wells—Hebrew Benevolent Cemetery
Michael Musick—National Archives
Richard Popp—Special Collections, University of Chicago
Mary Michals—Illinois State Historical Library
Dr. Wayne C. Temple—Illinois State Archives
Mark W. Sorensen—Illinois State Archives
Paul Brockman—Indiana Historical Society
Dr. Richard J. Sommers—USAMHI
Michael Winey—USAMHI

INTRODUCTION

Camp Douglas was not meant to be a prison. Construction began on a military depot at the southeastern limits of Chicago in the fall of 1861. Barracks and stables were prepared for about 8,000 troops. Suddenly, in that bitter winter of 1861-62, some men appeared at the edge of the city. These strangers felt like foreigners, with their accents and thin clothing. They wondered what sort of place had they come to? What chance did they have to survive in the arctic climate? As they would soon find out, Chicago would become the largest Confederate burial site outside of the South.

To Die In Chicago describes the reaction of the citizens and Confederates as thousands of prisoners were dumped on the camp after Union victories in the west. I specifically wrote this book to go beyond statistics and to probe the feelings and experiences of the Southerners in an alien climate, often without sufficient food, clothing, shelter, or medical care. Extensive research in archives, libraries, historical societies, and newspapers, has developed important new information on the camp, especially since the only other book about Camp Douglas was published in 1865:

The Henry Morton Stanley Hoax. Historians have relied upon his harrowing account of life as a Confederate prisoner of war at Camp Douglas before he became a famous explorer; his story was a fabrication.

The Black Prisoners of War. Heretofore an unpublished story: black Confederates were imprisoned at Camp Douglas, with some held there illegally by the army until late in the war.

The University of Chicago. Inadvertently placed in the line of fire by a bequest of Senator Douglas, it was separated from the camp by only a country lane, its life threatened throughout the war by the Camp's diseases and controversies.

The Religion Issue. Conflicts constantly arose between Chicago clergymen and the commanding officers over a chapel and access to the prisoners for preaching and evangelical work.

The Fate of the Confederate Dead. Historical detective work tracks the remains of prisoners to five cemeteries in and around Chicago and discloses the indifference and mismanagement attending the burials.

The Commanders. Biographical sketches of the nine men who served as commandants from 1862-65 became one of the organizational themes of the book, and there is a full description of how their different personalities and goals affected the lives of the prisoners.

The Parolees. Union prisoners of war captured by the South in the debacle at Harper's Ferry found themselves prisoners at Camp Douglas, treated no better than Confederate POWs.

Other major areas of interest. Great escapes and near misses: the quartet of Nazi-like guards; running-water toilets and a hospital years ahead of their time; the beef scandal, involving President Lincoln's brother-in-law, and the cover-up to protect him; a judicious examination of the famous "Chicago Conspiracy" to free the prisoners at Camp Douglas.

This book is the first complete and accurate picture of the prisoners and Camp Douglas, itself.

-George Levy
January, 1994

TABLE OF CONTENTS

1.

CHICAGO, WAR CAPITAL OF THE WEST

Chicago, more than any other city in the North, was responsible for the Civil War, according to President Lincoln. When Joseph Medill, editor of the *Chicago Tribune*, requested the president to lower the draft quota for Chicago, Mr. Lincoln turned to him with a "black and frowning face."

"After Boston, Chicago has been the chief instrument in bringing this war on the country," Lincoln said. "The Northwest has opposed the South as New England has opposed the South. It is you who are largely responsible for making the blood flow as it has. You called for war until we had it. You called for emancipation and I have given it to you. Now you come here begging to be let off from the call for men which I have made to carry out the war you have demanded."[1]

Surely, the president exaggerated. However, it is true that most Chicagoans supported the war enthusiastically, and per capita supplied more volunteers than any other city in the Union. Mr. Medill went home after his meeting with the president and raised 6,000 more men, for a total of 28,000 soldiers out of a population of 156,000.[2] It is fair to say that Chicago Republicans engineered Mr. Lincoln's nomination by bringing the convention to their city in 1860 and building the famous Wigwam Convention Center. The Fort Dearborn settlement had become the power-broker of 1860.

Lacking any railroads, it required seven days to make the trip from New York to Chicago in 1848. There were no sewers or sidewalks; in bad weather streets were impassable, and the city was deprived of its mail for a week at a time. There was no gas or water supply, and six blocks away from the court house was considered out of town, "where wolves were yet occasionally seen prowling about, and residents lived in true country fashion."[3]

Completion of the Illinois and Michigan Canal in April of 1848 brought in thousands of tons of freight. This set off a building boom from 1851 to 1853, which included the combined court house and city hall. By 1856 there were 145 stores, several hundred residences, and five hotels. Telegraph service opened in 1848, and the gas works were completed in 1850, with service to 2,000 consumers by 1855.[4]

At this time, the railroads coming into Chicago caused a rapid transition from an agricultural to an industrial and commercial society. The city's slaughterhouses, meat-packing industry, textiles, and storage silos could feed and clothe many troops and prisoners of war. There were 2,933 miles of railroad track touching Chicago, 10 trunk lines, and 11 branch lines. The Michigan Central hauled 3,400 immigrants into town on a single day.[5] Chicago's transportation axis was also responsible for Camp Douglas becoming a military base, and later a prisoner of war camp and collection center for parolees.

The growth of lake traffic was almost as spectacular as railroad expansion. Lumber, iron, and goods from the east moved to wharves on the Chicago River, while farm crops were carried away to mills in New York and New England.[6] Construction on a water tower and a timber crib built 600 feet out in Lake Michigan began in 1853. Water was conducted into a well near the water tower and pumped 136 feet to the top. Reservoirs were built around the city to hold one night's water supply and connected to the tower. Water began flowing in 1854.[7]

Meanwhile, streets, alleys, and vacant lots reeked with filth. The trash and slop from houses were tossed into the streets, and the city drank water which was polluted by manure piled on the lakefront. Chicago had the highest death rate of any city in the United States in 1855. Later, this had serious consequences for Camp Douglas when the Chicago Common Council ordered the city to supply it with water free of charge. The city also had another major problem; it was sinking into the mud because it was only four to six feet above the river.[8]

Mrs. Joseph Frederick Ward described the situation as frightful with deep holes in the streets marked "No Bottom." "A frequent sight was a cart stuck fast and abandoned. I remember one such cart deeply imbedded in the mud just in front of McVicker's Theater."[9]

Medicine in Chicago was primitive when at least six Chicago doctors would be treating prisoners at Camp Douglas. They subscribed to the "miasma" theory of medicine, that a vapor rising from decomposing matter carried diseases through the air. When a railroad mechanic sought medical treatment for his wife's ear-ache, a Chicago doctor prescribed roasted onions.[10] Her husband does not say whether she was supposed to eat them.

Beside the commercial and industrial forces, there was also a religious movement revived by the Panic of 1857, which carried over into intense Fundamentalist activity among the prisoners.

"During the pitiless winter of 1857-58 men of the cloth spoke in daily meetings and by mid-March, 1858, recorded over 250 conversions. Morning and noon prayer meetings brought about striking manifestations of the Spirit's power. Testimonials from gamblers, drunkards, and degenerates of all stripes added to the gatherings, something wholly new in the annals of Chicago."[11]

The plank roads that carried freight had been replaced by the rails of the Galena & Chicago Railroad, and the Illinois Central Railroad had built its way into the city to become the longest railroad in America, a conduit between Chicago and the victorious Union armies in the West.

In spite of the Panic of 1857 (really a depression), the Chicago Board of Trade had increased its membership to 600 in 1860. The population of the city stood at 109,206. Chicago real estate was worth $37,053,512. This was one of a quarter billion dollars in today's money, and the city and county were collecting $373,515 yearly in real estate taxes.[12] Citizens could boast of a dozen newspapers, a fire department, four district schools, a mechanics' institute, a medical college, and 15 churches.[13] In addition, the town possessed the infrastructure for a war capital: a foundation of roads, power plants, transportation, and communications. Moreover, a supply of skilled labor, tools, and construction materials was available to construct a military base.

Five streets had buildings as far out as two miles from downtown in 1860. Otherwise, nothing reached further than a mile and a half from the Court House. However, the young city was now raised, drained, and connected to every part of the country by rail and wire. Streets were made of planks, cobblestones, and wooden blocks. Swing bridges spanned the river and horse-drawn street railways began to operate. Gas, water, coal, and stone were plentiful.[14]

Municipal government was based upon the election of two aldermen per ward in the Common Council, for a total of 32 when the war started. The mayor served only a two-year term. The people had a good deal of input, electing every department head including the city attorney, city physician, police board, and fire chiefs.[15] The firing on Fort Sumter, April 12, 1861, inspired an immense meeting in the city to voice the sentiments of the people.

"The speech of Mr. Lovejoy was followed by the Star Spangled Banner sung in splendid style by Frank Lumbard, the vast audience swelling the chorus with an intensity of feeling and effect we have never seen equalled."[16]

Chicago held a double war meeting a few days later. "It would be impossible to describe the wild enthusiasm of the double meeting at Bryan and Metropolitan Halls last evening, called to procure subscriptions for the immediate expenses of our volunteers. The money came down like rain, and the people rushed forward in unprecedented numbers at the various military headquarters to enroll in defense of the flag."[17]

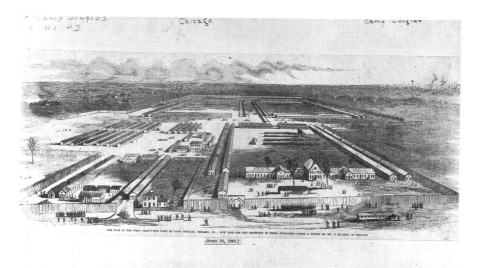

Early lithography of Camp Douglas, circa April 26, 1862. (courtesy Chicago Historical Society).

The Wigwam Convention Center was renamed the National Hall, and at a meeting there on April 20, 10,000 people occupied all available space, and half as many were turned away. Because it was rumored that traitors were present, a judge administered the oath of allegiance to the meeting en masse. No doubt this war fever was common in many northern cities, though it had special significance for Chicago, where some 27,000 prisoners would arrive. [18] How the city immediately reacted to them is an essential part of the Camp Douglas story.

Senator Stephen A. Douglas was only 48 years of age when he and his wife, Adele, reached the Tremont House in Chicago on May 1, 1861. The next day he became ill. On June 3, 1861 he was dead. He had worked too hard, eaten too much, drank too heavily, and chewed tobacco.[19]

It is ironic that his name was given to the camp that became notorious in the South. In 1859, he had written to an autograph seeker "that this Union can exist forever divided into free and slave states, as our fathers made it, if the Constitution be preserved inviolate." However, he supported

The Graves homestead with Cottage Grove Avenue in the foreground circa, 1872. Note street car tracks (courtesy Chicago Historical Society).

the North in the war, and his "Save the Flag" speech to the Illinois General Assembly on April 15, 1861 made him popular to Union sympathizers.[20]

The government made heavy use of Douglas property near the camp, although is unlikely that any rent was paid. The camp's smallpox hospital was located there, and about four rows of garrison barracks opposite the south fence may have occupied the property sometime between 1862 and 1864.[21]

Records show that the stockade included 30.5 acres owned by Henry Graves. The area was known as "Cottage Grove" because of the Graves' cottage and the grove in which it stood. In 1851 there were only two houses nearby. Ten years later there were a dozen houses in the vicinity. Mr. Graves did not consent to the taking of his land and refused to move. The property had been leased at the time, and his tenant had allowed the state to take it over.[22] The stockade enclosed the Graves' residence on all sides except Cottage Grove Avenue. He and his wife stayed throughout the war.

One reason for locating the camp there was the prairie that extended around for miles. The isolated area was located four miles southeast of downtown Chicago. Nearby Lake Michigan meant an abundant supply of

Henry Graves, circa 1880 (courtesy special collections, Chicago Historical Society).

water, and Judge Allan C. Fuller, acting for Illinois Governor Yates, selected the site.[23] An army engineer would have been a better selector because of the numerous problems associated with it.

The stockade fronted Cottage Grove, then ran west four blocks to Kankakee Avenue, now Martin Luther King Drive. Henry Graves and others met on June 4, 1878 to find the site and thought that the western fence sometimes extended two blocks further west.[24] It was bounded on the north by East 31st Street (Ridgley Place), and on the south by East 33rd Place (College Place). The enclosed area measured eighty acres. A wooden sewer was located at the foot of east 33rd Street (Cook Place), as well as the posts to the main entrance of the camp.

Camp Douglas changed constantly, but usually had three divisions (page 8). The eastern division with the flagpole was "Garrison Square," containing officer's quarters, a post office, post headquarters, and a parade ground. Adjoining it to the south was the Graves' residence and "White Oak Square," so called because it housed the infamous White Oak dungeon.

The enlisted men's quarters were in White Oak Square, and housed prisoners also until Prison Square was built in the western division of the camp. White Oak was later merged with Hospital Square, which contained the prison hospitals and a morgue. The western division held the post hospital, warehouses, and surgeon's quarters.[25] Not visible on the map are two roadways that intersected the camp from north to south and east to west. Water entered through a hydrant in the northeast corner of camp.

Surrounding the camp and separating the various compounds within were three miles of high board fence.[26] The height of the fence has been a matter of controversy, but it appears that 6 feet is the most accurate estimate for the year 1862. However, this was not the extent of Camp Douglas. Troops camped outside the stockade as far as four blocks west. The irregular shape of the camp marked the boundary lines of a few abutting land owners.

The main entrance was on Cottage Grove. Access to the Douglas property was through the gate in the south fence. Illinois Central tracks, which brought many prisoners to Chicago, were about 200 yards east, and the camp soon had its own railway station.

Originally, Camp Douglas was a series of regimental camps with several names. The opening of the new Camp Douglas for recruiting, organizing, and training is described by the *Tribune* on September 30, 1861. "Arrangements have been made with the Illinois Central to give a new crossing and secure ready access to the lake shore. The water in the camp will be supplied direct from city hydrants on the grounds. The City Railway Company are to carry, free, officers and soldiers on the business of the camps." This railway ran on a single track with horse-drawn cars that came out from downtown Chicago.[27]

Public transportation to the area began in 1860, due to the influence of Senator Douglas, who had invested in a large tract of land called Oakenwald and built a home there. His land faced the camp for three blocks on the east side of Cottage Grove, from where it extended to railroad tracks on the shore of Lake Michigan about 200 yards east. Douglas land was also located on the west side of Cottage Grove and abutted the camp's south fence. The old University of Chicago was established on this property before the war.

No one knew that Camp Douglas would also serve as a major prisoner of war camp. First of all, the problem with the foul drinking water was serious enough. In addition, the site lacked sewers, power, and gas, and the prairie could not absorb the human and animal waste generated by thousands of men and horses. The site was a serious mistake.

The first commandant of the new Camp Douglas, and the person responsible for building it, was Colonel Joseph H. Tucker. Born in 1819, he arrived in Chicago in 1858 from Cumberland, Maryland, where he had headed a bank. He was successful in different types of speculative trading in Chicago, was a partner in a commodities firm, and sat on the Chicago Board of Trade by 1861. While his main occupation was business, he enjoyed part-time military life as a Colonel in the 60th Regiment Illinois State Militia. Illinois Governor Yates appointed Colonel Tucker in the summer of 1861 to take command of the Northern Military District of the State of Illinois.[28]

This district comprised the northern 24 counties of the state of Illinois. The Post meant creating Camp Douglas and command responsibilities as a military base, a prisoner of war camp, and camp for paroled U.S. troops waiting to be exchanged. Under future exchange agreements between the North and South, prisoners were returned to their respective sides on parole until exchanged according to a formula. The camp enclosure was not large enough to hold more than 8,000 troops and 2,000 horses.

Barracks were built in October and November 1861, mainly by troops called the Mechanic Fusileers. These buildings were wooden structures, designed after the customary army barracks of one story, 105 feet long, 24 feet wide, with nine-foot walls divided into three rooms, each containing two stoves. Each housed 180 men, and cost $800 to build. They were made "of a single thickness of pine boards, without plastering or ceiling."[29] The seams of the upright pine boards were covered by narrow wooden strips, and the roofs were covered with tar paper.

A young recruit named Benjamin J. Smith arrived at camp by street car on October 11, 1861 to find "long lines of barracks newly constructed, and clean and comfortable."[30] Double bunks were arranged along one side of the barrack. In the rear of each barrack was a kitchen with a long table and benches for 100 men. It is possible that these structures were combined later into one building about 300 feet long. The state attempted to press the fusileers into service as infantry after the barracks were completed, and they mutinied on December 18, 1861. Smith saw action sooner than he had expected, and described it to the folks at home.

"A regiment called the Mechanics Fusileers mutinied last night and our boys were ordered out to put the laws in force. They had torn down about 40 yards of fence and burned it, and altogether it was quite a rebellion, but the sight of our bayonets had a very soothing influence on them, and they went to work and built the fence up again."[31]

The story had a positive ending when the fusileers paraded in Chicago, and stopped at a saloon downtown for a fill of lager beer, before being discharged. However, the Fusileers' chaplain had left his congregation to take the appointment, and now was unemployed. He wrote to President Lincoln requesting an appointment at Camp Douglas because of the fusileers being discharged. "I therefore feel that I have some claim to an appointment which many other clergymen have not."[32] He was not successful.

On November 15, 1861 there were 4,222 troops on hand from 11 regiments.[33] Serious cases of measles were present by December 15, 1861. A recruit who had been suffering in the hospital for a week wrote, "The provisions that they furnish is nothing extra Betty. I am very weak. It is all that I can do to hold my pencil." Measles remained a serious problem as late as October 21, 1863, when a prisoner wrote to his mother that his health was good, but expressed fear of getting the measles for himself and his brother, also a prisoner.[34]

The consolidated morning reports in 1861 show an astonishing death rate for troops who were in excellent condition, especially compared to the prisoners.[35] Private Benjamin Smith's bunk mate caught a bad cold and died on January 18, 1862. The recruits suffered 42 deaths from disease in four months, a bad omen for the future prison camp.

NOTES TO CHAPTER 1.

Note: All endnotes use the following abbreviations:

CHS — Chicago Historical Society
CWTI — Civil War Times Illustrated
ISHL — Illinois State Hisotrical Society
LOC — Library of Congress
NA — National Archives
OR — Official Records of the War of the Rebellion
RG — Record Group in the National Archives
USAMHI — U.S. Army Military History Institute
VRC — Veteran Reserve Corps.

[1] Emmet Dedmon, *Fabulous Chicago* (New York : Random House, 1954), 70.

[2] Dedmon, *Fabulous Chicago,* 70.

[3] John Moses and Joseph Kirkland, *History of Chicago,* Vol. I (Chicago: Munsell & Co. 1895), 119.

[4] Moses and Kirkland, 1:119-20.

[5] Herman Kogan and Lloyd Wendt, *Pictorial History of Chicago* (New York: E.P. Putnam & Co., 1958), 85.

[6] Harold Mayer and Richard Wade, *Chicago: Growth of a Metropolis* (Chicago: University of Chicago Press, 1969), 42.

[7] Moses and Kirkland, *History of Chicago,* I:120-21.

[8] Lloyd Lewis and Henry Justin Smith, *Chicago, The History of Its Reputation* (New York: Harcourt, Brace & Co., 1929), 65-66; Common Council Proceedings, 21 October 1861, File 0190, Illinois Regional Archives Depository, Northeastern Illinois University.

[9] Caroline Kirkland, *Chicago Yesterdays* (Chicago: Doughaday & Co., 1919), 88.

[10] *History of Medicine and Surgery and Physicians and Surgeons of Chicago* (Chicago:Biographical Publishing Corp., 1922), 73; Diary of Robert Tarrant, ms., CHS.

[11] Bessie Louise Pierce, *A History of Chicago* (Chicago: University of Chicago Press, 1940), 376.

[12] Moses and Kirkland, *History of Chicago,*I:146.

[13] Moses and Kirkland, *History of Chicago* I: 119.

[14] Lewis and Smith, *Chicago,* 95; Joseph Kirkland, *The Story of Chicago* (Chicago: Dibble Publishing Co., 1892), 255.

[15] Weston A. Goodspeed and Daniel D. Healy, *History of Cook County,* Vol.I (Chicago: Goodspeed Historical Ass'n, 1909), 306.

[16] Goodspeed,*History of Cook County,*I:434-35.

[17] Goodspeed and Healy, *History of Cook County,*I:436-37.

[18] E.B. Long, Camp Douglas: " A Hellish Den," *Chicago History* (Fall 1970): 94.

[19] Wayne C. Temple, Ph.D, *Stephen A. Douglas, Freemason* (Bloomington: The Masonic Book Club, 1982), 52.

[20] Robert W. Johannsen, *Letters of Stephen A. Douglas* (Urbana: University of Illinois Press, 1961), 437; Temple, *Stephen A. Douglas,* 49-50.

[21] Prints and Photo Dept., CHS.

[22] Chicago Title and Trust Co., (Pre-fire records, Tract book 340), 185-89, 192-95; Philip M. Hauser and Evelyn M. Kitagawa, *Local Community Fact Book for Chicago, 1950* (Chicago: University of Chicago, 1953), 146; Charles Cleaver, in *Reminiscences of Chicago During the Forties and Fifties,* Mabel McIlvaine, ed. (Chicago: Lakeside Press, R. R. Donnelley & Sons Co., 1913), 59; R. G. 92;

[23] William Bross, "History of Camp Douglas." Paper read before the Chicago Historical Society, June 18, 1875, in *Reminiscences of Chicago During the Civil War,* Mabel McIlvaine, ed. (Chicago: Lakeside Press, R.R. Donnelley & Sons Co., 1914), 164; Chicago Tribune, 28 Feb. 1862.

[24] Bross, *History of Camp Douglas,* 163.

[25] Camp Douglas newspaper file, CHS.

[26] Joseph L. Eisendrath, Jr., "Chicago's Camp Douglas," *Journal of the Illinois State Historical Society,* 55 (Spring 1960):37-63.

[27] Jesse L. Rosenberger, *Through Three Centuries* (Chicago, University of Chicago Press, 1922), 83.

[28] Unidentified newspaper clipping, 24 Oct. 1894, CHS; Elias Colbert, *Chicago. Historical and Statistical Sketch of the Garden City* (Chicago: P.T. Sherlock, 1868), 93.

[29] *Official Records of the War of the Rebellion* (Washington: U. S. Government Printing Office, 1901), Series II-Volume III, 56; B.R. Froman, "An Interior View of the Camp Douglas Conspiracy," *Southern Bivouac* 1-No.2 (Oct. 1882): 64.

[30] Benjamin J. Smith, 51st Illinois Infantry, Co. C. "Recollections of the Late War," 9. msc, Illinois State Historical Library

[31] James Buckley, Co, f, 45th Infantry Regiment Illinois Volunteers, Courtesy of Alan C. Hunt, Springfield, IL.

[32] *Chicago Tribune,* 6 Feb. 1862; Reverend James Bassett, 30 May 1862, ISHL.

[33] *Report of the Adj. Gen. of the State of Illinois,* 1861-66, (Springfield: H. W. Rockker, 1886) Vol. 1, 122.

[34] Letters of George Russell, Douglas Brigade, ISHL; Frank Wintersmith to his mother; Manning-Biggs Family Papers, 1863-1939. University of Kentucky, Lexington.

[35] "Consolidated Morning Reports for Camp Douglas," Illinois State Archives, Springfield.

2.

TROUBLE AT CAMP

A rumor was flying about that orders had been received to put Camp Douglas in readiness for the accommodation of 5,000 rebel prisoners. In a classic case of bad timing, the *Chicago Tribune* lampooned it as the joke of the season, but made an amazing prediction.

"The idea of keeping five thousand prisoners in a camp, where the strongest guard couldn't keep in a drunken corporal is rich. The whole population would have to mount guard and Chicago would find herself in possession of an elephant of the largest description."[1]

Camp Douglas could not keep its own troops from going AWOL. There was never any question of prisoners escaping, only how many would. The poor quality of some volunteers exasperated Colonel Tucker. He complained that "recruits are being brought into the camp who for various causes are utterly unfit to be sworn into the service," and charged that "the lack of discipline on the part of the men is due to the utter incompetency and entire negligence of the company officers."[2]

Many officers dressed like enlisted men and lived in their barracks instead of occupying officers' quarters. From January 1, 1862 through the end of August, 1,037 men were court martialed for drunkenness, insubordination, fighting, playing cards with the prisoners, and shooting an officer.[3] Theft, destruction of property, and desertion was rampant. A deserter from the Irish Brigade had to be bound hand and foot to get him back to camp.[4]

Chicagoans were more in danger from the garrison than from the prisoners. "Careless handling of guns had wounded one citizen while he was sitting in his home. A bullet smashed into a school house, and would have killed some children were any present. "Hen houses around camp were rifled, soldiers robbed citizens of watches, and Union deserters were on the prowl." An officer of the Irish Brigade menaced passengers with his pistol on the State Street car going to Cottage Grove. When a policeman attempted to interfere, the officer and several of his comrades locked him in White Oak dungeon.[5]

One marvels that the North ever gained the final victory. It seems that the prisoners were not the only ones who had seceded from the Union. Surprisingly, these undisciplined rowdies went on to compile impressive combat records, not the least of whom were the Irish Brigade. Meanwhile, they created serious security problems at camp, although they were a minority of the 40,000 recruits who came there for outfitting and training.

A school teacher at camp named Tebbets wrote his parents that he enlisted because his fellow townsmen had given up everything to go to war, "and we staying at home like cowards until those rebels tear down and destroy the best government that ever was; a government for which our forefathers fought bled and died. I have left a loving & beloved wife and five little children but I will not attempt to describe to you the sorrow it has caused but would only say that it is a great sacrifice."[6] Private Tebbets was knocked down by a bullet at Fort Donelson and narrowly escaped death by shell fire. He was killed in action at Shiloh on April 6, 1862.

The battle of Fort Donelson on February 16, 1862 set General Grant on the road to the White House and caused the name "Camp Douglas" to fill narratives and reminiscences well into the next century.[7] Word of the surrender of the Confederate stronghold thrilled the North as its first major victory of the war. No thought was given about what to do with the 12 to 15 thousand prisoners. It was General Grant's duty only to collect them, but the prisoners became the immediate responsibility of General Henry W. Halleck in St. Louis, who commanded the Department of Missouri.

The Confederates were poor candidates for a trek to the frozen North. A storm of rain, snow, and sleet struck during the battle. Men inside the fort had no overcoats, and those outside had left coats, blankets, and knapsacks behind at another camp. "Many a stout fellow felt that the wind was about to turn his blood into icicles."[8]

Colonel Tucker was on duty in Springfield, Illinois, when he wired General Halleck that Chicago could hold "8,000 or 9,000 prisoners." It was a serious miscalculation. Camp Douglas was a logical choice because the Illinois Central Railroad had a terminal at Cairo, Illinois, 300 miles south of Chicago. Another reason may have been that the camp was already a well developed installation, and the captor usually selects a distant prison site to discourage escape attempts. Downstate Springfield, Illinois was a possible location, except that the influential Governor Yates did not want the prisoners there because "there are so many secessionists at that place."[9] His feeling was correct, as the many Southerners in Chicago proved to be a security hazard for Camp Douglas throughout the war.

This would be the Union army's first experience in collecting and transporting other Americans to prison camps in such large numbers, and the number of messages sent for the next six days was overwhelming despite the primitive telegraph system.[10] Confederate General Buckner angrily wired Grant that the "ignorance" of some Federal executive officers caused his men to stand nearly all day in mud and cold without food. Governor Morton of Ohio said that he could take 3,000 prisoners. The governor of Iowa offered to handle 3,000 at 16 cents each per day. Halleck decided that 500 sick and wounded would go to Cincinnati. Grant confided to Halleck that he "was truly glad to get clear of them. It is much less a job to take than to keep them." Meanwhile, many prisoners were escaping in the confusion.

The heaviest burden fell on Brigadier General George W. Cullum, Halleck's chief of staff at the scene.[11]

Cairo, February 19, 1862, to Major-General Halleck: "Eight steamers with 5,000 prisoners here. Shall I send 3,000 to Indiana as proposed yesterday? Telegraph reply immediately."

A second telegram from Cullum followed: "About 9,000 prisoners had gone to Saint Louis before receiving your dispatch. One thousand left for Chicago this evening and 500 follow tomorrow morning"

He sent a third wire advising that none of Halleck's telegrams had reached him until after he had made disposition of the prisoners. "I am completely fagged out, and being among the little hours of the morning I must say good night."

The code of chivalry added to Cullum's problems. Captured Confederate officers arrived at Cairo wearing their pistols and swords.[12] General Grant agreed to it in the surrender terms. The United States had collapsed, but some men still cherished ancient ideas of courtesy between foes. Regarding the sick and wounded prisoners, Halleck ordered: "Treat friend and foe alike. It is simply a question of humanity." General Cullum disarmed the officers, but the enlisted men were not thoroughly searched. Two weeks later a small arsenal was collected from them at Camp Douglas.[13]

The War Department directed the Illinois Central to move 7,000 prisoners to Chicago.[14] They numbered much less, but no one knew this for days. Steamboats carrying the prisoners to Cairo, Illinois were described as "filthy" by Andrew Jackson Campbell, an officer in the 48th Tennessee Infantry. The trip was also dangerous, as the boats were fired upon from the shore and several prisoners were wounded. The shooters were not identified. However, the difficult, cold journey had some compensations when the Confederates were met with great enthusiasm at St. Louis. Women, especially, defied the Federal guards and showered the prisoners with food and tobacco.[15] The Confederate officers were also gratified to learn that General Halleck would honor the code of chivalry to the extent of returning their swords.

An enlisted man later reported that memories of the boat trip "made his hair stand on end." He spent a week aboard a "rickety old craft" which was in constant danger of catching fire as the prisoners used a wood stove in the engine room to cook their meat, and the blaze from the drippings reached the underside of the upper deck. Writing a half-century later, a former private described the craft as "old hulks of steamboats that appeared to be rotten from top to bottom," and the men had to eat and sleep on piles of coal.[16]

Halleck realized that the situation was out of control and wired desperately to General Fuller in Springfield, Illinois that the prisoners were traveling without enough security. He ordered Fuller to obtain temporary guards to meet the trains at Chicago and Indianapolis. He did not know when these trains would arrive, but ordered: "Be ready for them."[17] Fuller, the one who had selected the site of Camp Douglas, was now Adjutant-General of the State of Illinois.

General Fuller was not "ready for them," because he was also short of men and requested time to raise a citizen guard. The Confederates would have welcomed the protection. One train was attacked by a drunken detachment of Union cavalry near Chicago, and prisoners were injured by bricks thrown through the windows. Two prisoners had been allowed to go searching for water and then were left behind. They ran after the train, shouting and waiving their hats, until they were taken aboard.[18] The two preferred a prison camp, over the barren and frozen prairies of Illinois.

First Sergeant Charles Edwin Taylor, 20th Mississippi Infantry, had no complaints as he rode up to Chicago in style. "We were very well provided for having good passenger cars to ride in in which was a good stove and plenty of fuel." He described his rations as "Crackers, Bakers bread, chip beef-fresh beef, Coffee already ground, sugar, beans, cheese & -very good barracks." The prisoners of 1862 were apparently better fed and housed than those who came later. By May 20, a prisoner was able to tell his wife that "I am as fat as a I ever was. My weight is 163 lbs."[19]

A major foul-up was the failure to coordinate with the Commissary General of Prisoners, because department commanders such as Halleck were not made aware of him. It is possible that fewer Fort Donelson prisoners would have gone to Camp Douglas.

The War Department created the office of the Commissary General of Prisoners in 1861. Lieutenant Colonel William Hoffman was appointed to this critical post, and his superior was Montgomery C. Meigs, Quartermaster General of the Union Army. This office became an agency of the War Department on July 17.[20]

Colonel Hoffman was a regular army officer born in New York City in 1807. He graduated from West Point in 1829 at age 22. His father was in the War of 1812. Hoffman fought in every major battle of the Mexican War and in most of the Indian uprisings that followed. "Hard bitten" would be too mild a term to describe him. He had one son named William, and appeared to have been a widower.[21]

Hoffman was also a paroled prisoner. Confederates had wrongfully made him captive in Texas before the war started. Montgomery C. Meigs, Quartermaster General of the Army, selected him for this high visibility post because of Hoffman's detailed report regarding the feasibility of a prison camp on Johnson's Island in Lake Erie. Hoffman recommended it because lumber was abundant and cheap, with plenty of fresh water in the area. Unfortunately, the old soldier's initial planning provided for only 1,000 prisoners.[22] He must have expected a short war.

Colonel William Hoffman outside his Washington Headquarters, circa 1864. The two men may be his assistants, Capt. Freedley and Sgt. Lazelle (courtesy Libtaty of Congress).

It was Meigs, then a young army lieutenant, who designed Fort Jefferson, which was to hold some famous prisoners of the Civil War.[23] His confidence in Hoffman was not misplaced. He was an obedient, intelligent, and tireless official.

Colonel Hoffman would be responsible for the supervision of prisoners, both military and civilian, and supervised correspondence and other business relating to Union prisoners of war confined in the South. The maintenance of camps for paroled Union prisoners was also his responsibility, and he had two assistants, Captains Henry M. Lazelle and Henry W. Freedley.[24]

The South did not develop a central prisoner of war authority until November 21, 1864. By then it was too late. The Johnson Island Prison would reflect the attitude of the government toward the prisoners at Camp Douglas and elsewhere. "In all that is done, the strictest economy consistent with security and proper welfare of the prisoners must be observed," Meigs told Hoffman on October 26, 1861. As far as practicable, the prisoners would have to furnish their own clothing. Meigs closed with, "Trusting much to your discretion and knowledge, and believing that your appointment will alleviate the hardship and confinement of these erring men."[25] It was to be otherwise.

Private Ryan of the 14th Mississippi Infantry retained bitter memories of being paraded through the streets of Chicago "for the people to see" after leaving the train. "Some would curse us and call us poor ignorant devils; some would curse Jeff Davis for getting us poor ignorant creatures into such a trap." One consolation was that they were were able to save their cooking utensils, such as "camp kettles, skillets, ovens, frying pans, coffee pots, tin pans, tin cups and plates."[26] The first group of prisoners arrived on February 20, 1862 and were surprised to find that there was no prison at Camp Douglas. They were housed with Union troops in White Oak Square.

On February 23, 1862, the troops were ordered to vacate the barracks, except one guard regiment. A recruit wrote home that "There is 4,500 secesh here they have full liberty here in camp and are more numerous than the blue coats."[27] A guard line was established between the barracks and the stockade. If a prisoner could run past it he usually escaped. This was called "running the guard." It would take years to develop a functional prison. At the same time, Union prisoners were held in factories and warehouses in the South or did without shelter.[28]

There was only one water hydrant in the northeast corner of camp, not enough pits for latrines, nor sufficient medical facilities to treat the sick. Colonel Arno Voss, who commanded a cavalry regiment leaving for the front, took temporary charge of Camp Douglas on February 18 and attempted to prepare for the prisoners.[29]

G. L. Wells of the 7th Texas Infantry liked his accommodations after a rough trip by boat and train. "I well remember the disembarking at Chicago before daylight on the morning of February twentieth. I recall how we stood shivering in the cold, crisp atmosphere waiting for the command to take up the march to the quarters that had been prepared for us. Colonel Mulligan was in command of the camp. With a foresight that does credit to the heart of him who suggested it, the stoves in the barracks into which we were ushered had been heated red hot and the barracks had been fitted with new hay. A more comfortable place under the circumstances I never saw."[30]

It is ironic that Wells credits Colonel Mulligan, who had successfully avoided the responsibility of commanding the camp. The flamboyant Mulligan was Chicago's resident war hero, and had declined the honor of Post Commander on February 14, 1862. The burden fell on Colonel Tucker, the banker and businessman who had never seen action. Tucker was ordered to return to Camp Douglas and take temporary charge on February 21, 1862. He was still acting under authority of Governor Yates, not the Federal government. Tucker was instructed by Adjutant-General Fuller to see that the Army Quartermaster at Camp Douglas issued food and supplies to the prisoners and guards.[31] The former judge must have known that he had no authority to give orders to the Federal government.

Confusion about the captives continued. Troops were ordered into the field while the prisoners were arriving, and the guards accompanying them were sent back to the front. There were no rules for providing food, shelter, medical care, or clothing, but the prisoners were organized into companies with their own senior sergeants in charge of requisitions. The men were warned to "use the sinks and not commit nuisances about the barracks."[32] Colonel Tucker faced a vastly different situation than when the camp's sole purpose was for the rendezvous and instruction of volunteers. His first order was to appoint officers to various posts. Mulligan became the censor of prisoner mail.

Bureaucracies take on a life of their own. Mail service between Camp Douglas and the Confederacy was only a question of how many stamps. Mail within the Union lines could come and go directly between the camp and the Prisoners' homes; and mail traffic beyond that went through "Flag of Truce" exchange points. Aiken's Landing on the James River was designated by the warring factions as such a point in March 1862.[33] A prisoner affixed three cents in Federal stamps and ten-cents in Confederate, if he had them; otherwise, he could enclose cash in an outer envelope. The Camp Douglas mail was then hauled to the downtown Chicago Post Office.

The Federal Post Office at Fort Monroe, Virginia was well stocked with Confederate stamps. Money for these stamps was removed from the outer envelope and postage attached before the mail went on to Aiken's Landing.[34] If the prisoner had no money the Confederate Post Office collected from the addressee. There was no free mail for prisoners of war on either side. This flow of mail sometimes had comic results. Often, the only paper and envelopes available at Camp Douglas carried patriotic markings, and it was not unusual for prison mail to go South bearing the Federal shield.

The army had yet to say who was responsible for the prisoners, the Federal government or the State of Illinois. Tucker notified Halleck that there were insufficient guards to prevent escape. "The prisoners are being made comfortable in barracks, but they arrive in much confusion—parts of regiments and companies together—and many are thinly clothed and some sick and no surgeons with them." [35] Sick prisoners were not supposed to be at Camp Douglas.

Fuller was also baffled and turned to Halleck. "Will you please advise me what character of discipline shall be enforced upon prisoners in our camps?. . . The mayor telegraphs me this evening that there is much indignation that the rebel officers have been feasted at the principal hotels. Shall I order a strong enclosure about the barracks?"[36] Loyalists in Chicago need not have been so indignant. Union officers were allowed to leave Libby Prison unescorted at Richmond, Virginia until some violated the code of chivalry and escaped.[37] Halleck ordered Fuller to confine all prisoners at camp. "It was contrary to my orders to send officers either to Springfield or Chicago."

The State's order to supply clothing and equipment to the prisoners confused Captain J. A. Potter, the Army Quartermaster at Camp Douglas. On February 21 he wired Washington, "Shall I do it?" Fuller advised Halleck that there was only one Confederate surgeon among the prisoners, and asked whether he should employ more medical officers. Halleck was irate. Confederate surgeons separated from their regiments would be sent on immediately. "Their separation was made by the stupidity of subordinates and contrary to my orders!"[38]

General Meigs finally settled the question of authority with a thundering telegram to Potter on February 22: "The prisoners are the prisoners of the United States! The supplies to be issued are the property of the United States. You are an officer of the United States. The State of Illinois

General Henry C. Halleck, circa 1864 (courtesy USAMHI)

has no more right to give you orders than the State of Massachusetts. State authorities have no right to give orders to an officer of the United States."[39] Meigs forgot that the United States was no more.

Julian Rumsey, the mayor of Chicago, was deeply worried. He notified Halleck on February 24 that the "7,000" prisoners were a danger to the city, with no stockade about their barracks and only a skeleton guard force. "I have seen two men guarding 300 feet with no other arms than a stick. The secession officers are not kept separate from the men, and our best citizens are in great alarm for fear that the prisoners will break through and burn the city." He was unduly troubled, because only 4,459 prisoners arrived from Fort Donelson.[40]

Fear of Union prisoners breaking out of Libby Prison and burning the city also worried the citizens of Richmond, Virginia.[41] It did not happen there, either. Halleck was a spiteful man who had caused Grant to request relief from serving under him. He petulantly told the mayor to guard the prisoners himself. "Raise a special police force if necessary," he lectured. "I have taken these Confederates in arms behind their entrenchments; it is a great pity if Chicago cannot guard them unarmed for a few days. No troops can be spared from here for that purpose at present."[42] General Halleck took credit for the victory at Donelson, which was won by Grant while Halleck was in St. Louis.

The mayor's fears were not well founded, according to G. L. Wells of the 7th Texas Infantry. He claimed that White Oak Square was secure. "The enclosure was surrounded by a high board fence, which was well guarded by sentinels day and night."[43] The mayor sent a large force to watch the camp "so that they may not get loose and come down into the city," according to one homemaker. Her husband, Enoch, had been there every night for the week on special duty. About 77 escapes had occurred by June, so the mayor had a point.[44] However, there was no report of escaping prisoners harming civilians.

It is not likely that many cared to escape at this time. A drummer boy named DuPree, 13 years of age, who had lost most of his clothing during the battle at Fort Donelson, recalled how it was when he arrived. "When we reached Chicago it was below zero. I stood in the crisp snow from 4 til 9 a.m. That first night was bitter cold, and from then until the end of winter, scores of men died daily of pneumonia." He was stretching it a bit. Men died daily, but not by the scores. The youngest prisoner to enter Camp Douglas was not DuPree, but J. Graves, Co. E. 1st Alabama Infantry, listed in the prison records as a "Child 12 years of age".[45]

The city was excited. "Camp Douglas was at an early hour besieged by thousands of citizens anxious to obtain a sight of the secessionists."[46] Visitors were barred, but "those with business at camp" were allowed in. The exception became the rule, and reporters from the often critical *Evening Journal* and the *Tribune* roamed about, as well as friends, family, and Southern sympathizers.

Prisoners also had the run of the camp, according to Frank Tupper, a recruit in training.[47] Camp Douglas was barely a minimum-security prison. Escapes were common, Tupper wrote. "Several have been shot in trying it and numbers have also got away and not been caught." He described the prisoners as "a motley looking crowd." One Mississippian told him that this was the coldest country he had ever been in. Tupper agreed. "A good share of them won't go to war again once they get home," Tupper wrote. However, "others were stubborn and say they will fight again." A reporter called the Southerners a "motley assemblage of humanity" because of their ragged and mismatched uniforms.

However, another described the men of the 7th Texas Infantry and 20th Mississippi as "dare-devil set of fellows and still full of fight." Two-thirds of them were glad to be out of the war, according to the reporter, while many were sullen and could not conceal their hatred. These prisoners believed that everyone in the North was an abolitionist. "Let us alone and the war will cease!" Confederate officers insisted. The *Tribune* reporter agreed that the Mississippians wished to fight on, while many Tennesseans did not. However, this did not mean that the North had won their hearts. Private John W. Robison confessed to his wife that her father was right in having advised him to stay home, but that it would be dishonorable to take the oath of allegiance at Camp Douglas. His wife maintained a stony silence, and John complained that "he had not even received the scratch of a pen" from her.[48]

Soap and water was furnished and the men were "washing and scouring" themselves while stripped to the waist in frigid temperatures. A Texan "profanely" remarked that they were being treated "a _____ sight better than we had a right to expect."[49]

Religion made an early appearance as prisoners continued to arrive. Dr. Pratt of Trinity Church preached the first sermon on February 23, 1862. A large number of prisoners gathered in the chapel. The minister assured them that he did not come to talk politics but to call their attention to the fearful day of final reckoning. "What would they do then if they still had doubts about religion?"[50]

An army recruiter claimed that he could enlist at least 500 prisoners at Camp Douglas. "Four out of every five are perfectly willing to take up arms for the Union and anxious thus to testify their loyalty."[51] There was no indication that Colonel Tucker knew about this proposal. Hoffman was at his New York City headquarters when he received a telegram from General Meigs on February 24. It set out the first regulations for the care of prisoners at Camp Douglas. The government would furnish blankets, cooking utensils, and clothing, but only enough to prevent real suffering. "Much clothing not good enough for troops has by fraud of inspectors and dealers been forced into our depots. This will be used."[52]

An incident occurred on February 25, 1862 affecting black prisoners of war. The Fort Donelson group included seven blacks.[53] Three were undoubtedly servants and four appear to have been soldiers. The arrival of black prisoners at Camp Douglas did not present any dilemma. Racism in the North was widespread, and blacks were severely discriminated against in education, employment, and civil rights.[54] Prison rolls did not list slaves owned by Confederate officers because they kept their property under the code of chivalry.

Colonel Tucker received peremptory orders from General Halleck to move Confederate officers to Camp Chase at Columbus, Ohio. He said nothing about taking their slaves with them. They left at 5 P.M. on the 25th. Six of the slaves were sent to Camp Chase that day with their owners.[55] This practice of returning slaves caught the attention of the president and congress. President Lincoln issued an order against it 18 days later. Many thought that this did not apply to servants captured with their owners. A Senate investigating committee soon discovered more than 70 slaves serving Confederate officers at Camp Chase in Ohio.[56]

The seven blacks listed on the prison rolls remained at Camp Douglas because three servants belonged to enlisted men, and the rest were either free blacks or slaves without masters. Some claimed that they were soldiers, others denied it.[57] "One thing is certain," the *Tribune* noted, "that many of them are as well dressed as the commissioned officers we have seen."

On February 26 the guard force was only 469 enlisted men and about 40 officers to hold back 4,022 rebel privates and 350 non-commissioned officers. Despite the danger, Colonel Tucker was ordered to Springfield, Illinois by General Halleck. The *Tribune* reported that Mulligan assumed command of Camp Douglas on February 26. This was probably true, because Tucker wrote to Mulligan on March 2, 1862 from downstate, requesting him to take charge of the prisoners and relieve Illinois of the expense.[58] Since Mulligan was a Federal officer, the camp became the government's responsibility. Tucker would return as commandant on June 19, 1862. Governor Yates, a powerful ally of President Lincoln, was still calling the shots despite General Meigs' directive. The new commandant would have much to contend with. Some problems would be of his own making, but the prairie camp site suffered from severe deterioration, and sickness and death among the prisoners reached epidemic proportions.

Contrary to Civil War romanticism, the Blue and the Gray at Camp Douglas did not feel as though they were brothers, or even fellow countrymen. Reverend Edmund B. Tuttle, Post Chaplain, described the prisoners as "poor white trash." He was struck by their attitude of being a "foreign foe" from another country that the North had invaded. Tuttle, unlike some bogus army chaplains, was an ordained Episcopal priest, and had served as rector of a church.[59]

Some Union soldiers agreed with Tuttle's opinion of the prisoners, as one reported to his hometown paper. "The secesh prisoners are as motley a looking set as you ever saw. There are of course among so large a number many intelligent faces to be seen, but their uniform (!) causes them to appear far worse than our common day laborers, when dressed in their every day working suit.

The prisoners jeered at the guards as "stay at home soldiers," not knowing that they were going into combat shortly. Many of them despised the Federals as abolitionists who were fighting to put southern whites under black rule, which was not so. "The more we see of the Yankees the more we hate them," a Tennessean wrote from camp on June 21, 1862.[61] Nevertheless, cataclysmic events would tend to lessen their differences.

A nun who lived on the main road to Camp Douglas reported mournfully, "During the greater part of this year, companies of Federal troops, shoeless, hatless, coatless very often; with squads of rebel prisoners, handcuffed singly or in pairs, in the same destitute condition, were crowding into Chicago from the different depots, marching to Camp Douglas. All the glory and panoply of war had departed from these processions."[62]

NOTES TO CHAPTER 2.

[1] *Chicago Tribune,* 14 Feb. 1862.
[2] G. O. No. 19, "Camp Douglas Order Book," 4 Dec. 1861, CHS.
[3] Compiled from the records of the Commissary General of Prisoners, Microcopy 598, Record Group 109, Roll, 58.
[4] *Chicago Tribune,* 3 Jun. 1862.

[5] Camp Douglas Order Book, 2 May 1862; Story, "Camp Douglas," 29-30; *Chicago Tribune,* 12 Jun. 1862. White Oak Square took its name from the dungeon located there.

[6] Paul M. Angle, "The Story of an Ordinary Man", *Journal of the Illinois State Historical Society,* 33 No. 1 (Mar. 1940): 230.

[7] Fort Donelson was located near the town of Dover in northwest Tennessee.

[8] *Battles and Leaders of The Civil War,* (New York: Thomas Yoseloff &. Co., 1956) I:410.

[9] O R Ser.II-Vol.III, 274; Friederike H. Lesser, *Civil War Prisons: A study of the conditions under which they operated* (Montgomery: University of Alabama, 1968); O R Ser.II-Vol.III, 277.

[10] O R Ser.II-Vol.III, 267-301.

[11] He was the author of the *Biographical Register of Officers and Graduates of the United States Military Academy at West Point* (1879), which is still considered a classic.

[12] O R Ser.II-Vol.III, 282.

[13] *Chicago Tribune,* 5 Mar. 1862.

[14] John F. Stover, *History of the Illinois Central Railroad* (New York: Macmillan Publishing Co., 1975), 95

[15] Diary of Andrew Jackson Campbell, edited by Jill K. Garrett, Columbia Tennessee (1965): 22-23. Special Collections, Chicago Public Library.

[16] J. T. Lowery. "Experience as a Prisoner of War," ms. colection, William R. Perkins Library, Duke University; Milton A. Ryan, 14th Mississippi Infantry, "Experience of a Confederate Soldier in Camp and Prison in the Civil War." CWTI coll., USAMHI.

[17] O R Ser. II-Vol. III, 288.

[18] O R Ser. II-Vol. III, 297; *Chicago Tribune,* 22 Feb. 1862. .

[19] Diary of Charles Edwin Taylor, 20 Feb. 1862, Courtesy of Medford H. Roe, Jr., Mobile Alabama; John Wesley Robison Papers, Tennessee State Library and Archives.

[20] Microfilm Publications. Selected Records of the War Department Relating to Confederate Prisoners War, 1861-65, Microcopy No. 598, R. G. 109, NA.

[21] Roger D. Hunt and Jack R. Brown, *Brevet Brigadier Generals in Blue* (Gaithersburg: Olde Soldier Books, Inc., 1990), 288; Cullum, *Biographical Register of Officers and Graduates of West Point,* 347; Collection of Civil War Pension Records, NA.

[22] William Best Hesseltine, *Civil War Prisons, A Study in War Psychology* (New York: Frederick Ungar Publishing co., 1930), 35; O R Ser.II-Vol.III, 54-57; Frank L. Byrne, "Prison Pens of Suffering," *THE IMAGE OF WAR*, Vol. 4, (Garden City: Doubleday & Co., 1983) 399; O R Ser.II-Vol.III, 57.

[23] Stephen Z. Starr, *Colonel Grenfell's Wars* (Baton Rouge: Louisiana State University Press, 1971), 275.

[24] Microcopy 598, R.G. 109, NA.

[25] Hesseltine, 168; O R Ser.II-Vol.III, 122-23.

[26] Ryan, "Experience of a Confederate Soldier."

[27] General Order No. 26 Camp Douglas Order Book, 23 Feb. 1862, CHS; "Dear Parents." F.W. Tupper letter, 3 Mar. 1862, ISHL.

[28] Hesseltine, 56-57.

[29] Goodspeed and Healy, *History of Cook County*, I:453.

[30] Chicago Inter-ocean, 25 May 1895.

[31] Camp Douglas Order Book, Special Order No. 36, Fuller to Tucker, 20 Feb. 1862; General Order No. 26, CHS.

[32] G. O. 1,2,3, Camp Douglas Order Book, 22 Feb. 1862.

[33] Harvey M. Karlen, Ph.D, "Postal History of Camp Douglas, 1861-1865," *The American Philatelist* 10 (Oct. 1979): 926.

[34] Karlen, 927.

[35] O R Ser.II-Vol.III, 297.

[36] O R Ser.II-Vol.III, 297.

[37] Hesseltine, *Civil War Prisons*, 60.

[38] O R Ser.II-Vol.III, 297; 312.

[39] O R Ser.II-Vol.III, 301.

[40] O R Ser. II-Vol.III, 315; Report of the Illinois Adjutant General. I:123-24.

[41] The Richmond Dispatch, 17 Feb. 1864.

[42] Mark Grimsley, "Ulysses S. Grant," *Civil War Times* 7 (Feb. 1990):32-34; O R Ser.II-Vol.III, 316.

[43] Chicago Inter-Ocean, May 25, 1895.

[44] Howard Kenneth Story, "Camp Douglas, 1861-1865 (M.A. thesis, Northwestern University, 1942): 15; Selected Records of the War Department Relating to Confederate Prisoners of War, 1861-1865 (Washington: National Archives) Commissary General of Prisoners, Camp Douglas, Ill. Military Prison, Microcopy 598, Record Group 109, Roll 54.

[45] Chicago Daily News, 24 Aug. 1968; Confederate Prisoners of War, R. G. 109, Roll 56.

[46] *Chicago Tribune*, 24 Feb. 1862.

[47] 3 Mar. 1862. Letters of Frank W. Tupper, 53rd Illinois Infantry, ISHL.

[48] Chicago Evening Journal, 21 Feb. 1862; *Chicago Tribune,* 24 Feb. 1862; J. W. Robison to his wife, 30 Apr., 6 Jul. 1862.

[49] Evening Journal, 23 Feb. 1862.

[50] *Chicago Tribune,* 24 Feb. 1862.

[51] O R Ser.II-Vol.III, 318.

[52] O R Ser.II-Vol.III, 316-17.

[53] Confederate Prisoners of War, 1861-65. Microcopy No. 598, R. G. 109, Roll 56.

"*James,* black. Co. H, 7th Texas Infantry. Property of W. D. Powell. Captured February 16 1862 at Fort Donelson." Remarks: "Enlisted." [Sgt. W. D. Powell of the 7th Texas was captured also].

"*Sam,* contraband. Co. H, 7th Texas Infantry. Property of J. S. Crawford. Captured February 16 1862 at Fort Donelson." No disposition given. [Sgt. J. S. Crawford of the 7th Texas was captured also].

"*Nathan,* contraband. Co. H, 7th Texas Infantry. Property of T. H. Cray. Captured February 16 1862 at Fort Donelson." Remarks: "Enlisted." [T. H. Cray is not shown on the prison rolls].

"*Peter Calloway,* negro. Co. D, 7th Texas Infantry. Captured February 16 1862 at Fort Donelson. Remarks: Released unconditionally September 10, 1862."

"*Joseph Matthews,* negro. Co. C, 20th Mississippi Infantry. Captured February 16 1862 at Fort Donelson. Remarks: Released unconditionally September 10, 1862."

"*G. Blackwood,* colored. Co. C, 3rd Tennessee Infantry. Captured February 16 1862 at Fort Donelson." No disposition given.

"*Isaac Wood,* negro. Co. E, 20th Mississippi Infantry. Captured February 16 1862 at Fort Donelson. Remarks: Exchanged Sept/29 62 via Cairo."

[54] Arthur C. Cole, *The Era of the Civil War* (Springfield: Illinois Centennial Commisssion, 1919), 225-29.

[55] Chicago Tribune and Chicago Times, 26 Feb. 1862.

[56] *Chicago Tribune,* 31 Mar. 1862.

[57] *Chicago Tribune,* 25 Feb. 1862.

[58] Report of the Illinois Adjutant General, I:124; Alfred T. Andreas, *History of Chicago, Vol. II* (Chicago: A.T. Andreas Co., 1885), 301; *Chicago Tribune,* 27 Feb. 1864; Mulligan papers, CHS.

[59] Edmund B. Tuttle, *History of Camp Douglas* (Chicago: J. R. Walsh & Co., 1865), 8, 19; Harpel Scrap Book obituary, 8:56, CHS.

[60] Ottawa Free Trader, Ottawa, Il., 15 Mar. 1862.

[61] "Dear Ma." G. A. Pope to Mrs. L. J. Pope. William R. Perkins Library, Duke University.

[62] *Life of Mary Monholland, one of the Pioneer Sisters of the Order of Mercy in the West.* By a member of the Order. (Chicago: J.S. Hyland & Co., 1894), 107.

3.

CREATING A PRISON SYSTEM

Colonel James A. Mulligan was born in 1830 in Utica, New York, and grew up in Chicago. He was a well educated lawyer. Like Colonel Tucker, he enjoyed military life in a local militia company while working at his profession. The young attorney had visited Central America on a railroad project, was a clerk in the State Department in Washington, and returned to Chicago to edit a Catholic newspaper.[1]

He helped form a military unit called the Irish Brigade when the war started. It was a brigade in name, only, and soon became the 23rd Illinois Infantry Regiment, with Mulligan in command. Just how Irish it was is questionable since a recruit named Israel Solomon joined on June 15, 1861.[2]

In September 1861, Colonel Mulligan, with 2,780 men, faced Confederate General Sterling Price at Lexington, Missouri.[3] The Confederate force numbered 18,000. Mulligan refused to retreat and fought for 52 hours before surrendering on September 21. It cost the North about 100 killed and wounded. His army was taken prisoner with Mulligan and five more colonels.

Also taken were 118 other officers, five pieces of artillery, two mortars, 3,000 rifles, numerous sabers, 750 horses, wagons, teams, and ammunition. The Confederates captured over $100,000 worth of stores, and $900,000 in cash that Mulligan had confiscated from a Confederate bank.[4] Colonel Mulligan was exchanged on October 30, 1861 and enjoyed great popularity upon his return to Chicago. His fame had spread much farther. A businessman requested Mulligan's autograph for his sister living in Boston. In a letter to another admirer, Mulligan boasted that General Price had 28,000 men.[5]

Mulligan's troops were paroled by the South upon their word not to take up arms again until exchanged. The North had to trade an equal number of Confederate prisoners or honor the parole under the code of chivalry. As no general exchange of prisoners was taking place, the Irish Brigade were discharged on October 8, 1861.[6] By this clever ploy the South escaped the burden of more prisoners and the North lost many veteran troops. Union General McClellan declared the Brigade exchanged two months later, and it was reassembled at Camp Douglas and placed on guard duty.

Colonel James A. Mulligan, circa 1861 (courtesy Library of Congress)

There were now close to 5,000 prisoners on hand. School children who had come to taunt a group of Confederates marching to camp from the depot became "still as death at the sight. We were filled with pity for the poor fellows when we saw their feet peeping out through their poor shoes on the day in February with a slight fall of snow on the ground—about two inches—and some with pieces of carpet and a pillow to keep them warm."[7]

A less sympathetic view was taken by a famous feminist. "They seemed a poorly nourished and uncared for company of men, and their hopeless and indescribable ignorance intensified their general forlorness. It was pitiful to see how easily they gave up all struggle for life, and how readily they adjusted themselves to the inevitable. Not less uncomplainingly than the camel, which silently succumbs to the heavy load, did these ignorant, unfed, and unclad fellows turn their faces to the wall, and breathe out their lives, without a regret, or a murmur."[8]

Their condition is not surprising, as the South claimed that it was unable to feed and clothe Union prisoners. In November of that year the Federal quartermaster shipped thousands of blankets, shoes, clothing, and food stuffs to Southern prisons. During the first week in March, the army delivered three tons of corn meal to Camp Douglas plus large quantities of blankets, clothing, shoes, and eating utensils. The cornmeal allowed for the difference in diet, being a Southern staple, while Northerners ate white bread.[9]

There was one ration per hundred men at this time, which consisted of ¾ pound of bacon or 1¼ pounds of beef, $1^1/_3$ pounds of white bread or 1¼ pounds of corn bread, $^1/_{10}$ of a pound of coffee, 1½ ounces of rice or hominy, $^1/_6$ of a pound of sugar, a gill [½ pint] of vinegar, one candle, one tablespoon of salt, and beans, potatoes, and molasses in small amounts.[10] The ration would change continuously, and much depended upon how many days the ration was to last.

Mulligan probably continued the guard schedule established by Colonel Tucker in December 1861. Three squads stood watch with two hours on and four hours of rest. The detail was housed in tents on the Old Fair Grounds, an area of two square blocks adjoining the fence on the west side of the camp.[11] Non-commissioned officers were responsible for ensuring that each squad was ready for duty. The first guard mount was at 9:00 a.m. Talking between guards and prisoners was prohibited, but it never stopped.

Colonel Hoffman inspected the camp around March 1 and commended Mulligan on his care of the prisoners. "The hospitals are well organized and the sick are having the best possible care taken of them." Chicago physicians also visited and praised Colonel Mulligan, but found many sick prisoners in barracks for lack of hospital space. Hoffman ordered Mulligan to stop admitting visitors. Friends could send packages, and provisions for the sick were to go to the hospital. Prisoners could also receive small amounts of money.[12]

Mulligan disobeyed Hoffman's order of no visitors, as he was to ignore many other of Hoffman's directives. Sergeant Charles E. Taylor of the 20th Mississippi had a full day with visitors on March 8. A Mr. Priestly with his wife and sister came calling, bringing "fruit cake, oranges, Biscuits and Milk." Following them came a Mr. Clark, a Mr. Howard, and Mr. Charles Pope, "nephew of General Pope of the U.S. Army."[13] Sergeant Taylor apparently was a musician, and Mr. Priestly made him accept a violin. Taylor mentions that others in his barrack also had visitors that day.

Visitors were coming in as late as March 20, when Taylor met with "Mrs. Waller (Mother of Young Waller whom I became acquainted with on our first arrival here)." Mrs. Waller was involved in the so-called "Camp Douglas Conspiracy of 1864" to free prisoners, and her son would be arrested. Colonel Mulligan finally did shut off the flow of visitors by April 12, when the Reverend Thilman Hendrick of Tennessee wrote home that it was useless to come to Camp Douglas without authority from Governor Johnson.[14] Otherwise, only physicians and ministers were admitted to the camp.

Captain Christopher, the Army Commissary of Subsistence, awarded the food contract to John W. Sullivan. His price of $10.85 per ration was not unreasonable. Hoffman had told Mulligan that the ration was "larger than necessary for men living quietly in camp, and by judiciously withholding some part of it to be sold to the commissary, a fund may be created with which many articles needful to the prisoners may be purchased and thus save expense to the government."[15] Hoffman would suffer much heartburn trying to get the prison fund going.

The plan was based on his experience in the regular army. "The Commissary General of Prisoners published from time to time the articles and quantities to be issued for consumption by the prisoners, and the difference between the money value of the ration thus issued and that of the full ration allowed by law to the United States soldier was set aside as a prison fund for the articles as were necessary for the health and comfort of the prisoners, and not expressly provided for by the Army regulations."[16]

At Camp Douglas, the unissued rations were sold back to the contractor or purchased by the commissary to generate cash for the prison fund. Hoffman's army experience was not an appropriate measure for Camp Douglas without yet knowing the number of prisoners and number of days the ration was to last.

The fund was controlled by the Commissary of Subsistence, who made disbursements on order of the commandant, and filed a monthly report with Hoffman's office showing expenditures.

It could pay for tables, cooking utensils, mops, brooms, and other cleaning equipment. Bed-ticks, straw, repair of barracks, lantern oil, and even stoves, or any other item that could benefit the prisoners came out of it.[17] Extra pay for the clerks who handled the prisoner's mail or money was justified, but some disbursements were to their detriment, when, as an example, detectives, spies, and informants drew their pay from the fund. Business taxes also went into the fund, as did money confiscated from prisoners, and money belonging to the deceased.

The post surgeon could draw on a separate hospital fund in much the same manner. It covered food supplements and underclothing, also, laundry, cleaning equipment, and other sanitary items. This fund never amounted to much because the sick needed all the rations they could get.

Intense heat in the South exhausted Union prisoners, while Confederates at Camp Douglas struggled through ice, snow, and the agonizing winds howling off the frozen lake during the winter of 1861-62. Adding to this was a shortage of water when the hydrant froze, and soon 200 to 300 prisoners were in the camp hospital. On March 4, 1862 the number reached 325. "A large barn in the camp has been comfortably fitted up, and yet there is not hospital room enough," the *Tribune* reported. On March 7, Colonel Hoffman told General Meigs that there were over 5,000 prisoners on hand, about 400 of whom were in the hospital. "There have been comparatively few deaths, and the attending surgeon thinks that now that the sick can be well taken care of the, number of patients will rapidly diminish."[18]

It was the fate of Camp Douglas to be plagued by miscalculations. In the coming months the death toll of Fort Donelson prisoners was severe. They were in camp the longest and suffered the worst weather conditions. One in eight died of pneumonia, pleurisy, colds, and bowel disorders. One Union soldier died of measles.

Mulligan had planned to drain the swampy camp by a series of ditches and trenches, as well as raising the stockade 12 feet with a guard mount on top. These projects had to wait due to the frozen ground. Colonel Hoffman naively told General Meigs that the prisoners "generally express themselves very well contented with their position and gratified for the kind treatment they have received, and there does not seem to be the least desire on their part to violate any restrictions placed upon them."[19]

Hoffman left after authorizing Mulligan to draw on the quartermaster all articles "absolutely necessary" for the health and comfort of the prisoners. As usual, economy was the watchword. He gave instructions regarding security matters and control of the prisoners. Visitors were already prohibited. Prisoners could receive "non objectionable" material, but there were no plans to reorganize the camp for better security.

Camp Douglas soon began to acquire the reputation that compared it to the Confederate death camp called Andersonville, and which filled survivors' accounts well into the next century. Public sympathy for the prisoners was aroused in Chicago, and Reverend Tuttle, the Post Chaplain, was elected chairman of a relief committee. "Collections were taken up in the churches; and we supplied medicines by the wagon load, and employed careful apothecaries to aid the post surgeon, Dr. Winer," Tuttle reported in his history of the camp. "I suppose I distributed clothing from Kentucky, the first year, to the amount of $100,000. It was mainly among the sick and dying."[20]

When he was a prisoner of the Confederates, Colonel Mulligan "received every possible courtesy from Confederate General Price and his staff." He reciprocated by giving Reverend Tuttle's committee some space in his quarters, and the Post Surgeon was permitted to bring in volunteer surgeons from Chicago. Meanwhile, three of the rebel surgeons sent by General Halleck refused to work because "they would not take orders from a Federal officer," and two resigned.[21] They were told that prisoners of war could not resign. A threat to send them to White Oak dungeon in irons quickly settled the matter.

The garrison resented the attention given the prisoners by the relief committee. "Have the good people of Chicago forgotten that there are such beings as Union soldiers in camp here!" they complained.[22] The committee furnished the prisoners with clothing, books, wine, and sweets, but the garrison received nothing. Donations even included wash tubs and wooden pails.

However, the committee's resources were meager in comparison to prisoners' needs. Survival at Camp Douglas depended upon many factors. Time and place of capture determined how much equipment and clothing a prisoner could save.[23] It was important to be with friends and form groups for mutual aid, protection, and conversation.

While hot weather would be intolerable without adequate sewage, drainage, and fresh water, the following winters were severe, and the prisoners required warm clothing and a good deal of fuel for their stoves. Colonel Hoffman originally had proposed two-story barracks for the prison with weather stripping and a ceiling on the second floor. This plan was rejected in favor of a one-story building made of a single thickness of pine boards without insulation or shingles, and no plastering or ceiling.[24] Tar paper covered a wooden roof.

In addition to his other problems, Colonel Mulligan became entangled in a dispute over the chapel. He had turned it into barracks, according to a group dedicated to bringing Christ to the prisoners. Dwight L. Moody came to Chicago in 1856 from Boston, bringing with him a heritage of Puritanism and anti-slavery zeal. Moody soon was part of the evangelical church movement through the Young Men's Christian Association. The YMCA built a chapel in Garrison Square in 1861 with Colonel Tucker's permission. A week after the first prisoners arrived, Moody went there to preach. "These meetings were kept up two or three weeks, and many were converted."[25]

It was this chapel that Mulligan appropriated. John V. Farwell, president of the YMCA, complained directly to Edwin M. Stanton, Secretary of War, on March 7, 1862. "While Providence has permitted our soldiers to fill this camp with our enemies we cannot but believe that we should preach the same gospel to them that we did to the brave fellows who in the march of events have turned the tide of battle in our favor."[26]

He was careful to exonerate Mulligan from any deliberate wrong doing. Stanton ordered Colonel Hoffman to see that the building be returned to the YMCA. It seems that Mulligan had made it into a hospital, not a barrack. Regardless, Hoffman ordered Mulligan to remove the sick prisoners.[27]

The diary of James Taswell Mackey, 48th Tennessee Infantry, echoes like the mournful tolling of a church bell counting off the dead each day. "To-day I have to chronicle the death of Mr. James S. Hodge, the most beloved member of our company. His manners were unexceptionable, his conversation mild and gentle, and his deportment toward his comrades unchangeably affectionate."[28]

The chapel dispute was the first time that a religious question arose, and Colonel Hoffman placed limits on it. He denied Farwell's request for undisturbed use of the chapel. Prisoners could attend when any minister offered to preach to them, not just YMCA clergymen, "but the prisoners only must attend the service on such occasions; there must be no mingling of our troops or visitors with them. The association cannot be permitted to hold meetings with the prisoners."[29]

Mulligan accordingly made peace with the clergymen, and the Chicago Bible Society prepared to donate 3,000 Testaments, stating, "thus we hope that these strangers among us may find their imprisonment the greatest blessing of their lives."[30] The question of enlisting prisoners at Camp Douglas arose again. Colonel Mulligan wrote to General Halleck that many were in the rebel army by compulsion, and from conversations with them many were loyal. "One Tennessee regiment, the Tenth, is composed almost exclusively of Irishmen, and they desire to enlist in some of the companies in my regiment."[31]

Without authority from Washington, Halleck authorized Colonel Mulligan to fill his regiments by enlisting prisoners of war. He advised Mulligan "to be careful as to the character of these recruits, and to make himself personally acquainted with each one."[32] This was good advice, as Mulligan may have been fooled by a few Irish names. The War Department vetoed the idea of enlisting prisoners, but Mulligan continued to do so, anyway. They were moved to separate barracks for protection from other prisoners.

Colonel Mulligan's determination to fill his regiment reflected his uncertain position. Was it his primary duty to prepare for action, or to manage Camp Douglas? His main responsibility was never made officially clear. Yet, he was held strictly accountable for his administration. The constant change of command prevented an orderly prison camp. Colonel Voss took over on the eve of his departure for the front. Colonel Tucker was ordered to Springfield in the midst of this turmoil. Now the camp had come under Colonel Mulligan who had lost his entire army at the battle of Lexington, Missouri.

This lack of professionalism was common in the prison system due to the practice of permitting governors to appoint camp commanders. The reason was strictly political. For example, Colonel Hoffman pleaded with the governor of Ohio to cease his frequent changes of command at Camp Chase. "It required a suitable officer to remain permanently in charge," Hoffman advised. Meanwhile, there were 5,500 prisoners on hand at Camp Douglas by March 17, 1862. No one knew how large the guard force should be. General Halleck planned to send 1,847 more prisoners, and the garrison consisted of only 510 men in the Irish Brigade and 451 in the 65th Illinois, Colonel Cameron's "Scotch" regiment. Mulligan protested, but Governor Yates thought that the guard force was sufficient.[33]

Colonel Mulligan was continually caught in a power struggle between outside forces because General Halleck interfered at Camp Douglas, weakening the authority of Colonel Hoffman. On March 18, 1862 Halleck ordered Colonel Mulligan to punish Confederate surgeons who did not work, while on the same day he countermanded Colonel Hoffman's order of no visitors. Hoffman complained about this to General Meigs. "General Halleck has given orders in relation to the prisoners taken at Fort Donelson, even when they were beyond the limits of his department." Meigs ordered appropriate instructions issued regarding Colonel Hoffman's authority.[34]

The prisoners became belligerent, sensing the lack of command, and suffering from Chicago's arctic cold, the open latrines, sickness, death, boredom and constraints. On March 19, one prisoner was stabbed in the 5th Tennessee Infantry. Two companies of the 10th Tennessee engaged in a savage fist fight, most likely caused by Confederate enlistments into Mulligan's Irish Brigade.[35]

More of Halleck's meddling at Camp Douglas brought Stanton's wrath down hard, even though Halleck's new idea made sense. He sent a commission to the various prisons to explain the oath of allegiance to the prisoners, and "the conditions upon which their discharge depended." The *Tribune* reported his activities at Camp Douglas on March 21, 1862, and Stanton had a fit when he saw the article. Halleck was ordered to recall his commission, and Stanton bluntly told him that only the President could order prisoners discharged. Halleck responded evasively that "no commissioners have been empowered by me to release prisoners of war."[36]

Nonetheless, the commission which consisted of a colonel, major, and first lieutenant claimed that 1,640 prisoners at Camp Butler were ready to desert the Confederate army.[37] The bulk of them came from Tennessee, and the remainder belonged to regiments from, Kentucky, Arkansas, Alabama, and Mississippi. Many of them were shipped to Camp Douglas, which was so deep in mud from rain and thawing that both prisoners and soldiers rarely ventured out of barracks.[38]

One prisoner begged a Union army colonel to obtain his release on the strength of the colonel's friendship with the prisoner's father.[39] In the meantime, Chicago was intrigued by a murder in barracks. Manslaughter would be a better term for the killing on March 30, 1862. William H. Kilpatrick of Co. E, 3rd Tennessee Infantry fatally struck Thomas M. Golden of Co. E on the head after Golden forced his way into the kitchen when Kilpatrick was on duty.

A former prisoner later claimed that Colonel Mulligan chained Kilpatrick outside in sub-zero weather for 10 days before the trial.[40] James T. Mackey confirmed the story, except it was not that cold according to him. "In the evening a large crowd gathered around Col. Mulligan's quarters to witness the spectacle of two men sitting astride a wooden horse for intoxication, and a Tennessean bound to a tree awaiting his trial for murder."[41]

Corruption added to Mulligan's problems. One of his lieutenants took a bribe to let a prisoner escape. However, Mulligan failed to prosecute and the man was not punished. Five Fort Donelson prisoners in the 3rd Tennessee Infantry paid a guard $10, (almost a month's pay), to let them cross his patrol area and reach the fence.[42] Another guard saw what was happening and opened fire. Only two prisoners escaped. Mulligan drummed the corrupt guard out of camp with his head shaved. However, Mulligan's guards made a regular business out of letting prisoners escape. One even sold civilian clothes to some prisoners for $7.50.[43]

Yet, public officials did their part to shield Mulligan from criticism. The Cook County Board sent up a hymn of praise for his "excellent hospital management and care of prisoners." The City of Chicago was less assured, and requested that the Board of Public Works contact Colonel Mulligan "to examine the privies and drains of Camp Douglas and if found to be in such a state as to endanger the health of citizens or disreputable to the city to notify the County of Cook for abatement."[44] Mr. E. G. Chesbrough, the Public Works engineer, reported that Colonel Mulligan personally took him on a tour of inspection, and he found conditions much improved. "The measures the Colonel was carrying out will make the camp neater and less offensive than it is practicable to keep many of the streets and alleys of the city," he said seriously.[45]

By March 31, the camp was again deep in mud from thawing snow and heavy rains. Colonel Mulligan put prisoners to work in a futile attempt to drain the ground. The citizen's relief committee furnished dried fruit and much cough syrup to the garrison and prison. Civil War cough syrup is reputed to have had more than medicinal value. Fortunately, only 40 more prisoners arrived during this period. Camp Douglas was not prepared to receive more, although the War Department did not care about what the prison could manage.

In a masterful understatement, the *Tribune* said that "The sanitary conditions of the camp, notwithstanding the pleasant weather for the past few days, is not so good as might be expected under the circumstances," and revealed that four more prisoners had just died.[46] This was despite the fact that General Meigs had ordered Hoffman to feed the prisoners the same rations as Federal troops and to issue blankets, cooking untensils, and clothing. "Much clothing not good enough for troops has by fraud of inspectors and dealers been forced into our depots," Meigs said candidly. "This will be used." He did not forsee that such clothing would futher undermine the shaky security at Camp Douglas.

NOTES TO CHAPTER 3.

[1] George L. Holderith, "James A. Mulligan," (M.A. thesis, Notre Dame University, 1932): 5.

[2] Report of the Adj. Gen. of the State of Illinois, Vol. 2.

[3] *Battles and Leaders of the Civil War*, (New York: Thomas Yoseloff & Co., 1956) I: 307-13.

[4] O R Ser.II-Vol.I, 182.

[5] Mulligan papers, 13 Apr. 1862; 29 Apr. 1862, CHS.

[6] Frederick H. Dyer, *A Compendium of the War of the Rebellion* (Dayton: Morningside Bookshop, 1978): II:1054-55.

[7] Francelia Colby, *Our Family*, 101, ms., CHS.

[8] Mary A. Livermore, *My Story of the War* (Hartford: A.D. Worthington & Co., 1889) 182-3.

[9] O R Ser.II-Vol.IV, 777; Hesseltine, *Civil War Prisons*, 66; Joan Marie G. Kubalanza, "A Comparative Study of Conditions At Two Civil War Prison Camps: Camp Douglas, Chicago, Illinois, and Camp Sumpter, Andersonville, Georgia" (Master's thesis, Department of History, De Paul University, 1979), 3.

[10] Hesseltine, *Civil War Prisons*, 43.

[11] Camp Douglas Order Book, 1 Dec. 1861, CHS; Seymour J. Currey, *Chicago, Its History and Its Builders* (Chicago: S. J. Clarke Publishing Co., 1912), 1333.

[12] *Chicago Tribune*, 3 Mar. 1862; O R Ser.II-Vol.III, 361.

[13] Diary of Charles Edwin Taylor.

[14] Taylor, diary; Jill K. Garrett Collection. Tennessee State Library and Archives.

[15] O R Ser.II-Vol.III, 361, 604.

[16] *Medical and Surgical History*, I:68

[17] *Medical and Surgical History*, 69.

[18] *Chicago Tribune*, 5 Mar. 1862; O R Ser.II-Vol.III, 360.

[19] O R Ser.II-Vol.III, 360.

[20] Tuttle, *History of Camp Douglas*, 11.

[21] *Chicago Tribune*, 3, 15 Mar. 1862.

[22] *Chicago Tribune*, 26 Mar. 1862.

[23] Mark W. Sorensen, "The Civil War Prisoner of War System" (Unpublished manuscript, Ill. State Archives, 1978) 32.

[24] B. R. Froman, "An Interior View of Camp Douglas, *Southern Bivouac*, Vol. I-No.2 (Oct. 1882): 64.

[25] Pierce, *A History of Chicago*, 377; William R. Moody, *The Life of Dwight L. Moody* (Chicago: Fleming R. Revell Co., 1900), 83-84.

[26] O R Ser.II-Vol.III, 362.

[27] O R Ser.II-Vol.III, 386

[28] James Taswell Mackey diary, 9 March 1862, ms., Eleanor S. Brockenbrough Library, Museum of the Confederacy, Richmond. James S. Hodge is buried in Chicago. *Confederate Soldiers, Sailors and Civilians Who Died as Prison-*

ers of War at Camp Douglas, Chicago, Ill., 1862-1865. Kalamazoo: Edgar Gray Publications.

[29] O R Ser.II-Vol.III, 386.

[30] *Chicago Tribune,* 12 Mar. 1862.

[31] O R Ser.II-Vol.III, 335.

[32] O R Ser.II-Vol.I, 174.

[33] O R Ser.II-Vol.III, 337, 383.

[34] O R Ser.II-Vol.III, 386, 389-90.

[35] *Chicago Tribune,* 26 Mar. 1862.

[36] O R Ser.II-Vol.III, 403,405.

[37] O R Ser.II-Vol.III, 388-89.

[38] *Chicago Tribune,* 21 Mar. 1862.

[39] "Dear Sir." Samuel L. Foute to Colonel Tragg, 9 April 1862. The Tragg Collection, Library of Congress ms. Division.

[40] *Confederate Veteran* 15 (May. 1907):234.

[41] Mackey diary, 30 Mar. 1862.

[42] O R Ser.II-Vol.IV, 323-24; J. T. Lowery, "Experiences as a Prisoner of War." ms. collection, William R. Perkins Library, Duke University.

[43] J. T. Branch, "Account of Escapes from Camp Morton," *Confederate Veteran,* 8 (Feb. 1900):71.

[44] Mulligan papers, CHS; Chicago Common Council Proceedings, File No. 0339, Illinois Regional Archives Depository, Northeastern Illinois University, Chicago.

[45] Common Council Proceedings, File No. 0003.

[46] *Chicago Tribune,* 25 Apr. 1862.

4.

THE CONFEDERACY IN CHICAGO

Cold winds were sweeping across Camp Douglas on April 1, 1862. Strong gusts blew down a section of the fence and two prisoners escaped. They were caught the following day, and Mulligan tied them to a tree. Eight other recaptured prisoners were required to parade with boards lashed to their backs reading, "Escaped Prisoners Recaptured."[1] James T. Mackey referred to Mulligan sarcastically as "His Excellency."

General Halleck instructed Mulligan to place recaptured prisoners in "close confinement," which meant the dungeon. This order remained in effect until the end of the war. The legal rights of prisoners who escaped or attempted to escape were not defined by the North until 1864, when the

Fort Donelson prisoners in barrack, circa April, 1862 (courtesy Chicago Historical Society).

army ruled that "An attempt on the part of prisoners to escape is not re-garded as a crime, but it justifies any measures necessary to prevent its recurrence.[2] This double-talk meant that an escapee was not a criminal, but could be treated as one. Halleck was finally vindicated.

A petition on April 10 from some Tennessee regiments at Camp Douglas requested permission to take the oath of allegiance and go home as "true and loyal citizens of the Union."[3] They appealed to Mulligan: "In view of your personal and political influence with the Federal Govern-ment." They knew how to address "His Excellency" to get his support.

One week later, 29 men in a Tennessee artillery battery claimed that they were only a "home guard" which had been pressed into the Southern army against their will.[4] They were anxious to take the oath, and were backed by Andrew Johnson, Governor of Tennessee, who wrote to Stanton on their behalf. Previously, the oath of allegiance included amnesty, meaning release. Early in the war, a Confederate prisoner could gain his freedom by exchange in the field or by taking the oath of allegiance.[5] Mulligan illegally recruited prisoners, presumably upon their taking the oath.

Succeeding commanders of Camp Douglas were cautious in granting amnesty, and looked to Hoffman for instructions. The oath differed from parole, by which the prisoner was free to fight again upon being exchanged. Taking the oath would make rejoining the Confederate army a capital offense if recaptured.[6] The White House often gave a parole of honor to Confederates with influence. They simply gave their word that they would not take up arms again and were released.[7] This type of parole also applied to a temporary release for a specific purpose. It was not unusual for Con-federate surgeons to go to Chicago on a parole of honor, purchase medical supplies, and then enjoy a few hours of relaxation.

It was the parole of honor that caused three more Confederate sur-geons at Camp Douglasto refuse to tend their own men. Mulligan had given them the parole while they were at Camp Douglas, but the commanding officer at Camp Randall, Wisconsin, refused to recognize the parole when they were transferred there.[8] Hoffman was outraged by the refusal to work and ordered them returned to Chicago. Mulligan was authorized to make the alternative to working "as little agreeable as possible."[9] Mulligan thought that the matter was overblown and recommended that they "be restored to their positions and paroled."

Chicago clergymen continued to provide comfort to the prisoners, once with amusing results. "One Sunday Dr. Eddy was reading a verse to them: Show pity, Lord, O Lord, forgive; the next line was, Let a repenting rebel live. He quickly read it, Let a repenting sinner live, but the verse was

The famous speech by Parson Brownlow in Garrison Square, circa April, 1862 (courtesy Chicago Historical Society).

well known to the prisoners. There was a roar of laughter and all serious attention vanished."[10]

One preacher came to talk politics. Parson William Gannaway Brownlow, a Southern minister of Union persuasion told the prisoners that "they were the dupes of designing leaders."[11] James T. Mackey was there. "In the evening parson Brownlow of Knoxville, Tenn. visited Camp Douglas. He was followed by General Cary of Cincinnati, O., who violently denounced the leading secessionists, but like his friend Brownlow expressed sympathy for we poor misguided prisoners who could neither read nor write."[12]

Meanwhile, Mulligan was not doing a good job of keeping up with his paper work. This was not for lack of workers, as there was plenty of talent among the prisoners, but employing them meant access to confidential records. On April 14, General Fuller was nagging Mulligan about his failure to file prison rolls in Springfield for three weeks. Many more prisoners were due to arrive, as General Grant's campaigns in Tennessee added 736 prisoners from the battle of Shiloh on April 6 and 7, 1862; eventually 1,709 more prisoners came from Island No. 10, a Confederate position on the Mississippi, and 700 were received from various hospitals. Camp Douglas soon held 8,962 Confederates.[13]

There was barely sufficient housing for 8,000 men, including the garrison, and stables became temporary barracks. These were collapsing and not fit for habitation. By April 18, some 219 prisoners had died.[14] The guard lines around the barracks and stables remained the only barrier to escape, as the fence was not manned. One young prisoner went over the fence with the help of a bribed guard. He walked to Cottage Grove and boarded a street car that was leaving for downtown Chicago. Soon he was enjoying the comforts of a good hotel with the help of Southern sympathizers. In 1863 an escaped prisoner simply looked up his brother who was studying medicine at Rush Medical College in the city. The future Doctor R. F. Stone took his brother to an excellent hotel and restaurant and then put him aboard a train.[15]

The presence of a Southern bloc in Chicago benefited prisoners throughout the war. Southerners invested in Chicago real estate and visited often. Confederate General Buckner, captured by Grant at Fort Donelson, was in Chicago managing his wife's property when the war started. Others migrated to the city and became part of the legal, medical, industrial, and commercial community. Cyrus McCormick came to Chicago from Virginia to build his farm tools and was most sentimental at a banquet given for Chicagoans in exile from his native state.[16] Carter Harrison I, an attorney, who served four terms as Mayor of Chicago after the war, was from Kentucky. Famous names in Chicago history, such as Honore, Winchester, Waller, and Rogers were all Kentuckians. Harrison's son, the first Chicago-born mayor, asserted that his mother never forgave the North for its defeat of her homeland.[17] Two prewar Chicago mayors from Kentucky were jailed at Camp Douglas on conspiracy charges.[18] Riverboat gamblers, criminals, and deserters from the South flocked to Chicago to escape Confederate military service and share in the wartime prosperity of the city.

The army once arrested three editors of the *Chicago Times* because of their Southern bias, and soldiers from Camp Douglas acting under Federal orders later seized the paper for a short time.[19] The majority of people in the city were anti-slavery. However, downstate Illinois did not feel that way, and some men from southern Illinois joined the Confederate army. Chicago businessmen formed the Union League of America in 1862 to guard against dissident groups such as "Knights of the Golden Circle," who were alleged to be engaged in pro-Confederate plots in the North.[20]

At Camp Douglas, there was no move by the army to bring William Kilpatrick to trial for the killing his fellow prisoner, Thomas Golden, although court martial boards were in session there almost daily. The "U.S." Attorney also washed his hands of the matter, but some show of enforcing the law had to be made. On April 22, 1862 the government ordered Mulligan to turn Kilpatrick over to civil authorities for trial, which began six days later in the Circuit Court of Cook County in downtown Chicago.[21] There was keen interest in the matter because it opened a window on how the prisoners lived at camp.

A surgeon testified that "if Golden would have had an ordinarily thick skull there would have been no injury." More sensation was caused when the body of the victim was lost for a time due to the camp's indifferent treatment of the Confederate dead. Kilpatrick was finally convicted on a lesser charge of manslaughter, and received one year in the former State prison at Alton, Illinois, then being used to house prisoners of war.[22] He may have won acquittal had he been tried by court martial at Camp Douglas, because Golden had started the dispute by invading the kitchen where Kilpatrick was in charge.

Vaccinations for the prisoners began on April 28, 1862, but this would not prevent smallpox from ravaging the camp. There were indications later that the vaccine was defective, and it was apparent that a mass escape was planned by the 49th Tennessee on April 25, when deaths reached 230. Colonel Mulligan found out about it and foiled the attempt by a show of force. The leaders of the plot were locked in White Oak dungeon.[23] According to Henry Morton Stanley, Camp Douglas was a killing ground of pestilence under Colonel Mulligan.

Henry M. Stanley's "Doctor Livingstone, I presume" was ten years in the future at the time he allegedly joined the Confederate army in 1861 and later became a prisoner at Camp Douglas. He claimed to have enlisted in Company E of the 6th Arkansas Infantry Regiment, although records do not show that a Henry Stanley from this company was at Camp Douglas, nor a John Rowlands, which was his real name.[24]

Maintaining that he was captured at Shiloh, his autobiography describes his alleged arrival at Camp Douglas on April 15 1862. "Our prison-pen was a square and spacious enclosure, like a bleak cattle yard, walled high with planking, on the top of which, at every sixty yards or so, were sentry boxes. About fifty feet from its base, and running parallel with it, was a line of lime wash. That was the 'dead line,' and any prisoner who crossed it was liable to be shot." Stanley charged that "the authorities rigidly excluded every medical, pious, musical, or literary charity that might have alleviated our sufferings."[25] The facts prove otherwise.

There was no sentry box on the fence until December, 1863, and it did not have a parapet until long after Stanley left around June 13, according to his writings. Confederate surgeons at Camp Douglas went to the city daily for supplies, and a Chicago law office channeled money to them from the Confederate government. The funds must have been substantial, for the doctors ordered new uniforms from a Chicago tailor on Lake Street.

Organized religion was active among the prisoners through the YMCA, just one of the many groups who reached out to the prisoners.[26] Stanley's description of suffering was as vivid as his tales of exploration, and perhaps just as fanciful. "Exhumed corpses could not have presented anything more hideous than these dead-and-alive men, who oblivious to the weather, hung over the latrines, or lay extended along the open sewer, with only a few gasps intervening between them and death and one insanely damned his vitals and his constitution, because his agonies were so protracted."[27] The story is a hoax.

The only Stanley in Company E of the 6th Arkansas Infantry was William H., who joined in 1861. He was 18, two years younger than Henry Stanley, and had enlisted 200 miles to the North of where Stanley said he was.[28] According to official records William H. was listed as missing at Shiloh, but was never at Camp Douglas. Henry M. Stanley may have written this account to explain why he enlisted in the Illinois artillery on June 4, 1862. However, a British subject did not have to enlist to escape the camp. Colonel Mulligan, without authority, was releasing Englishmen by order of the British Consul in Chicago. In addition, there was no Henry Stanley, or H. Stanley, in Battery L, 1st Illinois Light Artillery, which he supposedly joined.[29]

In later years, former comrades expressed their views about the then famous explorer. One writer claimed that Stanley escaped at Shiloh by swimming the river. Another branded him as a thief and a deserter. A third affirmed that the "great African explorer and newspaper correspondent was captured at Shiloh and taken to prison at Camp Douglas." However, he refers to a Stanley in the 13th Arkansas. Writing 67 years later, a fourth veteran believed that Henry Morton Stanley was a prisoner at Camp Chase, not Douglas. It is difficult to tell whether these aging veterans were reshaping the truth or revealing it.[30]

A contrary account of the camp was given by William Micajah Barrow, Corporal, Company C, 4th Louisiana Infantry, who was taken prisoner at Shiloh on April 7, the same day that Stanley claimed he was taken.

Barrrow suffered severe hardship after his capture. He sat on the ground for three days, exposed to rain and chilly weather, and with very little to eat. "Lord deliver me from such hardships," Barrow wrote.[31] It was not until April 11 that he boarded a steamer for the trip to St. Louis.

Barrow was a literate and ardent Southerner, who read Dante and the bible. For him the major hazards at Camp Douglas were boredom and over-eating, as compared to the hardship following his capture. "We are well fixed off for prisoners," he found to his surprise. "Our quarters are plenty large enough and we are permitted to go out and walk in the enclosure. Today I read and slept the day away. I took a dose of medicine before going to bed. They treat us as if we were their own soldiers give us the same rations and everything that is necessary."[32] He seemed to have recovered by May 1 when he was the cook. "My imprisonment is beginning to pass away a little better than when I was sick." For dinner he had beans, fried beef, and Irish potatoes.

"May 14th 1862. This morning after breakfast I read Travels in Denmark & Sweden; we got some books through the kind ladies in St. Louis, and we got books at this place through a parson (Presby) by the name of Tuttle. Our dinner today was very good for prisoners of war; we had beef-steak, mashed-Irish-potatoes, and a bread pudding with a nice sauce. The beef steak and potatoes was the ration but the sauce was not."[33] His major complaint was about cold rainy weather on June 1. "How people can live in such a climate I cannot conceive. I am reading the Count of Monte Christo which is very interesting."

There was an invasion by the inevitable body lice, which he described as being "horrid!" It is improbable that Corporal Barrow was serenely reading the bible and several novels while his comrades were suffocating in their own waste. His dysentery was under control and he enjoyed a good appetite in spite of the boredom. It would be inconsistent for him not to mention the agonies reported by Stanley, especially since Barrow was at camp until September 6, 1862. Barrow wrote that prisoners could walk about freely in the "enclosure," which was probably White Oak Square. It was surrounded "by a high board fence" with a guard line inside. His mess was 15 men, which was larger than later groups of prisoners, and there was only one cook. The prisoners had their own library, which was probably the reading room at the chapel in Garrison Square.

The truth about the camp can be difficult to learn as prisoners failed to keep records, or deliberately distorted and exaggerated their experiences. An example is a letter from a prisoner to his beloved niece that summer. He reassured her that "This is as pleasing a prison as there is."[34]

Barrow would have disagreed, since he was enraged at the theft of money and valuables by Chicago police who searched barracks by order of Colonel Tucker on June 23. Newspapers often were so partisan that they made untrue statements about the camp.

James T. Mackey continued to eloquently record the deaths of his comrades: "Mr. George D. Armstrong, a man loved by his friends and respected by his enemies, to-day closed his eyes upon the pleasures and pains of this world. Thomas J. Johnson breathed his last to-day. The King of Day had just commenced his course across the azure sky when his gentle spirit took its flight to him who gave it. Last night Joseph C. Nichols breathed his last. He was a prepossessing youth, beloved by all his company and his acquaintants. Peace to his ashes. Flowers must wither."[35]

On May 2, Colonel Hoffman rescinded the order permitting prisoners to have money in their possession because they could combine their funds to bribe guards. This money was now deposited in their names at headquarters. By the end of May, 1862, the camp looked like a permanent military base, with a post sutler for the prisoners and a regimental sutler for the troops, each paying a tax of $75 per month.[36]

The Camp Douglas sutlers were not the fabled characters appointed to a regiment, sometimes by graft or corruption, and who accompanied Union troops to the war front. Their wagons, loaded with good things to eat, drink, smoke, and chew, were often deep in enemy territory. These larcenous peddlers sometimes became battle casualties or prisoners of war in their relentless pursuit of free enterprise. The drab sutlers at Camp Douglas resembled them only in their high prices. Colonel Tucker had appointed regimental officers to a Council of Administration in 1861 in an attempt to control them.[37]

Other businesses paid less taxes monthly to operate: a photo studio, $5; a barber shop, $1; a news stand, $4; a shoe maker, $5; a grocery store in Garrison Square, $10. Milk and butter peddlers with wagons paid $5, and vendors who carried milk and vegetables in by hand paid no tax. Laundresses could charge 50 cents for 12 items of enlisted men's wear. Officers paid 75 cents because their clothes required ironing.[38]

Talk of exchange was the favorite rumor. Families in the North and South pressured leaders to begin exchanging prisoners. The Lincoln administration was reluctant to do so because this would be a tacit recognition of the Confederacy. Therefore, only special exchanges were taking place between commanders in the field, or for specific individuals.[39] Both Colonel Mulligan and Colonel Hoffman were examples of special exchanges. The idea of trading prisoners in the middle of a war seems odd, because today prisoners do not come home until the war is over or peace negotiations are in progress. Many months would pass before the Union and the Confederacy began a general exchange. Meanwhile, conditions at camp deteriorated, and the depressing record of disease, death, and attempted escapes escalated.

On May 17, 1862, Hoffman ordered Mulligan to close the prison bakery because of fuel costs. He submitted a formula by which outside contractors "can with great profit to themselves take twenty ounces of flour and return twenty-two ounces of bread."[40] Profit would be even greater by substituting corn bread for wheat. In June, Hoffman discovered that there was no prison fund because Mulligan ignored his order to save on rations. He bypassed Mulligan and submitted Camp Morton's scale of rations to Captain Christopher, advising that "they have a fund of $2,400."

Christopher apparently told Mulligan, who directed an angry and impertinent letter to his superior. "Have you issued any orders in regard to shortening the rations of the prisoners in this camp further that [than] those given to myself?"[41] Hoffman would not forget this, and soon caused serious trouble for Mulligan, which ultimately led to an order for his arrest because of shortages in the prisoners' personal accounts. Colonel Mulligan may have been wise in not reducing rations, because his garrison numbered only one-tenth of the 8,962 prisoners in camp on June 9.[42] Of these, 5,717 prisoners came from Fort Donelson, 736 from Shiloh, 1,809 from Island No. 10, and 700 received from St. Louis and other hospitals. They equaled one-half the size of the army Mulligan had faced at the battle of Lexington, Missouri. It was the Colonel's fate to be hopelessly outnumbered by the Confederates until the day he died.

NOTES TO CHAPTER 4.

[1] Mackey diary, 1, 2, April, 1862,

[2] O R Ser.II-Vol.III, 433; Vol.VII, 898.

[3] O R Ser.II-Vol.III, 457-58.

[4] O R Ser.II-Vol.III, 459-60.

[5] Jonathan T. Dorris, *Pardon and Amnesty Under Lincoln and Johnson* (Chapel Hill: University of North Carolina Press, 1953) 20.

[6] The Oath of Allegiance:

"I _____ of the County of_____, State of _____, do solemnly swear that I Will support, protect and defend the Constitution and Government of the United States against all enemies, whether domestic or foreign; that I will bear true faith, allegiance and

and loyalty to the same, any ordinance, resolution or laws of any State, convention or legislature to the contrary notwithstanding; and further, that I will faithfully perform all the duties required of me by the laws of the United States; and I take this oath freely and voluntarily, without any mental reservation or evasion whatever."

[7] *Chicago Tribune,* 9 Apr. 1862.

[8] O R Ser.II-Vol.III, 632.

[9] O R Ser.II-Vol.III, 542.

[10] Kirkland,*Chicago Yesterdays,* 108-09.

[11] Chicago Historical Society, ms. collection. Source unknown.

[12] Mackey Diary, 10 April 1862.

[13] Fuller to Mulligan, 14 Feb. 1862, Mulligan papers, CHS; *Shiloh.* Near Savannah, Tennessee, on the Tennessee River. *Island No. 10.* A Confederate stronghold guarding the Mississippi River below Columbus Ky. which fell to Union forces on 7 April 1862; Ill. Adj. Gen. Report, I:124.

[14] Kubalanza, "A Comparative Study," 8; Goodspeed and Healy, *History of Cook County,* I:451-52.

[15] W. C. Keady, "Incidents of Prison Life at Camp Douglas. Experience of Corporal J. G. Blanchard." *Southern Historical Society Papers,* 12 (1864): 269-73; *Southern Bivouac* 2 (Oct. 1882):410.

[16] Papers of Malcom McNeill, 1853-1874, Folio 1359, Elizabeth Winston Collection. North Carolina State Archives, Raleigh, N.C; Goodspeed and Healy, *History of Cook County,* I:466; Stephen Longstreet, *Chicago, 1860-1919* (New York: David McKay Company, Inc., 1973), 52-53.

[17] Carter H. Harrison, *Growing Up With Chicago,* 11, 14, 17.

[18] Levi D. Boone and Buckner Morris.

[19] Herman Kogan and Lloyd Wendt, *Chicago, A Pictorial History* (New York: E. P. Dutton & Co., 1958), 97-99; Goodspeed and Healy, *History of Cook County,* I:470-71.

[20] Lewis and Smith, *Chicago,* 91; Arthur Charles Cole, *The Era of the Civil War,* (Springfield: Illinois Centennial Commission, 1919), 228, 262, 310-11; Bruce Grant, *Fight for a City,* (Chicago: Rand McNally & Co., 1955), 13-18.

[21] Mulligan papers, CHS; Chicago Tribune, 28 Apr. 1862.

[22] *Confederate Veteran* 15 (May. 1907):234.

[23] Chicago Tribune, 29 Apr. 1862.

[24] *Autobiography of Sir Henry Morton Stanley,* edited by his wife, Dorothy Stanley, (Boston: Houghton Mifflin Co., 1909), 264; Confederate Prisoners of War, R. G. 109.

[25] Stanley, 209.

[26] Dennis Kelly, "History of Camp Douglas," 74; O R Ser.II-Vol.IV, 247; Goodspeed and Healy, *History of Cook County*, I:454; Chicago Tribune, 9, 19 Jul. 1862; A. T. Andreas, *History of Chicago*, vol. II (Chicago: A. T. Andreas Co., 1885), 511.

[27] Stanley, 209-10.

[28] War Department Collection of Confederate Service Records, NA.

[29] Richard Hall, *Stanley, An Adventurer Explored* (Boston: Houghton Mifflin Co., 1975), 130; Confederate Prisoners of War, R. G. 109, Roll 56; Report of the Illinois Adj. Gen., vol. 8.

[30] *Confederate Veteran* 2 (Nov. 1894):332; 3 (Jan. 1895):16; 18 (May. 1910):205; 37 (Mar. 1929):84.

[31] Confederate Prisoners of War, R. G. 109, Roll 54; Civil War Diary of Willie Micajah Barrow, *The Louisiana Historical Quarterly* Vol. 17, No. 4 (Oct. 1934): 722-31. His diary is presented as written; Barrow, 10, Apr. 1862.

[32] Barrow, 27-28 Apr. 1862.

[33] Reverend E. B. Tuttle, Post Chaplain; Barrow, 14 May 1862.

[34] "Dear Emma". John L. Williams to his niece, 18 July 1862. Library of Congress ms. Division.

[35] Mackey diary, 3, 6, 24 May 1862.

[36] Camp Douglas Order Book, 20 May 1862. CHS.

[37] James M. McCaffrey, "A Short History of the Civil War Sutler," *Civil War Times* 4(Jun. 1985):36; Dennis Kelly, "History of Camp Douglas," 94.

[38] Camp Douglas Order Book, 20 May 1862; Kelly, "History of Camp Douglas," 98.

[39] Hesseltine, *Civil War Prisons*, 30.

[40] O R Ser.II-Vol.III. 549-50.

[41] O R Ser.II-Vol.III, 647.

[42] *Chicago Tribune*, 9 Jun. 1862.

5.

CHARGES OF MISMANAGEMENT

The "kind treatment" described by Colonel Hoffman in March, 1862 vanished. As Mulligan's troops were preparing to leave for the front, a drunken soldier fired into a group of prisoners, wounding three badly, and one fatally. The soldier was immediately arrested. On the same day a guard killed a delirious prisoner as he ran from the hospital and crossed the "dead line." This brought the number of dead to 499 since the first arrivals.[1] The death rate was a little over 5%, not the worst record for Camp Douglas.

Describing Mulligan, one paper stated that "He allowed the prisoners to go the full length of their privileges, and promptly and fully punished the slightest infraction thereof. A 'showing of teeth' was out of the question." An example of this was when he put a prisoner in the guard house "for speaking his true sentiments in regard to the U.S. Government." Nevertheless, an officer among the prisoners captured in April, 1862 reported that "the Confederates liked" Mulligan, but not Colonel Tucker.[2] Captain Harder of Co. D, 23rd Tennessee Infantry, had managed to conceal his rank, and remained at Camp Douglas as an enlisted man.

Sergeant Taylor of the 20th Mississippi recorded an unusual incident just before Mulligan left, the murder of a sentinel by one of the prisoners: "he was found this morning on his beat with his throat cut."[3] If true, this was the only such incident in the camp's history. The *Tribune* made no mention of it. Taylor did not say if the alleged victim was a member of the "Chicago Home Guards," whom he claims took over guard duties on June 3.

Mulligan's administration was the least distinguished of any commander who had charge for this length of time. He was not to blame. There is no indication that Mulligan could have made any improvements at this time. It was a dirty job, and one he did not wish to do. Mulligan had not received much help from the army since he took command. Hoffman only made a cursory inspection the first week of March. Then there were friendly visits by Cook County and the City of Chicago, but no assistance was offered.

Colonel Mulligan was happy to leave Camp Douglas on June 14, 1862. Now he could get on with the war. The Irish Brigade marched up Michigan Boulevard to the train depot, where a band played "The Girl I left behind me." The regiment would fight many battles in the East, but returned without its leader. The war ended for Colonel Mulligan on July 24, 1864, while leading his tiny regiment against the center of a 30,000-man Confederate army in Virginia.[4] He received his general's star posthumously. The Colonel would not have wanted it any other way.

Some statistics are available for when he commanded Camp Douglas, although the "Official Records of the War of the Rebellion" did not compile data before July, 1862. By then, close to 500 prisoners had already lost their lives, and the prison rolls showed 77 escapes. It is possible that the sutler was involved. A message to Secretary of War Stanton on June 24, 1862 from Columbia, Tennessee told of escaped Camp Douglas prisoners arriving there. "The sutler in the camp knowingly sells them clothing to disguise themselves."[5]

Mulligan simply turned the camp over to Colonel Cameron when he left. There was no need to notify Hoffman, because he had nothing to say about it. Cameron departed for the front five days later, on June 19, 1862, after turning command over to Colonel Joseph H. Tucker, who happened to be at camp recruiting a new regiment. There were about 8,000 prisoners on hand, but Cameron was unable to give Tucker any information about his duties.[6] The casual manner in which Tucker took over Camp Douglas for the third time is remarkable. He was only a State militia officer, and this was the largest prison camp in the North. Many of its departments were headed by Federal officers, like the Quartermaster. Meigs' previous reprimand to Potter, "that the State of Illinois could not give orders to a U.S. officer" would come home to roost through lack of cooperation. This would be the longest summer of Tucker's life.

Security was not much better than when the prisoners first arrived in February, and Tucker felt that he had to take immediate steps. His most decisive act earned him the most criticism. He brought in Chicago police for a massive "shakedown" of the prison on June 23, 1862. He was justified in not trusting the volunteer army to do the job, and subsequent commanders felt the same way. The prisoners thought that using Chicago police was simply not fair, especially because of their thievery.

Willie M. Barrow: "then the yanks came with police from Chicago went around in the prisoners quarters. Took watches, money, Guata Percha rings [fashioned from coal] sigars clothes etc. Then the Police robbers came through our ranks and searched us, takin pocket knives and money." He claimed that because of this incident a company of Tennesseans who were thinking of taking the oath "concluded that the Confederacy was the best government." James T. Mackey wrote that a renegade prisoner aided the police and stole a daguerreotype; for this he was expelled from the Federal company he had joined. "A fate deserved," said Mackey. The *Chicago Evening Journal* published a letter about the search, supposedly from a prisoner. "We have suffered all the insults and indignities that an ignorant and ill-mannered city-rabble could heap upon us," the writer concluded.[7]

On June 27, 1862, a directive came from Washington that would make escape attempts more likely. Secretary of War Stanton put a stop to amnesty by local commanding officers.[8] Only the War Department could authorize a release from prison or elsewhere. Prisoners could still take the oath of allegiance, but that would not bring about their release. Almost immediately, over 300 of the prisoners remembered that they were British subjects, and managed to get word to the British Consul in Chicago. The consul wished to go to the camp and investigate these claims. Hoffman happened to be at Camp Douglas when this came up. "I object!" he wired to Stanton. His boss was not frightened by the British lion. "This Department recognizes no right in the British consul to visit prisoners of war taken in arms with rebels against this Government!" he fired back on June 28.[9] No one could charge Stanton with diplomatic double-talk.

Hoffman had been ordered to Chicago on the 27th of June because of the report that a Camp Douglas sutler was running an escape ring. Tucker had already placed two detectives among the prisoners.[10] Hoffman ordered "the inquiries to continue," although the prisoners were not deceived by the spies.

A prisoner in the 49th Tennessee wrote to his father for $20 in gold: "If you can get it if you can send me that amount it will enable me to get home all persons that has money here is making thear escape." Money had to be sent to "Frederic Hutson" [Frederick Hudson] "one of the Express Company in Chicago" who would "fetch it to camp." He warned his dad that "if the money is sent to Camp Douglas the commander pais us in tickets."[11] The *Tribune* concluded that Mulligan's officers had a good thing going.

Hoffman reported to the army that "There has been the greatest carelessness and willful neglect in the management of the affairs of the camp, and everything was left by Colonel Mulligan in a shameful state of confusion." Vital information about the prisoners was lacking. He complained that relieving Mulligan was against his orders. The command passed to Colonel Cameron, who "knew nothing of the affairs of the prisoners."[12] The instructions given to Mulligan appeared to have been lost, so he had to educate Tucker about his duties. Tucker was to organize the prisoners into companies or divisions. The number of prisoners present and those who were sick, discharged, escaped, or died had to be shown on a daily morning call. Tucker was lectured about the prison fund, "which will be created by withholding such part of the rations as may not be necessary, the surplus to be purchased by the commissary." The only visitors allowed were near relations ("loyal people") of sick prisoners.

The sutler was under Tucker's control, and "you will see that he furnishes proper articles and at reasonable rates." They had to pay a tax to the prison fund for doing business on post. Regarding mail: "Prisoners will not be permitted to write letters of more than one page of common letter paper, the matter to be strictly of a private nature or the letter must be destroyed." Hoffman and Tucker discussed the need to purchase horses and wagons for service in camp, and a portable saw for sawing wood. Other priorities were necessary repairs of fences and barracks, construction of a bake-house, and the need for a running water sewer system.[13]

Colonel Tucker was overwhelmed. His business experience did nothing to prepare him for ongoing crises at a major prison camp. Doctor B. McVickar, the Post Surgeon, warned him on June 30, 1862, that "the surface of the ground is becoming saturated with the filth and slop from the privies, kitchens and quarters and must produce serious results to health as soon as the hot weather sets in." There were 326 patients in the hospital, with many more in barracks. The situation worsened when 16 Confederate surgeons were released on June 6, 1862 by orders from Washington. Dr. McVickar estimated that he would need at least "five surgeons and four assistants to perform the medical duty at the camp in a proper manner."[14]

Coincidentally, Henry W. Bellows of the U. S. Sanitary Commission sent a negative report on the camp to Colonel Hoffman the same day.[15] "Sir: The amount of standing water, of unpoliced grounds, of foul sinks, of unventilated and crowded barracks, of general disorder, of soil reeking with miasmatic accretions, of rotten bones and the emptying of camp-kettles is enough to drive a sanitarian to despair. I hope that no thought will be entertained of mending matters. The absolute abandonment of the spot seems the only judicious course. I do not believe that any amount of drainage would purge that soil loaded with accumulated filth or those barracks fetid with two stories of vermin and animal exhalations. Nothing but fire can cleanse them."[16]

The report made no distinction between the quarters for the Federal troops and the prisoners. Further, he indicated that the size of the camp should be limited to 10,000 men. Bellows' remark about cleansing the camp with fire was prophetic. Later that year it was burned, not by prisoners, but by Federal troops. However, conditions at Camp Douglas were not unusual for a Civil War prison; in the South, the Surgeon General of the Confederate army also warned of pestilence resulting from the crowded and unsanitary conditions in the Richmond prison.[17]

Colonel Hoffman authorized Tucker to employ four private physicians, "and four assistants at not over $50 per month," with leave to request a fifth physician. The Official Records list 589 prisoners sick in July 1862 and 558 in August, but only 57 sick Union soldiers.[18] Many were suffering from diseases of the lungs and bowels. The barracks had between 200 and 300 men sick, and attended by only four assistant surgeons.

Prisoners had been there four months, and the camp was running out of space for latrines and garbage pits. Colonel Hoffman returned to his headquarters in Detroit on July 1, 1862, and drew a dismal picture for General Meigs. Guards and prisoners alike suffered from the mud. Sinks had been reused and were overflowing. At least one guard regiment had to be moved outside the stockade, and were living in tents. Camp Douglas was on low, swampy ground, and was difficult to drain. Hoffman proposed a running water sewer system connected to the lake "to float out the filth of all kinds. The sinks should be connected with the sewers," he advised, "so that during the summer the camp and neighborhood would be relieved from the stench which now pollutes the air."[19]

He placed the cost of building new barracks and repairing the old ones at between $5,000 and $8,000, and installing the system of pipes and drainage about as much more. Hoffman now had the Bellows' report and agreed with the idea of abandoning Camp Douglas, but concluded it was too late. "The hot weather of summer is just upon us and if something is not done speedily there must be much sickness in the camp and neighborhood if not a pestilence," he told Meigs.

Colonel Hoffman's report to General Meigs brought a blunt response on July 5, 1862. "I cannot approve the expenditure involved in the improvements suggested in your letter. Ten thousand men should certainly be able to keep this camp clean, and the United States has other uses for its money than to build a water works to save them the labor necessary to their health."[20] General Meigs also cited the abuse of Union prisoners held in the South as additional grounds for rejection.

On July 7, Colonel Hoffman issued a lengthy memorandum to all prison commandants. He set standards for sanitation, security, record keeping, and roll calls, including a monthly report to his office.[21] New arrivals would be designated as "joined" in the monthly status report. The prisoner rolls which accompanied them had to be accurate. The senior surgeon in charge of the hospital answered to the commanding officer. Hoffman's office was to approve all clothing requisitions for the prisoners issued by the commander to the quartermaster. With typical stinginess, Colonel Hoffman ordered that "from the 30th of April to the 1st of October neither drawers nor socks will be allowed except to the sick."

Quartermaster General Montgomery C. Meigs, circa 1864 (courtesy Library of Congress).

A general prison fund would be collected "by withholding from their rations all that can be spared without inconvenience to them," and selling this surplus to the commissary. This officer would hold the funds so earned subject to the order of the commanding officer. The sutler was still under the commandant's control and would pay a business tax. Purchases at the sutler had to be marked on a voucher and kept with the prisoners' accounts. Family and friends could contribute articles for the prisoners' welfare, and only the critically sick were allowed visitors. Letters were limited to one page on common letter paper. Finally, only the War Department or Colonel Hoffman could order a prisoner released.

However, Colonel Hoffman quickly reversed himself about his proposed improvements in the face of General Meigs' displeasure. He was glad to be relieved of the responsibility of deciding that Camp Douglas could not have the large expenditures made to improve its sanitary condition, he told Meigs on July 10. "The condition of the camp excited the apprehensions of the officers and of the neighbors, and I felt bound to submit the plans which had been projected for the improvements, though I was doubtful of the necessity of it to the extent suggested."[22] The prisoners may have agreed with him. Lack of sanitation was not an issue in postwar literature on Camp Douglas. The Confederates had used primitive sinks before, and probably understood the difficulty of waste disposal in a confined area.

Tucker had to contend with security problems, an unhealthy camp, and decaying barracks. Moreover, his nerves were frayed by peremptory orders from Hoffman on how to run the prison. At the same time he was finding more unexpected problems. "There is scarcely a record left at camp and it will be difficult to ascertain what prisoners have been at the camp or what has become of them," he advised Hoffman. He could not furnish the names or the number of those prisoners who escaped, were sick, had died, or who were discharged before June 19, 1862.

Tucker began reconstructing records from the memory of some remaining guards who made roll calls. He then pressured the Confederate noncommissioned officers to verify the new rolls from their memory, and asked for their records regarding deaths, escapes, and discharges. This work was transcribed onto official forms and in the camp ledger. "Thus two persons are writing, and one calling off constantly," he proudly told Hoffman.[23]

Statistics about this period remain doubtful. Much to their relief, 21 prisoners listed as dead were later exchanged. Mulligan had also failed to preserve the orders issued by Hoffman and the War Department. It was not certain whether he took records with him or never made copies, although the latter is more likely. Yet the lack of records was not much different from other Northern prisons. At Camp Butler, near Springfield, Illinois, Captain Freedley, Hoffman's assistant, also resorted to asking the prisoners to verify the rolls.[24]

Tucker found that there were 7,807 prisoners on hand. According to the Post Surgeon, 650 had died by July 5, there were 260 prisoners in the hospital, and many were sick in barracks. On July 9, Tucker told Hoffman that there was a shortage of $1,450.79 in the prisoners' personal funds collected by Mulligan.[25] This is where Mulligan proved to be vulnerable, although he had not taken the money. The shortage was arrived at when Tucker received only $2,628.88 from Colonel Cameron, representing the balance of funds owned by the prisoners. Cameron was not held responsible due to the few days he was in command. After deducting "worthless bills," and the amount drawn by the prisoners, the total deficiency was $1,450.79. For Tucker, a banker, it was a nightmare. "In order to gain time and not compromise the colonel" he limited prisoner withdrawals to $5, and credited them with only one-half the balances shown in their accounts. Tucker considered the prisoners to be creditors of Mulligan to the extent of their loss. He asked Hoffman whether "they will have claims against the United States or Colonel Mulligan."[26]

Tucker also requested permission to release prisoners who were dying and those who could prove "that they were forced into the rebel service." Hoffman disregarded the amnesty request, but asked the army if the money could be refunded. There was no response. James T. Mackey went to claim $4.70 left in his account according to the ledger. However, his name was omitted from a posted list of balances. "So I will have to lose my money," Mackey reflected, "unless Col. Tucker takes the ledger instead of the list of balances."[27]

From then on, a special clerk would manage the prisoners' private funds. Tucker appointed Private W. H. Bushell, "who handled nearly a million dollars of their money over the next four years with an accurate accounting," Reverend Tuttle boasted.[28] This was an exaggeration, for imbalances in the fund continued. On July 9, Tucker was told that there would be no improvements made to the camp. Meigs' harsh language was translated into: "The Quartermaster General does not approve of the system of sewage and introduction of water pipes." Barrack repairs were also out. Tucker was to fill the old latrines and dig new ones with "shed houses over them," using prison labor.[29]

Meanwhile, Colonel Hoffman challenged General Meigs about providing better shelter. "Some prisoners are living in old leaky stables which should be rebuilt, and the south fence could be moved further in which is now no obstacle to the escape of the prisoners." Old lumber and prison labor could be used to cut expenses, he suggested.[30] Meigs gave a grudging nod. "Whilst the expensive, not to say extravagant, arrangements for sewage, water supply, &c, could not be authorized, the department will approve the reasonable repair of the sheds to make them waterproof." He said that the quarters at Camp Douglas were much better than those of Union prisoners in the South. This was true, as the South did not build barracks or even huts for prisoners, and tools and lumber were seldom furnished.[31]

Hoffman was concerned about the Bellows report because he had allowed him to inspect the camp. "I do not agree with him as to its fearful condition, nor do I think that it is past being put in a wholesome condition. When he asked for my permission to visit the camp in his official capacity I granted it, with the request that he should make no report on its condition, as I should do that myself."[32] Bellows accused Colonel Hoffman of a cover-up, and the Colonel dared him to release his report.[33] Bellows did not do so, because this would have damaged his relations with people in high places. The Sanitary Commission was a private organization which required the cooperation of the administration in order to operate. Hoffman must have realized this, and the report remained a secret. The seasoned soldier was fast becoming a skilled politician.

Colonel Tucker continued to insist on the need for the sewer system. "I regard it of vital importance to the health of the camp and safety of the prisoners of war," he warned Hoffman on July 11. The water supply was insufficient because the only hydrants were in the northeast corner of the camp. This created a security problem, "and the water is setting back under the walls of Mrs. Bradley's house adjoining camp."[34] Incredibly, mail service between Chicago and Detroit, Hoffman's present headquarters, only took one day, and Hoffman sent a fault-finding response on July 12.[35]

The sewer system was a dead issue, and Hoffman was angry about the Bradley news. He had given the woman his word that her house would suffer no further injury. Hoffman had felt sure that the horse carts and other equipment had been obtained and "that the work of putting the camp in a wholesome state of police was by this time well in progress if not already completed." In other words, he expected Tucker to correct six months of neglect in less than 30 days. However, Tucker was to cancel the purchase of a saw as a general exchange was imminent, and "to prevent such a waste of water as has been tolerated." The water lines had to be extended away from the Bradley property, but no additional hydrants were authorized. Major repairs would not be necessary if there was to be a general exchange.

Meanwhile the death rate increased dramatically to 146 in July, 21 more than Mulligan's worst month of March, 1862.

There were several reasons why the camp was not moved or improvements made in 1862. First and foremost, the government had to economize; soldiers had not been paid for many months and were destitute. Even the president of the Illinois Central Railroad complained to Congress that the line between Chicago and Cairo had been appropriated by the military, but the company was not being paid. Hoffman had to stop prisoners from baking bread because of fuel costs. Under the Enrollment Act of March, 1863, the North resorted to selling draft deferments.[36]

Other reasons included the enormous expense of maintaining the prisoners as they had been, for a total of $2,000 per day by the end of February 1862.[37] Rations cost over $1,000 for prisoners and guards, fuel was $400, and the balance went to paying guard personnel and incidental expenses. Also, Washington's attitude towards the prisoners was hardening due to negative reports about Southern prisons received from escaping Union prisoners. "The Confederacy would be bankrupted by the proper feeding and care of Union prisoners," according to its Commissary General of supplies.[38] This was not true. The South had the means to carry on the war for three more years. However, the Northern blockade probably made it more difficult to channel resources into the prison system when they were needed elsewhere.

There had been a furious round of correspondence and inspections after Colonel Mulligan's departure. For the first time, authorities had some idea of what was required to make the camp habitable. Still, nothing was done. The main concern was security, not improvements. Therefore, a state of martial law was declared in the area around Camp Douglas on July 12, 1862. Colonel Tucker's brother, Hiram A. Tucker, who sat out the war on the Chicago Board of Trade, referred to the Colonel derisively as "The Jailer."[39] No doubt Hiram was referring to an incident which reached the White House.

NOTES TO CHAPTER 5

[1] *Chicago Tribune,* 9, 16: June, 1862.

[2] William H. Harder, (undated memoir): 36, Tennessee State Library and Archives.

[3] *Chicago Evening Journal,* 5 Jul. 1862; Taylor diary, 31 Mar., 11 Jun. 1862.

[4] *Chicago Tribune,* 16 Jun. 1862; *Battles and Leaders of the Civil War,* 1:313.

[5] Confederate Prisoners of War, R. G. 109, Roll 54; O R Ser.II-Vol.IV, 62.

[6] O R Ser.II-Vol.IV,111.

[7] Barrow diary, 23 Jun. 1862; Mackey diary, 23 Jun. 1862;O R Ser.II-Vol.IV, 193.

[8] O R Ser.II-Vol.IV, 90.

[9] O R Ser.II-Vol.IV, 93.

[10] O R Ser.II-Vol.IV, 111.

[11] *Chicago Tribune*, 30 Oct. 1862. Hudson probably worked in the Adams Express office at camp.

[12] O R Ser.II-Vol.IV, 111. Colonel Daniel Cameron commanded the 65th Illinois Infantry at Camp Douglas.

[13] O R Ser.II-Vol.IV, 102-03,172.

[14] Dr. Brockholst McVickar was a pioneer Chicago physician. Thomas Neville Bonner, *Medicine in Chicago, 1850-1950* (Madison: American Research History Center, 1957), 72. He did not have to be at Camp Douglas, but was pressed into service by Colonel Tucker on 23 June 1862. He was the only civilian to serve as post surgeon; O R Ser.II-Vol.IV, 107-08.

[15] Maxwell, *Lincoln's Fifth Wheel, The Political History of the United States Sanitary Commission*, 8.

[16] O R Ser.II-Vol.IV, 106.

[17] O R Ser.II-Vol.III, 698.

[18] O R Ser.II-Vol.VIII, 986-1003.

[19] O R Ser.II-Vol.IV, 110.

[20] O R Ser.II-Vol.IV, 129.

[21] O R Ser. II-Vol.IV, 152-53.

[22] O R Ser.II-Vol.IV, 166.

[23] O R Ser.II-Vol.IV, 154-55.

[24] Confederate Prisoners of War, R. G. 109, Roll 54; O R Ser.II-Vol.IV, 248.

[25] O R Ser.II-Vol.IV, 180.

[26] O R Ser.II-Vol.IV, 166-67.

[27] O R Ser.II-Vol.IV, 179; Mackey diary, 14 Jul. 1862.

[28] Tuttle, *History of Camp Douglas*, 20.

[29] O R Ser.II-Vol.IV, 162.

[30] O R Ser.II-Vol.IV, 166.

[31] O R Ser.II-Vol.IV, 238; Hesseltine, 126. Belle Isle in the James River is an example. So is Andersonville.

[32] O R Ser.II-VolIV, 166.

[33] O R Ser.II-Vol.IV, 178-79.

[34] O R SerII-Vol.IV, 172-73; Mrs. Jane Bradley was the widow of Henry Graves' brother and received 11 acres of the Cottage Grove property by will. It

abutted the camp on the north, from Cottage Grove to present Vernon Street. *Chicago Title and Trust Co., (Pre-Fire Records)*; Chicago Historical Society, ms., "Abstract of Title to former Camp Douglas land."

35 O R Ser.II-Vol.IV, 185-6.

36 *Chicago Tribune,* 26 Nov. 1862; Letter Book of William H. Osborn, Illinois Central Archives, Newberry Library, Chicago; O R Ser.II-Vol.III, 549-50; Eugene C. Murdock, *One Million Men: The Civil War Draft in the North* (Madison: State Historical Society of Wisconsin, 1971).

37 *Chicago Tribune,* 27 Feb. 1862.

38 Hesseltine, *Civil War Prisons,* 114.

39 O R Ser.II-Vol.IV, 188; Unidentified news clipping, 24 Oct. 1894, CHS.

6.

THE CONSPIRACY OF 1862

The declaration of martial law seems to have affected Camp Douglas only, and not other Northern prisons. Careful guidelines were laid down by Colonel Hoffman. The decree had to be posted outside the camp and published in the local papers. A line of stakes 50 feet apart and close to the camp would mark the boundaries of martial law.

A buffer zone around the camp seemed desirable in view of Southern sympathizers in Chicago. An incident involving a clergyman, who was arrested for talking to a prisoner through the fence, seems to have triggered the idea. A judge in Chicago agreed that this was a restricted zone. That gave Hoffman the idea of pushing Stanton to issue the decree. Colonel Tucker published it on July 12, 1862.[1] The notice read: "Any person violating military authority within said line will be subject to punishment by short confinement or trial by court-martial at the discretion of the commanding officer."

Tucker was authorized to impose martial law "for a space of 100 feet outside and around the chain of sentinels." This created a loophole which allowed Tucker to extend the zone as far as he liked by throwing out his picket lines. This way the decree ran as far as State Street six blocks to the west, and probably included the old University of Chicago across the road on the Douglas property. The idea was to keep civilians away from all sides of the camp except Cottage Grove, and Colonel Tucker placed 200 posters around the neighborhood.

The *Chicago Evening Journal* gleefully warned the public not to misbehave on the State Street cars, and charged Tucker with petty acts, such as banning peddlers.[2] It warned that in the likely event of a mass escape, the country "would be devastated by pillage, incendiarism, rapine, and all the risks which stare us in the face." Tucker was unduly sensitive to such criticism and complained to Colonel Hoffman, who soothed him and advised Tucker to put the blame for the restrictions on Colonel Mulligan.[3] However, Tucker now had the authority to ban disloyal papers from camp.

Simultaneously, Tucker became entangled in political clout. The Honorable Schuyler Colfax of Indiana, member of the "U.S" House of Representatives, had secured an unconditional release for a Camp Douglas prisoner. He acted for "Friend Spencer," probably a newspaper publisher, to free William Pinckney Jones, 3rd Mississippi Infantry. Colfax was Speaker of the House from 1863 to 1869, and a future Vice President of the United States. As a close supporter and advisor of President Lincoln, Colfax was given the release by Stanton as a personal favor, "which will open his prison doors," Colfax boasted to Spencer.[4] "P.S.—As the temper of our people is not in favor of releasing rebels and as I would not have done it but to oblige you make no reference to it in the paper."

At Camp Douglas, Private Jones demanded to know if the release allowed him to cross the Union lines into Mississippi. It did not, so Tucker kept him prisoner. Hoffman was petrified. "The Secretary of War's orders give you no discretion in the matter!" he thundered.[5] Hoffman wanted Jones booted out of camp at the point of a bayonet if necessary. The old war horse liked his job, if Tucker did not. Tucker was angry; there was no answer when he requested permission to release dying men, and those who deserted the Confederate army at Camp Douglas were left to rot.

However, it was not unusual for prisoners to be released through political influence, if not corruption. Even President Lincoln interceded in 11 cases at Camp Douglas, 10 of them at the request of influential Kentuckians and other friends. Governor Yates acted once.[6] Influence peddling became a regular business for a Kentucky law firm with ties to the President. The two law partners charged $100 for each case, and were successful 20 times in releasing prisoners at Camp Douglas. They had the audacity to send business cards there. Captain Shurly, the adjutant, was so offended that he complained directly to Hoffman. "I presume that accounts for the release of so many prisoners of war who have never made application to take the oath of allegiance," he snapped.[7] Hoffman kept quiet.

The troublesome prison fund held only $369.48 on July 14, 1862, which suggests that Colonel Tucker was not selling many rations. He was not as petty a tyrant as the papers claimed. An astonishing incident was discovered on July 16. Five young women and a child were found among prisoners who had arrived on May 28, 1862 from Madison, Wisconsin. There is no indication that Colonel Mulligan knew of their presence. For almost seven weeks the women had solved problems of food, clothing, bathing, sleeping arrangements, and hygienic needs for themselves and the child. The latrines at this time were shallow pits, "many of them merely surrounded by a few poles and brush insufficient to afford privacy."[8]

Most likely they were disguised as men, but that does not explain the child. The guards may have been bribed, and of course they were lax in calling the roll. Officers did not take over this task until later by Colonel Hoffman's orders. Even the Chicago police did not find these women during their search on June 23. When Tucker reported the group to Hoffman's headquarters in Detroit, he did his best to put them in a good light.[9] They were not camp followers, but respectable ladies, he described as:

1. Rebecca Parish, about 28 years of age, from Sumter County, Ga. She was at Island No. 10 where her husband and two children died in April. "Since then she lived under the protection of her brother, a Confederate soldier."

2. Harriet Redd, about 24 years of age, from Pike County, Ala. "She was taken prisoner with her husband at Island No. 10 while an invalid."

3. Araminta Palmer, a widow, about 33 years of age, from Great Bend, Meigs County, Ohio. She was a cook in the Confederate hospital at Island No. 10 when taken prisoner on April 8. She was sickly and "her parents were good Union people."

4. Amelia Davis, about 33 years of age, from Vermont. She and her husband were employed as cook and stewardess on board a steamer when taken at Island No. 10, and both were sent prisoners to Camp Douglas together with a little boy eight years of age.

5. Bridget Higgins, from Galway, Ireland. She followed her husband after they were taken prisoners at Island No. 10. She had no relatives in this country and "was in delicate health."

The little group was known to the officers at Camp Randall, Madison, Wisconsin, and could have had their freedom. Their presence among the prisoners was not reported to Camp Douglas. It was a matter of kindness. Colonel Hoffman decided that the women could remain at camp as nurses or laundresses, but not as prisoners. If they accepted employment they had to stay within the camp. Otherwise, they could live outside at government expense, or they had the option of free transportation to the limits of the Union lines. No mention was made of the child.[10]

These generous terms reflect a warmer, softer side of the iron soldier. There is little information about the outcome of this incident. The prison rolls list Mrs. Redd and Mrs. Davis and her child at camp on September 10, 1862.[11] It is certain that the women were waiting for their husbands to be released from the hospital; healthy prisoners were gone by this time.

The Camp Douglas order book reveals that Tucker still had concerns about lack of discipline among the garrison. Officers were leaving camp without passes, and packages were still being delivered to the prisoners. He prohibited this practice and all unnecessary conversation with prisoners. He nagged about troops shopping at the wrong sutler, and ordered the Articles of War to be read immediately, with selected sections read every Sunday.[12] No one could accuse him of courting popularity.

On July 20, 1862, Hoffman ordered Tucker to pull in the fence line on the south side of the camp and to rebuild and strengthen it. His plan called for sentinel walks on top at intervals of 50 to 75 feet.[13] The supports had to be on the outside "so that the sentinel may have a good view of all inside the fence near his post." With short-sighted stinginess, Hoffman ordered Tucker to use old lumber laying about the camp. "Let it cost as little as possible." He gave no specification for the height of the fence. Officers were to be permanently detailed for the roll call, or assigned by the week. A major or officer of higher rank was required to supervise the entire operation and make a morning report to Tucker.

A significant development outside the camp was the Dix-Hill Cartel of July 22, 1862, providing for a general exchange of prisoners. Meigs could now defer the sewer system, additional water hydrants, better medical care, housing, and security, which would cost the prisoners dearly in terms of health. Colonel Hoffman was quickly exchanged as a paroled prisoner and returned to full military status. Ironically, Article 4 of the Cartel prohibited paroled prisoners from performing military duties, but Hoffman was paroled before the Cartel.[14]

Both governments had consented to the negotiations between General John A. Dix for the North and General D. H. Hill for the South. The Cartel was a lawyer's document with complicated formulas for exchanging men of unequal rank. Only good will could make it work; therefore it was doomed to failure. The most critical clause called for parole of all prisoners within ten days of capture. This was violated by both sides almost immediately. Another clause stated that prisoners then in custody were to be released at once. The North had 20,500 Confederates. Camp Douglas, holding 7,800, was the largest camp.[15] However, the document failed to mention either government by name. It was though the war were raging on another planet.

There was also a new postal agreement between North and South. "Flag of Truce" was relocated to City Point, Virginia, and prisoner mail was to be marked "examined" or "approved."[16] Now, prisoners at Camp Douglas could write to other prison camps, also. One wrote to his commanding officer, a prisoner at Johnson's Island, reporting that the lack of "vegetable food have rendered our camp somewhat unhealthy." The censor probably let this comment stand because the letter was going to another prison.

Incoming mail was also censored for derogatory or political matter. Often, prisoners received empty envelopes.

In spite of strong rumors about exchange, Camp Douglas prisoners made a serious escape on July 23, rushing the fence with three scaling ladders constructed rudely of boards and cleats.[17] Gunfire broke out while off-duty sentinels were camped in tents adjoining the stockade. A young recruit in the 67th Illinois Infantry recalls, "We went off in the darkness at a double quick and soon arrived at the point of disturbance just in the nick of time to prevent a general escape. Some sympathizers had arranged with the prisoners by some means that at a certain signal a rush on the guard line should be made."[18] A hole was found dug under the fence at another point.

The *Tribune* reported that "Parties were seen skulking about in the Cottage Grove Woods" before the attack, and that an officer fired his pistol at one of them. The paper called for a "Home Guard" to reinforce security at camp. The alarm reached as far as downtown Chicago and terrified Mrs. Ward, at that time a young woman living at home. She was with some friends "when a troop of cavalry turned off State Street, came to position in front of our house, and were there put through the manual of the saber, sharp and quick, to be addressed in very strong language by their commander, after which they turned about and went jingling down State Street."[19]

The women were not concerned until the bell rang later and a man shouted that armed prisoners were out. They changed from summer dresses to walking-suits; "we gathered up a few things in hand-bags, turned out the lights and sat in the dark, stunned and stupid with fear, and waited. Suddenly there was a volley of musketry-another-a third-then cannon-then all was still."

Colonel Tucker reported that a treacherous guard from the 67th Illinois left his gun and equipment and fled with 21 prisoners. There were no injuries. The Colonel pointed out that Camp Douglas, by its structure and form, was unsuitable for the confinement of prisoners, and the guard detail had only one captain, seven lieutenants, 13 sergeants, 24 corporals, and 382 privates. Besides this, there was a patrol that ranged as far as three miles. All told there was no more than 450 men to guard the prisoners. The two 90-day units on guard duty, the 67th and 69th Illinois Infantry regiments, apparently were regiments in name only.

The losses amounted to 25 escapes, but 20 were recaptured within two weeks.[20] It was fortunate for the citizenry that the escapees meant them no harm. Tucker had an astonishing solution to the security problem. "I have no hesitation in saying that in my opinion martial law should be declared over the city of Chicago and the command vested in the commanding officer of this camp."[21] It was one way to become the mayor of Chicago, but Washington did not respond.

There was more to this incident than reported. A few men in the 67th Illinois panicked and fled when they the heard the shots and pandemonium at camp, but the vast majority did their job. One prisoner dismissed the affair as "a highly exaggerated account of a rebellion in Camp."[22] The 67th Infantry was not released when 90 days expired, but served a total five months. Most of the men re-enlisted for three years and fought throughout the war.

Guard lines were drawn tighter around the prison barracks because of the escapes. This left the stables on the south side of White Oak Square uncovered. Some prisoners hid there hoping to flee, but were discovered. Meanwhile, the prisoners' ragged condition continued because of poor communication by Tucker. The army reject-clothing promised in February never arrived, and on July 24, 1862 Colonel Tucker made an emergency requisition for clothing. "Many of the prisoners are destitute and without a change, while others have portions of citizen's dress which they had received before I assumed command."[23] He wished to replace their civilian clothing with captured Confederate uniforms, which in case of an escape would be easily recognized.

Tucker had to cope with the major prison break and then deal with Hoffman the next day about security and the prisoners' health and welfare. Hoffman suggested ways to improve security, but their nature is unknown. Also on the 24th, Tucker sent Hoffman an estimate by S. S. Greely, a Chicago firm, for building a sewer and water system at camp.[24] It would have rivaled anything in downtown Chicago.

The sewer would be 3,250 feet long, made of oak, and have three-inch water lines connected to the privies and hydrants. Three 500-gallon water tanks were designed to help flush waste through the system. Ten privies were thought to be sufficient. This was only one of the miscalculations. It was designed to handle surface water and human waste, but not for the 18,000 more prisoners who would arrive by war's end. Nevertheless, it was a well thought-out project, costing $8,257.18.

Claims of coercion to join the Confederate army were becoming common among the prisoners at this time. Many excuses were given to gain their freedom. One prisoner claimed to be "working" in the South when he was conscripted. Petitions from Rockford, Illinois arrived in another case. The mayor wrote that "John Hayes would not voluntarily of his free choice join the enemies of his country, because his oldest son had been in the Union army for the past year."[25] Tucker interviewed the man and recommended to Hoffman that he be released. This was not likely without political clout.

By July 27, 10 prisoners were recaptured from the escape of the 23rd. A "lad" named Charles Ellis, 20th Mississippi, returned and gave himself up. He would not be the last to do so. Meanwhile, nothing had been heard from Colonel Mulligan concerning his accounting problem at Camp Douglas. On July 28, 1862, Stanton ordered Mulligan's arrest at New Creek, Va., "and be called to account for the charges made against him in the enclosed letter from Col. J.H. Tucker."[26]

Tucker also was in a quandary when many more prisoners asked to take the oath, believing that this would mean going home. He requested instructions on July 30. Some men claimed that they enlisted from fear of being drafted or jailed for refusing to serve. Others admitted that they enlisted voluntarily, "yet profess to be tired of the rebellion now and desire to return to their loyalty and to their homes," Tucker advised. Stanton denied amnesty for them, but agreed that prisoners could take the oath to avoid being exchanged.[27]

The next day, July 31, Tucker was ordered to prepare up-to-date prison rolls, and he had only four days to do so. This was a monumental task, considering the 8,000 prisoners on hand. However, the stingy Hofffman did allow the hiring of additional clerks. Chaplains held as prisoners were to be released immediately. Yet, even the "imminent" prospect of exchange did not slow Hoffman's constant charges of mismanagement at Camp Douglas. On August 4, he demanded to know why only $5 out of $25 recently sent to a prisoner had been credited to his account. James T. Mackey also asked about the same problem regarding his money.[28] Mulligan's "shortage" becomes more understandable when the magnitude of keeping the accounts is understood.

In that momentous summer of 1862, General McClellan floundered near Richmond, and General Lee began his disastrous invasion of Maryland. The Confederacy had yet to furnish clothing to its prisoners, and at Camp Douglas, 283 Confederates died and 1,147 became ill during June and July. The dreaded scurvy returned in August, and Colonel Hoffman again charged that the camp was being mismanaged.[29] "The presence of scurvy among men where there is an abundance of vegetables and antiscorbutics is a novel state of things to me, and I fear grows out of a want of attention somewhere." Medical inspector Keeney reported in September, 1862, that he "was inclined to believe" there was a shortage of vegetables at camp, but did not verify this.[30]

Tucker probably wished that he were back at the Board of Trade, because it was Hoffman who had omitted the order to buy vegetables.[31] Hoffman was irritated about another report from Dr. McVickar that the camp was in poor police, and again accused Tucker of neglect. The bedding had to be aired out at least once a week, with "free use of lime everywhere to neutralize all impurities. There can be no excuse for noncompliance with this order," Hoffman warned.

Colonel Tucker was probably a poor administrator, and he had less excuse for not solving the problems at camp than Mulligan, who commanded during a terrible winter and spring. Then why did Hoffman not simply remove Tucker? Strange as it may seem, he never had the authority to appoint or fire prison commanders, although he asked Stanton for this power on September 19, 1863.[32] "I beg leave to respectfully suggest that it would facilitate the management of the affairs of prisoners of war . . . if the commanders of stations . . . could be placed under the immediate control of the Commissary General of Prisoners." Hoffman also wanted command of all surgeons serving in prison hospitals. He was never given these powers.

Another reason for Tucker remaining at Camp Douglas was Governor Yates, the ally of President Lincoln, who had named Tucker the camp's first commanding officer. Hoffman was aware of Yates' influence as seen in a cringing letter in which Hoffman informed Yates that he has directed Freedley, his assistant, to inspect Camp Butler, near Springfield. However, Freedley was to confer with Yates first, "and any suggestions you may please to make will be carefully carried out."[33] The steely veteran was finding that shot and shell was one matter, politics was another.

Imagine Hoffman's embarrassment on August 2, 1862 when he accompanied Governor Yates on an inspection of Camp Douglas and a prisoner shouted "Hurrah for Jeff Davis!"[34] The mischief-maker was Private Joseph M. Rainey, Co. C, 48th Tennessee, the same unit as James T. Mackey, who wrote the moving obituaries about his comrades. Rainey was hauled off to the dungeon. Tucker questioned recaptured prisoners from the escape of July 23rd and made an astonishing discovery. The money to bribe guards came from Dr. Levi D. Boone, a wealthy and influential man in the city. Colonel Tucker promptly jailed him at Camp Douglas on charges of conspiring to free prisoners.

Jailing of civilians by the military was common in the North and the South. Yet, it is odd that Tucker did not request permission beforehand. He uneasily notified Secretary of War Stanton and Colonel Hoffman on August 4, 1862 that he had "arrested a prominent citizen named L. D. Boone." Dr. Levi D. Boone was a physician and was Mayor of Chicago from 1855 to 1857. He was related to the Daniel Boone clan of Kentucky, where he lived before coming to Illinois. "It is ascertained beyond any doubt that considerable sums of money have been given to prisoners contrary to the regulations of the camp," Tucker charged.[35] Boone had access to the camp under Colonel Mulligan for the purpose of bringing relief supplies to the prisoners. This continued long after Hoffman had prohibited Mulligan from admitting visitors.

Tucker also had in custody an ex-prisoner named Warren, who had been paroled as a chaplain. Warren admitted giving money to the guards, but refused to say where he got the funds. A recaptured prisoner named Greene said that he received $50 from Dr. Boone. The accused doctor admitted giving Greene $20 dollars, but claimed that the additional $30 was given to Greene without his authority by a third person with whom he had left it. The doctor claimed to have been 300 miles away at the time, but Tucker continued to detain him.[36]

Hoffman approved of Tucker's decisive action on August 6. "It is plain that all persons who interfere in any way to endanger the safety of the prisoners under your charge, or to disturb the good order of the camp render themselves amenable to arrest and punishment." As usual, however, Hoffman would retreat in the face of political pressure. Boone was a trustee of the University of Chicago, separated from the camp by only a country lane. A fellow trustee was Hiram. A. Tucker, Colonel Tucker's brother, who had been Lincoln's personal banker before the war.[37] This was not all. Lincoln knew Dr. Boone, and had argued law cases in Chicago when Boone was mayor. Both served in the Black Hawk War.[38] Another bizarre twist is that Dr. McVickar, the present Post Surgeon at Camp Douglas, had shared medical offices with Dr. Boone, and when Boone was elected mayor, McVickar was elected City Physician.[39]

It was difficult for prisoners from the deep South to obtain funds, since mail from beyond the Union lines could cross only at "Flag of Truce" meeting places. Moreover, it was not likely that family or friends in the deep South had any Federal money to send. That is where Dr. Boone came in, by helping to furnish money to the prisoners. This incident makes the famous Camp Douglas Conspiracy of 1864 look like the farce that it was. Forty-five prisoners were able to escape in July 1862, a number which would be surpassed only twice in the future. No one managed to escape during the alleged Conspiracy of 1864.

With the emergency over, Colonel Tucker vigorously defended his administration against Hoffman's charges of mismanagement. It was Hoffman's office that gave him a late start in providing vegetables, and Dr. McVickar meant in his reports that a water drainage system was required to cure sanitation problems, and not that Tucker was doing a poor job. Dr.

Oil painting of Dr. Levi D. Boone (1808–1882), circa 1866 (courtesy Chicago Historical Society).

Company C, 48th Tennessee Infanry at Camp Douglas, circa Hune, 1862. Circled at top is James T. Mackey, the writer, and below is Joe Rainey who cheered for Jefferson Davis (Courtesy Confederate Veteran*).*

McVickar confirmed that it was lack of sewers and water that caused the sickness. The doctor did not have to be at Camp Douglas, but was pressed into service on June 23, 1862 by Colonel Tucker. He was the only civilian to serve as Post Surgeon at this camp. Colonel Hoffman must have respected the doctor, because he again approached General Meigs. The prisoners would be willing to work on the proposed sewer system, he told him, "and I believe that they have not at any time refused to work even in cases of doubtful propriety, such as putting up fences that we may hold them with greater security."[40] The prison was difficult to manage because the commandant was responsible for both administration and security. Infantry and artillery regiments were training, and of course there was no room for them in the stockade. Soon, tent cities were springing up outside. Adding to the stress of clothing the prisoners and improving living conditions, the many escape attempts required almost all of Tucker's attention. Meanwhile, Hoffman pressed the matter of Mulligan's shortage in the prisoners' funds, and court martial charges were filed against Mulligan on August 12, 1862.[41] Truly, the War Department had more important matters than chasing a fighting officer for a small debt, especially one that Mulligan angrily denied to the Adjutant-General of the Army: "My character, sir, has never been sullied, and I am impatient of the undeserved reproach of this arrest—impatient to vindicate to you and your department that I am an honest man and an obedient officer. I therefore respectfully demand an immediate trial or that the War Office upon the accounting shall vindicate me as publicly as it has wronged me."[42]

Private G. B. Byrns, prisoner of 1862 still wearing his frock coat. Back of photo confirms it was taken at Camp Douglas (courtesy Richard H. Shogren).

Dr. Brackhurst McVickar, Post Surgeon under Colonel Tucker, circa 1870 (courtesy the Newberry Library).

While this was going on, Hoffman complained that Tucker had not given him the clothing estimates he needed for the prisoners, and was sharply critical of him for not returning the requisition papers.[43] "What have you done to supply this clothing; or are the prisoners still suffering for want of clothing?" He seems to have changed his mind about requiring the prisoners to furnish their own clothing. On August 13, Hoffman went ahead without Tucker and ordered 3,000 each of pants, hats, coats, and shirts. This shipment met half the prisoners' needs. Another set of 3,000 each was stopped later in August because exchange appeared imminent. It is possible that Colonel Tucker was being sabotaged by Captain Christopher, Assistant Commissary of Subsistence. Hoffman advised Washington that the Captain bypassed Tucker in submitting reports to Hoffman's office. Christopher "was unwilling to recognize the authority of Colonel Tucker," Hoffman charged.[44]

Censorship of the mail was severe under Colonel Tucker, in fact almost paranoid. When William M. Barrow wrote home that "I am going to join the army again," the censor inserted the word, "not," and thereby changed its entire meaning. Nonetheless, censorship was no protection against corruption among the garrison. In one bribery scheme, a soldier obtained Federal uniforms for two Confederates, but the trio was stopped by a suspicious guard before they reached the fence. A party of Kentuckians gave a private $165 to distribute to certain prisoners plus $10 for himself. This was sixteen months' pay. He was not seen again.[45]

Meanwhile, everyone waited for exchange, and the delay was costly in lives, for 117 prisoners died in August, 1862. More than one-third were from Fort Donelson. Camp Douglas also cost Colonel Tucker the life of one of his sons who was serving with him.

FUNERAL OF CAPTAIN TUCKER.

The funeral obsequies of Captain Lansing B. Tucker, son of Col. J. H. Tucker, were observed yesterday afternoon, at two o'clock, in the grove of the University grounds at Cottage Grove. A large number of his friends from the city were in attendance to pay a last tribute of respect to the young officer who has lost his valuable life in consequence of the exposures incident to the camp.[46]

TABLE 1.
FORT DONELSON PRISONERS WHO DIED.[47]
1862

February 3
March 125
April 96
May 68
June 69
July............................... 78
August........................ 42
September 37

TOTAL
518 + one killed in barracks

Money belonging to deceased prisoners was deposited in the hospital fund. The prospects of exchange dimmed as the Cartel continued to break down. Federal commanders declined to parole prisoners, and the South charged that three summary executions had occurred in Tennessee.[48]

Colonel Tucker was concerned about having sufficient time to settle prisoners' accounts and observing proper banking procedures. Suddenly, on August 28, 1862, he was directed to begin transferring prisoners for exchange "as soon as practical." They were to leave in parties of 1,000, by regiments, via Cairo, Illinois to Vicksburg, Mississippi.[49] Prisoners who had engaged in guerrilla warfare were excluded, and each group would be guarded by one company of troops and have rations to take them only as far as Cairo. Escapes were to be prevented and the prisoners protected from outsiders; their personal money was due at Cairo with proper balance sheets.

Prisoners could refuse exchange by taking the oath of allegiance to the "United States," and be discharged at Camp Douglas. A total of 918 did so. This loyalty oath violated the Cartel, as there was no provision included for giving such a choice. Added to the 918, were the 228 prisoners recruited by Mulligan and Cameron, so that the Confederate army suffered a 13% desertion rate at Camp Douglas.[50] The causes were not always the same as those that decimated the Confederate army in the field.

For example, Camp Douglas prisoners from the western armies of the Confederacy appear to have suffered more hardship and deprivation than the eastern troops, and there were many from Kentucky who had strong ties to the North and did not mind switching sides. The Europeans and English among the prisoners did not care much about who won the war. Then there were those who hoped to profit from the upheaval and later decided that the price was too high. Conscripts also took this opportunity to desert.[51] Those who had harbored a romanticism about the South found that war was not an adventure for those who stand face-to-face with it. Captain William H. Harder of the 23rd Tennessee Infantry, a former prisoner at Camp Douglas, noted ruefully in his memoir that many of his men who were eager "at the beginning of the affair, after seeing the tusk of the elephant, cease to love war and resolve to do anything but die for the South."[52]

Colonel Tucker kept Dr. Levi Boone prisoner at Camp Douglas throughout this turbulent time. Finally, Secretary of War Stanton heard from President Lincoln on September 1, 1862. "I personally know Dr. Levi D. Boone, of Chicago, Illinois, who is not in close confinement, but on limits, on parol, under bonds, and oath of allegiance. From my knowledge of him, and the open, and rather marked part he has taken for the war, I think he should be at least, enlarged generally, on the same terms. If the Sec. of War concurs, let it be done. Yours truly, A. LINCOLN." [53]

Stanton passed the responsibility on to Colonel Hoffman, who reported that "There seems no reason to doubt Dr. Boone's loyalty."[54] The aging veteran had learned his Washington politics. Imprisonment for 37 days did not affect Dr. Boone's standing at the University of Chicago. On July 1, 1864 he was named to a nominating committee to seek a new Board member.[55]

Colonel Hoffman was supposed to come to Chicago and help prepare the prisoners for exchange, but never arrived. Tucker did very well without him. The first ones to take the oath were out the gate on September 1, 1862. The first group bound for Cairo was on the road the next day. By September 27, all prisoners were gone except those in the hospital. Of these, 71 did not survive.[56]

Black prisoners captured at Fort Donelson exercised different options. Three slaves enlisted in Federal service. Two of the soldiers took unconditional releases. They were not entirely safe in Chicago. President Lincoln's Federal Marshals were zealous in rounding up blacks under the Federal Fugitive Slave Act, and they were also subject to arrest and possible enslavement under the Illinois "Black Code" of 1853, which prohibited the migration of blacks into the state.[57] Private Isaac Wood chose to be exchanged.[58] It was probably for a white Union soldier, as the South was not holding black prisoners of war at this time. The Federal exchange officer at Cairo may have been astonished to see a black prisoner answering the roll. Richmond would not have allowed it, had it known. The South was concerned about slaves without masters and especially free blacks serving as soldiers in the Confederate army, since this undermined the basic assumption about slavery.[59] G. Blackwood was the victim of bad record keeping at Camp Douglas and his fate is unknown.

The freight cars of the Illinois Central were drawn up almost daily, about 200 yards east of the camp gate on Cottage Grove. "It was a spectacle long to be remembered to see these multitudes of men in gray and butternut garb, ragged and threadbare, trooping to the long lines of freight cars drawn up on the lake front, from which point they started on their journey in hilarious spirits."[60]

However, the road back proved lethal when one train, consisting of an engine and five cars, ran off the tracks 120 miles north of Cairo, Illinois at Centralia. One prisoner was killed and 10 were injured.[61] The wreckage was cleared in four hours and a new locomotive was hooked onto the cars. Otherwise, the operation went much smoother than the one seven months before which had brought the men to Camp Douglas.

Reports differ regarding how 7,192 prisoners traveled down the Mississippi river. There was a flotilla of eight or nine Federal transports waiting for them at Cairo on September 8. These were guarded by one or two gunboats. Private Terrell of the 49th Tennessee Infantry estimated that at least 600 prisoners were crammed aboard each boat, but some must have held more.[62] The boats flew a large white flag and only traveled during the day, anchoring in mid-river at night. The prisoners were greatly heartened when they stopped to refuel at Memphis on September 10. "Multitudes of wimmin crouded around and hallowed for Jeff Davis and the South," Private Terrel remembered. "Tha give meny Gifts of tobaco apples and peaches candy and all sorts of grappess. The boys gave them rings in return whitch was very acceptable to the Tenn girls."[63] Several men died on the boats, and Vicksburg was unprepared to receive the prisoners. Clinton, Mississippi, a college town 34 miles east of Vicksburg, was selected as a rendezvous point.

Everything was scarce in Clinton or too costly for the exchanged prisoners. Watermelons cost one dollar each, shoes sold from $15 to $20 a pair. Sweet potatoes went for three dollars a bushel. Their mess consisted of pickled pork, flour and meal, much worse than the rations at Camp Douglas, and they soon learned the universal truth that the road back is not an easy one for prisoners of war. All between the ages of 18 and 40 were immediately conscripted into the Confederate army for two years or longer without furloughs.[64] They quickly commenced drilling, and would have to again face the confident Federal armies in the west.

Corporal William Micaja Barrow, who devoured much food and many novels at Camp Douglas, left on September 6. His family was divided on the war, according to his last letter: "I hope better luck will be my part next time. At any rate my love for my Grandparents will always be the same, if we do gain our independence. Well I must close as we leave now in an hour so good bye and may God bless and protect you is the sincere prayer of your most affectionate nephew." He rejoined the Confederate army and died of dysentery 15 months later at Resaca, Georgia.

James Taswell Mackey left on September 7. "The day dawned beautiful and bright," he recorded, "and found many glad-hearted rebels making preparations to leave a place associated with the most melancholy events of their lives." He was promoted upon returning to the Confederate army, and remained loyal to the South, dying of smallpox on January 6, 1865 while a prisoner of war at Fort Delaware. A poetic voice was stilled without a farewell.

As the prisoners departed, Camp Douglas claimed the life of Private C. W. Dozier, Co. I, 40th Tennessee Infantry. How could he have known when he left his home to follow the Confederacy that one day he would merit an obituary in a powerful Yankee newspaper?

> **THE LAST REBEL GONE.** The last rebel remaining in the Camp died yesterday. He stated in his last moments that he had now three sons in the rebel army, besides four who had been killed in the rebel service. He was an inveterate traitor and maintained his treason boldly to the last minute. He declared that he was dying of grief because he had been so unsuccessful in his attempts to root out the Yankees. The surgeon insists, however, that he died of diarrhea, which is probably the case, accelerated perhaps by his profound melancholy.[65]

Private Dozier is buried in Chicago. Dozier was not "the last rebel gone," however. Private William H. Kilpatrick, who fatally struck Thomas M. Golden, was serving time for manslaughter in the former State prison at Alton, Illinois. He would not be leaving for at least one year.[66] Kilpatrick symbolized the common soldier caught up in forces that he did not understand, and which, in turn, did not understand him. He did what he had to do according to the code of Maury County, Tennessee, but a Chicago jury could not comprehend this.

Tucker's poor performance as commanding officer from June to September 1862 may have resulted from paying too much attention to his own business, rather than the camp's. A Chicago banker remembered him being "in and out" of the bank all the time "and more or less after he went out to take the position of commandant at Camp Douglas."[67]

The administrations of Colonel Mulligan and Colonel Tucker reflected their different goals and personalities. Mulligan was anxious to get back to the war, while Tucker's interests were local. Mulligan made no permanent contribution to the camp, but Tucker obtained plans for a water and sewer system that would one day revolutionize it. Mulligan made his own rules to keep the prisoners in line. Tucker went by "the book." Mulligan's popularity shielded him from personal attacks. Tucker had to suffer them. Mulligan boldly rejected Hoffman's formula for reducing rations. Tucker achieved the same result by giving it lip-service.[68] Hoffman was frustrated and angry about their failure to build a prison fund when he issued his final report on the camp to Washington in November, 1862. He mostly blamed Captain Christopher, who had the right as commissary of subsistence to cut rations and prevent "the consequent great waste of provisions and loss to the Government!"[69]

TABLE 2
PRISONER MORTALITY IN 1862
Deaths from February 23 to September 29

Disease 977
Prisoners killed by guards 2
Prisoner killed by another 1

TOTAL
980

The *Tribune* listed 976 deaths by disease beginning March 1, omitting three men who died in February, and perhaps not listing Pvt. Golden, who was killed in the barracks.[70] This does not agree with Tucker's reconstructed records, which count 781 dead through August 1, 1862. He added 22 more by August 10, and 36 additional mortalities were listed on August 26. Another 71 deaths occurred in the next 30 days, for a total of 910, plus Dozier is 911.[71] The *Tribune*'s figures may be more accurate because it kept a continuing count. Prisoners died at a rate of about 11.225% to 12.2250%, or one out of every eight. Deaths among the Union troops were not negligible at 240.

The Official Records accepted Tucker's figure of 7,192 prisoners exchanged.[72] However, the *Tribune* had reported 8,962 at camp on June 9, 1862, a difference of 1,556 men. About 290 had since died, leaving 1,480 unaccounted for according to the *Tribune*'s figures. Of these, 584 were released, mostly by taking the oath, and three were transferred to other depots.[73] This still leaves 893 missing. One explanation is that the *Tribune* had based the number of prisoners on Mulligan's records, not Tucker's. Tucker, for example, had brought up-tp-date, as best he could, the total number of dead, escaped, and released beginning in February, 1862. Another answer is that more were released upon taking the oath than the records show. A third reason is that some deaths were unreported.

The second phase of Camp Douglas was now over. First it was a camp for recruiting, rendezvous, equipping, and training recruits. Next, it was a also a prison camp. The *Tribune* remarked that the camp was lively "in spite of the absence of the secesh." Barracks are described as "being left in a most filthy condition" and were being repaired. "It is no wonder they died so rapidly. It is only a wonder that the whole eight thousand of the filthy hogs did not go home in pine boxes instead of on their feet." Medical Inspector Keeney found the barracks to be dark, dingy, and poorly ventilated.[74]

Colonel Tucker shipped out the last of the prisoners who were able to travel on September 29, 1862, but peace and quiet did not return, and there would be no rest for Tucker or the garrison. Camp Douglas was entering its third phase as a camp for Union prisoners of war paroled by the South under the Dix-Hill Cartel. They were more raucous, insubordinate, and destructive than the Confederate prisoners had ever been. A historic relic named General Daniel Tyler commanded this lot.

NOTES TO CHAPTER 6

[1] Dennis Kelly, "A History of Camp Douglas," 110; OR Sev. II–Vol IV, 194.

[2] O R Ser.II- Vol.IV, 194-95.

[3] O R Ser.II-Vol.IV, 223-24.

[4] O R Ser.II-Vol.IV, 147-48; *Dictionary of American Biography*, American Council of Learned Societies (New York: Scribner's & Sons, 1928-32) VI:298.

[5] O R Ser.II-Vol.IV, 147,154.

[6] *The Collected Works of Abraham Lincoln*, VI:532; VII:66, 100, 129, 257, 430; VIII:30, 86.

[7] Jonathan T. Dorris, *Pardon and Amnesty Under Lincoln and Johnson* (Westport: Greenwood Press, 1953), 60-61; R. G. 393, v. 235:291.

[8] O R Ser.II-Vol.IV, 230; Goodspeed & Healy, II:455; The Medical and Surgical History of the War of the Rebellion, Vol.I, Part III, Medical History (Washington: U.S. Govt. Printing Office, 1888): 50.

[9] O R Ser.II-Vol.IV, 228-29.

[10] O R Ser.II-Vol.IV, 228,247-48.

[11] Confederate Prisoners of War, R. G. 109, Roll 56.

[12] Camp Douglas Order Book, 5, 11, 19, Jul. 1862; 6 Aug. 1862, CHS.

[13] O R Ser.II-Vol.IV, 247.

[14] O R Ser.II-Vol.IV, 266-269.

[15] O R Ser. II-Vol. IV, 278.

[16] Karlen, "Postal History," 928.

[17] O R Ser.II-Vol.IV, 278.

[18] J. Seymour Currey, *Chicago: Its History and Its Builders*, vol. II(Chicago: S. J. Clarke Pub. Co., 1912), 134.

[19] *Chicago Tribune,* 25 Jul. 1864; Kirkland, *Chicago Yesterdays,* 110-11.

[20] O R Ser.II-Vol.IV, 278-79; *Chicago Tribune,* 5 Aug. 1862.

[21] O R Ser.II-Vol.IV, 279.

[22] Currey, *Chicago: Its History and Its Builders,*II:124; Karlen, 928.

[23] Mackey diary, 28 Jul. 1862; O R Ser.II-Vol.IV, 279.

[24] O R Ser.II-Vol.IV, 280-281.

[25] O R Ser.II-Vol.IV, 229.

[26] O R Ser.II-Vol.IV, 293-94; O R Ser. II-Vol.IV, 301. The letter referred to is Tucker's report to Hoffman on 9 July 1862 describing the shortages in detail, Ser.II-Vol.IV, 180.

[27] O R Ser.II-Vol.IV, 312-13, 335-36.

[28] O R Ser.II-Vol.IV, 339; Mackey diary, 19 Jul. 1862.

[29] Hesseltine, 65; Story,"Camp Douglas," 21; *Scurvy:* Severe disorder due to lack of vitamin C; evidenced by internal bleeding, sallow skin, bleeding and ulcerated gums, and fetid breath. *Black's Medical Dictionary,* Edited by C. W. H. Havard, MA, DM, FRCP, Thirty-fifth edition, Totowa: Barnes & Noble, 1987) 604.

[30] O R Ser.II-Vol.IV, 324-25; Medical and Surgical History of the War of the Rebellion, Vol. I, Part III:49.

[31] O R Ser.II-Vol.IV, 263.

[32] R. G. 393, IV:41.

[33] O R Ser.II-Vol.IV, 112.

[34] Mackey diary, 2 Aug. 1862.

[35] Thomas Neville Bonner, *Medicine in Chicago* (Madison: American History Research Center, 1957) 72. Dr. Boone invested in real estate, railroads, and commercial ventures; O R Ser.II-Vol.IV, 339-40.

[36] O R Ser.II-Vol.IV, 339-40; *Biographical Sketches of Leading Men of Chicago* (Chicago: Wilson & St. Clair, 1868), 277-78.

[37] O R Ser.II-Vol.IV, 347; *Halpin & Bailey's Chicago Street Directory* 1862-1863; Basler, *The Collected Works of Abraham Lincoln,* III:203n.

[38]8. A charismatic Indian leader named Black Hawk invaded Illinois in 1832 with a force of 400 to 500 Sauk and Fox warriors to reclaim lands they had signed away in 1804. They were opposed by regular army troops and Illinois militia to which the future president and Dr. Boone belonged.

[39] Bonner, *Medicine in Chicago.* 72, 160.

[40] O R Ser.II-Vol.IV, 324, 353.

[41] O R Ser.II-Vol.IV, 376.

[42] O R Ser. II-Vol.IV, 432.

[43] O R Ser.II-Vol.IV, 385.

[44] O R Ser.II-Vol.IV, 758-59.

[45] Barrow diary, 6 Sep. 1862; *Chicago Tribune,* 21 Feb., 22 Sep. 1863.

[46] *Chicago Tribune,* 21 Aug. 1862.

[47] Compiled from the Records of the Commissary General of Prisoners, R.G. 109, Roll 54.

[48] O R Ser.II-Vol.IV, 414-15.

[49] O R Ser.II-Vol.IV, 458-59.

[50] O R Ser.II-Vol.IV, 551-52, 615.

[51] Dorris, *Pardon and Amnesty Under Lincoln and Johnson, 61.*

[52] Harder, 40.

[53] *The Collected Works of Abraham Lincoln,* Roy P. Basler, ed. (New Brunswick: Rutgers University Press, 1953) vol. V, 403.

[54] Vol. IV, 504.

[55] *Chicago Tribune,* 1 Jul. 1864.

[56] Confederate Prisoners of War, R. G. 109, Roll 55 & 56.

[57] R. G. 109, Roll 56; Cole, *Era of the Civil War* 225, 233.

[58] Confederate Prisoners of War, R. G. 109, Roll 56.

[59] O R Se.II-Vol.IV, 551-52, 892-94.

[60] Currey, II:129.

[61] Spot F. Terrel, 49th Tennessee Infantry, "A Confederate Prisoner at Fort Donelson, *The American Historical Revue* (New York: Macmillan Co., 1926):482-83.

[62] Journal of Marion F. Baxter, 20th Mississippi Infantry, III:3. Baxter coll., USAMHI.

[63] Terrell, 483.

[64] Terrell. 484.

[65] *Chicago Tribune,* 4 Oct. 1862.

[66] R. G. 109, Roll 56; *Confederate Veteran* 15 (May. 1907):234.

[67] Unidentified newspaper article, 24 Oct. 1894, ms. CHS.

[68] O R Ser.II-Vol.IV, 758-59.

[69] O R Ser.II-Vol.IV, 758-59.

[70] *Chicago Tribune,* 19 Nov. 1862.

[71] Confederate Prisoners of War, Microcopy 598, R. G. 109, Roll 55 & 56. The Official Records do not provide returns from the camp before July 1862.

[72] R. G. 108, Roll 56.

[73] O R Ser.II-Vol.VII, 986-1003.

[74] *Chicago Tribune,* 22 Sep.1862; *Medical and Surgical History,* I, Part III:49.

7.

THE IRON RULE OF GENERAL TYLER

Camp Douglas moved along easily through the beginning of Autumn, 1862. Eight regiments of infantry and three companies of artillery were training and caught up in the Civil War.[1] Dress parades took place every afternoon. The food was fair, and the pride the men took in their new skills made it all seem worthwhile. Funds were finally allotted to Colonel Tucker to clean up the camp. As usual it was too late for improvements. Tucker's plans were wrecked by events taking place 800 miles to the southeast. The North suffered one of its worst defeats of the war on September 15, 1862. Almost an entire army corps surrendered at Harper's Ferry, Virginia.[2]

The event ushered in a period of mutiny and disarray at Camp Douglas. About 8,000 men paroled by the South under the Cartel began arriving September 28, 1862. Only 1,000 of them were from Illinois. Secretary of War Stanton had charged Brigadier General Daniel Tyler with organizing and moving them to parole camps. However, Camp Douglas had 8,000 troops in training at that time, leaving little room in the stockade. There were now two regiments outside in tents. Stables previously constructed west of the stockade were pressed into service as barracks for the parolees.[3] This created another camp named Camp Tyler, after the commander of the parolees, and extended two blocks west of the stockade to present Giles Avenue, in an area then called the "Fair Grounds."

General Tyler at age 64 belonged to another century. His father had fought at Bunker Hill. Tyler was born in Connecticut in 1799, and graduated from West Point in 1819. Denied promotion because of his rigid honesty in dealing with government contractors, he resigned in 1834.[4] Tyler re-entered the army as Brigadier General at the onset of the Civil War, but was discharged after incurring blame for the Union defeat at First Manassas. Recommissioned in 1862, he appears to have been ideally suited for his assignment at Camp Douglas.

Tyler complained to Washington that the railroads had moved the parolees in freight cars without water or toilets. Yet, they charged the passenger rate of two cents per mile instead of one cent for freight, at a cost of $632.80 to move 8,000 men. "I am bound to say that the price paid for the service is the most outrageous I have ever known!"[5]

The paroled troops consisted of the 60th Ohio; 32nd Ohio; Colonel Cameron's 65th Illinois; 39th New York; 111th New York; 115th New York;

General Daniel Tyler, circa 1865 (courtesy SAMHI)

125th New York; 126th New York; 9th Vermont; 1st Independent Indiana battery; 15th Indiana battery; 19th Ohio battery; 5th New York battery; and Phillip's Chicago battery.[6]

Colonel Tucker clashed with mutinous parolees on September 30, when the 9th Vermont groaned loudly and refused his order to go on guard duty. Tucker called out the 93rd Illinois Infantry and prepared to enforce the law with bayonets, but the parolees gave in. However, General Tyler relieved Tucker of command that same day.[7] He became commandant of the post by virtue of his rank. Tucker remained to organize and train volunteers. For the first time, the camp was under an officer sent by the War Department.

A lieutenant who straggled into camp from Harper's Ferry found his regiment quartered in "horse sheds" at Camp Tyler. "The floors of the apartment were laid in mud and the roofing perforated so as not to exclude the refreshing rain," he quipped.[8] Since the parolees were used to the hills of Virginia, "large quantities of garbage, rotting hay, etc. was thrown in heaps before the sheds," he added.

The stables were divided into stalls 10 to 15 feet square with eight men to a stall.[9] Private De Graff, of the 115th New York Infantry, conceded that "they do not look very inviting, but all hands set to work forthwith to make them as comfortable as possible." The stalls lacked bunks, which even the Confederates had enjoyed, but piles of clean hay were provided to sleep on. Captain Ripley, of the 9th Vermont, preferred the stables because the barracks "are filled with vermin, even if you can keep them as clean as you can."[10] This reflected on the condition of the just-departed prisoners. In addition, the stables had been used for only a few days to house horses during a recent fair. One drawback was the lack of windows. Natural light had to filter in through cracks in the roof and walls.

Unfortunately for Tyler, The *Chicago Tribune* published the Dix-Hill Cartel on October 5. Paroled troops were not to perform military duties under the agreement. "If we comply with this paragraph it appears to me it leaves little else for us to do with the men but feed and clothe them and let them do as they please," Tyler complained. The parolees took it to mean that they did not have to drill or perform guard duty, but the General thought otherwise; they were denied furloughs and made to go into training, police the camp, and pass inspections. His problems increased when the officers sided with the enlisted men.[11]

This resulted in a state of insurrection exceeding the prison break of July 23. The parolees set fire to barracks and fences at Camps Tyler and Douglas, and made frequent escape attempts, "and during that whole period the citizens of Chicago slept insecurely. They felt that a volcano existed at the camp which might at any time break forth and overwhelm the city." Camp Douglas suffered $7,652.70 in damages, and $7,937.84 worth of buildings and fences were destroyed at Camp Tyler.[12]

New fences were torn down by the parolees as soon as they were built. The guard house was also destroyed, to everyone's satisfaction. Oddly, 125 men from the 9th Vermont were put on guard duty with useless weapons, and the mutinous troops drove them away with rocks.[13] Several in the guard detail were badly hurt, and one suffered a broken leg. Private DeGraff confirmed that enough barracks burned to accommodate four regiments. "Our boys are very unruly, and do not want to drill or do anything else." However, he reported the rations to be excellent on October 18. "Fresh beef nearly every day. Plenty of coffee, and excellent bread and butter." This did not last, as the *Tribune* reported later that the "Beef is musty and in some cases completely spoiled."[14]

Tyler brought in regular army troops on October 23, 1862 to quell the parolees. He ruled with an iron hand and probably would have done the same with prisoners of war had any been there. At least two parolees were shot by guards as they scaled the fence at Camp Douglas. Nevertheless, many escaped into the city, which Captain Benjamin W. Thompson of the 111th New York Infantry described as "one vast beer saloon." He and fellow officers had to hunt their men every night "out of the saloons—and worse places." Chicago seemed to be a rat-infested rickety place to him. AWOLs had gotten out of hand to the extent that General Tyler enlisted the aid of the Chicago police in rounding them up in the city. The Provost Marshal promised to back up the police with his own troops.[15]

Ironically, the remark by Mr. Bellows of the U. S. Sanitary Commission about cleansing the camp with fire had come true. Medical inspector Keeney was delighted by "the immense destruction of animal life, in the form of lice, and had less of the filthy and rickety quarters been spared still greater salutary effects would have been the result." Thirty-five of the parolees died between October 8 and November 7, mainly of diphtheria, typhoid, and pneumonia. The sick were short of clothing and lying in filthy bunks. Refuse and trash lay every where, and pools of stagnant water made the place a quagmire.[16] A succession of Federal troops and prisoners had worn the place out. Substantial repairs would be required to make Camp Douglas resemble the proud military base it had once been. General Halleck, who was moved upstairs as General in Chief of the Army, issued a terse order on October 27, 1862 for Mulligan to report to Washington and settle his accounts. Mulligan was already there, according to his diary.[17] He saw Colonel Hoffman in Washington that day, who told him that General Halleck would decide what to do. On October 28, Mulligan noted in his diary that

"Colonel Tucker has done his best, poor fellow, to the extent of his limited ability to straighten out his accounts—a very weak Joseph Tucker is our Colonel." Mulligan apparently blamed Tucker for the problem.

That same day, Mulligan paid Hoffman $1,384.21 in full settlement of the prisoners' accounts at Camp Douglas. It is not likely that this money found its way back to the prisoners. There the matter ended, as well it should have. Union prisoners in the South would lose many thousands of dollars as they were shifted around to avoid the approaching Federal army. A Confederate officer in charge of these funds stole $3,000 after Richmond fell.[18]

Dwight L. Moody, the evangelist, returned to Camp Douglas at the beginning of November, 1862 to preach and help ease the plight of the parolees.[19] Private Belknap of the 125th New York credited him with "working for the poor soldiers nearly all the time in providing for the wants of their families." Moody also distributed a little book entitled *The Great Redeemer.*

Some officers sought relief from the dreadful conditions by going to the theater in Chicago. Captain Ripley saw John Wilkes Booth in *Hamlet* on December 10, 1862. "It was a happy evening. I never enjoyed anything half so well. I never heard the Elder Booth, but the Younger is certainly 'some,'" Captain Ripley marveled.

Meanwhile, the Chicago Sanitary Commission reported that the original latrines at camp were overflowing, causing a terrific stench and making the nearby barracks unbearable. A relief effort was started by Chicagoans to aid the parolees, but on November 11, Colonel Hoffman ordered part of their rations sold, as though the parolees were Confederate prisoners. Tyler refused, explaining that the parolees were training "and in a healthy state of discipline," and that he did not wish to interfere with any of the government allowances.[20] Colonel Hoffman continually suffered frustration in trying to take food out of the mouths of prisoners at Camp Douglas. In Tyler-like fashion, the General prohibited credit sales by the sutlers, and crushed another tradition by not allowing them to collect their debts out of a soldier's pay.[21]

General Tyler was replaced around November 20, 1862, after the government conceded that drilling and training the parolees violated the Cartel.[22] Colonel Daniel Cameron, now a paroled prisoner of war from Harper's Ferry, took command of Camp Douglas again by direction of the War Department. This also violated the Cartel, which meant that the army got rid of Tyler to appease the parolees. It was significant that the command did not revert to Colonel Tucker again. Dr. Park of the 65th Illinois Infantry replaced Dr. McVickar as Post Surgeon. No civilian would ever again hold this position at Camp Douglas.

Cameron was Colonel of the 65th Illinois, the so called "Scotch Regiment." Descended from the Camerons who fought the British at Culloden in 1746, he emigrated to America in 1851 at age 23. He was a Democrat, a friend of Senator Douglas, and founded the *Chicago Times,* a pro-Confederate paper. However, he had sold his interest in 1861.[23] Cameron and his men could not have imagined that they would return as paroled prisoners of war as they left camp in 1862 to battle the Confederates. This time he only served 23 days as commandant. Halleck requested that Cameron be relieved because "he does not think it proper that an officer on parole should command at Camp Douglas, Chicago, Ill."[24]

Colonel Daniel Cameron, circa 1863 (courtesy USAMHI)

The difference in mortality between the prisoners and the parolees in 1862 is significant because they were almost equal in numbers. The Confederates suffered a death rate of from 11% to 12%, while the parolees died at a 2.5% rate. The parolees faced the same diseases, poor medical care, and primitive living conditions as the prisoners. However, the parolees were in good physical condition and warmly dressed. This appears to have counted heavily. Captain Ripley blamed typhoid fever for most of the deaths among the Vermonters.

While the Confederate prisoners had departed Camp Douglas in high spirits, the parolees were in a sullen mood when they left. On November 22, 1862, the 39th New York and the 125th New York exchanged gunfire aboard the train leaving Chicago, and a sergeant in the 39th was seriously wounded.[25] There may have been bad blood between them over responsibility for the fires at Camp Douglas and Camp Tyler. They could envision not drawing another day's pay until the damage was paid for. Another cause may have been that "There was plenty of liquor aboard," according to Private Belknap. The Confederates had been lacking in that department.

All parolees, except Cameron's 65th Illinois Infantry, Phillip's Battery, and the 9th Vermont, were exchanged by November 30, 1862. Cameron would be stuck at Camp Douglas until April 19, 1863. Both he and Adjutant-General Fuller protested bitterly, without success.[26] His long stay is suspicious, since his veteran 65th Illinois was needed at the front, and normally Illinois packed tremendous clout at the White House. Perhaps Cameron's standing as a national Democrat kept him at Camp Douglas, and certainly his strong support of Senator Douglas did not endear him to the Republican administration.

Captain Ripley of the 9th Vermont had no doubt that favoritism played a major role in deciding which regiments were exchanged first.[27] The Governor of Vermont felt called-upon to go to Washington himself to see about the matter. However, the War Department, incredibly, authorized the regular army to go to Camp Douglas and recruit the 9th Vermont away from its volunteer officers. Captain Ripley was enraged by the loss of 100 to 150 of the best men.[28] Only some farsighted advice kept him from resigning his commission and taking himself out of the war.

Cameron had some ideas about running the camp, and recommended to Governor Yates that a permanent commander be appointed.[29] Of course, Yates was happy to surrender further responsibility there. Other reforms the Colonel mentioned were the arrest of deserters, and a method of distributing clothing to the troops. Also, he recommended that the State should supervise recruiting instead of using several recruiting districts.

The year 1862 was the busiest one for the camp. Besides 8,962 prison-ers in 1862 the number of parolees rose to 8,226. By now, approximately 42,000 men had occupied Camp Douglas since it had opened in Septem-ber, 1861.[30] About 17,000 were Confederate prisoners and parolees, and 25,000 were troops in training. Tents on the outside reached six blocks west to State Street, south toward Hyde Park, and one mile to the north. Camp Douglas had become a very large military base.

TABLE 3
FATAL DISEASES AT CAMP DOUGLAS IN 1862

Typhoid Fever: Causal Bacteria are related to food poisoning and dysentery and are spread by exposed sewage and contaminated milk and drinking water. *(Contagious)*
Diphtheria: Infection of the tonsils and back of the throat caused by many varieties of organisms, particularly streptococci which grow freely in milk. *(Highly contagious)*
Small Pox: Caused by a virus. *(Highly Contagious)*
Cholera: Caused by a bacillus (micro organism) communi-cated in contaminated drinking water and by flies which contaminate food with infected human feces. *(Contagious)*
Consumption: Tuberculosis which may infect the lungs or any other organ; caused by a bacillus and has been known since 400 B.C. *(Highly contagious)*
Dysentery: Caused by a bacillus spread by flies, by direct contact, or pollution of water by feces from infected patients. *(Highly contagious)*
Measles: Acute infectious disease known since the Tenth century. It spreads rapidly by infected droplets from the nose and throat coughed and sneezed into the air and can cut down large populations. *(Highly contagious)*
Pneumonia: Acute inflammation of the lungs which attacks persons with lowered bronchial defenses and less resistance to infections. Caused by a multitude of organ-isms or a virus following influenza.[31]

NOTES TO CHAPTER 7

[1] *Chicago Tribune,* 23 September 1862.
[2] *Battles and Leaders of the Civil War* (New York: Thomas Yoseloff & Co. Inc., 1956), II:604.
[3] Andreas, *History of Chicago,* II:302.

[4] Ezra Warner, *Generals in Blue* (Baton Rouge, Louisiana State University Press, 1964), 514-15.

[5] O R Ser.II-Vol.IV, 595-96.

[6] *Chicago Tribune*, 4 Oct. 1862.

[7] *Chicago Tribune*, 1 Oct. 1862.

[8] E. B. Sherman, "A Letter from Camp Douglas," 4 Oct. 1862, ms. Division, LOC.

[9] Nicholas De Graff, 115th New York Infantry, Civil War Diary, CWTI coll., USAMHI.

[10] Otto Eisenschiml, *Vermont General, The Unusual War Experiences of Edward Hastings Ripley, 1862-1865* (New York: Devin-Adair Co., 1960): 46.

[11] O R Ser.II-Vol.IV, 600; *Vermont General*, 50.

[12] Colbert, *Chicago. Historical and Statistical Sketch of the Garden City*, 93-94; O R Ser.II-Vol.V, 214-15.

[13] *Vermont General*, 58.

[14] De Graff, 16 Oct. 1862; Chicago Tribune 18 Nov. 1862.

[15] O R Ser.II-Vol.IV, 645; Benjamin W. Thompson, 111th New York Infantry, Civil War Diary. CWTI coll., USAMHI; Chicago Tribune, 9 Oct. 1862.

[16] *Medical and Surgical History*, Part III, I:49; Chicago Tribune, 10 Oct., 11 Nov. 1862.

[17] Mulligan diary, 27 Oct. 1862, CHS.

[18] Dennis Kelly, "A History of Camp Douglas," 23; Hesseltine, 235.

[19] Charles Wesley Belknap, 125th New York Infantry, Civil War Diary. CWTI coll., UASMHI.

[20] O R Ser.II-Vol.IV, 698-99, 710-11.

[21] Kelly, 95.

[22] O R Ser.II-Vol.V, 106.

[23] Andreas, *History of Chicago*, II:226-27.

[24] O R Ser.II-Vol.V, 130.

[25] Belknap, diary.

[26] O R Ser.II-Vol.V, 105-06.

[27] *Vermont General*, 66-67.

[28] *Vermont General*, 68.

[29] R. G. 393, v. 233:138.

[30] Story, "History of Camp Douglas," 42.

[31] *Black's Medical Dictionary*.

8.

GENERAL AMMEN AS COMMANDING OFFICER

The Union war machine began picking up steam in 1863. Due to Grant's movements in the West, Camp Douglas became a prison again when more destitute and hard-luck prisoners arrived. This violated the Cartel that called for immediate parole of captives. The camp was officially still considered only a "temporary prison." The remaining parolees from Harper's Ferry, being the 9th Vermont, 65th Illinois, and Phillip's Battery, watched them come with sinking hearts. These new prisoners meant that they were doomed to stay on as guards. The colonel of the 9th Vermont and some of its officers resigned their commissions and left.

At the end of 1862, Confederate President Davis had warned that black Union soldiers would not be treated as prisoners of war. This gave the North an excuse to end exchanges, no matter what the cost to Union captives in the South. Camp Douglas officials ignored paroles carried by the new prisoners. It was ironic that the entry of blacks into the Union army stranded thousands of Confederates in Northern prison camps. Men would die needlessly on both sides because of indifference by politicians to the fate of the common soldier.[1]

Colonel Tucker resigned his commission on January 1, 1863, and returned to the Chicago Board of Trade. No photograph of him can be found. One could expect Tucker to look stiff-necked and humorless, a martinet without the imagination or charisma to lead men, but that was not so. Tucker led a hand-to-hand assault against rioting and looting Union troops at the camp on December 23, 1861, and successfully put them down. He ended with his uniform torn and his face scratched and bruised. Private Benjamin J. Smith, who was at his side, describes him with a good deal of respect, and mentions that he was a "classy dresser," although Smith refused Tucker's offer of a job in the garrison.[2]

The army ordered General Jacob Ammen to take command on January 6, 1863. The Federal Government had seized control of Camp Douglas for the remainder of the war. General Ammen was a West Pointer. Although born in Virginia in 1808, he grew up in Ohio. He was an instructor at West Point, and taught mathematics after resigning from the army. Reentering Federal service in 1861, he commanded a brigade at Shiloh and was credited with helping to reverse the impending Union defeat.[3] Then he commanded a division against Confederate General Bragg in Kentucky.

General Jacob Ammen, circa 1864 (courtesy USAMHI)

General Ammen ran Camp Dennison in Ohio, and was the first commandant at Camp Douglas with such administrative experience. The Department of Ohio, which included Chicago, thought he was suitable to command Camp Douglas because of his rank and background. He and General Tyler were similar in that they belonged to an older generation. Also, like General Tyler, he insisted on discipline, banned liquor, and put a stop to speculation in Confederate currency at camp.[4]

The first prisoners of 1863 were 1,500 Confederates captured at Murfreesboro, Tennessee (Battle of Stone's River) on January 5, 1863. They resembled the Fort Donelson prisoners, except that they were not as able-bodied, ranging in age from 15 to 68, and many were conscripts. They also lacked warm clothing as did the prisoners of 1862. A reporter observed that they were covered by pieces of carpeting and hearth rugs in place of overcoats. They even wore "coffee sacks and grain bags, with holes cut in the ends and sides for the head and arms, linen sheets, bed quilts, bed blankets, horse blankets, etc, etc. Their hats and caps were every conceivable shape and style—and quite a number were bareheaded, while others covered their heads and bodies with the same quilt or carpet."[5]

More Confederates were captured on January 11, 1863 at Arkansas Post, also called Fort Hindman, which guarded the Mississippi River in East Central Arkansas. The Union officer there refused to parole the prisoners as required by the Cartel because "it would seem to me criminal to send the prisoners to Vicksburg. To send them there would be to re-enforce a place with several thousand prisoners at the moment we are trying to reduce it."[6]

The Confederates had been exposed to cold rains in fending off the Union attacks at Arkansas Post, and stood in ice-water to their waists. The confusion of 1862 about where to ship the prisoners was repeated, and they were left on an island near St. Louis in freezing weather without shelter. Many did not reach Camp Douglas until January 27. These troops were mostly from Texas and Arkansas, described as "poor white trash in the main, poorly clothed and overjoyed at the sight of a fire."[7] Upwards of 1,000 of them were receiving medicine at camp, according to the *Chicago Tribune.*

Captain Ripley disagreed with the newspaper's opinion of the prisoners. "The Texans here are the finest Southern troops I have run across," he wrote home.[8] In fact, the 9th Vermont and the Texans knew each other from Harper's Ferry. In a repeat of 1862, Ripley discovered that many of the prisoners were still armed, and he planned to search them again. "If you want an Arkansas bowie knife," he told his father, I'll set aside a peck or more for you."

About 200 Southern sympathizers had attempted to free the Arkansas Post captives when their train stopped in Chicago for transfer to the Illinois Central. Whiskey was passed through the windows and some rowdies attempted to open the doors. Like the Conspiracy of 1864 it was all talk, and ended with the police making two arrests while the 34th Iowa guard regiment fixed bayonets to their well-worn rifles. The Iowans were a tough bunch who had fought in General Sherman's brutal "Chickasaw Bluffs" campaign in Mississippi at the end of December, 1862, sometimes called 1st Vicksburg, and then were thrown into the assault against Arkansas Post a week later.[9] They had killed one prisoner earlier in the trip, and it was fortunate for the crowd that the police intervened.

Forty carpenters had been at work on barracks at Camp Douglas since January 24, and "had all in good order." The assistant quartermaster spent $15,000 trying to repair the damage of 1862. Thirty-six stoves were also being repaired at a cost of $89.00. There were about 3,000 prisoners in camp by January 30, 1863. One group of 1,500 was described remorselessly as "being more poorly clad, dirtier, and more cadaverous than any that have been in camp before."[10] They included young boys of 14, Cherokee Indians, Mexicans, and more black prisoners. "There are a large number of sick among them, and there seemed a continuous cough from one end of the procession to the other." Camp Douglas was again a dumping ground for the deprived, the sick, and the destitute. Luckily, no more prisoners would be sent.

Captain Potter, the Assistant Quartermaster, had warned Colonel Hoffman that the camp could only hold well prisoners. Hoffman disregarded this advice. The result was an urgent message from Ammen on February 2 repeating the familiar story of 1862, that the prisoners were sick and poorly clothed for the arctic winter.[11] A *Tribune* reporter interviewed prisoners on February 3 regarding charges in the *Chicago Times* that three of them froze to death. "No!" the men responded. "They were sick when they came," which could be considered faint satisfaction.

Life in barracks was not easy, the *Tribune* conceded. A prisoner slept with one or perhaps two other men on a bunk of pine boards, without bedding, a mattress, or blankets, unless he had his own. A bunkmate could have been quite ill with a cold or a more deadly virus. Hay was plentiful and there was an 18-hour supply of coal piled on the floor, but the barracks sat on the icy ground, so that it took two blazing stoves to keep it warm. Rags and clothing were stuffed around the windows and the door. The one water hydrant was frozen, drinking water scarce, and cleanliness impossible. Dirty clothing, haversacks, and equipment hung from the rafters. It was more like a mission shelter than an army barrack. Yet, mail traffic was heavy despite the dismal conditions. Many prisoners had blank business forms looted from various towns, and the Post Office was busy.[12]

Mortality was soon out of control, as 387 died in February 1863, according to the Official Records. At 10%, this was not the highest death rate. However, the camp's reputation for "extermination" was now firmly established. Captain Ripley noted as early as February 4 that "Mortality among them is undiminished. At this rate we shall have our responsibility all underground before the last of Spring. Their blood is so thin, and they have so little vitality, that their blood seems to stop flowing and curdles when when exposed as they suddenly have been, half naked, to this piercing cold."[13]

Ripley was critical of eight Confederate surgeons among the prisoners who refused to help them, and noticed how brutal the prisoners had become. "If one happens to die, another will roll him outside no matter what the weather and take what he can from the poor wretch." Another Vermonter also drew a grim picture of life at Camp Douglas as the third year of the Civil War began. He thought that the Union troops were as much prisoners as the "Johnnies" because all were in the same enclosure. "The mercury often fell to 20 degrees below zero," he remembered. "The sight of four sallow men, clad in butternut, bearing the corpse of a comrade to the dead house was an almost hourly spectacle. They looked as though they were clothed in sack cloth and ashes, doing penance for their sins."[14] However, he claimed that the prisoners "were as well fed and comfortably quartered as their guards." He attributed their high mortality to being "poorly clad, uncleanly, and sickly."

One soldier in the 104th Illinois Infantry was defensive about the terrible death toll among the prisoners, and claimed that "They were provided with as warm and comfortable quarters as our own."[15] This may have been true, as prisoners and guards lived side by side in White Oak Square. However, he loses credibility by claiming that "they were fed the same rations, had the best medical attention when sick," and received clothing and blankets.

Captain H. W. Freedley, Hoffman's assistant, reported $1,115.34 accrued in the prison fund by cutting rations in February. Ammen was the first Commanding officer to turn a profit, as this was the largest fund to date. Freedley gave no percentage of the reduction in rations; therefore, it is difficult to estimate the food loss suffered by the prisoners. The opposition *Chicago Times* guessed it was one-third of their ration. It appears to

Hoffman told Ammen that it was not necessary to accumulate a large fund, but "to relieve the Government as far as possible of the expense of their keeping." They had been well satisfied with the food on February 1, especially the coffee.[16]

Prisoners were not starving, but it was almost a criminal act to reduce rations during the Chicago winter, when they were without adequate clothing or medical care. The food contractor was William F. Tucker, a hotel owner in Chicago. He was no relation to Colonel Tucker, but his son was married to the daughter of General John W. Logan of Illinois, a powerful Democrat who was credited with keeping southern Illinois in the Union, and Lincoln was indebted to him.[17] This is probably why Tucker had the contract.

There was an unprecedented assault on Camp Douglas around February 1. A woman by the name of Mrs. Finley defied the male hierarchy in camp by opening a contraband food stand. She began operations from a shack on Jane Bradley's property abutting the northeast corner of the fence where the hydrant was located.[18] The determined woman cut a hole in the fence large enough for a service window and dealt food and beverages to all comers inside the camp. When officers boarded up the window, she reopened it. This happened 12 times before the lady was finally locked out. She would return.

General Ammen submitted an estimate of prisoners' needs to Hoffman on February 11 with the comment that "they suffer severely with the cold." Ammen turned the prisoners' chapel into a hospital, as Colonel Mulligan had done, and this time there was no interference from Washington. Like Colonel Tucker, Ammen called in Chicago police on February 15 for a shakedown. The results were surprising. They confiscated about $12,000 in gold and greenbacks, and a caché of hand saws, hatchets, and small axes in the barracks.[19] Later, headquarters admitted sheepishly that the tools were there for the prisoners to cut firewood.

Amnesty for prisoners was suddenly restarted, and on February 18, 1863, commanding officers were authorized to release enlisted men who were willing to take the oath of allegiance. "A careful examination will be made in each case," Hoffman warned, "to ascertain the sincerity of the applicant." The penalty for violating the oath was death, and each one taking the oath was warned that he could be drafted into the Union army. They were safe, as it turned out. When the Colonel of the 16th Illinois Cavalry tried to enlist prisoners at Camp Douglas, Hoffman sternly warned him that Stanton "forbids the enlistment into our ranks of prisoners of war who have been released upon taking the oath of allegiance."

Ammen personally interviewed these applicants and asked the famous four questions designed by President Lincoln:[20]

"First. Do you desire to be sent South as a prisoner of war for exchange?

Second. Do you desire to take the oath of allegiance and parole, and enlist in the Army or Navy of the United States, and if so in which?

Third. Do you desire to take the oath and parole and be sent North to work on public works under penalty of death if found in the South before the end of the war?

Fourth. Do you desire to take the oath of allegiance and go to your home within the lines of the U. S. Army, under like penalty if found South beyond those lines during the war?"

A prisoner's choice was reduced to writing, signed, and witnessed. Their reasons for being in the Confederate army and their attitude towards the war were closely questioned. Ammen reported that the prisoners from Texas and Mississippi "are very hostile and do not wish any terms except to fight it out." Records show 51 prisoners discharged in February, with about 100 still in line.[21]

It was likely that those who sought amnesty required protection from the loyalists, because Hoffman ordered them placed in separate barracks.[22] He also provided "in all cases where you have to employ prisoners as laborers, whether allowed compensation or not, give these prisoners the detail, if they desire it." This may explain the large number of hired prisoners at Camp Douglas. Those who threatened these men were to be severely punished, but Hoffman did not say how.

General Ammen believed that his main job was security, and the camp was locked down as never before; officers needed a special pass to get out and visitors ceased to exist. Charitable gifts had to be left at the gate. Persons who claimed to be Ammen's friends received no favors. A measure of the man was the statement that his only friends at camp carried guns.[23] The result of his actions was the lowest escape rate ever, with only 14 in three months, and some of these were chargeable to Colonel Cameron.

In addition, Ammen was a strong administrator. Captain Freedley reported to Hoffman that "he has confined himself strictly to your instructions and they are rigidly enforced." Books and records were properly kept.

Freedley inspected the camp March 11, 1863 and saw nothing wrong. "I find the condition of the prisoners at Camp Douglas much improved. The barracks have all been repaired. The fence which was partly torn down by the paroled men has been reconstructed. The barracks are not crowded and are comfortably heated. Each one is provided with a comfortable bunk, and the prisoners are in every way as comfortably provided for as our own troops."[24]

The guard force was composed of the 63rd and 104th Illinois Infantry, the 9th Vermont, and Phillip's Battery. This force of 1,737 enlisted men was the largest one so far to guard the prisoners.

Freedley was confident that health care was satisfactory under Dr. George H. Park, 65th Illinois Infantry, as Post Surgeon. "I found the hospitals generally neat and clean and are well supplied with cots and bedding," he told Hoffman. "The sick prisoners are well cared for. The medical supplies were sufficient."[25]

To the contrary, civilian doctors who inspected Camp Douglas on February 18, 1862 called it an extermination camp in a complaint filed with the Secretary of War. They drew an unrelenting picture of "wretched inmates; without change of clothing, covered with vermin, they lie in cots without mattresses or with mattresses furnished by private charity, without sheets or bedding of any kind except blankets often in rags, in wards reeking with filth and foul air." The stench was oppressive, and the hospital so inadequate that 130 prisoners had died in barracks, with 150 more waiting for hospital beds. "Thus it will be seen that 260 out of the 3,800 prisoners had died in twenty-one days, a rate of mortality which if continued would secure their total extermination in about 320 days."[26]

The doctors also warned Stanton about a newspaper article which claimed that 100 more were dead at the end of March. Like the Bellows report, this one also remained a secret. It is difficult to believe that Freedley and the civilian doctors were talking about the same camp. Perhaps their disagreement resulted from opposing perspectives. The doctors probably compared the camp to civilian hospitals, while Freedley may have thought that the sick were doing fine measured against other prisons.

Neighbors living near the camp were not as complacent as Freedley and appealed to the Chicago Board of Health about the smallpox hospital established on Douglas estate property.[27] Three physicians, including Dr. McVickar, were appointed to investigate. General Ammen, anxious to reassure the citizens and protect his reputation, appointed his own surgeons to meet with the Chicago doctors on March 11.[28]

They reported the smallpox patients as well cared for, and recommended building a new smallpox hospital further west. A smallpox cemetery was required, with victims had buried at least six feet down. Clothing had to be burned and a vaccination program started. Security was important to prevent infected prisoners from escaping. "With these precautions, we feel that our citizens may yield all alarm."

Chicago's fears were justified. At least two patients escaped each month from the smallpox hospital. More than a year later, the epidemic was still raging at camp and claimed 32 prisoners in the week of November 22, 1864 alone.[29]

The University of Chicago trustees across the road felt that the camp was a major factor in declining enrollment and passed a resolution on March 26, 1863: "That the Hon. Thomas Hoyne be requested to draw a petition to Government on the subject of the removal of Camp Douglas. To be officially signed and communicated to the Secretary of War."[30] Such a petition did reach Washington, but did not have much chance of success.

Freedley conceded that smallpox was prevalent. "The mortality of the prisoners is quite large, but this is to be attributed to their wretchedly broken down condition. Their general health has greatly improved since their arrival at the camp." Besides the 387 dead in February, he reported 262 prisoners in the hospital. Many sick were lying in barracks, and 125 smallpox cases needed space. The *Tribune* reported only 56 cases at this time, which meant some covering-up was going on.[31] One-third of this number were Union troops.

Freedley gave high marks to Dr. Park and the four civilian surgeons, but took a chance in permitting four alleged doctors among the prisoners to work as surgeons. Their credentials were not verified by any prison roll.[32] Hoffman failed to question their employment, and the four would later be blamed for allowing smallpox cases to leave Camp Douglas.

The prisoners were drawing salt meat almost exclusively with their rations, and Freedley recommended that fresh beef be issued five days a week because it was both healthier and cheaper. The previous May, John Sullivan, the food contractor at the time, advised Colonel Mulligan that "cured meats, such as bacon, &c." made up four-fifths of the prison meat ration.[33] Freedley also thought that the prisoners should begin baking bread. Apparently Hoffman had changed his mind since the previous year when he closed the bakery, and now allowed them to bake corn bread. However, the continuing rise in fuel costs closed the bakery again.

The army furnished little clothing, and only in extreme cases. It appeared that Meigs and Hoffman were carrying out the old Johnson's Island plan of requiring prisoners to furnish their own clothing. Large contributions of underwear and outer clothing came from friends and family.[34] These donations were insufficient to clothe 3,540 men.

Union and Confederate smallpox victims were buried in a cemetery "near Camp Douglas." It abutted the west side of the smallpox hospital opposite the south fence, now 34th Street and Rhodes Avenue. On March

28, 1863, Major General Burnside, who commanded the Northern Department, asked Halleck about closing the camp.[35] Halleck responded that only Stanton could order it, which meant that the camp would stay open.

Everyone now considered the site to be a mistake. The environment had crumbled under the unprecedented war-time use, and the former prairie was a swamp one day and a dust bowl the next, depending upon the season.

By March 31, mortality was again out of control. Smallpox and other diseases had claimed 700 prisoners, it was charged. If true, the toll in two months was only 277 short of the 1862 record, which took eight months to reach 977. The Official Records deny it, listing 464 dead for the entire time. Obviously, this figure is too low, as 387 died in February alone. Suspiciously, there are no Camp Douglas returns in the Official Records for March, 1863. The *Tribune* appears to have counted the dead carefully, and indicated that the toll could have been "upwards of 700."[36]

Prisoners of war did not die this quickly until a Confederate prison named Andersonville opened in Georgia on February 27, 1864. Exchange was the only hope for prisoners everywhere, as it had been in 1862. Manpower needs pressured the Confederacy to unilaterally restart the Cartel. On March 31, 1863, the U.S. exchange agent, Lieutenant Colonel William H. Ludlow, sent an urgent wire to Colonel Hoffman. "The Confederates are making heavy delivery of prisoners, and it would be very desirable to get our paroled men declared exchanged as soon as possible. When will the Arkansas Post and Murfreesborough prisoners arrive?"[37]

Vicksburg was no longer an exchange center because of the fighting there. Camp Douglas prisoners would go to City Point, Virginia east of Richmond. This was a long trip to the East, through Pittsburgh, Baltimore, and Washington to Fortress Monroe. The first group of 600 prisoners left Camp Douglas on March 31, 1863, only two months after arriving.[38] They were guarded by companies of the 9th Vermont Infantry, who had been at camp for six months.

Ripley, newly promoted to Major, left Camp Douglas as commander of this detachment. He wrote to his father that 30 Vermonters had to be left behind in the hospital, "and over 60 poor fellows under ground, who found the mud and surface water here more fatal than any exposure in Virginia." He only had 90 men to guard the prisoners. Their former Uncle Sam was sending the Confederates back in good passenger cars, and the seats could be converted to sleepers at night.[39]

Major Ripley was an insufferable snob, but had some concern about the prisoners. When they were kept awake by boisterous brakemen after the train stopped for the night on April 3, Ripley rounded up the workers and enforced the peace with bayonets. On the other hand, he considered the trip ruined by "Lousy high scented Secesh" surrounding him, "for our efforts directed to teaching them sanitation and arousing in them any ambition to cleaning themselves up, were a dismal failure."[40] However, the *Tribune* had reported a shortage of water at camp due to frozen hydrants.

He clashed with the wife of a rebel officer in the train station on Chesapeake Bay when she attempted to talk to the prisoners and give them money. He threatened to transport her to Baltimore as a prisoner, but ended by "politely" escorting her to her carriage. A more potent danger was the pro-Confederate population of Baltimore.

Ripley was reinforced by 100 men of the 151st New York Infantry and 40 police when the prisoners reached the city on April 4, 1863. Streets were filled with welcoming crowds, and deep feeling for the prisoners was evident. Major Ripley, a bachelor, noticed that "many a handsome Secesh Girl quietly placed the corner of an embroidered handkerchief to her face, to figuratively brush away the tear that stood in her dark blue eye."[41]

However, the road back proved once again to be most difficult for prisoners of war, and Ripley soon struggled with one army SNAFU after another. Not one particle of food had been placed aboard the steamer ready to take the prisoners to Fortress Monroe, where they would transfer to another boat for the trip to City Point, and Ripley had to run around for hours to cut the red tape and obtain five days' rations.

The next surprise occurred when Colonel Ludlow, the Federal exchange agent, had the glad news that Ripley's rebels were "neither paroled nor exchanged," and that Ripley would have to write up almost 600 paroles by himself. He had the job done by the next day, April 5, but then became entangled in Confederate red tape. The rebel authorities refused to allow the Camp Douglas prisoners to land at City Point on the morning of April 7 because they had no transportation, and expected Ripley to feed the prisoners while they remained aboard the steamer.[42] Ripley refused to issue the rations because he saw no reason for the Confederate government to shirk responsibility for its own men. As usual the common soldier was caught in the middle, and the road back was strewn with boulders. A train finally arrived later that afternoon to take the hungry men to Richmond, but it was not likely that any rations were aboard.

Ammen reported to Hoffman on April 6 that the last shipment of prisoners had left on April 3. The number forwarded was 2,534. About 350 sick were still at camp, and Ammen was not hopeful that all would recover. He mentioned that there had been difficulties and troubles, but did not elaborate.[43]

So far it appeared that Ammen had performed his duties competently. However, a storm was about to break. There was great alarm in Baltimore when smallpox cases from Camp Douglas were discovered the first week in April, 1863. Ten prisoners and one guard were found infected and were removed to a hospital. Hoffman learned of it from the medical director there, and he hastened to wire the news to Stanton's office on April 8.[44]

Hoffman blamed the alleged Confederate doctors. "Examination of the sick was entrusted to the rebel surgeon who was attending on the prisoners and he suffered nine slight cases to be brought with the well men." A "slight" case died in Baltimore on April 8. Hoffman did not disclose that many squads of Camp Douglas prisoners had passed through Baltimore without the knowledge of the medical inspectors there.[45]

Secretary of War Edwin M. Stanton, who wielded harsh authority, was already in a rage about 25 other smallpox cases at Fortress Monroe.[46] "I think it is outrageous that the commissary-general of prisoners should allow infected persons to travel through the States and be introduced to our posts," he charged, and demanded an immediate report from Hoffman.[47]

Hoffman was out to do bodily harm to whomever had damaged his reputation. Harping on the rebel doctors would be foolish. He wanted to place the blame on Camp Douglas headquarters, but his inquiry was blocked by the continuous changes at camp. The situation was now worse than when Governor Yates controlled appointments. General Ammen was transferred to Springfield, Illinois by the army on April 13, 1863. Colonel Cameron was in command again.

When Hoffman demanded to know from Cameron the name of the Post Surgeon responsible for smallpox cases leaving Camp Douglas, it was too late. Cameron had left camp for the last time on April 19. Hoffman did hear from the new commanding officer, Captain John Phillips, Co. M, 2nd Illinois Artillery, who was starting his seventh month at Camp Douglas. His investigation showed that the prisoners were not examined for smallpox before leaving camp. "I find no record of any order from General Ammen (who was then commanding post) for an examination of prisoners."[48] On May 4, Phillips was preparing a final shipment of well prisoners to City Point, Virginia, and he left eight days later. Colonel Hoffman had so little control over appointments that he was ignorant of who was managing the prisons and hospitals at any given time.

Hoffman notified Stanton on April 20 that General Ammen and his principal surgeon had to be held responsible for the shipment of the infected prisoners. General Ammen responded that he did order the prison-

Edwin M. Stanton, Secretary of War, circa 1862 (courtesy USAMHI)

ers to be examined for smallpox. Hoffman argued that this was untrue because Ammen allowed the four rebel surgeons to "take with them all whom they were not forced to reject." Hoffman failed to mention that he had permitted their employment, but pointed out to the Secretary of War that Camp Douglas should be closed if smallpox were taken seriously.[49]

The old warrior ended his telegram with a refreshing show of bravado in the face of a powerful politician. "In closing my report I must beg leave to express my deep regret that my untiring efforts to perform the various duties of my office with ability and promptness should meet only with such harsh censure as is contained in your telegram."

It is not known how many smallpox cases left Camp Douglas and returned to the Confederate army. That is where the matter rested. A more amusing incident at this time shows how little communication there was between the two sides in the war. Dr. Park had seen an emaciated prisoner just out of the hospital eating a pie, and warned him: "You ought not to eat those pies, don't you know they are poison to you?"[50] The prisoner took this literally, not knowing it was a Northern expression. Soon after he was exchanged, the *Richmond Examiner* ranted: "Not satisfied with putting our men to death by suffering and torture, the Yankee demons have taken to poisoning them!"

The sanitation crisis at camp was beyond solution, as there was no ground left for latrines or garbage pits. Now, Colonel Hoffman realized the significance of Camp Douglas as a depot for trainees, prisoners, and parolees. There had to be a serious reorganization. He again requested General Meigs to spend the money on a sewer system, reminding him of Tucker's plans submitted in July, 1862. Hoffman thought the project was a good idea except during the winter, when the present system would likely freeze and sinks needed to be used. "The cost is estimated at $5000, but in this calculation it was expected that the labor of prisoners of war then at the camp might be used," Hoffman advised. About $2,000 could be spent from the prison fund.[51]

Secretary Stanton also felt that the prison system could not continue as in the past. By April 23, Hoffman was submitting suggestions for building a new prison near Lake Michigan, either in Indiana or Illinois.[52] Hoffman's belief in an early victory was gone, and he planned for the new depot to hold 10,000 prisoners. Nothing came of this, which meant that Camp Douglas would continue as a prison.

On April 24, the surviving Arkansas Post prisoners were quartered near Petersburg, Virginia. A citizen suggested that they be put to work on the defenses.[53] By May, 1863, they were back in service without furloughs. The road back home beckoned in their fitful dreams, but it would be many years, if ever, before they saw their loved ones in the southwest.

```
┌─────────────────────────────────────────────────────────┐
│                      TABLE 4                             │
│           CAMP DOUGLAS PRISON STATISTICS                 │
│            JANUARY THROUGH APRIL, 1863                   │
│                                                         │
│   Total Prisoners Received ......... 3,932[54]           │
│   Died.................................................. 700?   │
│   Released Upon Taking the Oath.229[55]                 │
│   Escaped ............................................. 14     │
│   Remaining Sick plus nurses .......... 350              │
│                   Causes of Death                       │
│              Smallpox, fevers, pneumonia                │
└─────────────────────────────────────────────────────────┘
```

If only 464 prisoners died, as claimed by the Official Records, this would be a little over 12%, about 4% higher than the camp average for the war. However, 464 deaths was catastrophic considering the short time span. If 700 is the true figure, which it appears to be, comparing the number of prisoners received and the number who left, this would be a 20% death rate, still not approaching Andersonville, that had yet to make its stain on history.[56]

There is no indication that the amount or quality of the food was the cause of so much mortality. However, Captain Freedley found the diet to be poor. The hospital had sufficient coal; barracks were not as well supplied, and they were in poor condition despite $15,000 in repairs after the fires of 1862.[57] The camp was still plagued by primitive sanitation, and there was a shortage of blankets during the severe weather. The failure of the Government to quickly furnish warm clothing and blankets was probably the catalyst that caused so many lives to go out.

Another explanation for the high mortality was the same as that of 1862. "Arriving just at the edge of winter, they were but indifferently fitted to stand the hardships of the barrack life in what was to them the far north. The fact is that there were too many crammed into the place, and, as a natural consequence, they died off like rotten sheep."[58] Reverend Tuttle thought that nostalgia could have been another cause.

Whether medical care under General Ammen met Civil War standards was a matter of controversy. Medicine of the time was not close to discovering causes or cures for the many diseases at camp. A commanding officer charged Camp Douglas doctors with incompetence the following year. A substantial amount of surgery was performed at camp, but doctors knew little about reducing wound infection and postoperative mortality. While smallpox inoculation had been effective in Europe, some Northern prison camps were receiving worthless vaccines.[59] Perhaps this is why the disease was prevalent at Camp Douglas as late as 1865.

Concern for the prisoners lessened as Northern losses escalated and its resources were strained. Significantly, there was no Chicago relief committee for the prisoners this time, and the respected U.S. Sanitary Commission claimed that "the suffering and privations of prisoners in the South were not due to causes the South could not control, but were rather purposely inflicted by the military and governmental authority of the Confederacy."[60] Camp Douglas would emerge as a model prison in the eyes of the North.

It appears that West Point graduates such as General Tyler and General Ammen knew how to enforce discipline and were good administrators. Ammen's error in permitting infected prisoners to be exchanged resulted from his reliance on Dr. Park, the Post Surgeon, who was indifferent to the danger. Volunteer officers such as Colonel Mulligan and Colonel Tucker were weaker in management. Colonel Cameron's main contribution was appeasing the parolees; otherwise he was never in command long enough have an impact.

Hoffman started to work on Stanton late in May 1863, reminding him of the Bellows report and the need for improvements. "It almost impossible to have instructions carried out at Camp Douglas because of the frequent changes of commanders," he complained. "There is no responsibility and before neglects can be traced to any one he is relieved from duty." He recommended permanent medical personnel for camps such as Douglas and permanent commanders with reliable guards assigned to them.[61] The only concession he received was appointment of a special medical inspector for prison camps. Their reports were to prove most valuable.

Meanwhile, the dying went on at Camp Douglas, with 42 of the sick prisoners answering the long roll in May.[62] Only 226 more prisoners were exchanged of the 339 on hand. A handful of from 40 to 50 remained during the summer of 1863 with two more deaths reported. Hoffman was now winding up matters at camp. Property purchased by the prison fund had to be protected.

A new amnesty policy began in May, 1863. Now, special authority was required from Washington to release prisoners.[63] No one knew what this "special authority" meant, although a power broker in Washington or Kentucky could do the job if a prisoner had enough money. On August 4, 1863, amnesty was further choked-off with tougher requirements. The applicant now had to prove that he was forced into the Confederate service, or have "loyal people" vouch for him. Youths would have to show that they were "led away by the influence of vicious companions, his Union friends guaranteeing his future loyal conduct."[64]

The year was not yet half over and Camp Douglas was almost empty. Federal troops moved on from there to fight in major battles of the Civil War. Over 30,000 men had been drilled and equipped at camp by June 1, 1863. Close to 12,000 prisoners had suffered through the brutal winter of 1862-63, when the temperature often fell below zero. From 1,400 to 1,700 of them lay dead, but only 615 could be counted in desolate graves far from camp.[65] Between 700 and 1,000 bodies had disappeared. Somehow, Camp Douglas was exterminating the dead as well as the living.

Hoffman had no jurisdiction at Camp Douglas during the short time that it held no prisoners or parolees. He could have closed his books on the camp had it returned to being solely a training base. However, it would soon become a prison again with the arrival of Morgan's Raiders, the most militant and troublesome prisoners ever to grace White Oak dungeon. This battered, ramshackle collection of huts, festering latrines, and sagging fences was to become a permanent prison. Never again would recruits be introduced to the manual of arms at this depot. Meanwhile, Hoffman began nagging Meigs again about the sewer and water project.

NOTES TO CHAPTER 8

[1] Lorenso, "The Cruel War Prisoner of War System," unpublished manuscript, Illinois State Archives, 1978; *Chicago Tribune,* 31 January 1863.

[2] *Chicago Tribune,* 27 Mar. 1863; *Recollections of the Late War, Private Smith's Journal* (Chicago: R. R. Donnelley & Sons, 1963), 15-16.

[3] O R Ser.II-Vol.V, 157; Warner, *Generals in Blue,* 6; *Battles and Leaders of the Civil War,* 1:567.

[4] *Chicago Tribune,* 3 Feb. 1863.

[5] *Chicago Tribune,* 28 Jan. 1863.

[6] Rossiter Johnson, *A History of the War of Secession* (New York: Wessels & Bissell Co., 1910), 277; O R Ser.II-Vol.V, 176.

[7] Hazel Hankenson, "Where Dixie Sleeps Farthest North," *Confederate Veteran* 33 (Aug. 1925):301; O R Ser.II-Vol.V, 203; Story, "History of Camp Douglas," 46.

[8] *Vermont General,* 74.

[9] *Chicago Tribune,* 31 Jan. 1863; *Battles And Leaders Of The Civil War,* III:460, 462, 471.

[10] *Chicago Tribune,* 28, 31 Jan. 1863.

[11] O R Ser.II-Vol.IV, 207; Vol.V, 235.

[12] *Chicago Tribune*, 3 Feb. 1863.

[13] *Vermont General*, 73.

[14] C. G. Benedict, *Vermont in the Civil War* (Burlington: The Free Press Assoc., 1888), II:210.

[15] William W. Calkins, *The History of the 104th Regiment, Illinois Volunteer Infantry, 1862-1865* (Chicago: Donohue & Henneberry, 1895), 79.

[16] O R Ser.II-Vol.V, 345, 367; Based upon a cost of $519.48 per day for rations, which indicates a loss of 7.60% per prisoner; *Chicago Tribune*, 3 Feb. 1863.

[17] Tucker owned the Briggs Hotel at Randolph and Wells Streets in Chicago. *Bailey's Chicago Street Directory*, 1864-65. *Harpel Scrap Book obituary*, vol. 9:179, CHS; Albert Castel,"Black Jack Logan," *Civil War Times* 7 (Nov. 1976):6, 8. Logan sponsored the Illinois "Black Code" in 1853, excluding blacks from Illinois under threat of being fined and sold into slavery in lieu of payment of the fine.

[18] *Chicago Tribune*, 10 Feb. 1863.

[19] O R Ser.II-Vol.V, 265; *Chicago Tribune*, 16 Feb. 1863.

[20] O R Ser.II-Vol.V, 281, 297; Vol.VI, 823.

[21] *Chicago Tribune*, 28 Feb. 1863.

[22] O R Ser.II-Vol.VII, 221.

[23] *Chicago Tribune*, 31 Jan. 1863.

[24] O R Ser.II-Vol.V, 343-45.

[25] O R Ser.II-Vol.V, 344.

[26] O R Ser.II-Vol.V, 588.

[27] Across the road from the south fence and on the west side of the University of Chicago.

[28] O R Ser.II-Vol.V, 346.

[29] Confederate Prisoners of War, R. G. 109, Roll 58.

[30] Minutes of Special Meeting of the Trustees, 26 March 1863, The Old University of Chicago Records. Thomas Hoyne was the mayor of the City of Chicago at the time and a trustee of the University. His son was a student there.

[31] *Chicago Tribune*, 21 Feb. 1862.

[32] O R Ser.II-Vol.V, 344.

[33] O R Ser.II-Vol.III, 604-05.

[34] O R Ser.II-Vol.V, 345.

[35] Confederate Prisoners of War. R. G. 109, Roll 58; The Chicago Sunday Record Herald, 6 Oct. 1912, Old University of Chicago Records, Special Collections, Regenstein Library; O R Ser.II-Vol.V, 400.

[36] Goodspeed and Healy, *History of Cook County*, I:469; O R Ser.II-Vol.VIII, 986-87; *Chicago Tribune*, 4 Apr. 1863.

[37] O R Ser.II-Vol.V, 415.

[38] O R Ser.II- Vol.V, 342; *Chicago Tribune*, 31 Mar. 1863.

[39] *Vermont General*, 85, 88.

[40] *Vermont General*, 89.

[41] *Vermont General*, 90

[42] *Vermont General*, 92.

[43] O R Ser.II-Vol.V, 440.

[44] O R Ser.II-Vol.V, 449.

[45] O R Ser.II-Vol.V, 450.

[46] Margaret Leech, *Reveille in Washington 1860-1865*. (New York: Time Incorporated, 1962) 197-98.

[47] O R Ser.II-Vol.V, 444.

[48] O R Ser.II-Vol.V, 548-9.

[49] O R Ser.II-Vol.V, 476-77, 495-97; Smallpox appeared in the camp as early as 10 November, 1862, Goodspeed and Healy, *History of Cook County*, I:469.

[50] Tuttle, 20.

[51] O R Ser.II-Vol.IV,28-81; Vol.V, 492.

[52] O R Ser.II-Vol. V, 511-13.

[53] O R Ser.II-Vol.V, 934.

[54] O R Ser.II-Vol.VIII, 986-1003.

[55] *Chicago Tribune*, 4 Apr. 1863. The Official Records show only 51 released, which cannot be correct.

[56] By the end of July 1864 Andersonville held 31, 678 prisoners, and 12,912 Union graves were found after the war, a forty percent death rate. Hesseltine, 146, 152.

[57] *Chicago Tribune*, 4 Feb. 1863; Story, "Camp Douglas," 46.

[58] Colbert, *Chicago, Historical and Statistical Sketch*, 94.

[59] Bonner, *Medicine in Chicago, 1850 -1950*, 34; *The Medical and Surgical History of the War of the Rebellion*, I:67.

[60] Mark W. Sorensen, "The Civil War Prisoner of War System," 6.

[61] O R Ser.II-Vol.V, 686-87.

[62] O R Ser.II-Vol.VIII, 990.

[63] *Pardon and Amnesty under Lincoln and Johnson*, 26.

[64] O R Ser.II-Vol.VI, 175.

[65] Story, "History of Camp Douglas," 55; Report of the Board of Public Works of the City of Chicago, 10 Apr. 1863, CHS.

9.

DARING ESCAPE FROM WHITE OAK DUNGEON

Confederate authorities at Andersonville left sanitation to the Union prisoners. As a result there were no latrines for six months after it opened. Then it was too late. The Surgeon General in Washington estimated that 7,000 prisoners "will pass 2,600 gallons of urine daily, which is highly loaded with nitrogenous material."[1] Camp Douglas was to hold 12,000 prisoners at one time.

This may have been what motivated the army to build a sophisticated sanitary system there in late 1863. It was to provide toilet facilities for the garrison, prison, and hospitals, which exceeded the standard of living for most civilians in the area. Another reason for the new sewer and water system was the belief that the depot would remain a training base and parolee camp for Federal troops. In addition, Camp Douglas was considered a hazard to the civilian population after the record mortality of early 1863.

Possibly, there was concern for the health and welfare of the prisoners; another consideration was that most of the money would come out of the prison fund. To Hoffman's surprise, he was notified on June 11, 1863 that the sewer project was approved by Meigs.[2] As usual, events overtook the camp and prisoners began arriving before improvements could be made.

On June 27, 1863, Confederate General John Hunt Morgan, with about 2,500 mounted men, had pushed rapidly northward through central Kentucky, via Burkesville, Lebanon, Springfield, and Bardstown, to Brandenburg on the Ohio River. He cut through Southern Indiana at Corydon, Lexington, and Vernon, and then headed east after reaching the suburbs of Cincinnati. His men pillaged, burned, and plundered, but were crushed by Federal forces in late July. "Many were drowned in the Ohio River and a few escaped. Most of the men were confined in Northern prisons."[3]

General Morgan was a Colonel Mulligan in gray, only to a greater extent. The Ohio raid was against the orders of Morgan's superiors, and was a frolic of his own.[4] However, he enjoyed the devotion of his officers and men, even after disaster set in.

Captain J. S. Putnam, in command of Camp Douglas since May 12, 1863, advised Hoffman on August 13 that "Camp Douglas is in good condition to hold 8,000 prisoners. I have 125 guards." Putnam was a former parolee from Harper's Ferry. Captain James A. Potter, Assistant Quartermaster, was thunderstruck by such inexperience and warned Hoffman that even 6,000 prisoners would be too many. "Please have a commandant sent," he begged, "also a good officer."[5] Presumably he meant that one person should have both qualities. Hoffman did not have the power to grant his request, and the next commanding officer appointed at Camp Douglas happened to be in the wrong place at the wrong time.

Among the Federal units chasing Morgan's men were six companies of the 1st Michigan Sharpshooters under Colonel Charles V. De Land, age 35. He entered the war as a captain in the 9th Michigan Infantry in 1861 and saw some hard soldiering for the next two years. Captured at Murfreesboro, Tennessee, he was the only Camp Douglas commandant to have been in a Southern prison. After being exchanged he organized the 1st Michigan Sharpshooters and was commissioned as its Colonel. One company of his regiment consisted of 76 American Indians, half Chippewas and half Ottawas.[6] He was a thin, balding man who had been a journalist and farmer in civilian life.[7]

Colonel Charles V. De Land, circa 1863 (courtesy New York State Library)

The 1st Michigan Sharpshooters returned home after Morgan's raid, and on August 16 the regiment was sent to Camp Douglas for guard duty. Colonel De Land innocently became the senior ranking officer at Camp Douglas, and thereby received an order from General Ammen to take command on August 18, 1863.[8] The following seven months would be the most trying time of the war for him, if not of his entire life. Colonel Hoffman was not consulted about De Land.

Amnesty was virtually ended, and applications to take the oath had to be submitted to Hoffman for approval. Local commanding officers no longer had any jurisdiction in the matter. The application could be speeded along by listing special circumstances, but taking the oath was no guaranty of being released. With the Cartel dead and amnesty dying, the new prisoners were stranded for a long time. There was scepticism anyway about whether they would honor the oath once they were released. Five of Morgan's men at Camp Douglas applied to take it, which earned them jobs as nurses in the hospital. They promptly began digging a tunnel in a closet and escaped.[9]

Private Curtis R. Burke, Co. B, 14th Kentucky Cavalry, arrived August 18, 1863 on the Illinois Central and saw two street cars and several carriages of sightseers waiting.[10] The camp appeared large to him, with a high fence around it. He counted a post office, barber shop, picture gallery, two sutler stores, a commissary house, and a chapel. His group was marched to White Oak Square, which was empty of garrison troops. He described the barracks in White Oak as long one story buildings, four of them forming a square. Burke kept a journal during his imprisonment.

"The barracks were divided into little rooms with from two to ten bunks in each, and doors and windows to match, also one long room with a row of bunks on each side of the room, mostly three bunks deep or high, and making room for about eighty men,"[11] Burke recorded.

There was also a large dormitory with three tiers of bunks on each side, and separate rooms for commissioned and noncommissioned officers. Outside, in the rear of each barrack, was a kitchen, mess room, and a latrine, or "sink."[12]

Burke's father, Edward Burke, was also a prisoner, and is referred to in the journal as "Pa." Pa was sergeant-major of Co. B, 14th Kentucky. Neither young Burke nor his father were Southerners. Curtis was born in Ohio in 1842, and his parents moved to Kentucky when he was nine years old. His father was involved in Kentucky politics as a Democrat while earning a living in the marble business.[13] Both considered the North a foreign enemy of their beloved South, which neither had ever seen.

Rations were slow in coming and there was a shortage of eating and cooking utensils. Burke and his friend, Henry White, were almost shot by an Indian guard while searching empty barracks for tableware. "You want to go back there now quick," the guard threatened, "or I'll blow your damned heads off!"[14] The "you want to" was a favorite phrase of the guards, and the prisoners were soon mimicking them.

Only one water hydrant supplied the entire camp. It was not working when 558 thirsty prisoners arrived on August 20, which forced them to drink from a contaminated well. A prisoner wrote home, "I took a notion at the start that I must go to fight for Southern Rights, and I have now got enough of them."[15]

Morgan's Raiders were different from the Confederates seen before at Camp Douglas. The earlier prisoners had been captured while defending strategic positions or in the brilliant stroke at Shiloh. Morgan's men had been squandered in a reckless escapade. Of course they did not see it that way, and considered themselves an elite group.

"Generally they are far better looking men than any of the secesh prisoners we had here before," a reporter conceded. "Those butternut suits and shapeless slouched hats, would make an ugly man of anybody. All the colors of Joseph's coat were represented in their wearing apparel: the butternut was worn by the careless quiet looking individuals, who had their horse blankets and tin cups strung across their shoulders. But the keen, black eyed out-and-out 'raiders' of the dare devil stripe, had either a suit of black broadcloth, or a portion of our own soldiers' blue uniform." [16]

Despite these romantic notions, Morgan's men were the only Camp Douglas prisoners who had made war on civilians. In one incident near Corydon, Indiana, Burke's comrades killed an elderly man who fought them with his bare hands to keep his home from being burned.[17] He was suspected of having fired at them from an upper story, killing one of the raiders. Other suspected "bushwackers" were threatened with summary execution. General Morgan had pointed the way for Sherman's march through Georgia.

Religion continued to play an important role in prison life. On August 26, 1863, the sermon was "Choose ye this day whom ye shall serve," apparently aimed at the many guests from the South. The chaplain of a guard regiment preached to 2,500 prisoners later that day, and there was much singing. Nonetheless, card playing in barracks was continuous, and disturbing to some. The prisoners did not rely entirely on Northern preachers and formed their own congregation "to improve the morals of the camp."[18] There was an ample supply of religious tracts thanks to the Chicago Bible Society and Reverend Tuttle.

Morgan's Raiders at Camp Douglas, Circa August, 1863. Probably taken by D.F. Brandon. Note their menacing look and ragged condition. The soldier in the upper right appears to be a youngster. (Chicago Historical Society)

Morgan's men continued to arrive until August 27, bringing their number to 3,100. Colonel De Land's guard force was then only 600 men. Prisoners recently captured at Cumberland Gap swelled the prison population to 4,234 by September 26, 1863.[19] The army's failure to furnish clothing at Camp Douglas continued, but this was not a problem for the Kentuckians. They were mostly affluent, and simply sent home a list of their needs.[20]

Colonel De Land's position was precarious from the start. Without warning he inherited a slum that rivaled the worst streets and alleys of Chicago, "its barracks, fences, guard houses all a mere shell of refuse pine boards," De Land complained.[21] While the city's poor may have accepted their lot, Morgan's Raiders did not. Ironically, the Confederates De Land had pursued began pouring into camp before he could loosen his tie. Add to this situation a cantankerous career-driven boss like Colonel Hoffman, and De Land was on his way to a case of ulcers.

De Land immediately issued comprehensive general orders to officers and enlisted men in his garrison, notwithstanding his lack of experience in managing such a depot. He expected strict discipline, and made it a serious offense to fraternize with the prisoners.[22] However, he still was frustrated by the poor condition of the camp and corruption among the guards.

He found two unsanitary sutlers named McBride & Van Fleet, and C.K. Winner & Son, who were selling in camp without authority and employing prisoners to solicit orders. Mrs. Finley, who had been shut down 12 times previously, was now operating a food stand in camp, after her persistence had caused Colonel Cameron to allow her inside the stockade. Colonel De Land condemned her food stand as a nuisance, and she was evicted along with the sutlers. She would be back, and so would the sutlers when Hoffman ordered them reinstated. They probably had political influence. De Land kept Hall & Treadwll, the sharpshooters' sutler.[23]

The "extensive repairs to barracks" in early 1863 was only a band-aid job, as it turned out. Some new prisoners had to be housed in outbuildings and kitchens. Hoffman recommended to Washington on September 23, 1863 "that the buildings burned down last winter not yet rebuilt may be put up with as little delay as possible."[24] His reason was economic; with the large investment in sewers, water, and fences, it made sense to prepare as many barracks as possible. He was now viewing Camp Douglas as a permanent prison.

Improvements were moving ahead, and the infantry prisoners were working on a ditch for water pipes by the middle of September, 1863. Food was drawn in messes of six men. Burke's mess equipped a six- by ten-foot room with shelves and other items. Cook houses were mentioned from time to time in various reports, but Burke's group cooked in the long room of the barracks.[25] A kitchen was later partitioned off from the dormitory, and one was added on to the barracks the following year.

The prisoners were astounded to learn that instead of receiving the cash sent from home, all they saw was the envelope with the amount noted on it. "Then we had to take the sutler's checks for it and pay whatever the sutler choose to ask for his goods, which made the profit very large," Burke complained. Equally astonishing was the free run of the camp. Prisoners were able to leave White Oak Square and go to the hydrants in the northeast corner of Garrison Square. They had to wait hours to get water because one of the three usable hydrants was reserved for troops.[26] This was a bone-chilling ordeal as cold winds frequently whipped through the camp.

No more applications to take the oath were being accepted after October, 1863. The reason was practical—there would have been no one to exchange for the thousands of Union prisoners in the South if Northern prisons were emptied. The question was no longer whether a prisoner could take the oath, but whether he could even apply. This made no difference to Morgan's Raiders, who were mostly loyal to the Confederacy, and Camp Douglas began to lose prisoners at a record rate. Two men in Burke's mess who had attempted escape three or four times previously were successful on the fifth, aided by civilian clothing and perhaps a corrupt guard.[27]

Colonel Hoffman opened a can of worms on October 1, when he requested Dr. A. M. Clark, Medical Inspector of Prisons, to inspect prison camps "to see how far the regulations are carried out." Hoffman received a distress call from Colonel De Land soon after. The camp was so dilapidated it could not house all of the prisoners. "I also desire the erection of an additional hospital building and a hospital laundry," De Land added.[28]

Dr. Clark made a wide-ranging study of conditions at Camp Douglas on October 9, 1863. There were 6,085 prisoners in camp, according to his report, but only 978 guards. These consisted mainly of the 651 men in the First Michigan Sharpshooters, and 309 in the Invalid Corps. The Invalid Corps was renamed the Veteran Reserve Corps on March 18, 1864. The Corps was recruited from oficers and enlisted men who were on duty but disabled by wounds and disease, men who were in the hospital or otherwise under medical supervision, and honorably discharged soldiers, also disabled, who wished to rejoin the military. Their primary duty was to guard prisoners, act as military police, or perform hospital duty.[29]

The water was described as insufficient, but "quality and effects, good," which showed how little Dr. Clark knew about Chicago water. He estimated that there was housing for 4,500 prisoners under the best of conditions. Barracks were without heat, flooring, or siding, and roofs badly needed repair. "There is not a door and hardly a window among them," Clark observed. The prisoners also lacked bunks and heating stoves, while the guard barracks were overheated.

Clark mentioned that prisoners were not required to work, but many volunteered. The three hydrants in Garrison Square continued to leak and created pools of water. Seven new hydrants were to be installed. Dr. Clark thought that the planned sewer system was inadequate to drain the camp. This turned out to be correct. His report denounced "the authorities," as Clark described "discipline in camp—very lax." Garbage littered the streets and open latrines fouled White Oak Square. "No attention was paid by the authorities to the cooking in barracks" or to policing the camp.

Dr. Clark did not explain what he meant about the cooking. True, "Johnny Reb" was a terrible cook at first. Southern newspapers attributed much sickness in the army to improper food preparation. However, by late

1862, he had become adept at preparing staple items and Southern specialties such as pies and baked "possum."[30] In addition, soldiers had developed a routine of cooking in messes of four to eight men. The prisoners appeared to have brought this method to Camp Douglas. It was likely that they lost many of their cooking utensils in the field and had not yet received new ones at Camp Douglas. Burke and Henry White had the previously mentioned run-in with a guard because they were looking for something to eat with.

Dr. Clark also charged that the number of deaths was not properly reported, which confirms suspicions about the figures published after the war. Prisoners were buried in City Cemetery, but he does not say how. About 1,200 prisoners were without blankets. Clark wrote that "some would be cleanly if they could, but most are filthy." De Land withheld army clothing because he was fearful this would aid escapes. Dr. Clark thought otherwise. "This should be looked to, for many of the prisoners are miserably clad, and already suffer much from the cold." De Land finally issued 1,000 blankets, 1,000 jackets, 1,000 pairs of pants, 2,000 woolen shirts, 2,000 pairs of drawers, 2,000 pairs of socks, and 1,000 pairs of shoes to the prisoners.[31]

The only bright spot in the report was the hospital, although too small for all of the sick, and 120 patients were without blankets.[32] The chapel became an 100-bed infirmary for the third time on October 4, 1863, the report discloses. Dr. Clark said that it was "against the protest of certain good ministers of Chicago, who claim that the prisoners' souls should be looked after at the expense of their bodies."

Believing with all of his soul that disease was carried through the air, Clark reported "ventilation utterly lost sight of" in the hospital. The main killer diseases were typhoid fever and pneumonia. Measles was also a problem. Fifteen patients were entirely recovered from leg amputations, which were performed elsewhere. A grave concern for him was the lack of "strict discipline" for the rebel nurses. Escapes were common.[33]

Dr. Clark described White Oak dungeon as "utterly unfit for that purpose." A hatchway in the ceiling opened an underground room about 18 feet square. A small barred window gave the only light, and a sink in one corner emitted an intolerable stench. He found 24 prisoners confined there because of attempts to escape. "The place might do for three or four prisoners," Dr. Clark estimated, "but for the number now confined there it is inhuman. At my visit I remained but a few seconds and was glad to get out, feeling sick and faint." Four prisoners had petitioned De Land the previous month to be released from there, promising "not again to attempt escape."[34]

De Land informed General Ammen on October 13 "of a stroke of bad luck in the loss of twelve prisoners on Sunday and Monday nights, and I strongly suspect collusion and bribery." The father of an escapee had been there for two days with a pass from Department Headquarters. De Land was fortunate in losing so few prisoners, considering the minimum security. The escapes had made the guards nervous, and they fired several shots at the prisoners on October 14 for trivial offenses. A substantial stockade to replace the old one was still under construction. On October 17, 1863, Hoffman promised De Land that no more prisoners would be sent and 1,000 would be transferred to a new prison depot at Rock Island, Illinois.[35] Both promises were illusory. Over 9,000 more Confederates came in the next 16 months.

Captain Charles Goodman, the Camp Quartermaster, purchased 150 pounds of tobacco to pay the hired prisoners working on the camp. He would buy 400 more pounds in the next four months. The prisoners favored chewing tobacco over the smoking kind. Either type cost about $1.50 per pound due to the war, and payment came out of the prison fund. Goodman had enough tobacco to put 500 men to work. The new fence was almost complete by October 17, 1863, with the parapet in place three-fourths of the way around the camp, and almost up to the hydrants in Garrison Square. Burke estimated the height to be 15 or 16 feet, and prisoners were drawing water from new hydrants near their barracks.[36]

One of the most desperate escape attempts occurred on October 18, 1863, when two prisoners entered the unfinished sewer, a wooden box-like duct two feet tall by 18 inches wide and filled with water. They emerged outside camp after 16 hours in this hellish box and escaped.[37] Both men were recaptured in Chicago, where they had lingered too long. The city was not only a commercial and industrial center, and a hub of religious revival, it was also a world-class den of prostitution, vice, saloons, and gambling hells.

"There were many fissions in the city's social pattern. Among them, the Prairie Queen, on State Street, which offered uninhibited dancing, erotic shows of Dionysian degenerate detail, dogfights, and a monthly prizefight, bare knuckle-style, for the pay of two dollars a fight and, for the winner, a free bed with one of the house whores."[38]

This is not to suggest that every escaped prisoner fled north to State Street instead of south to Dixie, although when 12 prisoners escaped in October, 1863 by bribing five guards in De Land's 1st Michigan Sharpshooters, one of them got drunk in town and revealed the entire affair. Eleven made good their escape, but not without adventures in Chicago.

They had the nerve to file police complaints against a taxi driver who over-charged them, which delayed their exit from the city.[39]

Ministers could have pointed out some fissions in the social pattern at Camp Douglas, also. There were 20 card tables going at the sutler.[40] Burke watched, but did not play. The sutler must have charged the prisoners for this, and made an additional profit on selling the playing cards. None of the Camp Douglas commanders were strong on religion, which may explain why Colonel De Land permitted the gambling.

Chicago had much to offer other than vice and gambling. Former prisoners William M. Barrow and James T. Mackey, for example, would have enjoyed fine acting at McVicker's Theater. John Wilkes Booth still appeared there in Shakespeare, and Chicago critics agreed that he was a star. "The simple announcement of his appearance will fill the theatre," one critic gushed.[41] Private Burke and his father would have liked the new game of baseball, played just west of downtown, or enjoyed a special racing day at the Chicago Driving Park when liquor was banned, and only the "best people could attend." Captured Confederate musicians at camp could have heard visiting orchestras in Chicago playing "Daisy Dean," "Babylon is Fallen," and "Before the Battle, Mother."

Colonel De Land could also have used some recreation. Dr. Clark's report exploded in his face on October 24, with Colonel Hoffman quoting the most derogatory parts to him. "All these deficiencies must be remedied at once," he lectured. This was to be at the prisoners' expense, paid for out of the prison fund. Even worse, Hoffman imposed restrictions that made management of the camp more difficult. Cooking, if one could call it that, was to be done in 40-gallon Farmer's boilers. This meant that the prisoners would lose their cooking stoves, a critical item for survival during the winter. Bread was to be baked in camp again, not contracted out. Hoffman ordered De Land to build two more hospitals with the prison fund. "The hospital affairs must be very badly managed if the hospital fund is not sufficient to purchase all the furniture of all kinds that is required for the hospital," he lamented. To the contrary, the fund was low because of the the large number of sick, and an increase in the cost of 100 rations from $14.80 to $18.42.[42]

Hoffman had told De Land to cut off the skirts, trimmings, and buttons from the army clothing before issuing them. Prisoners did not appreciate this idea because it made the clothing ugly, and they still had their pride. Did De Land have any pride? Hoffman demanded a report from him within six days on how he had remedied the shortcomings in Dr. Clark's report. Why did he take Hoffman's abuse? Camp Douglas was not De Land's responsibility. He could have resigned as commandant and demanded a

Edgar Druilhet, 30th LA Inf., cica, 1862. Note the two cent revenue tax on the photo, which was the same charged for a deck of playing cards. (courtesy Lewis Leigh, Jr.)

Coleman Pattie, Comp.A, 8th Ky, Cavl., circa 1862 by D.F. Brandon, Camp Douglas. (courtesy The Filson Club)

R. Simcoe, 10th Ky. Cavl., circa 1862, by D.F. Brandon, Camp Douglas (courtesy The Filson Club)

Samuel J. Sullivan, Co. B., 3rd Ky. Cavl., Circa 1862, by D.F. Brandon, Camp Douglas (courtesy The Filson Club)

transfer for himself and his regiment, or he could have resigned his commission and gone home. As it turned out, De Land was simply not a quitter. Colonel Hoffman's criticism did have some effect. Beginning October 25, prisoners were required to clean up the barracks and the kitchens, and to police the grounds immediately after roll call.[43]

A total of 151 escapes plagued De Land, the worst record of any commanding officer at Camp Douglas. There were many reasons for this. The small garrison was not able to patrol the city for escaped prisoners. The need for troops at the front took precedent throughout the war, and Camp Douglas guards were also employed in returning hundreds of deserters to their units.[44] Inexcusably, the army added to De Land's security problems by issuing visitor permits to relatives and others.

At one point, De Land had refused to allow the visitors in, and barred a minister who had a pass. This action resulted in a loud complaint from the army department in Cincinnati to General Ammen. "De Land has no authority to limit permits to visitors at Camp Douglas," the army charged. Ammen did support De Land in one case in which he warned him about a Reverend John Frimble "who is agitating to get into Camp Douglas to convert souls."[45]

The martial law decree of 1862 around Camp Douglas was being ignored, though. De Land told Ammen that "It is known to the prisoners that a large number of persons are constantly outside the prison." Colonel Hoffman came to De Land's rescue in regard to passes with a special order on October 15.[46] He ruled that De Land must have complete discretion and control in this regard, and neither the army nor Ammen could issue a pass for anyone to enter Camp Douglas.

General Morgan's men often filled White Oak dungeon, and it was from here that 26 prisoners made an extraordinary escape at the end of October, 1863. They cut a hole through the plank floor, then dug about four feet into the sink, according to De Land's report.[47] From there they dug ten feet underground past the fence, right under the feet of the guards. The nature of the tools they had used and how these were obtained was not revealed.

De Land refused to take the blame. "For six weeks I had less than 600 effective men as garrison," he pointed out. "During all the time we have been building, fencing, laying sewers, water pipes . . . Prisoners have slid out of the holes in the dark, have passed out as workmen, and in a variety of ways have eluded the vigilance of the guards . . . Several have been killed and others wounded, and yet some escapes could not be prevented."

He added that the sewers, water pipes, and the fence were nearly completed. "Three or four days more will make Camp Douglas so safe and secure that not even money can work a man out. The only danger then will be in tunneling and that will not be tried often." This was a disastrous prediction.

De Land was sick at the end of October, 1863, but made a vigorous defense of his administration against Dr. Clark's report on November 3.[48] The situation was similar to the time when Colonel Tucker had to explain Dr. McVickar's report of a health crisis at camp. De Land insisted that the poor condition of the hospital was due to terrible overcrowding. "How could it be otherwise with so many sick thrown upon our hands?" Food preparation was difficult for lack of utensils. However, garbage disposal had improved, two new hospitals and a laundry were being built, and the new sewer system would go into operation in three days.

It consisted of 10 sinks constructed over the sewers. Forty funnels from each sink connected to a soil box. A movable hydrant would flush out these boxes each day.[49] Three 500-gallon water tanks were to wash the filth through the sewers and into Lake Michigan (drawing page xx). The City laid a large water main under Cottage Grove to serve the new system, but three-inch pipes inside the camp proved to be a serious defect.

The prison camp at Elmira, New York had similar sanitation problems after it opened about July 1, 1864. Lack of a water supply defeated a plan to build water closets.[50] Pits were dug at the edge of a pond that quickly became a cesspool. Colonel Hoffman authorized only $120 to connect its sewers to a river one half mile away. In desperation the commandant did the job at a cost of $2,000.

De Land was blunt about the the boilers which were supposed to replace the cooking stoves. "We have tried the Farmer boilers and they are a failure," he warned Hoffman, and suggested that the prison kitchens be provided with the same brick and iron cooking stoves used by the garrison. Their stoves were "a range built of brick and covered with an iron top, with holes like a cook stove, on which pots, camp kettles, and frying pans could be used; each range three feet wide and twelve feet long, with sixteen holes to burn four-foot wood."[51]

De Land thought such stoves would be cheaper and more efficient than the boilers. He was right, but had not considered the paranoia gripping Colonel Hoffman and the War Department. The stoves were too good, and did not conform to the new policy of retaliation against the prisoners.

De Land had a nasty surprise for Hoffman in regard to baking bread at camp. It was now beyond De Land's control, as all rations at Camp Douglas had come under the jurisdiction of a captain in Springfield named Ninian W. Edwards, who managed subsistence for Illinois army bases and prisons by order of the Commissary Department in Washington.[52] Edwards may have been closer to President Lincoln than any other man, and owed him his commission.

Ninian Wirt Edwards, born in 1809 in Kentucky, was a lawyer by training and a merchant and politician by profession. He had pushed a State school law through the Illinois legislature in 1855. Proud and aloof, he was married to the elder sister of the future wife of Abraham Lincoln, with whom he had long been associated in politics. It was in the Edwards home in Springfield that Lincoln met Mary Todd; it was Edwards who encouraged the turbulent engagement, and it was in his home that they were married.[53]

His contractors furnished rations directly to the prisoners, and by-passed the camp commissary. One such contractor furnished the equipment for the prisoners to make "johnnie cakes."

Curtis R. Burke, of Morgan's Raiders, commented about the low quality of these rations. "We draw fresh beef every other day, but it is not a number one article being mostly neck, flank, bones, and shanks."[54]

De Land had spent $20,000 for improving the camp, employing 100 prisoners daily. They were paid in clothing and tobacco. "This cost the government nothing," De Land boasted, "as the tobacco was purchased with prison funds and much of the clothing came from Kentucky." He closed his report by assuring Colonel Hoffman that Camp Douglas was to be a model military prison by the end of November, 1863. "If I fail, the fault shall not be mine." [55]

Nevertheless, Dr. Ira Brown of the 65th Illinois Infantry reported to De Land on November 1 that the amount of square feet per prisoner in the barracks was far below government standards. Such overcrowding made it impossible to keep them sanitary. Tar paper covering was missing from the roofs, many barracks were boarded up for lack of windows, and some had no bunks for the men to sleep on.[56]

Another calamity occurred when one of De Land's officers carelessly "lost" 11 prisoners who were being transferred to Camp Douglas from Louisville. Hoffman chewed De Land out as though he were a private. "It is your duty to see that those under you perform properly their duties assigned to them!" Hoffman raged. "It is not sufficient that you give these orders, but you must see that they are obeyed!"[57] Pressure mounted for De Land to plug the security leaks, but conditions were against it. The garrison consisted mainly of disabled veterans, and his own 1st Michigan Sharpshooters were prone to corruption. Also, maximum security was impossible, given the layout of the camp. These problems ushered in a new era of brutality at Camp Douglas.

It began with the killing of a black prisoner. "The first prisoner they shot after we were put in was a small, fourteen year-old negro boy," a writer identified only as J.M.L. reported to the *Confederate Veteran* in 1897. "I saw him the next day in the dead-house, and the rats had eaten off his ears." J.M.L. provided accurate details about the camp, indicating that he was there at the time.

NOTES TO CHAPTER 9

[1] Kubalanza, "A Comparative Study," 35-36; OR Sev II–Vol. VIII, 604.

[2] O R Ser.II-Vol.VI, 4.

[3] J. G. Randall, *The Civil War and Reconstruction* (Chicago: D.C. Heathe & Co., 1937) 532-33.

[4] *Battles and Leaders of the Civil War*, 3:634.

[5] O R Ser.II-Vol.VI, 200, 206.

[6] *Record of Service of Michigan Volunteers in the Civil War*, Michigan State Historical Library, Lansing; *Loomis Index*, Michigan State Archives, Lansing; *Chicago Tribune*, 19 Sep. 1863.

[7] *Brevet Brigadier Generals in Blue*, 157.

[8] Dennis Kelly, "History of Camp Douglas," 51.

[9] O R Ser.II-Vol.VI, 212; *Chicago Tribune*, 28 Oct. 1864.

[10] Curtis R. Burke's Civil War Journal, *Indiana Magazine of History*, Pamela J. Bennett, ed., Vol. 66 (June, 1970): 121. Vol. 65 (Dec., 1969): 283. He was 21 years of age and a thin five feet seven inches when he entered the camp. His diary is presented as written. The "14th Kentucky Cavalry" is not listed with the official regiments in Morgan's command. *Reminiscences of General Basil W. Duke, C.S.A.* (New York: Doubleday, Page & Co., 1911).

[11] Burke, 120-21.

[12] Kelly, 79.

[13] Preface, Burke's Journal.

[14] Burke, 24 Aug. 1863.

[15] *Chicago Tribune*, 21, 24 Aug. 1863.

[16] *Chicago Tribune*, 19 Aug. 1863.

[17] Burke, 9 Jul. 1863.

[18] *Chicago Tribune*, 1 Sept. 1863; Burke, 2 Oct. 1863.

[19] O R Ser.II-Vol.VI, 434; A strategic gap in the Cumberland Mountains seventy five miles north of Knoxville, Tennessee linking east Tennessee and east Kentucky with Virginia. *Battles and Leaders of the Civil War* III (New York: Thomas Yoseloff, Inc., 1956) 62-69.

[20] Burke, 11 Sep. 1863.

[21] O R Ser.II-Vol.VI, 434.

[22] R.G. 393, v.244:1-22.

[23] R.G. 393, v.233:175; Dennis Kelly, "Camp Douglas," 96.

[24] O R Ser.II-Vol.VI, 314.

[25] Burke, 14 Sep., 24 Nov. 1863.

[26] Burke, 14 Sep. 1863.

[27] *Pardon and Amnesty Under Lincoln and Johson*, 25, 27; Burke, 7 Sep. 1863.

[28] O R Ser.II-Vol.VI, 332, 363.

[29] O R Ser.II-Vol.VI, 371-74; Gary L. Todd, "An Invalid Corps," *Civil War Times* 8 (Dec. 1985):16.

[30] Bell Irvin Wiley, *The Life of Johnny Reb* (New York: Bobbs-Merrill Co., 1962.), 105.

[31] Kelly, 145.

[32] O R Ser.II-Vol.VI, 371-74.

[33] *Chicago Tribune,* 31 Oct. 1864.

[34] R. G. 393, 237:18.

[35] R. G. 393, v. 233:38-39; Burke, 14 Oct. 1863; O R Ser.II-Vol.VI, 390.

[36] R.G. 393, v.244:266; Burke, 15 Oct. 1863.

[37] *Chicago Tribune,* 19 Oct. 1863.

[38] Longstreet, *Chicago 1860-1919*, 30-31.

[39] *Chicago Tribune,* 25 Oct. 1863.

[40] Burke, 31 Oct. 1863.

[41] *Chicago Tribune,* 7 Jun. 1863.

[42] O R Ser.II-Vol.VI, 417-18, 464.

[43] Burke, 25 Oct., 4 Dec. 1863.

[44] R.G. 393, v.243:491.

[45] R.G. 393, v.233:172; R. G. 293, 243:39; R.G. 393, v.422:16.

[46] R.G. 393, v.233:167; *Chicago Tribune,* 19 Oct. 1863.

[47] O R Ser.II-Vol.VI, 434-35.

[48] O R Ser.II-Vol.VI, 461-64.

[49] O R Ser.II-Vol.VI, 462.

[50] O R Ser.II-Vol. VII, 605-607.

[51] O R Ser.II-Vol.VI, 463.

[52] O R Ser.II-Vol.VI, 461-64.

[53] *Dictionary of American Biography*, American Council of Learned Societies (New York: Scribner's & Sons, 1928-32) VI:42-43.

[54] O R Ser.II-Vol.VI, 461-64; Burke, 21 Oct. 1863.

[55] O R Ser.II-Vol.VI, 461-64.

[56] Kelly, 76.

[57] Dennis Kelly, 54.

10.

CRUELTY UNDER DE LAND

A serious shooting occurred on November 3, 1863 because of an escape tunnel found under the 8th Kentucky Cavalry barrack. A prisoner named T.D. Henry charged that the regiment was lined up and the guards were told to shoot "if any sat down." A guard fired when a sick man fell, according to Henry. "One man was killed dead, two others were wounded, one of them losing an arm, as it was afterwards cut off," Henry claimed. Curtis R. Burke investigated and found that "there was at least a dozen different reasons given for the shooting," and he could not learn the truth about the affair. "Some fifteen or twenty finally stept out and acknowledged being the principal diggers and were sent to the dungeon."[1]

Colonel Hoffman received a tardy answer from Washington on November 7 regarding his proposal to build as many barracks as the camp could hold. Stanton's rejection reflected the hardened attitude in Washington. "The Secretary of War is not disposed at this time, in view of the treatment our prisoners of war are receiving at the hands of the enemy, to erect fine establishments for their prisoners in our hands."[2]

Women were suddenly in the news about Camp Douglas. A woman named Sarah C. Goodwin from Kentucky was imprisoned at camp on November 7, "charged with plotting and conspiring to obtain the release of five prisoners of war." A young woman was arrested on the same charge a few weeks later, but was allowed to live in an officer's home. It was reported that "she belongs to a family of high respectability in Kentucky, and her brother is one of Morgan's men." Other women, perhaps less respectable, gathered on Douglas estate property near the camp, "to indulge in the grossest licentiousness with soldiers" near Douglas' grave.[3]

Northern preachers at camp were more concerned with propaganda than with sin. On November 8, 1863, Chaplain S. Day of the 8th Illinois Infantry held a special service for the prisoners. His message was clear. "Chaplain Day spoke to them from the words of the Prodigal, I will arise and go to my father, —giving a brief resume of the parable—the departure from home of the prodigal—the sad consequences it involved—and the return and reception of the erring son. Chaplain Day assured his audience as hearty a welcome from their heavenly Father as the prodigal received—on his return home, —provided they came to God, through Christ, with the sincerity and patience which this sinning son manifested."[4]

Colonel Benjamin J. Sweet, commander of the 8th Regiment of the Invalid Corps at Camp Douglas, suddenly challenged Colonel De Land's authority on November 9, 1863. Sweet was an ambitious politician who realized that Camp Douglas was a high-visibility post. He complained to Colonel Hoffman that he should be in command of the camp because his commission from Wisconsin predated De Land's from Michigan. De Land responded that the government had recognized his commission first. "I do not wish to remain in command unless clearly entitled to it. I neither court nor shrink from responsibility, but it will be a pleasure to yield the command to any officer you may direct." he assured Hoffman.[5]

This was not the first time that Colonel Sweet had tried to undermine his commanding officer. While serving in the 6th Wisconsin Infantry he had made derogatory remarks about his colonel which resulted in a request that Sweet go home and raise his own regiment.[6]

A serious fire in Garrison Square on November 11 showed how flimsy prison security was. Some fences burned down and there was nothing to prevent prisoners from leaving adjacent White Oak Square and escaping. A company of Indians was sent to block off White Oak Square and force the prisoners into their barracks. They were ordered to shoot if necessary.[7] Burke estimated that 300 feet of barracks and fence, as well as the sutler's shop, were destroyed in Garrison Square. "The fire was accidental and caught from a stove pipe," he reported in his journal.

On November 12, General Halleck, without warning, ordered De Land and the 1st Michigan Sharpshooters to the front. Captain Potter urgently wired Hoffman "to stop it," as this would leave only 300 guards for 6,000 prisoners. Hoffman did stop it, but it is significant that De Land did not protest the order to ship out.[8]

Colonel Hoffman settled the De Land/Sweet dispute with a curt order for De Land to remain in charge. It is surprising that Hoffman sided with him in the power struggle. Perhaps he was influenced by De Land's optimistic report of November 3, 1863. It is also possible that this decision was made by Hoffman's superiors. The old warrior seemed to have regained his composure by November 9, when he told the beleaguered commander that he was "pleased" to learn about his reforms. However, he continued to insist on using the boilers for cooking. "A Farmer's boiler, which cost $25 to $35, will cook for 120 men, with a very small supply of wood," Hoffman said sternly, "and there can be no plan so cheap, and if they have failed at Camp Douglas it is because those who used them did not want to succeed."[9]

In addition, Hoffman warned De Land that the prison fund was low because previous commanders had not followed his orders for economies. "Now I must insist that my instructions shall be strictly carried out." Rations were to be be cut according to his formula, and the savings sold to benefit the prison fund. Hoffman was no longer willing to gamble his career on the uncertain quality of volunteer officers at Camp Douglas, and intended to exercise control.

Hoffman defied Captain Ninian Edwards by ordering De Land to contract for bread with a Chicago baker, but to cut the weight by two ounces per loaf to save money. Edwards' contractors were not to be consulted. He wanted the bakery ovens repaired so that the prison could produce its own bread. Fuel costs canceled this plan, as usual. De Land was told that he could hire a baker at "$75 to $100 a month" and he would soon have a savings of from $200 to $300 per month. "I depend on you, colonel, to put my plans into successful operation."[10]

Many prisoners were bribed with liquor to clean up the camp for an expected visit by Colonel Hoffman. He came to Chicago to inspect the fire damage of November 11, and arrived at camp on November 15.[11] Hoffman suggested to Secretary of War Stanton, with customary stinginess, that only the enlisted men be compensated for the loss of clothing in the fire, and that should be limited to one issue. Hoffman had secret talks with Colonel Sweet during his visit about Sweet replacing De Land as commanding officer. Sweet was confident that he could do the job with about 1,000 men. Hoffman was skeptical. He thought the Invalid Regiment was inefficient, with only two-thirds being available for duty at any time because of their disabilities. His meeting with Sweet did not lead anywhere.

Prisoners were still quartered in cook houses and the hospital was perpetually overcrowded. Hoffman thought about sending 1,000 men to the new prison at Rock Island, Illinois. It did not happen, any more than the new hospital. However, the sewer system was working and the camp was clear of trash and garbage.

Retaliation against the prisoners at Camp Douglas began on on November 16, 1863 in response to the reported ill treatment of Union prisoners in the South. Now, only families were allowed to send clothing to prisoners, "nothing from friends and sympathizers," which reflected the psychosis taking hold. "If a prisoner has a suit he can wear, nothing more can be given to him," Hoffman's order read.[12] Personal funds were limited to two dollars and later raised to 10 dollars. More than likely, these restrictions were Stanton's idea.

Prisoners who had Federal money were allowed to buy flour at this time for 20 dollars a barrel, eight dollars over the market price in Chicago. Once, the sutler accidentally delivered a barrel of sugar to the prisoners instead of flour, and the the camp was soon deluged with "vinegar pies," a Southern delicacy. Burke's mess joined with another one to buy a cooking stove and utensils in Chicago for 12 dollars on November 16, 1863 and were well satisfied.[13]

General Ammen, who commanded the district from Springfield, reorganized the morning roll call at Camp Douglas. Each squad of prisoners was listed by a supervising sergeant. A rebel sergeant in charge of the squad also filled out a morning report and the two lists were checked against each other.[14] Shortly, five Confederate officers were found among the prisoners. Their purpose was to help plan and to lead escapes.

The escalating escapes caused De Land to take extreme measures against the prisoners, and he hung three of them by their thumbs for allegedly threatening an informer. They stood it for over half an hour in silence and then began groaning and crying out.

"It made me almost sick to hear them," Burke recorded. "Several times the Yankee officers asked them if they were ready to tell what they knew, and they answered that they knew nothing to tell. A Yankee surgeon examined them to see how much they could stand. There were some citizens there and they tried to get Col. DeLand to take the men down. The men were taken down after having been tied up so that they had to partly tip toe for an hour. One of the boys fainted, and another threw up all over himself. Their names were James Allen, John Sweeney, and Wm. Wason." [15]

De Land lectured the prisoners on threatening informers and hung two more by the thumbs. "They were let down when this traitor Stovall said that he forgive them," Burke wrote. Another prisoner swore that the punishments under De Land were severe; he knew of recaptured prisoners being hung by their thumbs to extract information.[16] Stovall did not return to the regiment.

Most Civil War soldiers considered hanging men by their wrists or thumbs an inhuman punishment. Sometimes comrades would cut the victim down at the risk of being subjected to the same punishment.[17]

De Land required stoves be put out at Taps, and AWOLs were to be considered deserters. The prisoners were frequently turned out of barracks while De Land searched for tunnels. The hired prisoners took over Burke's entire barrack on November 24. "We call them the chain gang," Burke sneered. These barrack changes were chaotic, as De Land did not arrange new quarters for those being evicted. Burke and his mess had to crowd in with a different regiment, but carried their cooking stove with them, which was some satisfaction. The food situation was not good, either. The prisoners complained to Captain Levant C. Rhines of the Sharpshooters about a shortage of rations, and he ordered the commissary to increase them.[18]

De Land took the time to strike back at Colonel Sweet in a sharply worded letter which demanded a written report about complaints that Sweet's men were being shorted on rations.[19] The inference was that Sweet was somehow profiting.

Guards had been armed with single-shot muskets, and Colonel Hoffman ordered 400 revolvers for them on November 27 to increase fire power to six shots. This did not prevent the greatest escape in camp history, which was caused by the barracks having been built right on the ground. The prisoners had found a natural ally in the sandy loam underlying the prairie surface. De Land's earlier prediction that he had put a stop to tunneling turned out to be an empty boast.

On December 3, 1863, Colonel De Land had the "disagreeable duty to report a serious break of the Morgan prisoners in this camp."[20] About 100 prisoners in White Oak Square succeeded in digging a tunnel to the outside. A hole was started under the floor of one barrack, and the dirt was pressed down between the floors joists underneath. It worked so well that daily inspections had failed to discover it. The tunnel ran the length of the barrack parallel to the fence. Once beyond the barrack, the tunnel made a right angle to the fence and went underneath it.

De Land retaliated. "In view of this I have ordered all the floors removed from the barracks and cook-houses and the spaces filled with dirt even with the top of the joist, he advised Hoffman. "This will undoubtedly increase the sickness and mortality, but it will save much trouble and add security." The angry garrison tore down the partitions in the barracks, turning them into one large dormitory. "They also tore up the floors except under the bunks," wrote Burke gleefully, "and we enjoyed ourselves by jumping around on the sleepers." Guards were so upset by the huge escape that one fired at a prisoner who was hard at work repairing the roof on a barrack.[21]

About 50 of the escaped prisoners were recaptured due mainly to the telegraph. Half had obtained civilian clothing. Communication behind Union lines was well organized, and escapees found that most railroad stations were connected to a telegraph line. By December 18, 1863, all but 20 escapees since August, 1863 were recaptured.[22] The breakout was historic in another way; it caused Camp Douglas to be redesigned into a more efficient prison the following year.

Secretary of War Stanton made life more unpleasant for Confederate prisoners on December 1, 1863 by shutting down trade with the sutlers at all prison camps. The sutler at Camp Douglas had sold everything except liquor, but "including cider, butter, eggs, milk, canned fruits, boots, and underclothing." Burke noted that the sutler closed on December 12, 1863. He would be back in business in 1864. The liquor ban was hard on the Kentuckians, and they persuaded a woman who sold milk from a tin can at 10 cents per quart to fill it with "something more in keeping with the needs of a grown-up individual."[23] Closing the sutler also meant the discontinuance of stamps, envelopes, and paper. However, these purchases could be made from the camp commissary.

A few days later, De Land confiscated warm coats sent to the prisoners from home. This was either to prevent escapes or as retaliation. Burke angrily denounced the replacements as "some thin cottonade pepper and salt jackets, and some thin black rediculous looking tight spade tall Yankee coats! Some photographs were even taken of our men."[24]

Meanwhile, De Land had to suffer through another inspection on December 7, 1863, this time by prison inspector Brigadier General William W. Orme, a future commander of Camp Douglas. Orme felt that the food ration was good "being three-quarters of a pound of bacon (1 pound of fresh beef three times a week), good, well baked wheat bread, hominy, coffee, tea, sugar, vinegar, candles, soap, salt, pepper, potatoes, and molasses all of good quality." To each 100 men there was issued daily 10 pounds of hominy, 10 pounds of coffee, 1ˇ pounds of tea, 15 pounds of sugar, and 4 quarts of vinegar. Each prisoner received 1ˇ pounds of candles, while 4 pounds of soap, 3ʃ pounds of salt, ˇ pound of pepper, 30 pounds of potatoes, and 1 quart of molasses went with each 100 rations. Beans and rice were added to the hospital ration, but no tea. The cost of the hospital ration was $18.42 per hundred and $14.08 for the regular. Rations were issued between 11 a.m and 4 p.m. Apparently, General Orme did not talk to the prisoners about the beef.[25] He soon would.

Orme indicated that the lack of any system for cooking had not yet been resolved. "The result is a great waste of food and fuel, the latter of which especially is a serious item of expense at the camp." Colonel Hoffman must have chewed his nails after learning about this report. Orme thought that the garrison was dangerously small at 876 men, and a "chain of sentries" was needed outside the fence. Colonel Tucker had maintained outside patrols when he was commanding officer. In De Land's favor was the clean condition of the camp and a good situation in the prison hospital.[26]

The closing of Northern prisons became a possibility when President Lincoln issued a general amnesty on December 8, 1863. He called for releasing all prisoners below the rank of general. It was a miracle that any prisoners were left at all at Camp Douglas, with so few guards available. On October 14, 1863, De Land had requested the army to return Company I of the Sharpshooters which was on duty at Detroit. On December 19, he reported that the guard regiments "are broken down from measles and lung disease."[27] Only 250 men plus 10 officers were available for guard duty through December.

The barber shop and newsstand were closed on December 17 as punishment for the escapes, and sales of stamps, envelopes, and writing paper were banned completely.[28] However, mail service continued for those who still had these items.

It is likely that the mounting escapes and De Land's administrative failures caused a change in command. General William W. Orme was ordered by the War Department to take over the Northern District of Illinois at Chicago, including Camp Douglas. He relieved De Land as commanding officer on December 23.[29] De Land was not entirely disgraced as he remained in charge of the garrison. Reinforcements arrived with six more companies of the Invalid Corps under Colonel James C. Strong.

General Orme was a favorite of President Lincoln because he was a law partner of Leonard Swett, one of Lincoln's intimate friends.[30] Lincoln regarded Orme as a most promising lawyer. Born in Maryland in 1832, Orme moved to Illinois and was admitted to the bar at age 21. He was elected Colonel of the 94th Illinois Infantry at Bloomington, Illinois in 1861, and was in combat until June 11, 1863. He became ill with tuberculosis during the campaign at Vicksburg, and was unable to continue in active service. This led to his post as Prison Inspector, and his later appointment at Camp Douglas.[31] His experience with the prison system made him highly qualified to run the camp. He had already perceived the need for changes in security during his previous visit.

Colonel De Land had been hit with a deluge of prisoners before he could sit down. Now, General Orme was caught up in an investigation of food contractors instead of settling into his new job. Oddly, the scandal surfaced due to a complaint by a Canadian, Montrose A. Pallen, about "great suffering in Northern prisons." Secretary of War Stanton ordinarily would have fired off a blistering denial. Instead, he ordered Colonel Hoffman to make a wide-ranging investigation of the prisons, including Camp Douglas. Stanton was probably seeking the good will of the Canadian government, because Confederate agents had set up bases in Canada for operations against the North. On December 19, 1863, Hoffman ordered General Orme to give him a report on Camp Douglas.[32]

General William W. Orme, circa 1863 (courtesy of Massachusetts Commandery Military Order of the Loyal Legion and the US Army Military History Institute)

Orme had already "found abuses" regarding the quality of the beef and other supplies. He moved swiftly by submitting written questions to the Confederate sergeant-majors on December 24, 1863. Critical areas, such as medical care, bunks, clothing, blankets, and the quantity and quality of the rations were questioned. Orme assumed that the Confederate sergeants were truthful men, which was justified. One prisoner even wrote a separate report to Orme to make sure that his sergeant-major was not misunderstood.[33] The sergeants of 24 squads drawing rations responded to the questionnaires. Among them was Burke's father, Edward, of the 14th Kentucky Cavalry.

The main problem, according to 14 of the sergeants, was the short weight and poor quality of the beef. Some answers included carefully worded understatements. "It is proper to say that there may be an honest difference in the scales. By our scales the bread holds out." "The beef does not weigh out with other rations, according to our scales." "I presume all are gentlemen connected with the department." "I rely on the gentleman in charge to do justice to the prisoners."

Captain Rhines of the 1st Michigan Sharpshooters confirmed the responses. "I most fully believe the prisoners have been shamefully treated by the contractor for fresh beef," he reported to Orme. The reports were sent to Colonel Hoffman in Washington, who concluded that the prisoners had been habitually cheated by the contractors and ordered General Orme to investigate further. Hoffman wanted to know to what extent the rations were inferior or short in quantity, and who benefited. Ironically, Hoffman had already cut rations by one quart of molasses and two ounces of bread the day before Christmas.[34]

The answers by the prisoners to Orme's other questions are surprising.

Medical care: All but two of the 24 squads reported prompt medical attention. One sergeant gave a fair rating, saying that his men would have "benefited by a more prompt admission into the hospital in several instances."[35] Another said dryly, "Not having had any sick cannot tell." Prescriptions were promptly filled, and the four Confederate surgeons were praised. Dr. Whelan of the Sharpshooters, who was Post Surgeon, received a grudging nod. No mention was made of the smallpox hospital.

Bunks and blankets: There were about 7,000 blankets for 5,822 men, which would average less than two blankets per man, not sufficient for winter. One sergeant reported that some of his men were without blankets. Two complained that many blankets were "much worn" or "light and ragged." Another sergeant added that the 400 blankets in his squad were "all sent by friends."

The situation regarding bunks was inequitable. The smaller squads of about 100 men were doing fine, though they slept three to a bunk. The larger squads, comprising almost an entire regiment, were in dire straights. Two of these regimental sergeants reported that their men had no regular quarters because of the bunk shortage, and could not be found for roll call. They had become vagabonds, drifting from barrack to barrack trying to find a place to sleep. In modern terms, they were homeless. One sergeant snarled, "There are bunks for all who stay in the workmen's quarters!"[36] The shortage of bunks caused Burke and his friends to steal a large pie cupboard which the sutler had naively left outside his shop, and it was quickly converted into a sleeper.

Clothing: These responses were the most dismal. Only the smallest squads of less than 100 men had received sufficient clothing since entering camp four months previously. In protest, eight sergeants refused to answer the question. Most of the larger squads of more than 200 men had received only one-third of their clothing needs, and this clothing was of poor quality. "The cottanade jackets, substitute for coats, are very uncomfortable for the season; many men are suffering for clothes," one sergeant stated bitterly. Many sergeants said that most of the clothing had come from home, which totaled about 2,000 suits. One squad of 233 men had received at camp only 22 shirts, 35 pairs of socks, 5 pairs of pants, 42 pairs of shoes, and 3 coats.[37]

Quantity of rations: The first response about whether rations were drawn regularly was, "I am informed by the commissary that we do." The disbelief was evident.[38] Another, dodged the question and said that the rations were drawn regularly, "but very irregular." Two hedged by saying that rations were drawn regularly "generally" or with "a few exceptions." Twenty sergeants agreed that the ration was issued regularly. None of them suggested that it was inadequate to feed the men. Considering that they spoke sharply on other issues, it can be assumed that there was no hunger or starvation among the prisoners.

In comparison to Camp Douglas, General Benjamin Butler was personally questioning the Confederate sergeants drawing rations at the Point Lookout Maryland Prison Camp on the same day, December 24, 1863.[39] The prisoners had been there only four months and were living 16 to a tent with few stoves. Six sergeants drew rations for 1,500 men each.

Unlike Camp Douglas, the Maryland prisoners had no scales to weigh rations and did not know what the official allowance was for each man. However, they "had complete trust" in their Yankee commissary sergeant, and felt comfortable with that. "We have got very fine beef," one responded, but he could only describe it as "from four and a half to five and a half quarters." The beef ration was insufficient, but they received turnips, beans, and carrots by the barrel, and thus scurvy was absent as compared to Camp Douglas.

The shortage of blankets and clothing at Point Lookout was the same as at Camp Douglas. A sergeant from General Lee's army had drawn only one pair of pants and one shirt since August 9, 1863. Unlike General Orme's inquiry, Butler wanted to know about brutality by the guards. There was no abuse reported, except in being forced to build barracks and work on the grounds, which was no longer a problem for them because there were soon many volunteers. Butler asked the sergeants to compare their standard of living at the prison to what they had known in the Confederate army. A sergeant in the 7th Texas felt that the western armies of the Confederacy had less to eat. One from the Army of Northern Virginia said that "we lived better in our army than we do here." The main complaint was lack of clothing.

Back at Camp Douglas, General Orme was trying desperately to get a grip on administrative problems beyond the beef scandal. On December 29, he wrote to Colonel Hoffman that he saw no regulations or directives on how to run the camp. It was a repeat of the situation found by Colonel Tucker after Mulligan left. Orme discovered two detectives being paid $100 per month out of the prison fund, and requested instructions.[40] De Land was the first commandant to put detectives on the prison payroll, while Colonel Tucker had used them only for special assignments.

General Orme convened a post council of regimental officers to audit the prison fund, and additional clerks were employed to organize the records. Hoffman was pleased. He was sure that Orme would "bring about all the necessary reforms so much needed and produce a state of discipline and police which will be highly satisfactory."[41] Hoffman did not know that Orme was suffering from a severe case of tuberculosis, and was dying.

Along with the ration reports, Orme wrote that all prisoners were now in barracks heated by coal stoves, and that "they are well cared for in the hospital and receive every medical attention."[42] He had kept Captain Rhines of the 1st Michigan Sharpshooters as Commissary of Prisoners. Rhines concentrated on using clothing to pay for prison labor to repair the camp. Much of this came through friends or family of other prisoners and was confiscated from those not considered "needy."[43] Since September 23, the needy received: jackets, 953; trousers, 796; drawers, 1,955; shirts, 2,033; stockings, 2,106; blankets, 1,280; and shoes, 1,114.

A class structure had developed among the prisoners. At the bottom of the scale were the infantry who had to work for additional clothing and food. Above them was the leisure class of Kentuckians who could buy what they needed, and continually received packages from home. They were given government clothing if theirs were taken. Prisoners considered "needy" were allowed to keep clothing sent to them.

Private Burke and his father were members of the leisure class, thanks to Mrs. Burke's family in Ohio. So far, father and son had received their packages without confiscation, probably because the parcels came from Ohio. The amount of confiscated items given to the workers was enormous. However, many prisoners were still without blankets, and Captain Rhines issued 1,280 more by December 26, 1863. Blankets were 100% wool and tended to wear out quickly under the hard usage at camp. Each bunk received 12 to 14 pounds of prairie hay monthly. Stoves were fed 1,412 cart-loads of wood, or 350 cords. They consumed 294 cart-loads of coal, amounting to 196 tons each month. Captain Rhines did not consider this sufficient in extreme cold weather.[44]

Burke was preparing a Christmas dinner as the year began to close. He did not dream that he would give another Christmas dinner at Camp Douglas in the coming year. He and his friend, Henry White, were flush with orders on the commissary because the sutler was closed. On December 25, they received "10 candles, one box of pepper sauce, two lbs. of coffee, 7 lbs. sugar, 1 paper of black pepper, 1 paper of allspice, 1 lb. butter, and 1 lb. lard," at a total cost of $2.45. Gifts were not expected, but Burke's father gave him a pair of buckskin cavalry gloves, a pair of socks, a fancy shawl pin, and a 50-cent sutler ticket.

Burke's dinner was late because other messes were also cooking. Apparently, Hoffman had not been successful thus far in eliminating the cooking stoves. Burke's menu was biscuits, tea, beans and bacon, buttered bakersbread, toasted molasses, boiled onions laid in water, cheese, peach pie, apple pie, onion pie, plain doughnuts, and sweet doughnuts. The old saying that "money talks" held true at Camp Douglas, and the commissary was well stocked for those who could afford it. The holiday mood even had affected a guard officer. While inspecting the barracks he asked humorously if there was any "go-fer" business going on.[45]

Cups, mugs, and glasses were filled and refilled with "something more in keeping with the needs of a grown-up individual," and Henry White offered the Toast of Morgan's Men:

"Unclaimed by the land that bore us,
Lost in the land we find,
The brave have gone before us,
Cowards are left behind,
Then stand to your glasses, steady,

Here's a health to those we prize.
Here's a toast to the dead already,
And here's to the next that dies."[46]

The new hospital was still under construction, and Henry White was able to steal some lumber from the site to make a new storage bin for their extra food. The year 1863 was noteworthy for the installation of the water pipes and the sewer system which had begun operating on November 6. However, the water pipes would soon have to be replaced with larger ones. Escapes by Morgan's men in 1863 set a record, and the mortality rate at Camp Douglas continued inexorably high. About 1,010 now lay dead since July, 1862, according to the Official Records, and Approximately 6,144 Confederates had arrived since August, 1863.

Disappointing news for the prisoners came from Washington on December 31. President Lincoln had changed his mind about a general amnesty for prisoners of war and said that it did not extend to them. At least that is what the army said. "A general jail clearing, as you express it, could not certainly have been contemplated by the President in issuing his proclamation," the Judge-Advocate-General said in answer to a question from a prison commander, "and such a result would, I think, be in every way to be deplored."[47] Camp Douglas would soldier on to the end of the war and beyond as a prison camp.

The proclamation of amnesty had already caused desertions among Confederate officers. One of Morgan's steadfast raiders wrote home from Camp Douglas on December 3, 1863: "I am sorry for our regiment. I do not know what we will do if all the commissioned officers take the oath. I believe it will play out entirely."[48]

General Orme, unexpectedly exonerated the contractors for the beef scandal as the year ended, and blamed their subcontractors. Orme was satisfied that the beef issue had been short for sometime. However, he believed that the original contractors were not implicated, as the beef was furnished by their subcontractor. "I am further induced to this belief by the character and standing of some of the contractors, whom I personally know," Orme said openly.[49] Was a whitewash or cover-up in the making? Meanwhile, General Orme instructed Captain Ninian Edwards to withhold payment ot the subcontractors. As an aside, Orme advised Hoffman that prisoners were employed of various contractors and businesses at camp, and asked, "Has this practice met with your sanction?" A free market economy was in effect at Camp Douglas.

NOTES TO CHAPTER 10

[1] T. D. Henry, "Treatment of Prisoners During the War," *Southern Historical Society Papers I* (Jan 1876): 227. He was in Co. E, 2nd Ky. Cav; Burke, 2 Nov. 1863.

[2] O R Ser.II-Vol.VI. 315.

[3] Confederate Prisoners of War, R.G. 109, Roll 53; Chicago Tribune, 18 Dec. 1863; Story, *History of Camp Douglas*, 82.

[4] Chicago Tribune, 9 Nov. 1863.

[5] R.G. 393, v.234:106,107.

[6] Alan T. Nolan, *The Iron Brigade* (New York: Macmillan, 1961), 52.

[7] O. R. Ser.II-Vol.VI, 633; Burke, 11 Nov. 1863.

[8] O R Ser.II-Vol.VI, 504.

[9] R.G. 393, v.234:124; O R Ser.II-Vol.VI, 489-90.

[10] O R Ser.II-Vol.VI, 490.

[11] Burke, 14, 15 Nov. 1863; O R Ser.II-Vol.VI, 633-36.

[12] O R Ser.II-Vol.VI, 525.

[13] R. T. Bean, "Seventeen Months in Camp Douglas," *Confederate Veteran* 22 (Jun. 1914):269; Burke, 16 Nov. 1863.

[14] R. G. 393, v.233:187.

[15] Burke, 22 Nov. 1863. John Swinney of the 14th Ky. died on 19 May 1864. William T. Wasson of the 2nd Ky. Cav. died on 3 May 1864. Both are buried in Chicago.

[16] T. D. Henry, *Southern Historical Society Papers*, 276.

[17] Bell I. Wiley, "The Common Soldier of the Civil War," *Civil War Times* 4 (Jul. 1973):50.

[18] Kelly, "Camp Douglas," 56; Burke, 19-20, 24 Nov., 1 Dec 1863.

[19] R. G. 393, v.234:132.

[20] O R Ser.II-Vol.VI, 637.

[21] Burke, 3, 5 Dec. 1863. A "sleeper" was the beam laid horizontaly on the ground to support the floor.

[22] Chicago Tribune, 18 Dec. 1863; E. R. Hopkins, "At Fort Donelson," *Confederate Veteran* 38 (Mar. 1930):85.

[23] O R Ser.II-Vol.VI, 625, 660; R. T. Bean, "Seventeen Months in Camp Douglas," *Confederate Veteran* 22 (Jun. 1914):268.

[24] Burke, 4 Dec. 1863.

[25] O R Ser.II-Vol.VI, 660-61; Story, "Camp Douglas," 62-63.

[26] O R Ser.II-Vol.VI, 660-61.

[27] O R Ser.II-Vol.VI, 680-682; R. G. 393, v. 234:47,150.

[28] Burke, 256.

[29] O R Ser.I-Vol. 52, Part I, 504; R. G. 393, v.244:24.

[30] Swett capitalized on his association with Lincoln after his death, and conspired with Lincoln's son, Robert, to have his mother declared insane in Chicago on 19 May 1875. The object seems to have been for Robert to gain control of Mrs. Lincoln's money. Samuel A. Schreiner Jr. *The Trials of Mrs. Lincoln* (New York: Donald I. Fine, Inc., 1987)

[31] Warner, *Generals In Blue*, 350-51.

[32] O R Ser.II-Vol.VI, 718; Peggy Robbins, "The Greatest Scoundrel," *Civil War Times* 5 (Nov.-Dec. 1992):56; O R Ser.II-Vol.VI, 778.

[33] O R Ser.II-Vol.VI, 779-98.

[34] O R SerII-Vol.VI, 779-98, 799-812; Story, "Camp Douglas," 61.

[35] O R Ser.II-Vol.VI, 786.

[36] O R Ser.II-Vol.VI, 797.

[37] O R Ser.II-Vol.VI, 785, 789.

[38] O R Ser.II-Vol.VI, 779.

[39] O R Ser.II-Vol.VI, 764-67.

[40] R. G. 393, v.234:162.

[41] Dennis Kelly, "History of Camp Douglas,"58.

[42] O R Ser.II-Vol.VI, 778.

[43] O R Ser.II-Vol.VI, 799-80.

[44] O R Ser.II-Vol.VI, 800.

[45] Burke, 25 Dec. 1863.

[46] Burke, 25 Dec. 1863.

[47] O R Ser.II-Vol.VI, 802-03.

[48] *Pardon and Amnesty*, 59, letter of Private Nathan B. Deatherage.

[49] O R Ser.II-Vol.VI, 804-05.

11.

Unfit for Use

The year 1864 started Chicago-style with a blizzard of unusual severity swept in. On January 1 the temperature fell to 18 degrees below zero in the morning and 25 below at night. The snow was as much as five feet deep, causing an emergency situation.[1] Six or seven guards were hospitalized, and Burke was cut off from Pa's barrack. "I put a pot of dried peaches to cooking on the stove to bake a big peach roll for dinner," Burke recorded. "The night was very cold, but the guards kept the coal stoves red hot all night, which kept the barracks warm, and we slept well."

M. J. Bradley, who described Camp Douglas as "that hellish den of iniquity" complained that the garrison had warm gloves, but would not help the prisoners haul wood to their barracks: "Many men were frost bitten and many perished." He was wrong. None perished, although R. T. Bean said he would have died coming back from the wood pile 400 yards away had guards not taken him into their barracks. Mr. Bradley was probably referring to two prisoners who went over the deserted fence and were found frozen to death nearby.[2]

Dr. Brunson, an able Confederate surgeon at camp, reported a childhood friend as "frozen to death" in barracks during the winter of 1863-64. Dr. Brunson headed a Confederate medical corps of 10 doctors established by Colonel De Land. Private T. M. Page, captured at Chickamauga on September 19, 1863, claimed that the Federal surgeons challenged the diagnosis, but backed down when Brunson requested an autopsy. This incident may have resulted in more heat in barracks. Private Page had an interior view of events as secretary to the Confederate surgeons. This coveted position was awarded to him by Dr. Brunson as amends for predicting that Page would die when he examined him at Camp Douglas.[3]

Page alleged that Federal guards stripped him of his blankets before arriving on October 4, 1863, and that prisoners who had been treated similarly were freezing to death in their bunks. His account, written in 1900, is faulty at times. For example, he charged that about 539 prisoners died in October, 1863, which is unfounded based upon all available information. Captain Rhines reported that he had made up the shortage of blankets by issuing 1,280 in December, 1863, but admitted that fuel was insufficient in extreme cold weather.[4]

The *Tribune* described how "supply trains make their regular trips, regardless of the weather, and immense wagon loads of beef, bread, wood and coal can be seen several times each day wending their way to Camp Douglas." The prisoners did not mention this rescue effort in their accounts. Coal companies were gouging the poor in Chicago from $1.50 to $2.00 more per ton than in 1863. Wood, likewise, was up $2.00 per cord. Mortality in Chicago for the year 1863 provides another explanation why so many prisoners died "like rotten sheep." Scarlet fever raged throughout the city killing 475 people; smallpox accounted for 215 victims; cholera, typhoid, typhus, dysentery, and diphtheria also came in for their share, like scavengers flocking to a kill.[5]

General Orme took steps on New Year's day, 1864 to release black prisoners in Morgan's command.[6] Morgan's officers had apparently ignored orders from Richmond to report the presence of blacks in their units.[7] They were held prisoner at Camp Douglas despite President Lincoln's Emancipation Proclamation, effective January 1, 1863, which declared that slaves captured with rebel forces would be "forever free." It was reinforced by a War Department order on April 24, 1863, which declared that slaves captured from belligerents were "entitled to the rights and privileges of free men."[8] It seems that these men were not considered slaves.

One had died previously at camp, and three were unaccounted for. Orme reported "These negroes have been at Camp Douglas for some time and I submit this statement to you for such instructions as you may deem advisable." Hoffman responded that their release depended upon whether they were slaves or soldiers. Orme was to release them if they were slaves. "If soldiers they are not to be exchanged against their will."[9]

Orme issued many restrictions on January 3. Mainly they related to security. Burke counted them off: "1st that we must only write every thirteen days and then only one letter of two pages of note paper each. The whole number of prisoners in camp was divided into thirteen squads each having a certain day to write. 2nd. That we can not visit the other squares unless we get a pass from the officer of the day. 3rd. That we must be in our barracks by five o'clock p.m. and put all lights and fires out at the beating of the drum at eight o'clock p.m. and no one allowed out side of the barracks till day, except to go to the sink."[10] Burke noted that while General Orme signed the restrictions, Colonel De Land and his officers "still remains in office."

Colonel De Land ordered guards to shout only one challenge to a prisoner seen near the fence or outside his barrack at night. The guard was to fire if the prisoner did not obey.[11] On January 3, there was an offer to release prisoners if they enlisted in the Federal navy.[12]

Morgan's men were the most prolific writers, and they caused the mail restrictions. Their letters numbered 500 per day. This clamp-down did not deter one smitten prisoner: "Fortunately I found a man of a Mississippi regiment whose name was the same as mine except for the middle initial. He allowed me to use his name in writing to my rebel girl in Kentucky." Prisoners with money might "persuade" the Yankee barrack sergeant to "take out five letters per day until the regular writing day."[13]

The guard schedule was different from Colonel Tucker's. Reveille and roll call were at sunrise, breakfast at 7:30, and sick call an hour later. Changing of the Guard was in Garrison Square at 9:30 a.m. There was drill and another roll call at 3:00. Two more roll calls were made by 9:00 p.m., with lights out for the garrison at 9:30. An officer supervised the garrison roll call. Company commanders were to make daily inspections of garrison quarters and mess halls.[14]

Orme devised a system of ground patrols to parallel the changing of the guard.[15] It was directed to break up crowds around the barracks, and he required his officers to inspect the prison quarters twice a day; he intended to go much further. His investigation of the mass-escape of 100 men on December 3, 1863 had convinced him that it was necessary to build a new prison at Camp Douglas.

He reported on January 20, 1864 that the arrangement of the camp was to blame for the escapes, and recommended that barracks be moved from the southeast side of camp, White Oak Square, to the western part. "I have the honor further to state that a prisoner of war, once beyond the camp lines, finds in this city so many active friends and sympathizers as to render his recapture almost impossible." Orme had already begun removing prisoners to the western end of the camp. All of them were to be in one place for the first time in a new prison square enclosed by a 12- to 14-foot stockade with a guard walk on top. However, the parapet would not be completed until March 15, 1864. Another innovation was roving guards to patrol the square 24 hours a day. They would be separate from guards on the fence and have an office in the square.[16]

By this time Hoffman had General Orme's letter blaming the ration scandal on the subcontractors. Hoffman rejected the attempt to shift responsibility. "The parties contracting with the government are responsible that its terms are faithfully complied with," Hoffman ruled.[17] This was something Orme had to know as a lawyer. Hoffman wavered on whether prisoners could work for the businesses at camp, but finally decided against it. Orme's report on the rations would go to Stanton when it was complete.

Rats were killed and eaten when a kitchen was demolished on January 10, 1864. The North denied these reports after the war. Burke said that he saw it: "Two of the men gathered them up to clean them and to eat them. I understand that rat eating is very extensively carried on in the other squares, but my curiosity has never made me taste any rats yet." A prisoner in his barrack named Stoton ate one as an experiment, and reported that it was "as tender as a chicken." Stoton survived the rat and Camp Douglas. Some anonymous characters recollecting the camp 37 years

View of Prison Square looking west, cicra September, 1864. Note guard behind the deadline at end of the street and barrack 13 on the left where Prairie Bull tried to kill Prince.(courtesy Illinois State Historical Society).

later said that they raised the kitchen floor to catch "big gray rats" which were made into rat pie.[18]

The great move from White Oak Square began on January 20, 1864. Burke had to vacate his barrack on January 27. Manpower was used to move the 300-foot-long barracks on rollers. Eventually, they would be cut to just 90 feet. At first the non-hired prisoners helped, but a dispute soon broke out between them and the Yanks, and they quit. As a result, many barracks were still on route as night fell. The guards retaliated by preventing prisoners from sleeping in them, and they had to use makeshift shelters in White Oak Square. The mud, the cold, and the many rats disturbed by the move made this a memorable night. The project was stalled without substantial help from the prisoners. Most of the garrison were disabled veterans not up to the task, and Orme was forced to bring in an outside contractor with horses on January 29. The time was coming, however, when prisoners would either work or be punished.

The move took about two months, and some prisoners remained in White Oak Square until April, 1864. The new square could hold about 12,000 men after it was completed. It stretched for two city blocks from north to south and two blocks from east to west, about 40 acres total. The square occupied the ground between present Vernon Avenue on the east and King Drive on the west, and ran from 31st Street on the north to 33rd Street on the south. The Olivet Baptist Church at 405 E. 31st Street stands today in the northwest corner of the former Prison Square. At Andersonville there were 35,000 Union prisoners confined on a field of 30 acres in August, 1864.[19] Only a third of them had some ragged shelter.

Numerous civilians were now employed at camp, with pay scales set by Colonel Hoffman. Doctors received $100 per month; the controller of funds was paid $50 per month; clerks earned 40 cents per day; copiers, who hand-duplicated every document sent or received at Camp Douglas, eked out a mere 25 cents daily.[20] Their work fills about 25 volumes in the National Archives, not counting the hospital records.

Camp Douglas was to be continuously inspected in 1864 by the Surgeon-General, the Inspector-General, and the War Department. Lieutenant Morris Briggs made 12 inspections pursuant to War Department orders. Briggs was a former enlisted man, as were many Invalid Corps officers, and was disabled at the battle of Perryville. He had commanded a company of convalescents who had chased Morgan. The inspectors, including Briggs, were no-nonsense types, not interested in gaining favor or protecting reputations. Often their reports reveal little known facts about the camp.

On January 18, Dr. Kittoe of the Surgeon-General's office made an extensive visit, and Colonel De Land conducted him about the camp. The pressure was on General Orme this time. The damp winds from nearby Lake Michigan soured Dr. Kittoe on the location. Noxious odors from meat-packing industries in nearby suburbs added to his dismay. The garrison was well off compared to the prisoners. Guards were living in new barracks raised off the ground, their rations were good, and their persons were clean, "also their privies."[21]

The prisoners' story was different. Many of Morgan's men were already in the new square, while others remained in White Oak. They were living in mud and filth in both places, caused by removal of the floors. Barracks were crowded and swarming with vermin in White Oak. Three of the 90-foot barracks were badly overcrowded with a total of 440 men, although this would become acceptable as the prison population doubled. De Land told Kittoe that "he finds it impossible to make these men observe the ordinary rules of decent cleanliness of persons or quarters." Dr. Kittoe blamed much of this on the dirt floors. The barracks occupied by Morgan's men in Prison Square "were pre-eminently filthy."

Cooking was deficient among the prisoners, and garbage littered the streets again. Kittoe graded the prison rations as "good and ample" but noted that the cooking arrangements were bad, so that the food was improperly prepared with much waste. There was no further explanation. He gave high marks to the hospital and the medical care for prisoners, but the 234 beds were filled, and 250 patients remained in barracks. A new hospital was still under construction. Like the barracks, it would be built of one-inch upright boards 12 feet long, with the seams battened, but it would be lathed and plastered inside.

Kittoe discovered that the old sinks had not been properly sealed, and waste was seeping through the ground. There were 5,616 prisoners present, with only 1,595 guards available for duty from the three guard regiments. The 1st Michigan Sharpshooters had 812 men, the 8th regiment of the Invalid Corps under Colonel Sweet had 447 men, and Colonel Strong's 15th regiment totaled 409.

Illness among the prisoners was an appalling 36%, with 57 deaths in December, 1863, according to Kittoe. Many of the garrison were also sick. Mumps, measles, pneumonia, and sinus infections were present in force. Guards stationed on the fence suffered a higher rate of respiratory disease because they were "exposed to the full sweep of the cold and damp winds." Camp Douglas was not an ideal place to be either as a guard or a prisoner.

Kittoe concluded that the camp was unfit for use. The unrelenting cold added its own misery to the barren landscape, so that any feeling of warmth in a prisoner's life became a distant memory. A nervous guard fired at a prisoner going to the sink one night, missed, and the bullet may have fatally wounded another prisoner. The perceptive Burke feared "that a great many prisoners will take the oath before exchange comes again."[22] He was not one to admit that any of Morgan's Raiders had a breaking point, but when that time came it would strike very close to home.

Corruption reduced the already under-staffed medical department. On January 28, 1864, General Orme named Dr. John D. Lee, a Chicago contract surgeon, as a co-conspirator in a bribery scheme, and he went to the guard house. "I have so much to contend with," Orme wrote to Colonel Hoffman, "in the way of attempts at bribery (and successful attempts too) of persons on duty at my camp that nothing short of severe punishment will stop it." Dr. Lee was exposed when a drunk, arrested near the Prairie Queen, turned out to be a Confederate officer carrying letters describing escape plans, and even a receipt for cash signed by Dr. Lee.[23] Lee then had the gall to request that Orme send his salary to his "destitute" family in Chicago.

With almost 6,000 prisoners in camp, Lee's arrest left only three Chicago doctors and about four Confederate surgeons to help the Post Surgeon. Medical Inspector Clark returned to camp on February 1, 1864, and confirmed the lack of cleanliness among the prisoners.[24] With the sewer and water system now working, Dr. Clark thought that "a little care would suffice to keep sweet and clean." He was critical of the lax discipline regarding hygiene. His remark is surprising, since the hydrants were often frozen, something he may not have realized.

At Andersonville, which was to open in four weeks, there was no discipline imposed on the prisoners. Disease and crime went unchecked. It became so bad that an inmate remarked, "our own men are worse to each other than the rebels are to us." Lawless bands of Union soldiers called "The Raiders" roamed about the stockade to prey on the disorganized and the defenseless. By comparison, when a guard at Camp Douglas robbed a prisoner of his money in White Oak Square, the criminal was arrested and the prisoner's property returned.[25]

De Land tightened control of the guard house on February 2, 1864 by requiring a morning report on the number of prisoners being held.[26] Similar to Colonel Tucker, he ordered army regulations and paragraphs from the Articles of War read to the garrison at guard mounts and reliefs. Burke also had some personal problems when Pa found a letter from a young lady to his son and read it aloud to the barrack. Burke did not appreciate the "joke," as Pa called it, which shows that parents can be difficult sometimes. Apparently there was a "pen-pal" network in the South, because Burke was writing to three young women "at their request."

Both Dr. Kittoe and Dr. Clark agreed that the drainage in camp was poor despite the new sewers, but "vaccination is thoroughly enforced." This was similar to De Land's belief that he had stopped the tunneling. Dr. Clark was unduly optimistic about containing smallpox. Burke and many others avoided vaccination because the infections which resulted were almost worse than the disease. He was correct in not trusting the vaccine, but there was "considerable uneasiness" among both the prisoners and garrison about the rise in smallpox cases. This avoidance of the doctors caused the prisoners to be marched out by regiments for vaccinations on February 14.[27] It happened to be Valentine's Day, and Burke mourned the loss of romance in his young life. "I see nothing here to remind me of such old times," he reflected sadly.

Dr. Clark could not understand why the barracks were not raised off the ground to prevent tunneling. His suggestion was followed. Burke's was in place in the new square by February 4, 1864. Two days later he helped place short legs on it and laid the floor; Pa moved in, and the transfer of barracks from White Oak continued.[28] They were placed around the sides of Prison Square, close to the fences. Kitchens were also near the fence, allowing prisoners to continue their tunneling.

At the same time, General Orme was busy trying to build a criminal case against the subcontractors. Colonel Hoffman was also engrossed in it and failed to mention the negative reports about the camp from various medical inspectors. Orme submitted his findings to Colonel Hoffman on February 8, detailing how four contractors had been supplying the camp since April, 1863, and took the firm name of one of them, E. S. Fowler. The same four continued under another one of their names when the contracts were extended on November 10.[29] The agreements allowed them to bypass the camp commissary and issue provisions directly to the troops and prisoners.

The beef ration from subcontractor Curtis was exactly as reported, only the poorer parts of the animal, and those in short weight. The beef was up to 40% below contract requirements, "and has inured to the benefit of the subcontractors," Orme reported. He placed no blame on Ninian W. Edwards, whom he must have known through their mutual ties to Lincoln. Edwards had been banished to Chicago around June 22, 1863 due to a serious problem which preceded the violations at Camp Douglas. In a significant letter of that date his superior, General Taylor, wrote to Edwards that he had just seen the President about him.

"The President does not doubt you in any manner or shape but is embarrassed by circumstances should you remain at Springfield," Taylor advised. "Therefore I have or will today direct Colonel Kilburn to locate you in Chicago, which will be very agreeable to the President, and under the circumstances, I hope will be agreeable to you.[30] The President would very much regret should you resign and I also would much regret to lose you from the Commissary Department."

There was something rotten in Springfield. Otherwise, why should Lincoln be "embarrassed by circumstances" and banish Edwards to Chicago, and why else did Edwards offer to resign his commission? Possibly, Edwards was financially involved with the contractors, perhaps as a silent partner in the government contracts, and had issued them without competitive bidding. The contractors were all from Springfield, where Edwards had long-time business connections. He owned a store there under the name N. W. Edwards & Co., and Lincoln had an account with him before the war.[31] The cover-up by the President and General Taylor was successful, and there was no mention of the matter in the newspapers.

This earlier problem was compounded by Edwards' presence in Chicago during the Camp Douglas violations. He tried to protect himself in this case by asking Colonel De Land to give his opinion regarding the rations. De Land responded on December 9, 1863 that he was "perfectly satisfied" with Edwards. "How any fault can be found is beyond my knowledge, unless it is because you are too strict & cautious to shield the government & its troops from pecuniary loss & from all cause for dissatisfaction."[32] De Land soon had cause to regret this letter.

Edwards also requested Orville Hickman Browning, an Illinois senator in Washington, to intercede for him. Browning was a lawyer and politician who filled Senator Douglas' seat from July 4, 1861 to January 30, 1863, and was Lincoln's floor manager in the Senate. Some historians believe that "The president's office and the president's secrets opened to Browning when they opened to no other." Browning was an unscrupulous influence peddler, who only needed to prepare an order for Lincoln to sign to secure the release of a prisoner from Camp Douglas or any other Northern prison.[33]

Browning wrote a revealing letter to Edwards on December 30, 1863 in regard to the Camp Douglas investigation: "Your several letters have been received. I have had repeated conversations with the President in regard to you, in all of which he has expressed himself most kindly, and as having unshaken confidence in your integrity and capacity." Browning also met with General Taylor twice, who "informed me that the whole thing was finally disposed of—that the last contract taken by Mr. Baker & others

(E. S. Fowler, R. E. Goodell, E. L. Baker, and John McGinnis, Jr.) would be rescinded- the contract relet and you continued in command at Chicago under the supervision of Col. Small, and to report to him, and that nothing further would be done. This I presume, will be entirely satisfactory. The General expressed himself in the kindest terms respecting you. You have had a hard time of it, but I trust now you will be let alone, and permitted to discharge your duties in peace. I suggest that you do not talk about this matter. It is not necessary that the public shall know that either you or the contractors have been subjected to annoyances."[34]

This was the second cover-up by President Lincoln and others in order to protect Edwards. The Camp Douglas scandal was not as dangerous to Lincoln since it merely looked like negligence on Edwards' part. However, the E. S. Fowler contract was finally terminated. Edwards retained control of Illinois subsistence, but not for long.

Orme found that the loss in defective beef amounted to $1,416.89. The Federal troops had received the same low-quality meat. There was some confusion about the bread ration because of three different size loaves. However, Orme lamely concluded there had been no intentional shortage and the bread was of good quality. Hints about the scandal did surface, however. The *Tribune* wrote defensively that "The rations daily distributed are the same as those given to our soldiers, notwithstanding the reports to the contrary."[35]

Later that year, bakers were selling bread to prisoners at 25 to 50 cents per loaf, in cash or sutler's checks. This was more than five times the price in Chicago. Where did the bakers get the flour, except by shorting the prisoners? It was at this point that one of Morgan's men wrote, "My Dear Dad: Please send at once $100 or a coffin." The camp censor sent it back endorsed "Do you think we are all damn fools up here?"[36]

Orme decided that pork and bacon were not deficient; beans had been watered down with peas, but at no profit to the contractors. Rice and hominy were good, and it was no surprise to find that ground coffee at ten cents per pound was terrible. Green coffee was good, except no one knew about it. The prisoners were not great tea drinkers, so not much was drawn. However, they had also been cheated on soap, pepper, and molasses. Vinegar, candles, salt, and potatoes were not deficient.

The contractors did not pay the contact price when they repurchased rations from the prisoners, thus reaping additional profits. Orme saw no violation here, since there was no obligation to buy back the rations. He considered only the legal, not the ethical aspects, and ignored the fact that the additional profits to the contractors represented less money for the

Ninian W. Edwards, cicra 1861 (courtesy Illinois State Historical Society)

prison fund. Surprisingly, hospital rations were in full compliance with con-tracts.[37]

Captain Arvin F. Whelan, the Post Surgeon, said that the ration in the prison hospital was the same as that for the garrison hospital, consist-ing of "bacon, beans, fresh beef, soft bread, potatoes, rice, tea, coffee, sugar, &c." The hospital fund also purchased butter, eggs, vegetables of all kinds,

chicken, oysters, fresh fish, and several varieties of fruit. The smallpox patients, though, did not see much of it.[38] While the prison hospital drew
underwear, shirts, socks, and bed linen, none of this reached the "pest
house." It appears that the new hospital was a showcase for inspectors, and
the smallpox infirmary was a poor relation.

Ninian Edwards' responsibility in the ration scandal was again omitted when Hoffman set the matter before Secretary of War Stanton in February, 1864, although Stanton could see that Edwards had signed the
contracts. No one now expected Lincoln to lose the next election, let alone
be assassinated. Hoffman recommended that the contractors make good
on all deficiencies, including the beef. He placed responsibility not on
Edwards but on Colonel De Land, and recommended that the commander
be court-martialed for "failure to see that his command received the rations which they were entitled to under the contract."[39] Stanton had no
objection to prosecuting De Land. Edwards was Mrs. Lincoln's brother-in-
law, and Stanton had his eyes on a Supreme Court nomination.

Colonel De Land became the second commandant whose reputation
was "sullied" at Camp Douglas. The contractors thought it was unfair to
require them to reimburse the government $1,416.89, and retained Orville
Hickman Browning to have the debt canceled. Browning went to Colonel
Hoffman's Washington office to see him about the matter on February 13,
1864, but did not find him in. He returned on February 19, but did not
record that he saw Hoffman. Browning's chances of success were excellent,
as he was urging Lincoln to appoint Hoffman's boss, Mr. Stanton, Chief
Justice of the Supreme Court.[40]

Edwards was stripped of command over subsistence in Illinois at the
end of January, 1864 despite Lincoln's belief in his "integrity and capacity."
The army now bought rations through competitive bidding. About two
dozen Chicago suppliers submitted bids in excess of $100,000 to supply
subsistence to the army and prison camps. "Chicago beef and Chicago pork
have an excellent reputation among soldiers," the *Tribune* boasted, "and
Government has come to appreciate this fact, and to govern itself accordingly." This did not solve the problem. A new contractor named A. P. & D.
Kelly was charged with furnishing inferior beef to the garrison and prisoners at Camp Douglas, and Captain Shurly was ordered to investigate.[41]

General Orme also concluded his investigation into the status of black
prisoners at camp. He found that Robert Marshall, Isaac H. Cox, and John
A. Rogan were slaves and released them on February 19, 1864. He decided
that Marshall Henry was a "free negro, not listed as a soldier and not having been in the Rebel army," and released him also.[42] Orme's findings were
based more on compassion than attention to facts. Marshall Henry was a

free man from a border state, captured with Confederate raiders near Cincinnati, Ohio. He hardly qualified as a tourist. Orme had referred to John Rogan as a "private" in his first report to Colonel Hoffman, but now labeled him a slave in order to effect his release.

One Union General protested the exchange of black prisoners, and thought they should be put to work. Hoffman had forwarded this letter to Stanton on October 8, 1863, recommending that "the negroes who have been slaves be released on taking the oath of allegiance."[44] This did not apply to black Confederate soldiers. Private Berry Black died at camp and was buried with his white comrades in Chicago. No inquiry was made into the fate of the three blacks who were unaccounted for. One of them was Henry Marshall, from the same unit as Curtis R. Burke, Co. B, 14th Kentucky Cavalry. Imprisonment at Camp Douglas had cost the lives of perhaps half of the black prisoners.

The indomitable Mrs. Finley was back at camp, and she expanded from a food stand to a sutler store in Prison Square on February 22, 1864.[45] This was without authority from Washington, as prison sutlers had been closed in December, 1863. Maybe that is why her goods were quite high. Apparently Orme and De Land had given up their efforts to keep her out. However, her outrageous prices soon caused Orme to shut her down for good.

The prisoners honored the memory of George Washington on his birthday, but the Yanks did not seem to care. Prisoners continued to die while attempting to escape, and one lost his life on the night of February 26, 1864. A major adjustment was made in prison square the following day. Barracks were jacked five feet high and supported by new six-inch timber legs.[46] This made it easier to detect tunneling, but the measure was ineffective to stop escapes because the buildings were still too close to the fence.

Another serious blaze in Garrison Square on February 29 showed that the camp required a fire department. A sutler's store and 200 yards of barracks and kitchens were destroyed. It is likely that the Chicago Fire Department had equipment nearby, because "Two steam fire engines and two hand engines were soon on hand."[47]

By the end of February, 1864, De Land had become longest serving garrison commander, but could not remain after Hoffman's charges. De Land had taken command under desolate conditions when the camp was not prepared for prisoners, and supervised many improvements. Completion of the sewer and water system and repairs of barracks and fences were critical. However, he made the barracks unfit for habitation by removing the floors. He found unauthorized and unsanitary sutlers in camp using prisoners to solicit orders, and cleared them out. Persistent escapes frustrated his management efforts, and led to serious cruelty and retaliation on his part. On the other hand, he had tried to have minors among the prisoners released, and had told General Ammen in 1863 that anxious parents in the South were willing to post bonds for them. The following year there were still 50 youths at camp, ranging from ages 14 to 17.[48]

De Land would not face a court-martial for the same reason that Colonel Mulligan did not. Veteran officers were a priority for the showdown in Virginia. De Land and his regiment, minus about 20 deserters, left for the front in mid-March, 1864. In May, he fought in the battles of the Wilderness and Spotsylvania, and was wounded twice.[49] Captain Rhines, who had supported the prisoners in the beef scandal, assumed command of the Sharpshooters.

Rhines, now a Major, was killed in action at Petersburg, Virginia on June 17, 1864.[50] De Land returned to duty on July 15 only partially recovered. He was wounded a third time in the Battle of the Crater on July 30. De Land returned to the fighting, again not fully healed, and went down with his fourth wound on September 30, 1864. This time he was left to die on the field, but fell into the hands of the Confederates and survived. The former commandant of a notorious prison camp, who had hung prisoners by the thumbs, was in enemy hands. However, there was no retaliation by the Confederates, and he was exchanged in February, 1865. His war was over, with a promotion to Brigadier-General.

Meanwhile General Orme was despondent over the situation at Camp Douglas, and thought of resigning his post and returning to active duty. His good friend, Federal Supreme Court Justice David Davis, also from Bloomington, Illinois, was aware of Orme's poor health, and wrote on February 19, 1864 trying to dissuade him.[51] Regardless, Orme was being eased out of his command. He notified Colonel Hoffman that "on the 1st of March a new set of officers were placed in charge of the prisoners." The War Department had bypassed General Orme in appointing Colonel James C. Strong, 15th regiment of the Invalid Corps, as commander of the garrison to replace De Land.

Strong had arrived at camp with his regiment in June, 1863. As the new garrison commander, he immediately prepared new prison rolls without regard to the old records. The count disclosed that 84 prisoners were unaccounted for. Orme reported that "the discrepancy is not as large as I anticipated." Hoffman must have had his own ideas about that. Orme remained in command of the District and the post, but Colonel Strong was the boss over the garrison. It was not a happy situation. Ninian W. Edwards was demoted to Camp Douglas as food commissary and treasurer of the prison fund.[52] Lincoln did not intervene.

The prisoners received new orders from Colonel Strong's officers:
1. To rise at sound of bugle at sunrise.
2. Roll call one hour later.
3. Dismissal and breakfast.
4. Work detail from 8 a.m. to noon.
5. Dinner at 12:30.
6. Work detail at from 1 p.m. to 5 o'clock.
7. Supper at 5:30
8. Lights out at 7 o' clock.[53]

Colonel Strong was a native of New York state and served in New York regiments until he was disabled by wounds in 1862. He then joined the Invalid Corps. He was mobbed by mistake at President Lincoln's funeral because of his resemblance to General Grant.[54] He preferred to live in Chicago despite Hoffman's orders to take up residence at Camp Douglas.

Strong was the first garrison commander to exploit forced labor, and barracks were continually searched to conscript prisoners for work details, according to Burke. "Our Yankee sergeant brought six spades, one rake and two wheelbarrows and called for a detail of nine men to dig a ditch in front of the barracks."[55] The men were called out in alphabetical order when no one responded. They worked until 1 p.m., and then another detail was conscripted until 5 p.m. Burke and John Curd were among those put to work, and they dug 150 feet of ditch under the close eye of the sergeant. The leisure class of prisoners existed no longer. This was far different from the previous January when prisoners were free to quit helping move the barracks from White Oak. However some prisoners volunteered to work because they did not wish to be idle when the improvements were for their own benefit. Medical Inspector Clark had reported as early as October 9, 1863, "Duties in camp—none required of the prisoners; many volunteer to work."[56]

Prison life was demoralizing in many respects. Burke's mess stole a barrel of coal from infantry prisoners on February 16, not thinking or caring about what this meant to men who were in the same situation. The following month prisoners broke into Mrs. Finley's shop as she was moving out, and then raided the new sutler's store.[57]

Stanton eased some restrictions in March without explanation. Prisoners could make purchases from a small room—not a sutler store—during the day from a list of authorized items such as: tobacco, cigars, pipes, snuff, steel pens, paper, envelopes, lead pencils, pen knives, postage stamps, buttons, tape, thread, sewing cotton, pins and needles, handkerchiefs, suspenders, socks and underclothes, caps, shoes, towels, looking glasses, brushes, combs, clothes brooms, pocket knives, and scissors. Groceries available were: crushed sugar, syrup, family soap, butter, lard, smoked beef tongues, bologna sausage, corn-meal, nutmeg, pepper, mustard, table salt, crackers, cheese, pickles, sauces, meats and fish in cans, vegetables, dried fruits, lemons, nuts, apples, matches, and yeast powders. Table furniture items also available were: crockery, glassware, and tinware.[58]

Business hours were from sunrise to sunset. The most critical items for sale were the vegetables necessary to prevent scurvy. Many prisoners had to sell their food to obtain articles from the sutler, which was in addition to their share of the rations sold for the prison fund. When Burke's mess was out of meat and sugar they easily solved the problem. "We buy from the infantry prisoners at the rates of ten cents per pound for sugar and from five to seven cents per pound for fat meat," wrote Burke with a small token of guilt. "The infantry from the extreme south need a little cash to buy things they cannot draw so they save up part of their rations and sell them."[59]

The ban on packages from friends was lifted on March 11, although excess clothing was forbidden. Stanton issued an unprecedented order on March 17, 1864 to form a board of inquiry when a prisoner was shot. "Rigid discipline must be preserved," he ordained, "but great care must be observed that no wanton excesses or cruelties are committed under the plea of enforcing orders."[60] He was not taken seriously at Camp Douglas, though the following day was one of great satisfaction to the Invalid Corps as they officially became the "Veteran Reserve Corps."

A curious contraption for washing clothes had arrived in barracks. It was a boiler with six feet of pipe attached, and "looked like locomotives on a small scale at a distance."[61] Each barrack had two, fired by wood or coal. They would be replaced by a central wash house later that year.

Cooking and roll call procedures were tightened considerably. Each mess now had three permanent cooks. The rebel sergeant-majors would have to account for missing men at roll call, and the prisoners could not leave ranks until the morning rolls were completed. They stood in line for over three hours once because one man could not be accounted for.[62] The Confederate sergeants petitioned Major Skinner to change the rules so that this would not happen in bad weather. There was no response. Skinner never answered grievances. Perhaps his crippling wounds at age 25 made him ill-mannered and bad-tempered.

Another ingenious escape plot almost succeeded in March, 1864. Some prisoners still living in White Oak Square started a tunnel through the large brick and iron stove in their kitchen. A trap door protected it while the stove was in use. An officer uncovered it one day, much to the "astonishment of the rebs." The prisoners suspected treachery, but they were wrong. Reverend Tuttle disclosed that Captain Wells Sponable discovered the hole after spotting a prisoner running to the kitchen at one o'clock in the morning.[63]

On March 22, 1864, Orme told Hoffman that the fence separating the new Prison Square from the rest of the camp was completed.[64] For the first time Camp Douglas began to look like a maximum-security prison, but it was not and never would be. Orme also created a permanent guard detail for Prison Square, composed of one captain, one lieutenant, 10 sergeants, 20 corporals, and 38 privates. Prisoners were not leave the square without permission.

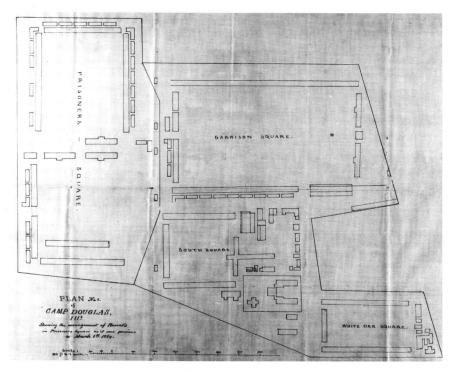

Plan of Camp Douglas, March 1, 1864, showing first arrangement of Prison Square, and three other squares. The gap between White Oak and Garrison Square was the Graves' property (courtesy the National Archives).

Regardless, 32 prisoners had escaped by the end of March, 1864, and 5,462 were present. General Orme had only 550 men available for guard duty that month. He realized that his design of the new square, with barracks placed near the fences, was defective because of tunneling by the prisoners, and the buildings were moved toward the center of the square. They were cut into 90-foot lengths, arranged on parallel streets, and put on five foot posts with double flooring. Tents were delivered with the consequent rumor that prisoners would have to live in them, although it never happened. Orme was serious again about resigning from Camp Douglas and returning to active duty. He received a frantic letter from Justice Davis on March 29 in which the judge warned "you must not go into the field anywhere! If you desire to remain in the army, remain in Chicago!" The jurist also informed his friend that he had seen Stanton to insure that Mr. Luman Burr, Orme's choice to be the new sutler, was approved.[65]

The new sutler's prices were "very high" when he issued his first checks. He intended to recover the losses suffered when the store had been raided by prisoners while he was setting up shop. His checks were "on thin paper and are steel engraved and harder to counterfeit than those used by the other sutlers."[66] Headquarters no longer issued sutler's checks; these were now the sutler's responsibility.

A new 225-bed hospital was finally completed in April, 1864 on the southeast side of camp between White Oak Square and Prison Square. It cost the prison fund $10,000.[67] There was no explanation about why it took eight months to build. The reason may have been a shortage of cash, considering the exorbitant price of the building. The exact nature of the hospital is difficult to learn because of varying descriptions.

It was first described as a two-story building with two wings, each containing four wards and 180 beds.[68] It had a mess room, kitchen, and adjoining two-story laundry. A furnace heated the water for laundry, bathing, and boiling clothes. Each ward had a running water toilet connected to the main sewer, and the entire place was whitewashed. Regardless, the cost of the hospital was at least double what it should have been. Economy was not the watchword when using the prison fund, and Chicago contractors took full advantage.

Although the hospital was well-equipped and modern, it was too small. At least 500 more beds would be needed as the prison population doubled. Two old buildings were added, amounting to 70 more beds. A hospital twice the size was built for the Camp Douglas garrison about this time, while smallpox patients had to suffer in a converted cavalry stable just west of the university.

Original University of Chicago looking northwest, circa May, 1863. Note construction work at entrance to main tower, and what appears to be the Camp Douglas smallpox hospital [circled]. (courtesy Chicago Public Library, Special Collections)

On March 28, 1864, Orme told the Quartermaster, Captain Goodman, to move the smallpox hospital to a place called "Adele Grove, one-half mile south of Camp Douglas." Adele was Senator Douglas' widow, so the hospital remained on the Douglas estate where the land was rent free. It contained two wards, and was in operation by April 15, 1864. Burke estimated it was 400 yards south of the fence. An inspector reported that it was only 200 yards away, although Burke was more accurate.[69]

General Orme further tightened security in Prison Square. Each barrack was controlled by a sergeant, two corporals, and five privates from the patrol. One of them named "Old Red" was reputed to be vindictive and dangerous.[70] This squad guarded the prisoners at roll call, prepared work details, and saw to it that rations and fuel were delivered to the barracks. They also patrolled the square at night.

Orme had attached many bright oil-burning reflector lamps to the fence, "so close together and the light so brilliant that it would be almost impossible to get to the fence without being discovered by the guards on the parapet." Bright reflector lamps were soon installed at the end of each street. The dead-line was a low railing about 18 inches high running around the square 10 feet from the fence. Guards also patrolled the area between the dead-line and the fence.

Discipline grew more rigid under Colonel Strong. On April 10, 1864, prisoners were made to stand on barrel heads after purchasing whiskey from a guard. Another punishment was to make a prisoner walk with his head sticking out of a box or barrel with a placard attached: "For disobeying orders," "For washing in barracks," "Lousy," "For meddling with other people's business," "For going to the other square."[71]

A dungeon of heavy timbers was built in Prison Square, measuring about eight feet square and seven feet high, with a door in front and two diamond-shaped windows or air holes on two sides. Previously the only dungeon was White Oak. This new one was located near the gate to Prison Square. Prisoners called it the "Four of Diamonds." Guards named it the "Monitor." Three men spent a night there for climbing on a roof to watch horse racing near the camp.[72]

The ball and chain were used extensively, consisting of a cannon ball weighing 32 pounds or more, with four or five feet of chain attached and a clasp to go about the ankle. Prisoners could carry it around by leather straps. They called the contraption their "time pieces." Several prisoners were punished this way after they applied to take the oath and changed their minds. Even sick prisoners were made to wear the time piece. "John Shackelford returned from the smallpox hospital with his ball and chain still on. On his way in, the 64 lb rolled out of the old ambulance nearly jerking his leg off before the ambulance could be stopped. At night he suffered a great deal with his leg."[73]

On April 16, 1864, General Orme's reputation was "sullied" by a mere Lieutenant-Colonel from the Inspector General's office. "General Orme gives very little attention to his command at Camp Douglas," said Inspector Marsh.[74] Orme apparently did not like Colonel Strong. "There is a want of courtesy on the part of the commanding officer toward the commander

A prisoner wearing his "time piece" at Camp Douglas, circa 1864 (courtesy Illinois State Historical Society)

of the garrison," Marsh noted. He was shocked by lax control of the four sutlers, one each for the 8th, 11th, and 15th V.R.C., and one for the prisoners. Only the sutler for the 15th V.R.C. had a price list posted. Marsh naively reported, "Sales restricted to articles authorized by law."

A private contractor came around every day or so to collect the garbage and grease from the kitchens. He paid prisoners with tobacco to carry it out to his wagon.[75] Barracks were in poor condition with floors ripped up, filthy bunks, bedding not aired, and the grounds wet and in poor police. "Colonel Strong and Major Skinner would be valuable officers serving under an efficient commander," Marsh advised. There were 5,435 prisoners, and Reverend Tuttle drove around camp in his buggy to distribute religious newspapers, although the prisoners were not altogether appreciative. "Some of the reading we respect," Burke reported, "but most of it, the abolition articles we read with the utmost contempt." [76]

Someone, possibly Colonel Marsh, told Orme to correct the problems at camp, and he suddenly resigned on April 29, 1864. Command of the District and post went to Colonel Benjamin J. Sweet of the 8th V. R. C. on May 2, 1864.[77] There was no explanation why Colonel Strong was not appointed. It is possible that his wounds prevented him from taking on the job.

Orme's main contribution to Camp Douglas was Prison Square. His investigation of the food scandal and other conditions at camp is memorable because he went to the prisoners directly. Orme's attempt to exonerate the contractors, and his disregard of Ninian Edwards' responsibility was an ethical failure. His post-war career in law and politics rested in Illinois, and he acted accordingly. General Tyler, who had commanded the parolees, may have acted differently.

Colonel Sweet was in an ideal position compared to past commandants. He had been at camp for seven months and went to school on the problems faced by De Land, Orme, and Strong. Unlike De Land, he did not face a deluge of prisoners before he could bite off the end of his cigar. Neither did he have to spend his energy on a ration scandal. He knew what had to be done, and the officers to carry out his plans were already in place. The former Wisconsin lawmaker saw his opportunity and would make the most of it. General Orme had but two years and three months to live.

NOTES TO CHAPTER 11

[1] Burke, 1 Jan. 1864; Goodspeed and Healy, *History of Cook County,* I:309.

[2] M. J. Bradley, "The Horrors of Camp Douglas as related by a prisoner," in Griffin Frost's *Camp and Prison Journal,* Quincy Herald Book and Job Office, (Quincy, 1867) 277; R. T. Bean, *Confederate Veteran* 22:270; *Chicago Tribune,* 8 Jan. 1864.

[3] T. M. Page, "The Prisoner of War," *Confederate Veteran* 8 (Feb. 1900): 63.

[4] O R Ser.II-Vol.VI, 800.

[5] *Chicago Tribune,* 8, 10 Jan. 1864.

[6] *"Isaac Cox,* negro. Co. L, 2nd Kentucky Cavalry. Captured 7-26-'63 at Talinnville, Ohio. Remarks: Released by order of Secretary of War, February, 1864." *Confederate Prisoners of War,* Roll 55.

 "Alex Bogan, negro. Co. I, Wood's Tennessee Cavalry. Captured 7-26-'63 at Talinnville, Ohio. Remarks: Unaccounted for." Roll 55.

"*Henry Marshall,* negro. Co. B, 14th Kentucky Cavalry [same unit as Burke]. Captured 7-26-'63 at Talinnville, Ohio. Remarks: Unaccounted for." Roll 55.

"*Marshall Henry,* negro. Captured 7-14-'63 near Cincinnati, Ohio. Remarks: Released by order of the Secretary of War, February, 1864." He was probably in the 15th Tennessee Cavalry]* Roll 55.

"*Robert Marshall,* negro. Servant of Dr. Marshall. Captured 7-15-'63 at Logan, Ohio. Remarks: Released by order of the Secretary of War [no date given]." Roll 55.

"*Berry Black,* negro. Co. D, 15th Tennessee Cavalry [Morgan's Command]. Captured 7-20-'63 at Cheshire, Ohio. Remarks: Died November 5, 1863." [Private Berry Black is interred in the Confederate Mound in Oak Woods Cemetery in Chicago under the name of Berry, Black. Pvt.]. Roll 55.

"*John A. Rogan,* negro. Captured 7-14-'63 near Cincinnati, Ohio. Remarks: Released by order of the Secretary of War [no date given]." Private Regan was in Co. I, 15th Tennessee Cavalry, Morgan's Command. Roll 55.

"*Reading Buffer* negro. Co. G, 15th Tennessee Cavalry [Morgan's Command]. Captured 7-20-'63 at Cheshire, Ohio. Remarks: Unaccounted for." Roll 55.

*The 15th Tennessee Cavalry on Morgan's raid is not the same Confederate unit as the 15 Tennessee Cavalry (Stewart's) or the 15th Tennessee Cavalry (Russell's). These were official units. *Gen. Marcus J. Wright, Tennessee in the War* (New York: Ambrose Lee Publishing Co., 1908) 90; *John B. Lindsley, Military Annals of Tennessee, Confederate* (Nashville: J. M. Lindsley & Co., 1886) 733-34. The one on the raid was not known in Richmond, although it was formed in September 1862 as part of Basil Duke's Brigade. It probably failed to file a muster in role.

7 O R Ser.I-Vol.XV, 556-57; Ser.II-Vol.III, 436-37; Ser.IV-Vol.I, 409, 529, 625, 1020; Charles W. Wesley, "Negroes As Soldiers In The Confederate Army", *The Journal of Negro History* IV (July, 1919-No. 3): 239-53; Luther P. Jackson, "Free Negroes of Petersburg, Virginia," *The Journal of Negro History* 12 (Jan. 1927-No. 1): 386-88; John D. Winters, *The Civil War in Louisiana* (Baton Rouge: Louisiana State University Press, 1963) 34-35; Merle R. Eppse, *The Negro, Too, in American History* (Nashville: National Publication Co., 1943) 225-26; Ira Berlin, *Slaves Without Masters* (New York: Oxford University Press, 1975) 386-87.

8 O R Ser.III-Vol.II, 584-85; Vol.V, 671-72.

9 R. G. 393, (Part 4, v. 234) Records of the U. S. Army Continental Commands, Camp Douglas Letter Book, 175; R. G. 393, v. 240:68.

10 Burke, 3 Jan. 1864.

[11] Kelly, 133.

[12] R. G. 393, v. 240:4.

[13] *Chicago Tribune,* 1 Sep. 1863; James S. Coke, *Confederate Veteran,* 14 (Oct. 1906): 38; Burke, 8 Jan. 1864.

[14] Kelly, 103, 104.

[15] Kelly, 105.

[16] Burke, 15 Mar. 1864; O R Ser.II-Vol.VI, 860-61; R. G. 393, 234:232.

[17] O R Ser.II-Vol.VI, 824.

[18] Burke, 19 Jan. 1864; "Doorstep Reminiscences," *Confederate Veteran* 10 (Oct. 1902):453.

[19] Burke, 29 Jan. 1864; R. G. 94, Plan of Camp Douglas, 1 March 1864, 8 August 1864, 1 January 1865; O R Ser.II-Vol.VII, 616.

[20] R. G. 393, v. 240:32.

[21] O R Ser.II-Vol.VI, 848-51.

[22] O R Ser.II-Vol.VI, 851; Burke, 14 Jan. 1864.

[23] R.G 393, v. 234:179; *Chicago Tribune,* 30 Jan. 1864.

[24] O R Ser.II-Vol.VI, 908-10.

[25] Hesseltine, 144; James R. Clark, "The Cost of Capture," *Civil War Times* 1 (Mar. 1992) 31:26; Burke, 16 Jan. 1864.

[26] Misc. ms., CHS.

[27] Burke, 14 Feb. 1864.

[28] Burke, 4 Feb. 1864. The barracks were arranged in long rows around the sides of the square.

[29] O R Ser.II-Vol.VI, 927-29.

[30] 0. Colonel Kilburn was chief commissary of the Department of the Ohio, which included Illinois; ms. Original Autograph Letters, v. 49:659, CHS.

[31] *The Collected Works of Abraham Lincoln,* v.II:188.

[32] *Autograph Letters,* v. 49:651, CHS.

[33] He was instrumental in winning over delegates to Lincoln at the nominating convention in Chicago in 1860. *Dictionary of American Biography,* III:175; *The Diary of Orville Hickman Browning,* Vol. I, Theodore Calvin Pease and James G. Randall, ed. (Springfield, Illinois State Historical Library, 1925) v. xix; Browning diary, 14 Dec. 1863, for the release of Henry N. Warfield from Camp Douglas. Warfield had escaped through the tunnel in December, 1863, but later surrendered.

[34] *Autograph Letters,* v. 49:663, CHS.

[35] O R Ser.II-Vol.VI, 927-29; *Chicago Tribune,* 8 Jan. 1864.

[36] Burke, 3 Nov. 1864; T. M. Page, *Confederate Veteran* 8: 64.

[37] O R Ser.II-Vol.VI, 929.

[38] O R Ser.II-Vol.VI, 798-99; Burke, 2-17 Oct. 1864.

[39] O R Ser.II-Vol.VI, 929.

[40] *Browning* diary, 17 Oct. 1864.

[41] *Chicago Tribune,* 27 January 1864; R. G. 393, v. 244:301.

[42] R. G. 393, 244:282.

[44] O R Ser.II-Vol.VI, 354.

[45] Burke, 22 Feb. 1864.

[46] Burke, 22, 27 Feb. 1864.

[47] Burke, 29 Feb. 1864.

[48] R.G. 393, v. 233; v. 233:160; *Chicago Tribune,* 1 Feb. 1864.

[49] John Robertson, *Michigan in the War* (Lansing: W. S. George & C., 1882)

[50] *Record of Service of Michigan Volunteers in the Civil War* (Brig. Gen. George H. Brown, Adj. Gen.) 2.

[51] Letters of General William Ward Orme, CHS.

[52] O R Ser.II-Vol.VII, 20-21; Karlen, "Postal History of Camp Douglas," 821; O R Ser.II-Vol.VII, 57.

[53] Burke, 7 Mar. 1864.

[54] Tuttle, *History of Camp Douglas,*34.

[55] Burke, 14 Mar. 1864.

[56] O R Ser.II-Vol.VI,372.

[57] Burke, 23-24 Mar. 1864.

[58] O R Ser.II-Vol.VI, 1014-15.

[59] Burke, 29 Mar. 1864.

[60] O R. Ser.II-Vol.VI, 1036, 1073.

[61] Burke, Mar. 14 1864.

[62] Burke, 22 Mar., 3 Apr. 1864.

[63] Burke, 27 Mar. 1864; Tuttle,17.

[64] R. G. 393, v. 234:232.

[65] O R Ser.II-Vol.VIII, 986-1003; R.G. 393, v. 234:238; Burke, 30 Mar., 2 Apr. 1864; Orme letters, CHS.

[66] Burke, 25 Mar. 1864.

[67] R. G. 393, 237:180.

[68] The Medical and Surgical History of the War of the Rebellion, v. I, Part III:49.

[69] R.G. 393, v. 244; *Chicago Tribune,* 15 Apr. 1864; Burke, 5 Oct. 1864; O R Ser.II-Vol.VII, 703.

[70] Burke, 3 Apr. 1864.

[71] Burke, 16 Aug. 1864.

[72] Burke, 16 Apr., 4 Jul. 1864.

[73] Bell I. Wiley, "The Common Soldier of the Civil War," *Civil War Times* 4 (Jul. 1973):49; Burke, 12, 18 Apr., 9 Dec. 1864.

[74] O R Ser.II-Vol.VII, 57.

[75] Burke, 11 Apr. 1864.

[76] Burke, 20 Apr. 1864.

[77] O R Ser.II-Vol.VII, 57-58; Vol.VIII, 102.

12.

CONDITIONS IMPROVE

Colonel Sweet was wounded in the critical battle of Perryville, Kentucky on October 8, 1862, leaving him with a crippled right arm. His 21st Wisconsin poured "a withering fire" into the ranks of a much larger rebel force, and received special mention in official reports.[1] He had played an important role in starting the Confederacy down the road to defeat long before Gettysburg.

His parents were farmers from Wisconsin where he was born in 1832. He was a lawyer and member of the Wisconsin Senate by 1859. Sweet volunteered early in the war, even though he had a wife and four children. It took a year for his wounds to heal, after which he took command of the 8th regiment of the Invalid Corps., and was assigned to Camp Douglas around September 26, 1863.[2]

He commanded the post from headquarters in Chicago after he became commander, and left Colonel Strong in charge of the garrison. Sweet saw to it that his plans were carried out at Camp Douglas, although there were restrictions set by Colonel Hoffman. The camp became much cleaner, with more internal discipline for the prisoners. This would benefit the prisoners in many respects. However, they would pay a price as breaking rules led to acts of cruelty. Sweet's refusal to live at camp is puzzling in view of his ambitions. This may have been due to his young daughter, Ada, who was living with him. She had just passed her 11th birthday.[3]

"About this time Colonel De Land was ordered to the front," T. D. Henry remembered. "He was succeeded by Colonel B. J. Sweet as commandant, Colonel Skinner as commissary of prisoners, and a fiend named Captain Webb [Wells] Sponable as inspector of prisoners. From this time forward the darkest leaf in the legends of all tyranny could not possibly contain a greater number of punishments."[4]

Sponable's small force in the square was about the same that Orme had established, two lieutenants, 10 sergeants, 20 corporals, and 38 privates. [5] These patrols did not have to account for their actions regarding the prisoners. They regulated the most important aspects of prison life, such as feeding, cooking arrangements, and work details.

On April 17, 1864, General Grant made a critical decision affecting the prisoners of war on both sides. With authority from Stanton, he canceled further negotiations for exchange of prisoners unless black Union

Colonel Benjamin J. Sweet, circa 1862

soldiers in Confederate hands were included. The prisoners at Camp Douglas probably read about it in the papers, but were "still more confident of the success of our cause," as April, 1864 came to a close. However, about 1,500 out of 6,000 men had applied to take the oath of allegiance.[6] There were persistent efforts by some prisoners to intimidate those who wished to enlist in Federal service or take the oath, which was called "swallowing the dog." Hoffman ordered severe punishment for any prisoner "who threatens or insults them in any way for expressing a desire to return to their allegiance."[7]

Sweet was the first commandant to reduce rations and supplies without orders, when hominy and candles were eliminated.[8] He believed that the candles were used for tunneling out. The light was highly prized during the long and gloomy Chicago winters. Reading or social activity became difficult for the prisoners after the short winter day ended, and Sweet also failed to consider that sick and dying prisoners in the barracks needed care during the night. Hoffman did not object to Sweet's actions. In addition, Colonel Strong's assistant, Major Skinner, wished to eliminate tea, and Ninian Edwards urged Sweet to take away rice and vinegar as well. The cutbacks started with the 10 days' ration issued on April 29. Meal was substituted for flour, and prisoners received pickled pork instead of beef three times of the last 10 days of April.[9]

At the same time, Union prisoners at Andersonville received "one pound of beef, or one-third pound of bacon, one and one-fourth pounds of meal, with an occasional issue of beans, rice, molasses, and vinegar." It is not known how long the ration was to last or how many men it had to feed. The Union prisoners lacked cooking utensils and were without shelter. A total of 1,026 men died in the 10 weeks after Andersonville opened on February 27, 1864. Robbers invaded the hospital tents since there was no protection by the authorities.[10]

In contrast, a Confederate prisoner was put in the new dungeon at Camp Douglas "for selling several suits of clothes that were sent to other persons in his care." When a prisoner named Joseph McCarney stabbed two brothers named Scroggin on May 12, 1864, he was badly beaten by the guards, tightly bound, and thrown into the Four of Diamonds. Burke reported that he was als balled and chained. One brother died on May 24, 1864, but took the blame for the fight and requested that McCarney be released. McCarney was in the dungeon wearing ball and chain until September 8. It was the worst such incident.

Also, the system of sutler's checks was protected from con-artists and thieves among the prisoners. Reverend Tuttle reported that sometimes

Riding the Mule at Camp Douglas, circa 1864. Some prisoners claimed that the plank was turned up edge-wise, not flat as shown here. (courtesy Illinois State Historical Library)

impostors would come to the sutler's cashier and claim other prisoner's checks.[11] If caught, they were made to ride the mule for a long time.

Colonel Sweet built on the experience of General Orme, and placed the increasing number of barracks along parallel streets in Prison Square. This was done by forced labor, with the guards constantly searching to find manpower.[12] Obtaining water was difficult again because the hydrants were not working properly due to the small three-inch pipes.

Surprise searches for contraband were made constantly, but prisoners usually succeeded in hiding their money. Pa was searched, although out of respect for his rank he did not have to take off his boots. The prisoners were warned to spend their sutler's checks on May 19, as he was closing his store. Burke was aware of everything going on. "Some of Colonel Sweet's friends are expected to succeed the present sutler, Mr. Luman Burr," he predicted. Two weeks later Sweet fired Burr and replaced him with Benjamin Nightingale. One observant prisoner claimed that Nightingale was Sweet's brother-in-law.[13]

On May 24, all prisoners were counted at once in a giant roll call. The men dressed in their best clothing because they expected a barracks search while they were out, when "excess clothing" was confiscated. Lines of prisoners filled the square in proud military formation. For a moment the 5,277 men were soldiers once more, and a picture was taken.[14] They could have added five regiments to the Confederate army had exchanges resumed.

Burke described the ration at this time: "May 30th 1864: The following is what my mess of eight gets for ten days: Meal 24 cups, pickle-pork 22 lbs, hominy 4 qts, fresh beef 18 lbs, light bread 24 loaves, parched coffee 4 pts, molasses 3 pts, sugar 5 qts, potatoes 1 peck. No soap, flour, candles, pepper, peas, beans, or vinegar were issued this time. Our beef and bread is not all issued at once, but we draw them in three different drawings during the ten days, so that we get them tolerable fresh."

Fresh beef amounted to only 2˜ ounces per day per man for the mess of eight. The potato ration provided about four ounces per day for the 10 days, not enough to prevent scurvy. The meal and bread were barely adequate at one-third of a cup of meal and one-third of a loaf of bread daily. With even the temporary loss of peas, beans, and flour, the charges of starvation leveled by some prisoners after the war is understandable. A mess likely ran out of food. Then the men went hungry unless they had funds to buy provisions at the sutler or from other prisoners.

Topsoil at camp was so eroded that the garrison was wearing "green goggles" against blowing sand and dust. Burke declared this part of the country unfit to live in. He was concerned about the Confederate dollar. Gold had risen to $1.9125 per ounce.

On June 1, Colonel Sweet completed the rearrangement of Prison Square into streets 50 feet wide, with four or five barracks on a street. This moved them away from the fence and prevented tunneling. The buildings sat on blocks and were white-washed inside and out. There were now 32 barracks. Each measured 90 feet long, including a 20-foot kitchen, and could house 165 men comfortably.[15] A long building in the square contained the express office, tool shop, and pharmacy.

The prisoners saw that the new arrangement of the square would make tunneling difficult, and there was an attack on the fence on the night of June 1. It was well coordinated, with some prisoners smashing the lamps and others rocking the fence so that guards on the parapet had difficulty firing. Another group attacked the boards with axes. Only one guard rifle discharged, but patrols on the ground ended the assault with revolvers. Miraculously, no one was injured. Colonel Sweet complained to Hoffman that the rifles had been condemned months before, and the prisoners knew this.[16]

A report made in February, 1864 revealed that the rifles were "an old and probably condemned lot of arms, unserviceable and positively danger-ous to the men using them." Only one company of the 8th V.R.C. had new Springfield rifles. The guards on the fence had revolvers besides rifles by July 2. The 500 replacement revolvers were also from a condemned lot. Prison security did not have highest priority in Washington. Sometimes the bullets did find their mark, however. Escapes fell sharply from 151 near the end of 1863 to only 92 for all of 1864.[17] This was mainly due to raising the barracks and moving them away from the fence.

A sutler's store and D. F. Brandon's photo studio were added to the square. Sweet was proud of the new prison, and argued for the erection of 39 more barracks on the same plan, "which would give a capacity to hold 11,880 prisoners, or would accommodate, by placing a few more men in each barrack, in round numbers, 12,000 men," he told Colonel Hoffman. The total cost including kitchens would be $19,600. Sweet knew that his boss would not agree to use the prison fund, and gave Hoffman a subtle warning: Authority for the expansion could be found in a War Department letter of April 29, 1864, Sweet wrote.[18] Precisely as Hoffman would not risk his career on volunteer officers, Sweet would not let him stand in the way of his own future. He was aware that the Surgeon General, the Adjutant General, and the Northern Department of the Army at Cincinnati were watching the camp.

Sweet had judged correctly, because Hoffman promptly ordered pris-oners to be housed in old tents. Sweet coyly replied that there were only new tents on hand, but old barracks in Garrison Square could be reno-vated and moved into Prison Square, "should you desire it." The garrison was about to receive new barracks. He had four more barracks in place in Prison Square by June 11, and it could hold a total of 82 such buildings. New barracks would cost $500 each plus $100 for an add-on kitchen. Un-aware of the additional barracks Sweet had just placed in the square, Hoffman ordered "worn" tents for 2,000 prisoners.[19] However, there is no record of prisoners living in tents at Camp Douglas, even temporarily, as they did at some other Northern prisons.

The War Department again reduced rations in June.[20] Tea, sugar, and coffee were restricted to the sick and wounded; molasses was eliminated. The gain would go to the prison fund. The tea, coffee, and sugar were eliminated at General Halleck's suggestion, "to reduce the ration to that issued by the Rebel government to their own troops."[21] There was no need for prisoners to eat better than the Confederate army. This was really a matter of retaliation, not economy. General Taylor, who had conspired with President Lincoln to hide the Edwards' affair, agreed with Halleck.

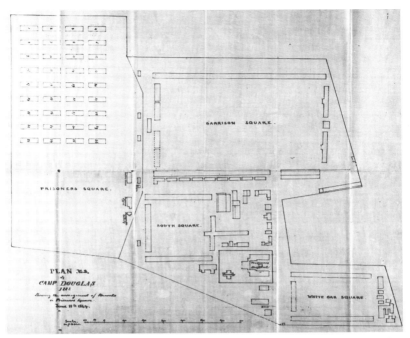

Plan of Camp Douglas, June 11, 1864, showing second arrangement of Prison Square, including sutler store, express office, photo studio, and new dungeon (courtesy the National Archives).

Each barrack was now required to furnish a work detail of six men for the day, "two to bring water and cut wood for the kitchen, two to keep the barrack and street in front well swept, two to carry out the waste water." Families were still allowed to send packages. When Burke received a box at the express office, the guard took a handful of cigars. It was common for these inspectors to take something for themselves. Otherwise, everything sent was there: for himself, a gray jacket and vest and some socks, soap, crackers, marbles, and two novels. Pa received a hat, socks, soap, thread, a pair of shoes, and part of a box of cigars. The package took only three days to reach camp from Kentucky.

Burke saw John Shanks, a member of his own regiment, working as a clerk in the express office. Shanks may have been a spy for Colonel Sweet at this time. He certainly was Sweet's agent in the coming Camp Douglas Conspiracy of 1864. There must have been something awry about the man, because the prisoners already had his number. They were intrigued by an incident on May 3, 1864, when a prisoner named William Calameze struck Shanks in the barrack.[22] Neither one would disclose the cause of the quarrel, which fueled more curiosity and suspicion.

Most of the square was out of food by June 6, "and it will be three or four days til we draw again," Burke guessed. By June 17 the men were living on scraps. After that the rations were only enough for two meals a day. R. T. Bean claimed, "I saw one poor fellow who had lost his mind for fear of starving to death, and his cries for bread were pitiful in the extreme."[23] The hunger was real, and anyone caught taking bones from the garbage was punished by having the bone fastened between his teeth, across his mouth, and then tied like a gag. "And then the poor fellow was made to fall down and crawl around on his hands and knees like a dog, a laughing stock for Federal soldiers, spies, and camp followers," Bean remembered with bitterness. "There is more inventive meanness in the Yankee composition, than any other nation upon God's green earth could conceive of during thousands of years!"[24]

A large issue of clothing was made on June 12, and the needy received shoes, dark blue pants, gray jackets or coats, high-crowned gray hats, cotton drawers, woolen shorts, and a few socks. Burke thought that he had a right to the clothing and was scornful of those who worked for it. He and Pa had been receiving "care" packages regularly from relatives in Ohio.

There was heavy drafting of prisoners to dig ditches, level off the ground, grade streets, and repair barracks. Burke did his best to dodge work details, and he loafed on the job at every opportunity. For him the war continued and any cooperation with the enemy was dishonorable. The uniform appearance of the many barracks in Prison Square was a source of hilarity as the prisoners often entered the wrong one. Soon each barrack had its own number painted on the front. However, the men turned on each other more often as hope of exchange faded. Arguments and fights were common by the summer of 1864. Something as trifling as a rusty plate could set off a battle.[25] There was seldom any damage because of quick intervention. No one wanted a repeat of the McCarney stabbings.

A major cause of tension and bickering was the bunk situation when one of the frequent barrack changes occurred. This resulted in a dash to the new quarters because the top bunks were the worst, due to leaking roofs. The bottom one was also undesirable because of the cold floor, leaving the second tier as first choice. There was talk among the prisoners of ending this "devil take the hindmost" mentality and drawing the new bunks by lot. Nothing came of it, but one prisoner named Jerry Murphy refused to sleep with anyone, and the other men tolerated him, although this meant less bunk space for others. One night he came back from the sink and found someone in what he thought was his bunk. His roar of anger awakened everyone, but Jerry had wandered into the wrong barrack in the darkness. The laughter could almost be heard in Chicago, as Jerry retreated very apologetic and embarrassed. Miraculously, he was not shot by the patrol or a guard.[26]

Burke was on a roof with a work detail one day and noticed a crowd at the race track nearby.[27] The country looked green and the houses were clean and comfortable. This caused Burke to reflect: "The people walking about as if there was no war going on, and here I have been wasting part of the prime of life in this miserable place a prisoner, and not knowing how much longer I will be forced to remain. I could not help envying them their liberty, yet I try to be contented." No doubt, many other prisoners felt the same way.

Sweet was baffled by the role of religion at camp and consulted Colonel Hoffman when the Catholic Bishop of Chicago requested permission to hold services among the prisoners. Hoffman advised him that Catholic clergy had the same limited rights as other clergymen to see the sick in the hospital or preach on Sunday, but Colonel Sweet barred Catholic nuns from the camp because he did not feel that they were included in Hoffman's order. The Mayor of Chicago prevailed upon him to allow the Sisters to distribute food on the hospital wards, and peace was restored. Sweet sent the Camp Douglas band to serenade the Sisters occasionally because Ada was a pupil at their academy near downtown. The nuns reciprocated with huge cakes for the 15th V.R.C.[28]

A Catholic Priest visited the camp and baptized more than 250 Confederates. Here are a few entries from his baptismal books: Bartholomew Server, Rebel Prisoner, Age 22 years, 54th Va.; George F. Reynolds, Rebel Prisoner, Age 44, 3rd Miss.; John L. Chadwick, Rebel Prisoner, Age 19 years, 39th Ala. Of those baptized, 77 soon died. This is the only Camp Douglas document that recorded the ages of prisoners. The youngest on the list was 17, and the oldest was 50. One was a captain in Forrest's Mississippi Scouts, who died at 38, one week before the war ended. The ladies of Grace Church in Chicago formed the "Camp Douglas Aid Society" to help the sick. Out of their experience they founded St. Luke's Hospital in Chicago in 1864, now part of the giant Rush-Presbyterian/St. Luke's Medical Center.[29]

The most devastating news a prisoner could receive was the death of a loved one. This was more so because the border states were within one day's travel on the Illinois Central. Depression was deepened by the short rations, mostly bread and water twice a day the third week of June, 1864. The sutler sold butter at the astronomical price of "65 cents per lb. and other things in proportion." Work details were demanding enough to make Burke stiff and sore when he could not escape conscription. Every day was nearly the same to him. "Time like a sweeping billow, rolls steadily on, and nothing as yet intervenes to break the dull monotony of our prison life." [30] Something would soon intervene.

A fearsome animal came to Prison Square on June 28, 1864. "The Yanks have fixed a frame near the gate [to Prison Square] with a scantling across it edge up, and about four feet from the ground, which they make our men ride whenever the men do anything that does not please them. It is called The Mule. Men have sat on it till they fainted and fell off. It is like riding a sharp top fence."[31]

The mule could be made more painful by adding weights. "Sometimes the Yanks would laugh and say, I will give you a pair of spurs," which was a bucket of sand tied to each foot. Other prisoners confirmed that men had to ride the mule in the worst winter weather. By 1865 it had grown to 15 feet tall and required a ladder to mount. There was a mule for the garrison in White Oak Square, except there it was called the "horse." Private Parkhurst of the 1st Michigan Sharpshooters was sentenced by Major John Piper of that regiment to ride the mule four hours on and two hours off during the day for seven days.[32]

New mess arrangements began at the end of June, 1864. A kitchen was partitioned off from the dormitory and cooking was being done for the entire barrack. Cooked food was then drawn in messes of 10. Burke's kitchen still had a cooking stove. By July 5, rations were ample for two full meals without breakfast. They were cornbread, pork, sour hash, beef, and pot liquor.

Patrols came down hard on unsightly conditions. Cooking utensils had to be scoured and the trash cleared out. Nearly all shelving was removed to get rid of everything not in immediate use.[33] This showed in the next inspection report. Colonel Sweet, however, was still living in Chicago.

Hoffman must have reported him to Secretary of War Stanton, who ordered Sweet to move his office to Camp Douglas "in order that your personal attention may be given to the affairs at that camp." Sweet's excuse was that in Chicago he was near the telegraph, provost marshal, and quartermaster. The real reason was probably his daughter Ada. There was no explanation for her not living in Wisconsin, unless she was in Chicago to attend school. Sweet moved to camp with Ada on July 15.[34]

Discipline was strict under Sweet's regime. This was necessary, except for the cruelty in enforcing it. "The Yanks make us keep the camp very clean, and are always on the alert to catch any prisoners that may break any of the rules and regulations." At Andersonville, the failure to impose any discipline on the Union prisoners was one of the causes for the high mortality rate, and the fighting, thefts, and murder which occurred among the prisoners. T. D. Henry wrote, "If the least sign of water or spit was seen on the floor the order was, Come, go to the horse or point for grub, which was to stand with the legs perfectly straight, reach over, and touch the ground with the fingers. If the legs were bent in the least, a guard was present with a paddle which he well knew how to use."[35]

M.J. Bradley confirmed Henry's report: "Another mode of punishment, was to make a man stoop forward, keeping his legs stiff, and touching his hands to the ground, remain in that position with the blood rushing to his head, and every vein in his body swelling until the protruding eyeballs became bloodshot, and almost bursting from their sockets with pain."

Garrison Square was festive on July 4, 1864, with speeches, fireworks, and bands playing. Prisoners could hear partying at a beer garden outside and racing at the Chicago Driving Park. They responded by singing their version of the former National Anthem:

"Oh say can you see, by the dawn's early light
What so proudly we hailed at the twilight's last gleaming
Whose cross bars and 'leven stars thro' the perilous fight,
O'er the breastworks we watched were so gallantly streaming,
And the rockets' red glare, the bombs bursting in air,
Gave proof thro' the night that our flag was still there.
Oh say, doth that cross spangled banner yet wave
O'er the land of the free and the home of the slave."[36]

Like Humpty-Dumpty in the old nursery rhyme, it would not be easy to put the Union back together again, but Colonel Strong was in a philosophical mood during the holiday. He compared the stimulation of battle to the dullness of guard duty, where "the soldier walks his lonely beat merely from a sense of duty and the earnest duty to perform it." He thanked everyone for the good condition of the camp and the low number of escapes. Colonel Sweet was on leave.[37]

There was little contact between Morgan's men and the infantry prisoners they called "web feet." The Raiders could hear singing in the infantry barracks every Sunday. "I suppose they have preaching," Burke said enviously. "I have never visited them to see. We have not had a sermon or even a hymn since we moved into this barrack."[38] Morgan's men were paying a heavy price for their false pride.

Colonel Strong received a sharp letter on July 27 ordering him to change his residence to Camp Douglas. He was reminded that Sweet had been required to do the same. Dissension also arose when headquarters tried to consolidate new prisoners into other regiments. This was fiercely resented, as the prisoners wished to maintain their regimental identity. It was the only refuge they had amid their degrading circumstances. Also, the Confederates continued the practice of electing non-commissioned officers, and strangers could use their vote to oust a long-time sergeant. This almost happened when 38 new prisoners were added to the 14th Kentucky Cavalry, and Pa barely won re-election as Sergeant-Major as the new men voted against him.[39]

Prisoners were allowed to go under the barracks during the day because of intense heat that summer. They were up-to-date on the war, due to the *Chicago Tribune, Post,* and *Journal,* which were sold at the sutler for 10 cents each, triple the price in Chicago which included home delivery. The *Chicago Times* was banned, but sometimes was thrown over the fence tied to a rock or smuggled in.[40] Prisoners could tell when a Confederate victory occurred because the newspapers were stopped. This did no good, as they had no trouble buying contraband papers from guards and the sutler.

Burke took the time to count his blessings as his second year of imprisonment began. "1st. My general good health with generally enough to eat, and 2nd. The privilege of corresponding with friends and receiving provisions, clothing, etc."[41] His remark about "generally enough to eat" conflicted with many reports, including his own, about hunger at camp. This may be explained by food packages he received along with money that enabled him to shop at the sutler. He had just received 10 dollars from his uncle, William H. Burke of Canton, Ohio, almost a month's pay for a garrison soldier.

Burke wrote all day to catch up on his journal and not lose scattered notes. He was upset because he received news on July 23, 1864, that his mother had moved back to Medina, Ohio, "in the neighborhood of her relations and purchased a little home for the present only, as Pa says he cannot live north and will not. And I say the same!"

The prisoners were excited by a *Tribune* dispatch from Washington, which described the arrival there of two disgraced officers of the 1st Michigan Sharpshooters. One was named De Land, and may have been related to Colonel De Land. Both men were convicted of cowardice and would be stripped of buttons and shoulder straps and go to the "Dry Tortugas," the prisoners read with satisfaction. "Such is the fate of men who assisted in tieing up prisoners by their thumbs to extract secrets, or supposed secrets last fall in this camp. We all say Amen."[42]

Camp Douglas received its best inspection report on July 25, 1864. Medical Inspector Alexander wrote to Colonel Hoffman. "Seeing the camp and hospital you would be pleased at the general condition and management." He gave no credit to Sweet or Strong, but to Major Skinner and Captain Sponable. As a sidelight he described how Major Skinner had confiscated money the prisoners earned by selling boots. The administration carried on a vendetta against boots, and none were permitted to reach the prisoners from outside.[43] It had to be a question of morale. Take away a man's boots and he does not feel as tall. There were now 170 men per barrack.

Alexander noted that the prison fund had $19,691.50, and more was owed to it. A substantial amount of rations was sold to earn this, although the fund had another source of income from the business taxes at camp. The hospital fund held $503.85. Alexander recommended six-inch water pipes to make the hydrants and sewers more efficient. Information about the smallpox hospital outside camp was skimpy. It does not appear that any inspector gave it a thorough examination, which is understandable. Alexander mentioned that it was still a stable "converted into a comfortable ward."

He described the new prison hospital, completed in April, as "a good two-story building adjoining a two-story laundry," and confirmed that it cost $10,000. It stood in a separate enclosure between White Oak Square and Prison Square. He reported that smallpox vaccinations had been stopped for some time because of unhealthy ulcers that developed, but it was resumed on July 21, 1864. Five men from Burke's regiment alone died of the disease since April. Alexander thought that the doctors were efficient. Sweet would soon think otherwise. Potatoes were the only vegetables issued.

The present system at the sutler was for a prisoner to give an order to draw on his personal account, with the sutler issuing the corresponding amount of checks. Dr. Alexander did not mention any gouging by the sutlers, but the greed of Mr. Nightingale was monumental. In an ironic incident concerning the sutler, Burke received a new gray uniform jacket. The Confederate buttons had been removed by an inspector, so the fanatical Burke had the option of either purchasing Union army buttons through the sutler or having none. He chose the Union buttons, and "two skeins of yellow sewing silk and a quarter of a yard of bright yellow cloth" to trim it with. Mr. Nightingale charged him four dollars for the order, a 300% profit.[44]

The prisoners were generous when they learned that a Mrs. William Brown had arrived from Georgia with two children, not knowing that her husband was dead. She was destitute and stranded in Chicago. The men raised $116.35 for her. She was very grateful, and took the list of donors home. Their compassion is striking, as was the fact that they had so many Federal dollars in their possession. One joker went to Captain Sponable and told him that he wished to surrender his money as required. It proved to be a 50 cent I.O.U. issued by the City of Sparta, Tennessee.[45] He suffered a few bruises and a shower of curses, and made himself scarce.

Colonel Sweet advised Hoffman on August 5, 1864 that the smallpox hospital was hazardous to both the camp and the University of Chicago.[46]

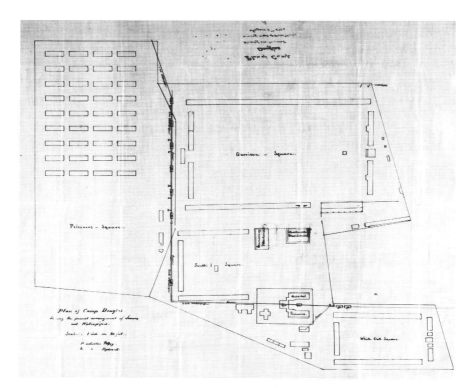

Plan of Camp Douglas, August 8, 1864, showing water hydrants and sewers, marked "h" for hydrant and "p" for privy (courtesy the National Archives).

"The Hospital is now too near the camp for safety," Sweet advised. "It has broken up two terms of school of the University and materially injures the property of the estate of the Hon. Stephen A. Douglas."

Sherman's Atlanta campaign and another raid by General Morgan sent almost 2,500 prisoners to Camp Douglas in July and August, 1864. They were questioned closely by the old hands. Surprisingly, the Confederate army had plenty of food, "and coffee every few days, with whiskey in bad weather." The arrivals caused a good deal of tension and upheaval in barracks. The old hands often refused to give up their quarters when ordered to do so, and had to be forced out by the garrison. Burke groaned about having "to move from our nice little room into the long room of another barracks with our regiment to make room for the newcomers." Some of the most stubborn, including Burke, were ungracious toward the new prisoners because they felt that "a good many of them did not try as hard as they might have tried to keep from being captured." About this time an escaping prisoner attempted to surrender and was shot anyway. There is no indication that this was pursuant to orders.[47]

Colonel Sweet requested reinforcements, because units of the 8th and 15th V.R.C. had been detached to other cities. Manpower at camp had been further reduced when patrols from the garrison began serving as military police in Chicago on May 14, 1864, demanding passes from all military personnel, including officers. Enlisted men without one were arrested.[48] The good old days when Chicago was a wide-open town for AWOLs and deserters had ended. Business at the Prairie Queen must have suffered considerably, and MPs probably accounted for some recaptured escapees.

Reprisal against the prisoners intensified because the South was allegedly refusing to allow clothing and other articles to reach Union prisoners in Confederate hands. A circular from Colonel Hoffman dated August 10, 1864 ordered that Confederate prisoners be treated in the same fashion. Only the sick could receive packages from outside. [49] "Prisoners will be allowed to receive clothing or other articles from relatives and friends residing beyond the lines, when forwarded by flag of truce, so long as the prisoners of war held at Richmond and other southern prisons are permitted to receive the same articles in the same manner from relatives and friends in the loyal states. No articles above referred to will be delivered to prisoners of war at this post after Aug. 25th, 1864." There was no word on whether banned packages would be returned to sender or confiscated. The latter was more likely.

That same day, sutlers at all prisons were limited to selling "writing materials, postage stamps, tobacco, cigars, pipes, matches, combs, soap, tooth brushes, hair brushes, clothes brushes, scissors, thread, and needles, handkerchiefs, towels, and pocket looking glasses." This eliminated vegetables and other foods that were essential to avoid scurvy, and caused tension between Sweet and Hoffman. The system of Sutler's checks was also terminated. Now, a prisoner filled out an order for the purchase and the sutler cashed it at the Post Cashier.[50]

Prisoners who relied on the sutler felt the restrictions more than others. "He has nothing to eat except sugar at 70 cents per pound," Burke complained. "We are getting boiled beef and sour light bread six days out of ten, and boiled pickle pork and sour light bread the other four and of course hominy for dinner extra." New prisoners felt hunger pangs more than the old hands and hung around the barracks begging for refuse meat and bread. "They have not worn the wire edge off their appetites yet," Burke observed. The hired prisoners had their own mess hall in a barrack with six long tables and benches. "They get coffee, sugar, etc. regular." The other prisoners hated the workers "nearly as bad as Yankees for humbling themselves to the Yanks," according to Burke.[51]

Did the prisoners eat a dog? Such stories are common in prison literature, both from the North and South. A small terrier owned by Lieutenant Fife was often in Prison Square, where Fife had his office just inside the gate.[52] According to the story, "this dog was a great favorite and pet of the prisoners, but one day the cooks in one of the barracks enticed the dog into their kitchen, killed and dressed it nicely, and cooked it; then invited quite a number of other prisoners to dine with them, as they had a rare dish for dinner—they ate the dog and drank the soup."

Fife posted a reward notice for the return of his dog, and someone wrote under it, "For lack of bread the dog is dead, For want of meat the dog was eat." Another prisoner said the dog belonged to a lady visitor. A third described it as a stray. The unfortunate creature came in with "a fellow delivering coal," a fourth man claimed.[53]

One former prisoner settled the question many years later. "Barrack No. 14 ate the captain's dog, and the inscription was written: 'For want of meat, the dog was eat.' We also ate all the rats we could catch. No doubt many died after the war from disease contracted on account of these things. I have written the foregoing in no spirit of ill will, but simply to state facts. It will not be long until we shall all pass under review in a better world than this. I am now sixty-three years old, and am crippled and helpless."[54]

The "dog was eat" legend still gripped men's imaginations 50 years after the war: "V.W. Hardt, of Cuero, Tex., wants to hear from someone who was in Camp Douglas, Illinois at the time of President Lincoln's assassination, also from any who read on the bulletin board, 'For want of meat, your dog was eat,' and he wants information of the sergeant who took out prisoners on May 4, 1865, escorted them to Cairo, Ill., and thence to New Orleans for exchange."[55]

Eating the dog may have had more to do with revenge than hunger. Lieutenant Fife commanded the patrols in the square who made life extremely miserable for the prisoners. In addition, he interviewed all who wished to take the oath. Of course, the gourmets in barrack 14 were soon discovered and their rations stopped. They had to scatter among the rest of the prisoners who fed them.[56]

Two prisoners were wounded by guards on the fence in alleged escape attempts, and an investigation took place on August 13, 1864. The inquiry concluded that it was not illegal to fire without warning, and the guards were commended.[57] The prisoners believed that the fence was paper-thin. Back on July 20, 1862, Hoffman had ordered Tucker to repair the fence with old lumber about the camp. "Let it cost as little as possible."

Elmira Prison Camp with fence and sentry boxes as they must have looked at Camp Douglas. Note guard walking his beat and the wreath of flowers in left foreground. (courtesy Chicago Public Library)

Much of the fence had been burned by the parolees. Colonel De Land found only a tattered strand of boards to keep the prisoners in. He rebuilt it entirely of oak. The height is uncertain. One report put it at 12 feet high, with sentinel walks two and one-half feet wide around the exterior and four feet from the top. The *Tribune* placed it at 14 feet, supported by 16-foot posts, with a three-foot guard walk. Curtis R. Burke estimated that it was 15 to 16 feet high.[58] He was too meticulous a reporter to be disregarded. Several sentinel boxes were added to the parapet in mid-December, 1864.

There was a rash of shootings as suicidal attempts to escape continued. Sweet reported five prisoners were shot in one week in August, one of whom died. A group of six working on a detail in Garrison Square tried to flee over the fence in plain sight. Only one made it. No investigation took place. The best way to escape was on the way to camp. Twenty prisoners disappeared out of a shipment of 503 coming from Alton, Illinois in August, 1864.[59] Alton was one of the principal 23 Federal prisoner of war camps.

Some prisoners sought an easier way out. One, who had obtained civilian clothing, went to the gate and told the guard that he would hang every "mother's son of the rascally secesh." The guard demanded a pass. When the pretended visitor said he had none, the guard kicked him out the gate instead of arresting him. A food vendor named Barney Hughes, who had a permit to sell food in the stockade in 1862, lent it to an "expert penman." Soon he was signing Colonel Tucker's name better than the Colonel did, and several prisoners who managed to obtain civilian clothing escaped with forged passes.[60] Later, a printed-form pass would eliminate the forgers.

Mr. Nightingale, the sutler, was tricked by his prison clerk into believing that a barrel contained sugar and could be sold in Chicago. The clerk had himself sealed in the barrel by other prisoners and was carted out of camp. He also stole "two or three hundred dollars from old Nightingale," Burke heard. The other prisoners working at the store were arrested, and the place closed. Another prisoner pulled a similar stunt by being sealed in an empty vinegar barrel and placed on a trash pile outside Prison Square. Ada Sweet remembers hearing about this "and being glad for the poor fellow."[61]

She personally wished a prisoner bon-voyage while living in Garrison Square. "The man slipped away from the other prisoners, and hid in our basement. At night when I came home from school I saw him hiding there behind a barrel. I just kept quiet and didn't say a word. About an hour later his absence was discovered. The alarm was given and a search was made, but it was too late. The man had run the guard and escaped. It was one of those things a child will do."[62]

In spite of Sweet's "excellent management," conditions in barracks were depressing, Burke recorded. August 6th, 1864: There were two candles burning all night, and several of the men sat up with the sick flux [diarrhea] patients. The barrack assumes the appearance of a hospital. Permission to have a light is often given in cases of extreme illness. I did not sleep much. August 7th, 1864: "Everybody walks light and speaks in whispers on account of the sick. About 11 o'clock John Duckworth of Co. D died, and about 3 o'clock Jessie T. Hunter of Co. D died.[63] Both died in their bunks of the flux. They were good soldiers and gentlemen. Duckworth is from Bath Co. Ky. and Hunter is from Wilkerson Co. Miss. They received all the attention that could be given them under the circumstances. Medicines of the right kind could not be procured."

The bodies were washed and laid out. An ambulance came with rough coffins and they were taken away. This was the last loving care they would receive. Mr. Page, secretary to the Confederate surgeons, accused the Post Surgeon of rejecting a request by the Confederate doctors to have medicines sent up from the South at no expense to the camp. Page's accusation appears to be true, for he blamed Dr. Whitehill, surgeon of the 11th Illinois Infantry, who was Post Surgeon at this time. "Respectfully disapproved,"

Whitehill said, "as all medicine is strictly contraband of war, excepting only such as is supplied by and through these headquarters." In 1862, medicines had been freely accepted from relief committees in Chicago. Whitehill wrote a memo 50 years later in which he claimed that the contract surgeons at Camp Douglas were incompetent, and that there was a 95% mortality rate among the smallpox patients. There may have been some merit in what he said, but he had not helped matters.[64]

Hoffman issued another order on August 13, 1864 to replace cooking stoves with kettles. Prisoners presented a petition signed by 41 men representing 44 barracks and included the doctors. The surgeons argued that many sick prisoners remained in barracks due to lack of hospital space and that only a stove could cook something for them. The petition was denied.[65]

Ada C. Sweet, circa 1882 at age 29 (courtesy Historical Society)

The prisoners offered to purchase their own stoves, but Hoffman rejected the idea because fuel was too costly. Arctic winters in Chicago had inflated the price. Prisoners could not bake their cornbread without the stoves, but not all had Southern tastes. The Irish among them called the cornbread "Yaller Hammers," and white bread was "gun wadding," which they preferred. Meanwhile, the 60-gallon kettles had the effect of boiling the rations to shreds when cooking for 200 men. One prisoner commented bitterly that "There was no more nutritious matter in it than an old dish cloth, for dinner one pint of bean soup and five ounces of bread, this was our living!"[66]

Colonel Sweet requested permission to move back to Chicago. No doubt he felt that Camp Douglas was not the best place for Ada. An officer remembered her as a "little girl" running in an out of headquarters. Hoffman's conciliatory rejection on August 21, 1864 shows a close relationship at this time. "I feared that in your absence from the camp it would necessarily fall into other and less reliable hands, and for this reason I asked for the change."[67] This type of soft-sell was out of character for the steely old widower. He did not mention Ada, and it is not likely that Sweet did.

Southern friends of the prisoners in Chicago were concerned about scurvy at camp. Burke recorded that "A good deal of flour, cabbage, potatoes and pickles were sent to the prisoners through the kindness of Mrs. Norrus [Mary Morris] of Chicago."[68] Mary Morris was a Blackburn from Kentucky, married to a prominent Chicago attorney, and whose brother-in-law was a Confederate general. Her brother, Luke, was charged in the "Yellow Fever Plot" against the North, and she would be arrested and jailed at Camp Douglas in the Conspiracy of 1864.

A large crowd gathered in Prison Square on August 27, 1864 to see a new fire hydrant tested (photo page 188). It could throw water 50 feet, and a guard amused himself by wetting many prisoners.[69]

Lieutenant Briggs' report on August 28, 1864 stated that the prisoners and the grounds were very clean, but that the three-inch water pipe could not supply enough water for 7,500 men. Sweet soon received permission "to substitute a 6-inch water pipe for the 3-inch one," and to install as many hydrants as required in all the squares.[70] However, nothing was being done to repair the roofs and windows and provide more clothing and blankets. Hospital space, as usual, was hopelessly inadequate, and would remain so to the end of the war.

Colonel Sweet did a good job of keeping the camp and the men clean, but could not cope with the major problems of health care, clothing, and housing. However, the prisoners' long hair did come under attack. John

Curd, in Burke's regiment, was appointed barber. "For every ten men he operated on he was to be excused from work detail one day."[71]

Atlanta was about to be occupied by Union troops, but many prisoners at Camp Douglas, especially among Morgan's command, did not believe that the war was yet lost. Escape attempts would continue as before, and Sweet did not have a rock-solid garrison behind him. He had received 802 men from the 196th Pennsylvania Infantry on August 13, 1864, but this was only an untrained 100-day outfit, and the prisoners would soon put them to the test.[72] Perhaps more important was the addition of the 24th Ohio Independent Battery of 145 men on August 29. They had six cannons pointed at Prison Square. It would seem that these guns were the best cards Sweet had in the deck. Surprisingly, Hoffman did not think so.

An inspector from the Northern Department of the Army reported on August 31, 1864 that an explosive situation existed at Camp Douglas. "There appears to be more than usual discontented feeling among the prisoners of war and a disposition, especially on the part of the Kentucky prisoners to escape." He joined many others in condemning the farmer's boilers. "It would be a matter of economy to place cooking stoves in the kitchen used by the prisoners, or even common camp kettles would be preferable." He may not have realized that the farmer's boilers were there for retaliation, not economy. In addition, prescriptions for medicine were not promptly filled: "the consequences, more sickness and more death."[73]

NOTES TO CHAPTER 12

[1] *Battles and Leaders of the Cruel War,* III: 38.

[2] Andreas, *History of Chicago,* II:310.

[3] John J. Flynn, *Handbook of Chicago Biography*(1893), 345.

[4] T. D. Henry, *Southern Historical Society Papers* I:276.

[5] Kelly, 105-06.

[6] Burke, 23 Apr. 1864.

[7] O. R. Ser.II-Vol.VII, 62-63, 221.

[8] O R Ser.II-Vol.VII, 142-43; Burke, 29 Apr. 1864.

[9] Burke, 29 Apr. 1864.

[10] O R Ser.II-Vol.VII, 125.

[11] Burke, 19 Apr., 12, 19 May 1864; Tuttle, *History of Camp Douglas,* 20.

[12] Burke, 13 May 1864.

[13] Burke, 19 May 1864; R. G. 393, v. 234:325; J. J. Moore, "Camp Douglas," *Confederate Veteran* 11 (Jun. 1903):270. Moore gives an excellent description of Prison Square, counting 64 barracks in 16 rows on 1 August 1864.

[14] Burke, 24 May 1864.

[15] O R Ser.II-Vol.VII, 184-85.

[16] Burke, 1 Jun. 1864; O R Ser.II-Vol.VII, 187-88.

[17] Original Autograph Letters, v.49, CHS; Burke, 2 Jul. 1864; Kelly, "History of Camp Douglas," 102; *Chicago Tribune,* 26 Sep. 1863; O R Ser.II-Vol.VIII, 995-99.

[18] O R Ser.II-Vol.VII, 184-85.

[19] O R Ser.II-Vol.VII, 195, 201-02; Vol.VII, 369.

[20] O R Ser.II-Vol.VII, 183-4.
The ration was modified as follows:

Meat

Pork or bacon in lieu of fresh beef	10 ounces.
Fresh beef	14 ounces

Bread

Flour or soft bread	16 ounces
Hard bread in lieu of flour or soft bread	14 ounces
Corn meal in lieu of flour or bread	16 ounces

Vegetables

Beans or peas per 100 rations	12° lbs.
or Rice or hominy per 100 rations	8 ounces
Soap per 100 rations	*4* ounces
Potatoes per 100 rations	15 ounces

For sick and wounded, only:

Sugar per 100 rations	12 ounces
Coffee per 100 rations	5 lbs. ground or 7lbs. green
Tea per 100 rations	1 lb.

[21] O R Ser.II-Vol.VII, 150-151.

[22] Burke, 3 May, 5 Jun. 1864

[23] "Seventeen Months in Camp Douglas," *Confederate Veteran* 22 (Jun. 1914):270.

[24] M. J. Bradley in *Camp and Prison Journal,* 270.

[25] Burke, 21 Jun. 1864.

[26] Burke, 26 Jun. 1864.

[27] Burke, 9 Jun. 1864. He saw the Chicago Driving Park, four blocks west of Prison Square, between Indiana and State Streets, and 32nd and 35th Streets. *Blanchard's Street Guide* (1866), CHS. "By war's end the Chicago Driving Park was the place to be seen in new duds, with new loves, new fortunes, followed by the busy pickpockets. Gay parasols revolved in dainty gloved

hands, as bodies in whalebone corsets went by dragging the trains of whores and society wives." Longstreet, *Chicago, 1860-1919*, 42.

[28] R. G. 393, Records of U.S. Army Continental Commands, Camp Douglas Letter Book, 340, NA; Life of Mary Monholland, 110-11; *Chicago Tribune*, 26 May 1895.

[29] Baptismal Records of The Reverend Patrick Joseph R. Murphy, 1864-1866, St. James Catholic Church, Chicago; Rev. Clinton Locke, D.D., Rector of Grace Church, 1859-1895, unpublished manuscript, (undated), Rush-Presbyterian-St. Luke's Medical Center Archives, Chicago.

[30] Burke, 23, 27 Jun. 1864.

[31] Burke, 164.

[32] T. D. Henry, *Southern Historical Society Papers* I:278; J. W. Cook, *Confederate Veteran* 16:406; Original Autograph Letters, V. 49, CHS. Major Piper was killed in action later that year.

[33] Burke, 29 Jun. 1864.

[34] Kelly, "History of Camp Douglas," 65; Report of the Adj. Gen., State of Illinois, v. 1:123.

[35] Burke, 170; William Best Hesseltine, *Civil War Prisons*, 144; Sorenson, "The Civil War Prisoner of War System," 38-39; T. D. Henry, *Southern Historical Society Papers* I:278.

[36] Burke, 4 Jul. 1864.

[37] Kelly, 66.

[38] Burke, 31 Jul. 1864.

[39] O R Ser.II-Vol.VII, 503; Burke, 24 Mar. 1864.

[40] Burke, 7 Jul. 1864.

[41] Burke, 19 Jul. 1864.

[42] Fort Jefferson military prison, about 80 miles off Key West, Florida; Burke, 22 Jul. 1864.

[43] O R Ser.II-Vol.VII, 496-97; Burke, 11 May 1864.

[44] Burke, 28 Jul. 1864.

[45] Burke, 28 Jul. 1864. William Brown, Pvt., Barnes Georgia Battery, died 25 May 1864 and is buried in Chicago; Burke, 20 Aug. 1864.

[46] National Archives R. G. 393, Records of the U.S. Army Continental Commands, Camp Douglas Letter Book, 462.

[47] Burke, 18 Jul.; 1, 6, 21 Aug. 1864.

[48] Kelly, 66; R. G. 393, v. 240:167.

[49] Burke, 19 Aug. 1864.

[50] O R Ser.II-Vol.VII, 573-74; Kelly, 97.

[51] Burke, 15, 30 Aug., 22 Sep. 1864.

[52] John M. Copley, *A Sketch of the Battle of Franklin, Tennessee, with Reminiscences of Camp Douglas* (Austin: E. Von Boeckman, 1893), 89. Lieutenant Joel A. Fife was wounded while fighting in the 5th Illinois Infantry and was assigned to the 8th V.R.C.

[53] R. T. Bean, "Seventeen Months in Camp Douglas,"*Confederate Veteran* 22 (June, 1914): 270; T. M. Page, "The Prisoner of War," *Confederate Veteran* 8 (Feb. 1900):64; *Confederate Veteran*, 8 (Apr. 1900):168.

[54] J. M. Berry, "Prison Life in Camp Douglas," *Confederate Veteran*, 11 (Apr. 1903) : 37-38. Sergeant Berry Co. I, 8th Arkansas Infantry, age 23, was captured 19 Sept. 1863 at Chickamauga and arrived Camp Douglas 4 Nov. 1863.

[55] *Confederate Veteran*, 23 (Jun. 1915): 286.

[56] Copley, 176.

[57] O R Ser.II-Vol.VII, 595-97.

[58] Kelly, 74; *Chicago Tribune*, 19 Oct. 1863; Burke, 17 Oct. 1863.

[59] O R Ser.II-Vol.VII, 595-96; Burke, 24 Aug. 1864.

[60] Tuttle, *History of Camp Douglas*, 14; E. R. Hopkins, *Confederate Veteran* 38 (Mar. 1930):85.

[61] Tuttle, 14; Burke, 6 Dec. 1864; *Chicago Tribune*, 26 May 1895.

[62] Camp Douglas newspaper file, CHS.

[63] Pvt. Duckworth is listed as 9th Ky. Cav. and is buried in Chicago; Pvt. Hunter, 14th Ky. Cav., was removed home.

[64] Page, *Confederate Veteran* 8:63; Tuttle, 48; Whitehill, CW Misc. Coll., USAMHI.

[65] Burke, 18 Aug. 1864.

[66] R. G. 393, v. 240:209;" Doorstep Reminiscences," *Confederate Veteran* 10:453; T. D. Henry, "Southern Historical Society Papers," 278.

[67] Julian Edward Buckbee papers, CHS; O R Ser.II-Vol. VII, 664.

[68] *Burke, 22 Aug. 1864.*

[69] Burke, 27 Aug. 1864.

[70] O R Ser.II-Vol.VII, 694, 767, 1083.

[71] Burke, 1 Sep. 1864.

[72] Edwin Greble diary, Dreer coll., ms. div., LOC.

[73] O R Ser.II-Vol.VII, 1067.

13.

DESPERATE ATTEMPTS TO ESCAPE

The 100-day men on the fence did not inspire much respect or fear among the prisoners.[1] "I notice a good many puny-pale gosling-looking boys on guard on the parapet," Burke sneered. "I understand that they are one hundred day men." On September 7, 1864, six men charged the fence at night with two axes, broke a plank, and escaped. Burke counted only two bullet holes. "Bad shots for fifty yards," he judged. At least three guards in the 196th Pennsylvania had failed to shoot.[2] This shortcoming would soon be cured with rigorous training.

At roll call on September 8, the prisoners received the "glad" news that they could no longer stroll around the square between the barracks and the dead-line. The penalty was shooting. They had to stay on the streets between the barracks as punishment for the escapes. Curiously, the North and South suddenly agreed to release all prisoners from close confinement. This emptied the dungeons at Camp Douglas and freed Joseph McCarney, who had killed Scroggin.[3] It was likely that he would have been tried for murder had Scroggin not exonerated him before he died.

The army inspector from the previous month was back in September, and found an increase in the water supply, barracks under repair, and the prisoners being forced to practice good hygiene. He was concerned about a mass escape. "There is an apparent restlessness that augers mischief among them if they are not well watched," he warned. In a prophesy of the alleged Conspiracy of 1864, he thought that the garrison was too weak for safety, "especially at this time, when everything tends to show that the prisoners of war expect succor from some quarter."[4] This perceptive officer also noticed another serious weakness: the garrison was housed too far away from the prisoners, at the east end of the camp. No one had thought of this before.

Lieutenant Briggs denounced the administration in his opening report for September, 1864, but did not indicate that he saw any danger of a major effort to escape. Instead, he complained that the new hospital was too small, leaving 200 sick in barracks, 12 of whom had died in the past week. The barracks were dilapidated, many prisoners lacked blankets, and the Farmer's boilers were a disaster.[5] Briggs confirmed the independent inspection report of August 31, saying that "the supply of medicine is insufficient for the actual wants of the prisoners."

On September 9, 1864, Union army General Benjamin F. Butler proposed an exchange of sick and wounded officers and men. This applied only to those who would not be fit for duty until after 60 days from date of evaluation by the captor. His idea may have come from a story about a delegation of Andersonville prisoners who were supposedly on their way to Washington at this time to see President Lincoln.[6] The South had allegedly released them to carry a petition detailing the horrible prison conditions and asking for immediate efforts to negotiate their release. While the petition charged the South with barbarities at Andersonville, it also pleaded the Confederate case to restart the Cartel despite the enslavement of black prisoners. "It is true that they are again made slaves," the white prisoners conceded in the document, "but their slavery is freedom and happiness compared with the cruel existence imposed upon our gallant men."

News of Confederate General John H. Morgan's death reached Camp Douglas on September 9, but his men did not believe it. The General had made another disastrous raid into Kentucky early in June, 1864, one year after the raid through Indiana and Ohio. Again, most of his command was destroyed or captured.[7] A few months later he began a third raid and was killed on September 4, 1864 at Greenville, Tennessee.

General Schoepf, the commanding officer at Fort Delaware, stopped the prisoners' mail about this time, and Hoffman demanded to know where he had the authority to do this. The officer responded that his clerks could not handle 2,000 letters a day. Hoffman dripped acid. Schoepf needed permission to stop the mail.[8] The point is that there was no reprimand when Sweet eliminated candles and cut rations at Camp Douglas, but mail service was apparently untouchable. It was so dependable that Confederate agents did not hesitate to mail coded messages to prisoners during the Camp Douglas Conspiracy about to break in November.

Some danger of a general escape occurred when high winds tore through the camp on September 9. There was substantial damage to the parapet, but the fence held. The new hospital near White Oak Square also suffered damage, and two prisoners were able to escape in the confusion.[9]

On September 14, 1864, prisoners at Camp Douglas were invited to join a regiment of U. S. Cavalry to fight the Indians. Burke saw a large crowd around the recruiting office all day, but did not know how many joined. This was one way to solve a shortage of 700 suits of clothing, 1,500 blankets, and a severe lack of hospital space. Burke noted on September 15 that "We deeply mourn the loss of John H. Morgan."

Colonel Hoffman finally answered Colonel Sweet's inquiry about filling Prison Square with barracks. It would have to be done cheaply, as much under $500 per barrack as possible. Hoffman thought the present barracks

Company H, 196th Pennsylvania Infantry, circa September, 1864, outside Camp Douglas. Soldier in right foreground has a violin and one or two prisoners appear to be in front (courtesy Chicago Historical Society).

were raised too high, and there was no reason why the seams in the floor could not be covered by lathing, using clay plaster as an insulator. The new barracks were nearly completed by November 30, 1864. By January 1, 1865, there were 60 barracks in the square, and four more were added shortly. They had a vestibule inside the outer door, six feet in length by four feet in width, with a door. While its purpose was to conserve heat, the patrol used it as a hiding place to spy on the prisoners. Spit boxes were available in barracks and the patrols were zealous in trying to prevent the men from staining the floor with tobacco juice.[10]

Barrack 41 in Prison Square was converted to a hospital. "It will accommodate about eighty men," according to Briggs. On September 17, 1864, workers began to install ventilators and chimneys visible on the barracks in photographs of Prison Square. However, Briggs wrote a dismal report of barracks without windows, roofs leaking, and needing new floors. Some prisoners had no blankets and many needed clothing.[11]

Colonel Sweet's wife and three children arrived at camp in the fall of 1864 for a winter visit. They lived in officer's quarters at the east end of the parade ground, near the gate.[12] The children were soon singing the words to all the bugle calls. For sick call: "Are you all dead yet? [very slow]. Are you all dead yet? [slower]. [Voice] Come get your quinine. Come get your quinine! Come!"

Sweet claimed that he had discovered a plot by the prisoners to make a concerted effort to escape on September 19. They were depending on draft riots in Chicago to help them. Sweet had planned "to let them make the effort and punish them in the act, and made dispositions accordingly."[13] Nothing happened. The prisoners probably knew that their plan had been discovered. Thousands of them had been there for over a year, and Sweet observed "that the prisoners are restive and inventive to an uncommon degree of late."

Private Greble of the 196th Pennsylvania Infantry confirmed that "Troops were alerted for a prison break." All weapons were loaded, and the two V.R.C. regiments took up positions outside the stockade. Greble heard reports that "700 rebels in Morgan's command have taken an oath either to regain their freedom or die in the attempt," and that the prisoners had killed an informer. He was skeptical. There were some pleasant moments for Greble when he saw the play, "An American Cousin" in Chicago. The city had an eerie preview of the Lincoln assassination with both John Wilkes Booth and the play Lincoln was watching at Ford's theater appearing in Chicago.[14]

Life was much harder for the prisoners at this time. Even an elderly Confederate surgeon was punished severely for a minor infraction he was unaware of. A new rule prohibited walking between the sutler store and the express office. Dr. Pettus, a Confederate surgeon, was sick in the hospital when the edict came down and did not know about it. Nonetheless, he was made to ride the mule on September 24, 1864. The doctor's health began slipping after this brutal incident, and he failed to diagnose a smallpox case the following week.[15]

Colonel Sweet made a rare appearance in Prison Square on September 26, but it was not a success. The prisoners chanted: "More bread! More bread!" so violently that he left. Three days later, a patrol fired two shots at a prisoner for the offense of starting toward the sinks before dismissal from roll call, but fortunately missed without killing anyone. Lt. Fife placed more restrictions on letters requesting packages from home for delivery by express. The new system was that two rebel clerks in the express office read the requests for packages, and a Yankee corporal told them what had to be stricken out. The workhands were cursed by the prisoners for "everything good or bad," including a two-hour roll call.[16]

Colonel Sweet returned to Prison Square on the 29th of September, and the prisoners again shouted: "More bread!" The bread ration was continuously short, and the men were often hungry because of it. The commander retaliated this time, and one barrack was marched out and made to mark time in place. Sweet had an unseemly interest in seeing a prisoner executed about this time. P. K. Thornhill of the 4th Alabama Cavalry was supposed to be shot on October 1 at Huntsville, Alabama for some unknown reason.[17] Sweet alerted Hoffman that he had not received orders to ship Thornhill, and was concerned that he might not reach Alabama in time. Sweet needed to curry favor with Hoffman in order to pay his detectives from the prison fund. This did not work with Hoffman, who bent only under political pressure.

Sweet's detectives were not doing a good job of detecting escapes, because prisoners struck the fence in a surprise attack on September 27.[18] This operation was unusual because 13 men spearheaded the assault, and came from nine different regiments consisting of infantry, artillery, and cavalry units. Normally, plans of such magnitude would have been betrayed or accidentally revealed.

It began when about 30 prisoners charged out of their barracks at 10:00 p.m. and made for the northwest corner of the square, where the Olivet Baptist Church stands today at East 31st Street and King Drive.[19] The leader threw a blanket over the light on the fence and took a bullet in the face. His squad pressed on and battered away furiously with axes and hammers. Meanwhile, the garrison drummer brought out security forces with a long steady roll. It was over quickly as patrols came up and fired into the corner. One more prisoner may have been wounded, and the others retreated into the darkness. The leader who was shot in the face was thought to be fatally wounded, but survived. The troops also fired at any prisoner coming out of barracks during the attempt, and two or three were wounded in this fashion, according to Greble.

The "puny boys" in the 196th Pennsylvania did much better this time. "Our men in Co. C fired at them," Greble wrote with satisfaction. Even more satisfying, their rifles had worked, while many of the V.R.C.'s did not go off. Twelve prisoners ended up in irons. This was almost a successful escape, and the prisoners proved again that Camp Douglas could not be a maximum-security prison without secure cell blocks. Colonel Sweet recognized this shortcoming by warning the prisoners of the artillery waiting for them outside.

Notices were nailed to the barracks the following day, September 28, announcing an easing of restrictions.[20] Destitute prisoners could now receive one suit of gray or dark material of inferior quality, and one change of underwear from home. All prisoners could be sent bed ticks and overcoats. However, the coats could not be taken with them in case of a prisoner exchange. As a result, some of the men stated that they would not request the coats. Because of the expected deluge of packages, all requests for express delivery had to be approved by Lt. Fife.

Sweet issued a bulletin the same day that revealed he knew about the "Supreme Council of Seven" at camp. "The Colonel Commanding has information, which leads to the conclusion that there is an organization among the prisoners of war at Camp Douglas, having for its object a combined attack, to overpower the guard and effect an escape," Sweet warned.[21]

This group was formed after the deadly winter of 1863-64. Many prisoners felt that their chances of survival were less than that on the battlefield. Six or seven of Morgan's men planned a mass escape in the early spring of 1864, and formed an escape committee called "The Supreme Council of Seven," according to B. R. Froman, one of Morgan's men. The Council members were all from Morgan's command and consisted of Clayton Anderson, Harmon Barlow, Ottway B. Norvell, A. W. Cockrell, Winder Monroe, John H. Waller (Waller was in Burke's Company B, 14th Ky.), and E. M. Headelston. They realized the difficulty of secrecy because of spies, traitors, and the indiscreetness among the prisoners. Therefore, the recommendation and the unanimous consent of the Council was necessary before anyone was approached. The candidate was sounded out and took an oath if he agreed to join.[22] R. T. Bean was one of those selected.

"The oath was administered to me by Mr. Waller, who, I thought was a Texan. We went under my barracks, and with my hand grasping a Bible, I repeated after him the most terrible, blood-curdling oath ever concocted by the brain of man. Every word seemed branded upon my mind with letters of fire, and for weeks afterward I hardly knew who or what I was."[23]

However, Mr. Bean later called the escape plans "wild and reckless in the extreme." The prisoners were too weak to walk back to the South, and there was little chance of stealing a train to travel that distance. Regardless, the Supreme Council was going ahead with its plans. Through bribery it was able obtain a report on guard strength and infiltrate Garrison Square to locate the weapons and munitions.

According to former prisoner Thomas S. Longwood, the Council recruited about 2,000 prisoners.[24] R. T. Bean believed the number was closer to 1,500.[25] "Many times the solemn ritual was interrupted by the guard, or a careless or too inquisitive prisoner," Bean recalled. Burke was probably not recruited due to his ill health. The plan was to flee west after smashing through the fence, and to free prisoners at Rock Island, Illinois, 120 miles away. This did not consider the communications available to the army, which could quickly block such a move. The idea was to unite prisoners from the two camps and attack Sherman's army in Georgia. It is difficult to imagine the weakened prisoners taking on Sherman's powerful army of well-equipped and hardened veterans.

The problem was too many uncoordinated escape committees. The attempted breakouts in 1864 appear to have been made by different groups, and the Supreme Council had no control over what was happening. It was so cautious that it became ineffective, almost paralyzed.

Camp commanders received orders from Colonel Hoffman on October 1 regarding General Butler's plan to exchange sick and disabled prisoners. Surgeons were to see who qualified. These men would be shipped to Cairo under guard unless they chose not to go. From there the Federal government agreed to transport them by boat to exchange points further south. The camp would supply three days' cooked rations, but invalids had to be stripped of all "U.S." property, including blankets. Meanwhile, the guards were going in for a little free enterprise, purchasing items for the prisoners outside the camp, and being paid for their services by "keeping the change." Greble also disclosed that guards rented their blankets to the prisoners "for a dollar a night," but the fee appears to be an exaggeration.[26]

Medical inspections for the exchange of sick prisoners proposed by General Butler began on October 2nd at Camp Douglas. Burke, barely able to stand and racked with chills and fever, was rejected. It is possible that he was reputed to be a die-hard and was being punished, because 14 of his friends, including John Curd, who were not as sick, made the list. However, all remained in camp.[27] The plan had cooled off. Only 60 men were released by the end of 1864, plus 162 more in January, 1865. Some of these may have been released for other reasons, so this humanitarian idea came to nothing.

If any prisoner should have left his bones in Chicago, it was Curtis R. Burke. Two infections and a case of smallpox did not stop him from living into the 20th century. On September 7, 1863, he underwent a tooth extraction with an unsterilized instrument without anesthetic or antibiotics. A week later he caught a severe cold, which could be fatal at Camp Douglas. He had the chills, and a hacking cough was treated with a stick of licorice. He remained in the barrack, which was not in good condition. October was a cold month during the war years, and Briggs' October 2nd report mentioned that barracks were under repair, but still in need of floors, windows, and roofs. Stoves were lacking and would soon be required.[28] However, the majority of prisoners made every attempt "to keep themselves neat and tidy."

On October 5, 1864, Burke was hospitalized with smallpox. An average of eight men died in the "pest house" each day. It was in the charge of the hard-pressed Doctor F. A. Emmons, a contract surgeon from Chicago. A red ambulance carried smallpox patients through the camp's south gate and traveled about 400 yards southeast to the smallpox hospital. The building was wider and longer than a barrack and was still located at Adele Grove on Douglas property, about two blocks south of the camp on Cottage Grove. Patients found to their surprise that the place had no hydrants or sewers, and that privies were the old fashioned pits.[29]

They were given a canvas cot with a mattress, and two blankets probably covered with the scabs of the prisoners who went before. No hospital clothing was issued, and patients slept in what they wore when they arrived. Only one stove was working on the ward, despite the many cracks and holes in the walls. An oil lamp hung from the ceiling, and the roof was open and airy, letting in the cold fresh air. Nevertheless, the stench from the sick was powerful despite the scrubbed floors.

Patients were discouraged from drinking water or washing, as "this was bad for smallpox." The three meals a day were the same: sliced bread, coffee, milk, sugar, crackers, and roast potatoes. About 13 male nurses, including three prisoners, ran the wards. The Yankee nurses were kind so long as patients did not give them any trouble. Two of the rebel nurses stole money and tobacco from the sick and escaped.[30] Several men were likely to die during the night and nurses tramped up and back with coffins. New patients were quite nervous, and happy to see the morning light when a brave woman came within a few feet of the hospital to sell sweet milk at 10 cents a quart, and buttermilk for 10 cents per gallon. Many patients were desperate for the milk, as water was practically forbidden, and the medicine was dark bitter stuff called "number one."

For the lucky ones, the bumps on their faces were getting dark spots and beginning to dry. They could go to the sink by themselves, but only in shorts and boots. The privy was a roofless shed set over an old style pit. The Chicago winter had come on early, and the patients shivered with sickness, and grew dizzy from the stench. One infectious patient wandered away from the sink and into the darkness and cold wearing only his shorts. He could not be found. While some of the sick were recovering, others were not. Every night the wards were filled with raving, ranting, cursing, and praying. One man spoke most eloquently against a death sentence from some imagined judge, and assured his family and sweetheart that he was innocent.[31]

A recovering patient was moved to the convalescent ward after two weeks. Dr. Emmons usually ordered a patient discharged about fifteen days after admission, ready or not, and some of them had running sores. He had no choice, given the number of sick and lack of facilities. There was no medical examination before discharge, and departure began with a bath, two men to a tub. The water was heated, but the wash house was a cold, dilapidated, roofless shed, and patients were thoroughly chilled. Old clothing was burned, and the hospital issued a new blue suit, thin shoes without socks, unlined pants without shorts, a good gray shirt, and a mutilated frock coat.

A returning patient barely recognized Prison Square because of the many improvements and new barracks that sprung up in only a few weeks. Comrades welcomed a prisoner as a hero for returning from the pest house alive, even though just barely so. Burke was very ill for the next two months and may have sent some of his comrades to answer the long roll.

T. M. Page accurately claimed that patients were discharged while still infectious and exposed to the freezing journey back to camp. Briggs confirmed that there was a serious shortage of hospital beds and men were dying in barracks. There was only the one smallpox hospital, and medicine was insufficient. The danger to the civilian population was not insignificant when 18 patients escaped from the smallpox hospital on October 11, 1864.[32] Meanwhile, the garrison was thoroughly vaccinated.

Burke complained of "soreness and slight pain on the left side of my neck under my jaw between the ear and apple of the throat. It increased so by night that I could hardly eat a couple of biscuits and cup of tea that Pa brought me." He had infected tonsils, probably diphtheria. Civil War medicine could only treat an infection locally. When the Confederate surgeon made his morning barrack call, he gave Henry White a prescription for nitrate of silver for Burke, and William Gibbons burned the ulcers for him. The pain was excruciating. Burke was still suffering with his throat the first week in November, burning the ulcers and gurgling with potash. The treatment was more agonizing than the illness. Poultices of lye, bread, onions, and vinegar were applied several times a day. Meanwhile, another one of his comrades died. Burke could not attend roll call for nine weeks. Convalescents from the smallpox hospital reported over 200 cases there, many lying on the floor and suffering frostbite. T. M. Page felt their suffering. "To the helpless agony of this situation smallpox added its own horror."[33]

Colonel Hoffman approved a plan to move the smallpox hospital to a mysterious place called "Dull Grove" so that the University could re-open. He required that the ground be rent-free, with the new building paid for by the prison fund. This would be the third move for the facility. It would have two wards like the present one, with windows for ventilation. Hoffman vetoed the idea of raising the building three feet from the ground, as this would be too expensive. "Dull Grove" cannot be found on maps of the area. T. M. Page claimed that "the victim was removed to an isolated hospital miles away out on a sandy waste, a removal which was a fatal journey to many men when the phenomenally cold winter of 1863-64 came on." Page was overstating the case. Medical Inspector Coolidge placed the new

Confederate officers in front of sutler store in Prison Square, circa September, 1864. Note the water and fire hydrants in the foreground. One of the prisoners standing on the extreme right appears to be a civilian. All look well fed (courtesy Chicago Historical Society).

Enlisted men in Prison Square, taken at the same time as the photograph of the officers (courtesy Chicago Historical Society).

hospital "one mile from the camp," and so did Burke.[34] This was probably southward on the lake front, and it was in operation by the end of December, 1864.

Barracks improved steadily, according to Briggs, but many needed windows and stoves. Prisoners were clean and comfortably supplied with clothing and blankets. "The kitchens are scrupulously clean and the messes are prepared as well as could be expected with the cooking utensils allowed them."[35]

Colonel Hoffman was promoted to Brigadier-General on October 7, 1864. There was probably some celebrating at the Washington office. On October 8, Camp Douglas had 7,402 prisoners on hand. Briggs reported that Prison Square was still dilapidated despite new barracks under construction and repair of the old ones. The prisoners were not only clean but "very neat in appearance.[36] Conditions improved steadily, but no one knew that the population would double in the next two months. The weak spot, as usual, was inadequate hospital space. This was no small matter, since the sick in barracks had "acute diseases" according to Briggs.

Between June 1 and October 1, 1864, about 304 prisoners died, with 1,354 sick. Another 1,000 were ill in barracks, which increased mortality.[37] Sweet was alarmed by the health problems after he had done so much to improve the camp and enhance his reputation. "In my opinion," he wrote to Hoffman, "this increase springs from three causes."

First: He claimed that the prisoners had been confined for a long time, "although they have the range of the prison square, which is kept in excellent sanitary condition." This caused depression and disease. Sweet was not accurate, as the prisoners were allowed to walk only on the streets between the barracks.

Second: Doctor A. M. Sigmund, a volunteer officer who became Post Surgeon on June 22, 1864, was not competent to run so large a medical department. Sweet complained about "a lack of efficiency" at the prison hospital and Prison Square. He gave no specifics, and none of the medical inspectors agreed with Sweet on this point. Dr. Alexander gave Sigmund good grades in his July report. Sweet's complaint is puzzling, since as commanding officer, he appointed the Post Surgeon. It was possible that this was now controlled by the War Department or the Surgeon-General.

Third: Hoffman was responsible because he had stopped the sutler from selling vegetables to the prisoners on August 10, 1864. "This want has been distinctly visible as a cause of disease," Sweet charged.[38] Potatoes were issued from time to time "upon surgeon's certificate, but not in sufficient quantities to stop scurvy."

Sweet recommended that competent medical officers be sent and that the sutler begin selling vegetables and other antiscorbutics to the prisoners. Many prisoners did not have the funds to purchase vegetables, and Sweet did not suggest that the government should furnish them. He bypassed Hoffman and complained directly to the Adjutant-General of the Army on October 11 that mortality at camp was up 35% since June.[39] Thirty-four died that month, 49 in July, 98 in August, and the September toll was 123 dead.

T. M. Page described how seed to grow vegetables was donated by Mary Morris in 1864, and prisoners grew a crop between the fence and dead-line. However, it was eaten by Federal officers and guards, according to him. His claim that the seed came from Mary Morris makes the incident probable. Burke described a vegetable garden 20 feet wide near the fence that belonged to the garrison. "A small squad of prisoners are often pressed to work in the Yankee garden," he complained in his journal.[40] It is possible that the garrison planned to seize the prisoner's crop; otherwise, it was not likely that they were permitted to go beyond the dead-line.

Interior of barrack in Prison Square, circa September, 1864, with a good view of the triple-tiered bunks (courtesy Illinois State Historical Library).

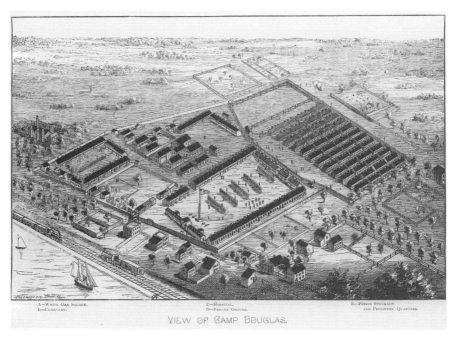

A—WHITE OAK SQUARE.
B—CEMETERY.
C—HOSPITAL.
D—PARADE GROUND.
E—PRISON STOCKADE
AND PRISONERS' QUARTERS.

VIEW OF CAMP DOUGLAS.

Lithograph, circa September 1864. The artist mistook the Graves homestead for a cemetery [B]. The University of Chicago is in the left foreground. Jane Bradley's house is to the right of Garrison Square, with a horse-car passing (courtesy Chicago Historical Society).

Why Colonel Sweet did not use the substantial prison fund to purchase vegetables is a mystery. He may have been hoarding it for the Democratic Convention. The Anti-Administration Party was suspected of promoting the alleged Camp Douglas Conspiracy which was about to break, according to Sweet's detectives. There was great interest among the prisoners in the convention scheduled for August 29, 1864 in Chicago.[41] They believed that the election of a Democratic president could end the war on favorable terms for the South.

The convention gave Colonel Sweet's detectives an excuse to make heavy demands for money. This caused a serious dispute on October 6, 1864, when Hoffman ordered Sweet to reimburse the prison fund $183.02 paid to them. Eleven days later Hoffman disapproved Sweet's request to put a detective on the camp payroll for $100 per month. Sweet had shown no proof that they had prevented a single escape. Hoffman said he would approve a lesser amount "if it can be shown that these detectives have rendered any services which have been of any value."[42]

Briggs found that major repairs and erection of new barracks were continuing as late as October 16. "The barracks are generally well policed; the floors are sanded every morning and dry rubbed," he reported. "The kitchens are in the best of order; their dishes, cooking utensils, and tables are scoured daily. Most of the prisoners wash their underclothing once a week. The supply of water is somewhat limited, supply of blankets and clothing is sufficient for present use."[43]

Hoffman responded to Sweet's complaints about Dr. Sigmund and the health problems by promising to lay the medical needs of the camp before the Surgeon General. He refused to relax his restrictions on the sutler, and suggested using the prison fund to purchase "a reasonable quantity" of vegetables, or to get the money by selling part of the meat ration. Colonel Sweet told him bluntly that he would not cut the meat ration because of winter coming on.[44] This must have surprised Hoffman because Sweet had cut rations and candles on his own. Any warm feelings between the two men were probably damaged.

By October 23, Briggs was concerned about the lack of stoves and fuel for the prisoners. However, a wash house with six large boilers was nearly complete, and workers were laying six-inch water pipes throughout the camp. Prisoners suffered without water while the hydrants were shut off. They sunk barrels in the ground to trap moisture, but with little success.[45] Briggs continued to criticize the farmer's boilers, but made no mention of the sutler, who was beyond his jurisdiction.

Mr. Nightingale charged the highest prices for shoddy goods. Inferior coffee was $1 a pound; poor quality black tea, $2.50 per pound; common brown sugar, 60 cents per pound; butter, 80 cents per pound; small apples, 5 cents each. Three large apples for 10 cents was a normal price. Nine envelopes and nine sheets of note paper went for 30 cents, double the normal cost. Consequently, the prisoners labeled Mr. Nightingale "a high priced singer." Meanwhile, scurvy reached a malignant stage, which brought an eloquent denunciation from R. T. Bean: "Lips were eaten away, jaws became diseased, and teeth fell out. If leprosy is any worse than scurvy, may God have mercy upon the victim! It was shocking, horrible, monstrous, and a disgrace to any people who permitted such conditions to exist."[46]

October 24 was a bad day for Colonel Sweet, with prisoners again pressing home successful escapes. About four rebels tunneled out from the cellar of the hospital adjacent to White Oak Square, all the way under the fence and parapet. An unknown number of other prisoners went over the fence by ladder, right past a V.R.C. guard. Sweet's detectives also failed to warn of a serious attack by the prisoners at the end of October, 1864. Captain E. R. P. Shurly was in charge at the time while Colonel Sweet was away in Wisconsin. Captain Edward Richard Pitman Shurly was a transplanted Englishman. He settled in New York and was commissioned First Lieutenant in the 126th New York Infantry early in the war. Shurly suffered serious wounds at the battle of Fredericksburg in 1862, and later joined the 8th V.R.C.[47]

A prisoner reported that an evening assault was planned on the western fence of Prison Square, "to be spearheaded by 100 prisoners with 11,000 to follow." His story was believed because there was an unusual amount of agitation in barracks that day.[48]

Captain Shurly placed the 8th V.R.C. outside the western fence of Prison Square after dark. Another regiment took positions at the eastern edge of the Chicago Driving Park, four blocks west. The prisoners attacked at eight o'clock p.m. and broke through the fence. The 8th V.R.C. fired a volley driving them back into the camp. As usual the guns did not do much damage. Ten men suffered slight wounds. Eighteen prisoners got away according to the official report, but were rounded up by troops advancing from the Driving Park. Shurly did not consider using the artillery. Hoffman was skeptical about the cannons, except for "overawing the prisoners, and its judicious use must depend on the ability of the commanding officer." Infantry would have to defend the guns, in Hoffman's opinion, making the 500 revolvers better.[49]

Sweet would have used the big guns. He said earlier that he was anxious to punish the prisoners while in the act of escaping. He had no confidence in the rifles, and he was right. Prisoners got by the V.R.C. despite the direct fire. Artillery would have shredded them at such close range, including those in the barracks who were not escaping.

The *Tribune* gave another account of the assault, dating it Friday, October 28, which was correct, according to Burke. The paper described how guards rushed in to fire at 25 to 30 prisoners in the square after the assault started. The fence was breached and four men escaped before troops arrived on the outside to seal the hole. Only one prisoner was wounded. The newspaper account concluded that this was a complete surprise and a close call. The *Tribune* guessed that the attackers were encouraged by the departure that day of 800 men in the 196th Pennsylvania, reducing guard strength by half. One of the leaders in the attack was Burke's friend, John Shackelford, who had been in irons twice before. This would be his third trip to the dungeon.[50]

Retaliation by Colonel Sweet was severe. The men were stripped of extra blankets and clothing to the extent that it took two wagon loads to haul the material away. Burke did not doubt that the "Yankees seem to be determined to reduce us to one suit."[51] This could be dangerous for the prisoners, with another brutal winter coming on.

The attack on the 28th reflected on the "Camp Douglas Conspiracy," which was an alleged plot by Confederate agents and Northern sympathizers to assault the camp one week later, on November 8, 1864. It is unlikely that those in the abortive attempt in October were aware of it, and the Supreme Council was ineffective to stop the attempt, if it knew. If it did not know what was going on, then the Camp Douglas Conspiracy had little chance of success.

It is ironic that on October 31, 1864, a report surfaced in which an inspector from the Northern Department disagreed with Hoffman about the cannons. He thought that two howitzers should be supplied in addition to the cannons at Camp Douglas, and that the farmer's boilers were fire hazards because of their worn out condition. Sweet was after Hoffman again regarding the detectives, reminding him about his statement that they could be paid out of the prison fund if "results were reported."[52] Sweet claimed that such employment "has given the names of rebel sympathizers, thus indicating where to look if they escape." Accordingly he presented the bills of two detectives amounting to $78.50 and $186.66.

They had discovered the "workings and the ultimate designs of the Sons of Liberty . . . a treasonable organization having for its main object the success of the rebellion and the overthrow of the Government of the United States," Sweet claimed, and he warned of an "intended insurrection among the inhabitants of this and other states." He also credited his operatives with the information about the planned insurrection at camp on September 19, 1864, which did not occur, and requested permission to continue employing detectives for the next three months.[53] Colonel Sweet was either a scoundrel or a fool to suggest that these dissidents could threaten a government that controlled the most powerful army on earth. He was no fool. Neither was General Hoffman.

NOTES TO CHAPTER 13

[1] The Northeastern states agreed to supply fully equipped men for 100 days to release veterans for combat. W. H. H. Terrel, *Indiana in the War of the Rebellion*, (Indianapolis, 1960): 43-48. The University of Chicago furnished many 100-day men from among the students, but more served at Camp Douglas.

[2] Burke, 15 Aug., 7 Sep. 1864; Greble diary, 6 Sep. 1864.

[3] Burke, 8 Sep. 1864; Kelly, 74.

[4] O R Ser.II-Vol.VII, 1067.

[5] O R Ser.II-Vol.VII, 703, 767.

[6] O R Ser.II-Vol.VII, 615-23, 793.

[7] *Battles and Leaders of the Civil War,* IV:424.

[8] O R Ser.II-Vol.VII, 795, 809-10.

[9] Greble diary, 9 Sep. 1864.

[10] O R Ser.II-Vol.VII, 834-35; Burke, 3, 30 Nov., 3 Dec. 1864.

[11] O R Ser.II-Vol-VII, 840-41.

[12] *Chicago Tribune,* 26 May 1895.

[13] O R Ser.II-Vol.VII, 861.

[14] Greble diary, 25 Aug., 20 Sep. 1864.

[15] Burke, 24 Sep. 1864.

[16] Burke, 26-29 Sep.; 3 oct. 1864.

[17] Burke, 26, 29, Sep.; 1 Oct. 1864; R. G. 393, v. 334:433.

[18] O R Ser.II-Vol.VII, 897.

[19] *Chicago Tribune,* 29 Sep. 1864.

[20] Burke, 28 Sep. 1864.

[21] Burke, 2 Oct. 1864.

[22] B. R. Froman, "An Interior View of the Camp Douglas Conspiracy," *The Southern Bivouac* 1-No.2 (Oct. 1882): 65.

[23] R. T. Bean, *Confederate Veteran* 22:311.

[24] Mr. Longwood settled in Chicago and became a successful businessman. He was president of the Confederate Veterans of Chicago and lobbied Congress for the erection of the Confederate monument in Oak Woods Cemetery.

[25] *Confederate Veteran* 22:311.

[26] O R Ser.II-Vol.VII, 907; Greble diary, 2 Oct. 1864.

[27] Burke, 2 Oct. 1864.

[28] O R Ser.II-Vol.VII, 913.

[29] Burke, 5 Oct. 1864.

[30] Burke, 9 Oct. 1864.

[31] Burke, 19 Oct. 1864.

[32] O R Ser.II-Vol.VII, 767; Greble diary, 11 Oct. 1864.

[33] Burke, 2-23 Oct. 1864; T. M. Page, *Confederate Veteran* 8:63.

[34] O R Ser.II-Vol.VII, 795; T. M. Page, 8:63; Medical and Surgical History, 49.

[35] O R Ser.II-Vol.VII, 913.

[36] *Brevet Brigadier Generals in Blue,* 288; O R Ser.II-Vol.VII, 959-60.

[37] O R Ser.II-Vol.VII, 954.

[38] O R Ser.II-Vol.VII, 954-55.

[39] R. G. 393, v. 234:458.

[40] *Confederate Veteran* 8:63; Burke, 14 Jul. 1864.

[41] Burke, 28 Aug. 1864.

[42] R. G. 393, v. 241:2:6.

[43] O R Ser.II-Vol.VII, 995.

[44] O R Ser.II-Vol.VII, 1006, 1058-59.

[45] O R Ser.II-Vol.VII, 1026-27; Burke, 27 Oct. 1864.

[46] Burke, 6, 10 Jun., 25 Oct. 1864; R. T. Bean, *Confederate Veteran* 22:270.

[47] Greble diary, 24 Oct. 1864; Francis B. Heitman, *Historical Register and Dictionary of U.S. Army Officers* (Washington: U.S. Government Printing Office, 1903), 885.

[48] Currey, *Chicago: Its History and Its Builders* 2:139; Andreas, *History of Chicago* 2:308.

[49] O R Ser.II-Vol.VII, 1083.

[50] *Chicago Tribune,* 31 Oct. 1864; Burke, 29 Oct. 1864.

[51] Burke, 31 Oct. 1864.

[52] O R Ser.II-Vol.VII, 1067; R.G. 393, v. 234:439.

[53] R. G. 393, v. 234:439.

14.

THE CAMP DOUGLAS CONSPIRACY OF 1864

The crime of conspiracy is peculiar in that it is punishable without committing the crime. If one person plans to rob a Federally insured bank and steals a getaway car, but decides to go bowling instead, he or she is only guilty of auto theft. However, if two people plan to rob the bank and steal a getaway car, they have committed a Federal crime by conspiring to rob the bank. Conspiracy law is useful in times of national stress to prosecute political dissidents or perceived enemies for alleged plots which do not have much chance of success.

There are opposing views about a Camp Douglas Conspiracy to free the prisoners in 1864. Some historians believe that the conspiracy existed. Others conclude that it was a hoax concocted by scoundrels and self-seekers.[1] It appears that the truth lies closer to the hoax theory. There were Camp Douglas conspiracies to free prisoners prior to 1864. The Levi Boone plot of 1863 is one, but none of them captured the attention of the media, or alarmed the North, as did the Conspiracy of 1864.

Perhaps there was some basis for believing the tale. Tension existed in the southern part of Illinois called "Egypt." One member of Congress suggested that Illinois be divided so that the southern half could join the Confederacy. There had been clashes there between draft officials and mobs opposing conscription. Guerilla bands in these rural regions attacked Unionists, and five men died in a battle on April 28, 1864. The "Clingman" gang caused much damage until it was broken up in 1864.[2] However, this strife involved the draft, and local feuds and animosities.

A bad situation for the South supposedly led to the plan for an uprising in the North by copperheads and Confederate agents. Movements of the Union army toward Atlanta and Richmond signaled doom for the Confederacy. It is claimed that on March 16, 1864, the Confederate government gave Captain Thomas Henry Hines, a former Confederate officer, an assignment to go to Canada. There he was to collect men from General Morgan's command. Hines supposedly engineered one prison break and had contacts among dissident groups in the North. In passing through to Canada he was to confer with friends of the Confederacy to persuade them to organize and render aid. "He will likewise have in view the possibility, by such means as he can command, of effecting any fair and appropriate enterprises of war against our enemies," the orders stated.[3]

Captain Thomas H. Hines, circa 1861 (courtesy the Filson Club)

Richmond also sent a commission to oversee the agents, headed by Jacob Thompson as the director and treasurer. In May, 1864, two more commissioners under instructions from President Davis to further the interests of the Confederacy arrived in Montreal, supposedly with $800,000 in Federal greenbacks.[4] This amounted to about $5,000,000 in Confederate money. It is not likely that a project with no plans or strategy was allotted such a huge sum.

Hines thought that Camp Douglas was the best choice for mounting an attack because of the large number of prisoners from Morgan's command, and because Chicago was supposed to contain large copperhead organizations, perhaps numbering 5,000 members. Confederate agents allegedly met in Canada with Clement Vallandigham, a prominent copperhead. He assured Hines and Commissioner Thompson that he controlled 300,000 men, many of them Union army veterans. They were ready at his command for an armed uprising to take over the state governments in Illinois, Indiana, and Ohio. "All that was needed was money." The Confederates conceded afterward that they were naive to believe this.[5]

The uprising was set for the Fourth of July, which was the day of the Democratic Convention in Chicago. Charles Walsh, an alleged leader of the "Sons of Liberty," would arm 2,000 of his followers to help attack the camp. Walsh was a successful businessman with a wife and 10 children, one of them an infant.[6] It was not likely that he would lead the attack.

The possibility of capturing a Federal gunboat on Lake Michigan and turning its guns on the camp was discussed. This never came up again. The plan expected that prisoners would be freed at other camps simultaneously with the attack on Camp Douglas, and the governments of the three Northwestern states would be seized.[7]

Yet plotters did none of the required planning for an attack on Camp Douglas. No assault positions were mapped out or assigned to any unit. Leaders went unnamed, and an opportune hour for the attack was never set. There was no discussion about weapons and munitions, or any provisions made for dead and wounded. No thought was given to escape routes or rear guard blocking units.

Small wonder that when the Democratic Convention was postponed to August 29 the Sons of Liberty decided to do the same with their plans. Hines, convinced that the promised troops were eager to fight, persuaded the copperhead leaders to make July 20 the starting date.[8] Again there was no planning for the promised assault.

The Chicago conspirators soon reneged on the July date, sending Hines word that they would not be ready, but giving no reasons. Another meeting allegedly took place in Chicago, and now August 16 was agreed upon as the new date. They soon requested another postponement. The copperheads argued that the Confederate army must attack into Kentucky and Missouri to divert Federal forces from Chicago. Hines and Thompson should have realized then that they were wasting money. Instead, the attack was reset for the day of the Democratic Convention, August 29, 1864.[9] Hines stipulated that there could be no further delays.

A major reversal occurred when Vallandigham withdrew from the plot and returned to Ohio. There went his 300,000 non-existent troops, limiting the uprising to an attack on Camp Douglas. Braggarts among the Confederates in Canada and sympathizers in Chicago boasted of an attack, not to mention the tales coming from spies and informers.[10] Several men, and perhaps women, on Union and Confederate payrolls were making a good thing out of the alleged plot.

This time Captain Hines made himself responsible for planning the assault. He came to Chicago, "and using the Walsh home as a vantage point, drew an accurate map of the camp and its approaches and planned the attack upon it as a textbook military operation. A night assault was aimed at three of the four sides of the camp; as soon as it started, the prisoners were to attack the guards from the rear."[11] Telegraph lines would be cut, and railroad employees bribed to transport the freed prisoners. The first stop was the prison camp at Rock Island, Illinois.

Omitting doubts about the railroad scheme, it is difficult to believe that Hines could rely upon civilians who had never fought as a unit, and expect them to mount a successful night operation without any training. Even more unbelievable, he paid no attention to the University of Chicago astronomical observatory towering over the camp. Colonel Sweet had taken notice and stationed one to two companies of riflemen there.[12] They could unleash devastating firepower on the camp and any attack force, provided their guns worked, and at the same time enjoy the protection of the stone tower. Captain Hines was overmatched before he had even started.

On August 28, 1864, the Confederate agents learned there would be no assault the next day. The copperhead army existed only in the imagination of John Walsh, or more accurately, in the imaginations of the Confederates. The many thousands of assault troops came to a mere 25 men.[13]

Initially the Supreme Council of Seven at Camp Douglas knew nothing about the Hines group. It had planned a mass breakout, probably for the spring or summer of 1864, but no date is given.[14] Before the time arrived, a coded letter was received from friends that Captain Thomas Hines was in Chicago, but otherwise the letter was unclear. Again, no date is given.

The Supreme Council postponed its plans, and a garrison officer accepted $130 to allow a prisoner named Joseph Grey to escape. He carried a code to Chicago for communicating by mail. This has a ring of truth because the bribe money was raised partly "by selling sutler's checks at enormous discounts to the Federal soldiers on duty as patrol guard." Friends in Chicago were to communicate with Council members. Soon, John Waller received a letter from Mrs. Sarah B. Waller (no relation) on August 4, 1864.[15] It was Waller who had invented the code.

The letter concerned a request for the prisoners "to contribute some curiosities of their own manufacture to be sent to a fair to be held in Liverpool, England for the Confederate prisoners' benefit," according to Burke. It was too much coincidence that this Southern woman, who had been active in prison relief work since 1862, sent the request to John Waller. One can assume that by August 4, 1864 Confederate agents were communicating with the Council. Sweet told Hoffman on October 11 that his detectives had discovered "channels of communication" between Chicago and a prisoner of war organization at camp.[16]

B. R. Froman wrote, "In this way we were informed that Captain Tom Hines, St. Leger Grenfel, Captain Castleman, and others, with about eighty of our comrades who had not been captured, were in Chicago, had come thither by way of Canada, for the purpose of liberating us, and they expected to be joined and aided by one or two hundred Copperheads, as they were then called, from Southern Illinois."

Mr. Froman gave no date for this; nor did he suggest that the Supreme Council received any further communications. He had wisely objected to postponing the escape attempt planned months before, but was overruled. Hines confirmed that "information had been conveyed to prudent prisoners that aid from the outside would come and they were to be watchful for the attack without as a signal for resistance within."[17] Such a signal never came, as the Sons of Liberty failed to produce an assault force.

Hines had perceived the Sons of Liberty as "being sincere and not lacking in courage." Now he realized that they had become timid and overestimated the reinforcements sent to Sweet. "It was necessary, therefore, to look beyond Chicago for a field of action," Hines decided. Supposedly, Hines and John Castleman suggested to the Sons of Liberty that they attack the Rock Island, Illinois Prison Camp and seize the state capital.[18] Castleman was a former Confederate officer who rode with Morgan.

The copperheads and dissidents did not respond to this suicidal suggestion, so "The Confederate officers accordingly deemed it wise to leave Chicago as the safety secured by the presence of the Convention was removed, and the agents of the Government had been aroused to greater vigilance and activity."[19]

That ended the Camp Douglas Conspiracy as far as the Confederates were concerned, but not if Colonel Sweet could help it. The rest of the tale was his invention, fabricated with the help of the so-called detectives and spies he employed. It is inconceivable that the few civilians ever intended to attack the camp. It was not their war, not their flag. They had no cause worth dying for.

Colonel Sweet, however, set out to convince his superiors that he was about to crush a dangerous uprising, and he intended to act without authority. When Colonel Tucker had proposed placing Chicago under martial law there was no response. When he arrested a prominent citizen it caused a furor. Colonel Sweet planned to do both. Where Tucker failed, Sweet would succeed, because Tucker was a businessman, while Sweet was a skilled politician. At 8:30 p.m. on November 6 he sent a message delivered by hand to General Cook, his superior in Springfield, because "he was not entirely sure of the telegraph." The real reason was to have time to act without being stopped. Stanton had given him authority to arrest only two "rebel agents."[20]

Cook was warned that "the City is filling up with suspicious characters . . . and others who were here from Canada . . . plotting to release the prisoners of war at Camp Douglas . . . I have every reason to believe that Colonel Marmaduke of the rebel army is in the city . . . and also Captain Hines . . . also Col G. St. Leger Grenfell . . . My force is only 800 men . . . to guard between 8,000 and 9,000 prisoners. I am certainly not justified in waiting to take risks . . . The head gone we can manage the body. In order to make these arrests perfect, I must also arrest two or three prominent citizens . . . I regret that I am not able to consult with you on my proposed action before acting without letting an opportunity pass which may never again occur . . ."[21]

Patrols left Camp Douglas on the night of November 6, 1864, and arrests began that night and continued into the morning, gathering in the supposed leaders of the plot, as well as the supposed foot soldiers. Martial law had come to Chicago. At 10:30 a.m. on the 7th, Sweet wired a list to Colonel Hoffman of the persons arrested

"Col. G. St. Leger Grenfell, and J.T. Shanks, an escaped prisoner of war at the Richmond House; Col. Vincent Marmaduke . . . Brig Gen. Charles Walsh, of the Sons of Liberty; Captain Cantrill, of Morgan's command, and Charles Traverse . . . at the house of General Walsh; Judge Buckner S. Morris, treasurer of Sons of Liberty . . . also capturing at the same time in Walsh's house about thirty rods from Camp Douglas arms and ammunition."[22]

Engraving of Buckner Morris, circa 1861 (courtesy Chicago Historical Society)

Sweet claimed that he had "complete proof" of Morris assisting Shanks to escape and plotting to release prisoners. "Their plan was to attack the camp on election night," Sweet claimed. His charges against Buckner S. Morris, a prominent lawyer, former Mayor of Chicago, and judge, proved to be false. His arrest was similar to that of Dr. Levi Boone by Colonel Tucker in 1862. On November 10, in response to an inquiry about Morris, General Cook repeated Sweet's charges against him, but admitted there was "no written order for his arrest especially."[23]

"In addition," Sweet continued, "the patrols aided by Chicago police arrested on 7 November 106 bushwhackers, guerrillas and rebel soldiers, among them many of the notorious Clingman gang of Fayette and Christian counties of this State with their Captain, Sears, and Lieut. Garland, all of whom are now in custody at Camp Douglas."[24]

His boast that Sears and Garland were at Camp Douglas was another lie. Only 81 alleged conspirators were listed at camp. Seventy-seven were from Illinois, and one from Georgia, Indiana, New Jersey, and Pennsylvania. Shanks was not among them, neither was Sears or Garland. Apologists for Sweet have put forward the tangled argument that it is a matter of punctuation, and that Sweet never claimed that Sears and Garland were captured, but only meant that they were the captain and lieutenant of the Clingman gang.[25] This is a preposterous reading of his report.

Colonel Sweet failed to mention that he had also arrested Mrs. Morris and that she was a prisoner at Camp Douglas. A story related that Colonel Sweet ordered Mrs. Morris sent to White Oak dungeon, but that Captain Shurly, the adjutant, defied him and housed the Morris couple in his quarters.[26] This would have been typical of Shurly, who considered himself a "Christian gentleman," which gives the story some credibility.

On November 7, General Hooker, commanding the Northern Department of the army, not knowing what Sweet had done, wired "I apprehend no attack on you." He advised Sweet to gather all of the military forces he could find and hold them ready until the crisis of the election has passed. "The Board of Trade and other loyal citizens will take care of Chicago, if necessary," Hooker said confidently. "This will leave you a handsome battalion to fight with, if required. I have requested General Cook to re-enforce you with two companies from Springfield."[27]

Stanton telegraphed his approval of Sweet's actions on November 7. On the same day, Governor Yates placed the Chicago militia under his orders. General Hooker fell into line and dispatched 500 more men to Chicago "under fighting officers."[28] The 48th Illinois Infantry arrived the following day along with "three car-loads of armed troops" from Camp Butler near Springfield. Sweet soon had 2,000 troops at his disposal.

President Lincoln sent no word. His humorous telegram to Frankfort, Kentucky on November 10 should have made him skeptical about the conspiracy: "I can scarcely believe that General John B. Huston has been arrested for no other offense than opposition to my re-election; for if that had been deemed sufficient cause of arrest I should have heard of more than one arrest in Kentucky on election day," Lincoln quipped. "General Burbridge will discharge him at once." The results of the conspiracy trials could have been different had Lincoln lived. It is no surprise that nothing was heard from General Hoffman. He had continuously denied Sweet's requests to pay his detectives, and believed that they were worthless.[29] Now Sweet's men seem to have triumphed.

By November 12 the hysteria in Chicago was so intense that Hooker's adjutant requested additional men from Springfield. General Cook reported that more weapons were found in Walsh's barn. "We have not touched bottom yet!" Cook warned sternly.[30]

On November 14, five more alleged members of the Sons of Liberty were arrested. One was Richard T. Semmes, whom Sweet claimed was a nephew of Confederate Admiral Semmes, which was untrue. Also taken was Doctor E. W. Edwards, who allegedly harbored Confederate agent Marmaduke. On November 15, a young Englishman from Canada was arrested "who proved to be a messenger" between the conspirators and guerrillas in Kentucky. Also arrested at this time was Edmund C. Waller. He may have been the son of Sarah B. Waller, who had sent the coded message to Camp Douglas a few months prior. Colonel Sweet advised the Adjutant General that Waller's family resided in Chicago and requested that he be held at Camp Douglas as a witness.[31]

The danger on November 6 and 7 amounted to seven alleged leaders and 106 more copperheads, soon reduced to 81 according to Camp Douglas records. Eight or nine more men were taken on November 14 and 15, and the total attack force was perhaps 96 men and Mrs. Morris. In addition, Colonel Sweet could name only 143 "prominent members of the Sons of Liberty" statewide.[32]

Chicago newspapers took sides depending on their politics. The pro-administration *Tribune* felt that Chicago had escaped a volcano. "A GENERAL SACK OF THE CITY INTENDED — PLUNDER, RAPINE— FIRE — BLOODSHED IN THE STREETS OF CHICAGO."[33] This came directly from Sweet's reports.

The pro-Confederate *Chicago Times* felt that there was never the slightest danger of an attack upon Camp Douglas. "That such an attack was contemplated by half a dozen rebels is probable, but that they could have relied upon any local assistance in the undertaking is wholly improbable." This was not an understatement. Colonel Sweet, however, used his reinforcements to extend the guard line outside Camp Douglas to one and one-half miles beyond the fence.

Sweet succeeded in his aims because, while Tucker only named Dr. Boone in the 1862 conspiracy, Sweet played on fears of an attack by thousands of traitors. Paradoxically, many prisoners escaped in the Boone plot, and that alarm was heard in downtown Chicago. Sweet's conspiracy barely made a ripple among the prisoners, who were busy darning their socks.

Burke heard that "There were rumors about arms, etc. being found near camp. At night we had unusually strict orders to keep quiet. The Yanks seem afraid of the rebs making a break."[34]

John Waller was in the same barrack. Perhaps he was also darning socks that night. The prisoners used yarn from warn-out socks, a darning needle, and a small stick about the size of a lead pencil. The damaged sock was sewn over the stick, which was then removed.

The arsenal of weapons and munitions stored by Walsh was the overt act required by law to support a conspiracy charge. Walsh claimed that he only intended to arm his local Democratic club to protect the polls on election day. His story is no more believable than any other about the conspiracy. Regardless, the arsenal implicated Walsh only. However, the other defendants were linked to him through the testimony of Shanks and three more dubious characters working for Sweet.[35]

Colonel Sweet saw the making of his career in the rumors of a conspiracy. He was promoted to Brigadier-General on December 20, 1864, and his post-war career was assured. He closed his reports on the conspiracy: "I respectfully recommend that the officers of the rebel army, and as many of the Sons of Liberty and guerrillas above mentioned, as the interests of the Government may require, be tried before a military commission, and punished."[36] His advice was heeded.

Buckner Morris, his wife, and others were sent to Cincinnati for trial by a military court. Proceedings began on January 9, 1865. Sweet requested that the trials be held in Chicago, but he was overruled because Major Burnett, the prosecutor in Cincinnati, was more experienced.[37] Holding the trials in Cincinnati would have been illegal in the past, when removing defendants to a different jurisdiction had been prohibited by the Sixth Amendment to the dead Constitution.

Benjamin M. Anderson, another "conspirator" sent to trial at Sweet's suggestion, committed suicide in jail, which was taken as an admission of guilt. Anderson was a deserter from a Kentucky regiment that had been part of Morgan's command. Co-defendant Grenfell claimed that Anderson left the army in September of 1862, "since which time I have never heard from him or of him."[38] This was probably one of few truthful statements made during the proceedings.

General Sweet's pretense that Shanks was not his agent, and that Buckner Morris had helped him escape from Camp Douglas, was his most devious lie. Sweet disclosed the truth in a letter to Hoffman on March 29, 1865, in which he requested permission to give Shanks one year's pay from the prison fund at $100 per month. "John T. Shanks had been employed for more than a year as a clerk in the office of the Commissary of prisoners without pay," Sweet wrote, "being a prisoner of war and was a very careful, efficient clerk—In November last at the time of the rebel raid from Canada he was taken into my confidence, went into the City of Chicago, detected the presence and identified the presence of some of the officers and prisoners engaged in the Conspiracy, and performed faithfully a very important public service for which on my application he was afterward released."[39]

Sweet thought that to pay him "is no more than a fair compensation for the amount of labor he performed." There is no record of Hoffman approving the request. Shank's questionable testimony against Grenfell and other defendants was damaging.[40] Sweet's role in employing Shanks remained buried in army files, and later lay undetected in the National Archives. Hoffman made no move to expose him, and General Sweet was the main attraction when he testified in Cincinnati. The trials lasted until April 18, 1865 with some strange results.

George St. Leger Grenfell: An Englishman and former Confederate officer, he was known for his wasted life and tall tales. Grenfell complained to Sweet that he was a British subject and inquired anxiously about his dog.[41] He was sentenced to death. Influential people, including General Sweet, interceded for him. The General already had Anderson's death on his conscience. The affair was no longer a comic opera. Grenfell's sentence was commuted to life in prison at Fort Jefferson off the coast of Florida. This was another death sentence. On March 6 or 7, 1868, after three brutal years of imprisonment, Grenfell escaped into the ocean and perished.

Except for the tainted testimony of Sweet's agents there is no evidence that Grenfell played a role in the so-called conspiracy. Certainly he was aware of it; otherwise, why was he in Chicago on November 7? His story that he just happened to be passing through town is absurd. Most likely he hoped to be employed by the Confederates in attacking the camp, since he was known to many of Morgan's Raiders. The fact that he was not warned when the plotters fled shows that he was an outsider.

John T. Shanks, 14th Ky. Cavalry: A man of flawed character and a tainted past, his main task on November 7, 1864 was to entrap Grenfell. He performed exceedingly well as a witness for the prosecution, and parried cross-examination with cunning and perjury.

Colonel Vincent Marmaduke: His role, if any, is unknown. Acquitted.

Richard T. Semmes: Originally from Maryland, he had refused to serve in either army. His downfall was belonging to a Democratic club that was the alleged center of the plot.[42] He received three years in prison, but was later pardoned.

John Walsh: An army veteran of earlier wars, he supported the war at first, and ironically, helped to raise Mulligan's Irish Brigade. He became bitter when Lincoln issued the Emancipation Proclamation, and his strong feelings about Negro suffrage may have led him to purchase weapons and munitions for the Confederates.[43] The court ordered five years imprisonment, and he was also pardoned.

Buckner S. Morris and Mary E. Morris: He was born in Kentucky in 1800 and educated in the law. As a member of the Kentucky legislature he introduced unsuccessful bills in the 1830s to abolish slavery in that state. Mr. Morris later moved to Chicago, and became mayor from 1838 to 1839. In 1855 he was the first judge in Illinois to allow scientific evidence in a murder trial. He was twice a widower with two grown daughters when he married Mrs. Mary E. Parrish of Frankfort, Kentucky in 1856 in a May-December marriage. She was strongly pro-Southern and used the Morris home recklessly as a center of Confederate activity in Chicago.[44] The judge was acquitted.

Mrs. Mary Morris, circa 1875 (courtesy the Filson Club)

Mrs. Morris was charged as a conspirator, but not tried. She took full blame for aiding prisoners to escape, and the military court banished her to Kentucky. The couple never lived together again, and she became first lady for her brother, Dr. Luke P. Blackburn, in the governor's mansion in Kentucky. Dr. Blackburn was the center of an infamous "Yellow Fever Plot" against the North during the war. The diabolical plan was to gather "infected clothing" from yellow fever victims for shipment to Northern cities.[45] A Federal warrant was issued for him, and the fiendish doctor was arrested in Canada. Fortunately, the "infected clothing" was no more dangerous than the Camp Douglas Conspiracy, since the disease is carried by mosquitoes.

Judge Morris died in poverty on December 16, 1879. Mary Morris returned to Chicago for the first time since the war in order to attend the funeral, but was prevented by sub-zero weather.

Lawyers for the conspiracy defendants had argued that a military trial of civilians was unlawful under the former U.S. Constitution, which required a Grand Jury indictment before a citizen could be tried for a "capital, or otherwise infamous crime." In 1866, the again U. S. Supreme Court ruled that trial of civilians by the military was unlawful and vacated a military death sentence against an alleged Indiana copperhead. This decision should have freed Grenfell, but it did not.[46]

Captain Hines was staying at the Morris home when the arrests began "and was saved from the patrol by being placed between two mattresses on a bed while two ladies reposed in apparent sleep upon the upper mattress, with suitable bed clothes." Legend also placed him at Dr. Edwards' residence when Marmaduke was captured, this time under the mattress of Mrs. Edwards.[47] Hines was compensated with a seat on the Kentucky Court of Appeals after the war.

The 81 suspects at Camp Douglas spent four and five months there; the last releases were on April 19, 1865. Twelve of them died, most likely of smallpox. This brought the toll to 14 dead in the Conspiracy hoax, counting Grenfell and Anderson. Some may have been put on trial at Camp Douglas. The *Tribune* reported: "A court martial has been sitting for some weeks at camp, trying the leading cases; it has now been adjourned. The findings are not made public." If the report was true, then General Sweet violated the "Articles of War," which prohibited secret verdicts. None of the court martial findings were ever released. Unfortunately for these prisoners, President Lincoln had suspended the Writ of Habeas Corpus on September 24, 1862 for persons in military custody.[48] The Writ, embodied in Article I, Section 9 of the fallen Constitution, was a well-known order issued by a judge to deliver a person from illegal confinement. No civilian court could now question the "probable cause" for the arrests.

Ironically, President Lincoln did not credit the conspiracy story, for he protected two high-ranking plotters from prosecution. John Castleman was caught, but never tried because his sister, Virginia, was married to Judge Samuel M. Breckinridge of St. Louis. The judge was a fellow Kentuckian and on a first-name basis with the President. Lincoln was happy to oblige "Sam" and "Virginia" by interceding for Castleman. In the final hours of his life, before going to Ford's theater, Lincoln ordered the warrant for Jacob Thompson, the leading Confederate commissioner in the alleged plot, torn up so that he could leave the country.[49] Compare this to the treatment accorded the ill-fated Grenfell.

Sweet continued to employ John T. Shanks, and on April 6, 1865, he placed the 6th U. S. Volunteer Infantry Regiment in his charge to march it to another camp.[50] This unit consisted of Confederate prisoners at Camp Douglas. Whether intended or not, Sweet had sent an unpleasant message to the new regiment.

 Camp Douglas may have seen its largest insurrection had the Supreme Council not postponed its own plans. Mr. Otway B. Norvell, Council member, claimed that any object that could serve as a weapon was hidden away, and they were ready by mid-summer, 1864.[51] Simultaneous attacks were planned for 3 a.m. on the guardhouse to arm themselves, the parapet, and the fence. Once through the fence, they would seize the artillery outside.

A sudden attack by close to 2,000 men against only 800 disabled guards had some possibilities. This would have been the first mass attack ever made on the garrison. By November 8, it was too late. It is ironic that the "interior conspiracy" had a better theoretical chance of succeeding than the exterior one. On the other hand, the Council had made some serious miscalculations. It believed that the garrison was composed entirely of "perfectly raw troops," and their assumption that the artillery would not immediately fire into Prison Square was unwarranted. Finally, the danger of betrayal seems to have been overlooked, because Sweet told Fuller on October 7, 1864 about a plot on the part of 400 to 500 prisoners working in Garrison Square to seize arms and munitions.[52] The information must have come from a prisoner; otherwise, Sweet would have given credit to his detectives.

Believing in the Camp Douglas Conspiracy is a matter of faith. Confederate agents wished themselves into believing they had created one and General Sweet made their dreams come true. It was the nature and the character of men like Grenfell, Hines, Castleman, and Sweet that gave life to the hoax. It was logical that such compatible enemies cooperated to achieve the same goal. With the conspiracy fading by the end of November, the forces of nature moved in to fill its place. Soon another dreary winter lay over the camp. Sleet and snow swirled off the nearby lake, while daylight fled the city as though it were a plague. Darkness fell on the hearts of guards and prisoners alike.

NOTES TO CHAPTER 14

[1] Stephen Z. Starr, *Colonel Grenfell's Wars* (Baton Rouge: Louisiana State University Press, 1971); Frank L. Klement, *Dark Lanterns* "Secret Political Societies, Conspiracies, and Treason Trials in the Civil War" (Baton Rouge: Louisiana State University Press, 1984)

[2] Cole, "The Era of the Civil War," 300, 305, 307.

[3] The term "copperhead" was applied to various anti-war and pro-Confederate groups in the North such as the Order of American Knights, renamed Sons of Liberty, and Knights of the Golden Circle; Starr, 148.

[4] Peggy Robbins, "The Highest Ranking Scoundrel," *Civil War Times* (Nov.-Dec. 1992:56-57; Starr, 150.

[5] Starr, 155-56.

[6] Klement, 196.

[7] Starr, 156.

[8] Starr, 157.

[9] Starr, 155, 157-58.

[10] Starr, 159.

[11] John Walsh resided on Ellis Avenue, one block east of the camp. *Bailey's Chicago Directory*, 1864-65. A report received at camp on 6 May 1864 that a Mrs. Walsh who lived near Camp Douglas was aiding prisoners to escape by using her small daughter probably referred to this family. R. G. 393,v.237:186; Starr, 166.

[12] 39th Congress, 2d Session, House of Representatives, Ex. Doc. No. 50, *The Case of George St. Leger Grenfel* (Washington: U.S. Government Printing Office, 1867) 191.

[13] Starr, 173, 177.

[14] B. R. Froman, *Southern Bivouac* 1 (Oct. 1882):67.

[15] B. R. Froman, *Southern Bivouac,*68; Burke, 4 Aug. 1864. Mrs. Sarah B. Walker, a "Southern lady" in Chicago, was appointed agent by friends of the prisoners to distribute goods to them at Camp Douglas. Andreas, *History of Chicago*, II:303.

[16] R.G. 393, v. 234:454.

[17] Hines, 573.

[18] "The Northwestern Conspiracy," *Southern Bivouac*, New Series 2 (Jun. 1886-May, 1887), 508, 574.

[19] Hines, 574.

[20] O R Ser.I-Vol.39, Part 3:678.

[21] O R Ser.I-Vol.39, 3:678.

[22] *Seized on 7 November:*

> 142 shot guns, double-barreled, loaded.
>
> 349 revolvers.
>
> 13,412 cartridges.
>
> 3 boxes cones
>
> 265 bullet molds for pistols.
>
> 239 cone wrenches for pistols.
>
> 8 bags buck shot, No. 4.
>
> 2 kegs powder,partly filled.
>
> 115 holsters for revolvers.
>
> 8 belts for holsters.

Seized on 11 November:

> 47 shot guns, double-barreled.
>
> 30 Allen's breech-loading carbines.
>
> 1 Enfield rifle.

[23] O R Ser.I-Vol.39, 3:739.

[24] Report of Colonel Sweet. Tuttle, 27.

[25] Confederate Prisoners of War, Roll 53; Story, "Camp Douglas" thesis, 94

[26] John A. Marshall, *American Bastille: A History of the Illegal Arrests and Imprisonment of American Citizens during the Late Civil War* (New York: Da Capo Press, 1970) 98-101.

[27] O R Ser.I-Vol.39, Part 3:696.

[28] O R Ser.I-Vol.39, 3:696-697.

[29] O R Ser.I-Vol.39, 3:739; R.G. 393, V. 234.

[30] Part 3:762.

[31] Klement, 208. Semmes was a resident of Chicago; R. G. 323, v. 235:13.

[32] Tuttle, *History of Camp Douglas*, 31-33.

[33] *Chicago Tribune*, 11 Nov. 1864.

[34] Klement, 213, quoting Chicago Times of 20 Feb. 1865; R. G. 323, v. 235:7; Burke, 7 Nov. 1864.

[35] Klement, 196; 211; Star, 227.

[36] *Brevet Brigadier Generals in Blue*, 599; Tuttle, 28.

[37] R.G. 393, v. 235:53.

[38] Klement, *Dark Lanterns*, 207, 233; Story, 96.

[39] R.G. 393, v. 235:261.

[40] Starr, 225.

[41] R. G. 393, v. 240:117-18.

[42] Klement, 208.

[43] Klement, 196.

[44] Winslow, "Biographical Sketches of Chicagoans, Vol. 4, 1770-79. ms Chicago Public Library; A. T. Andreas, *History of Cook County* (Chicago: A. T. Andreas, Publisher, 1884) 256; Henry Raymond Hamilton, *The Epic of Chicago* (Chicago: Willett, Clark & Co., 1910) 293-94.

[45] Starr, 230; Nancy D. Baird, "The Yellow Fever Plot," *Civil War Times* 7 (Nov. 1974):16-18.

[46] *Ex Parte Milligan*, 4 Wall 2, 18 L. ED. 281 (1866). Lambdin B. Milligan was tried by court martial and condemned to death. The Supreme Court ruled that where civil courts are open a citizen cannot be tried by the military, and vacated the sentence.

[47] Froman, *Southern Bivouac*, 69; Story, *Camp Douglas*, 94.

[48] R. G. 109, Roll 53; *Chicago Tribune,* 4 Apr. 1865; Collected Works of Abraham Lincoln, v. V:437.

[49] *The Collected Works of Abraham Lincoln,* v. VIII:123; Peggy Robbins, "The Greatest Soundrel," 90.

[50] R.G. 323, v. 244:16.

[51] Otway B. Norvell, "Secret Order in Camp Douglas," *Confederate Veteran* 11 (Apr. 1903):168-71. Mr. Norvell was a member of the Council and confirms Froman's account of the interior conspiracy in every important respect.

[52] R. G. 393, v. 234:448.

15.

Social Life among the Prisoners

The turmoil in Chicago did not stop Briggs from writing an inspection report criticizing Morgan's men for lack of cleanliness. Otherwise, the camp was finally in excellent condition, he thought, and "the guards performed their duty well." Belatedly, the barracks had sufficient coal stoves with plenty of fuel, and the sick "have plenty of attendants, the hospital is well supplied with food necessary for the sick." However, smallpox patients were not doing well. Briggs suggested that the prisoners be allowed to receive from home "uncooked garden vegetables, such as onions, potatoes, cabbage, turnips, &c." The continuing retaliation scuttled this sensible idea. Clothing, bedding, and ticks could again be shipped from home, "but no articles the sutler sells."[1] Nightingale must truly have been Sweet's brother-in-law.

Hoffman's policy of providing vegetables only to the hospital caused tension among doctors at Camp Douglas. Hospital surgeons refused to discharge patients because of the scurvy in barracks. As a result, Prison Square was swamped with the sick who needed those hospital beds, and the surgeons in the square were pulling their hair out.[2]

Scurvy at Elmira Prison Camp was just as bad. Hoffman did not authorize fresh vegetables even for the hospital, and he rejected needed repairs on barracks. This explains why Elmira is considered worse than Camp Douglas. There were far fewer escapes there, but it had an appalling sick list. "In March 1865 an average of sixteen prisoners died daily. Out of the total of 12,123 soldiers imprisoned at Elmira, death claimed 2,063, nearly one out of six."[3]

The stockade in Prison Square was reinforced with more lumber in mid-November, and large reflector lights were installed at the end of each street. This was in addition to the lamps already there. The work on the fence was described as "an extra coat of plank." It was nailed "as high as a man can reach" on both sides of the fence. Conscripted prisoners had to carry planks, and were furious with the hired hands who did the carpentry "for hiring themselves to the Yanks to nail themselves and us up." Meanwhile, the water was shut off again to repair water pipes, and the men had to gather snow to brew tea or coffee. The supply of snow around the barracks was soon exhausted, and they had to brave the dead-line to gather it. Patrols fired at them, and one prisoner was severely wounded in the head.[4]

Three POWs from the Tennessee Infantry, all captured at the Battle of Frankin, Tennessee. Note the new uniforms and clothing, which may have been sent by General Beal (courtesy Mike Miner).

General Hoffman lost his Washington office on November 15, 1864, and was given supervision of lesser prisons west of the Mississippi River. The Washington office went to Brigadier-General H. W. Wessells as Commissary General of Prisoners for Prisons east of the Mississippi River.[5] The situation did not last long. Hoffman reoccupied his Washington office on February 1, 1865. Perhaps he had been ill or worn out.

His absence benefitted affluent prisoners at Camp Douglas, because the sutler was selling vegetables by November 22. This may have been authorized by General Wessells. However, Sweet did not buy vegetables for the indigent. He did try to force rebel cooks to use flour owned by prisoners for the general mess, but the cooks rebelled. Those who had flour used the coal stoves to bake their pancakes, while keeping a sharp lookout for the patrol. The efficient express office became a casualty, as inspectors now stole many articles from packages sent to prisoners.[6]

Colonel Sweet organized the Camp Douglas Fire Department on November 28, 1864.[7] It had one captain, one lieutenant, five sergeants, 10 corporals, and 135 privates. With five fire engines, it rivaled the Chicago Fire Department. There is no record of the prisoners ever setting a fire, although this probably happened accidentally from time to time. They were never deprived of matches for cooking and smoking materials, and there may have been an unspoken agreement that arson was not fair play.

Burke again objected to favoritism shown a group of prisoners, but these were not the paid workers who had always received special treatment. "The Reb free Masons (Master Masons and higher) have been rubbing their heads together and have succeeded in getting a barrack to themselves where they will have a lodge," Burke fretted. "It was obtained through the influence of Yankees who are free Masons and free Masons outside."[8]

They received barrack 49 for themselves. Pa was a Mason and his son visited him there. The privileges must have been substantial, because Pa gave up his stripes as Sergeant-Major in the 14th Kentucky to live in 49. Another eagle had fallen. Burke could not hide the hurt and disappointment he felt at Pa's desertion. A. W. Cockrell, a member of the Supreme Council of Seven and prosecutor in the prison trials, was also living in 49, and became president of the "Prisoners Masonic Association of Camp Douglas, Ill." The Yankee guard assigned there was also a Mason, and Burke observed with disapproval that "they all appear to be getting along as well as could be expected under the circumstances!"[9]

Briggs, whose duties brought him into barracks daily, requested more meat for the prisoners, and also bed sacks because they did not have enough blankets. Many had only one, "which will not keep them comfortable during the winter months."[10] He found the "quality and quantity of the food good," which was contradicted by prisoner accounts, and Briggs soon changed his mind about the rations.

Destitute prisoners from General John B. Hood's army, captured in the battle of Franklin, Tennessee arrived on December 5, 1864. The remaining Confederate forces under Hood were shattered in the battle of Nashville, on December 15 and 16, 1864, ending his invasion of Tennessee. These prisoners had to undress outside the gates to be searched after a freezing journey in box cars. The men stood for a long time in ice and snow while the guards robbed them of their valuables, according to John M. Copley.[11]

Copley saw the final arrangement of Prison Square. Its appearance had changed considerably during the past year. "There are fifteen rows of barracks with four to each row, and number from one to sixty," Copley noted. "Two hundred men are assigned to each barrack . . . Each barrack had a kitchen attached to one end . . . The main door or place of entrance to the barrack was near the center in one side." The interior was similar to earlier barracks, with "bunks from the floor to the roof, in tiers or rows above each other the entire circumfurence of the barrack, divided by narrow strips of plank."[12] The kitchen was partitioned off and had a square opening with a sliding panel for issuing rations. Prisoners called it the Crumb Hole. Copley likened it to a teller's window in a bank.

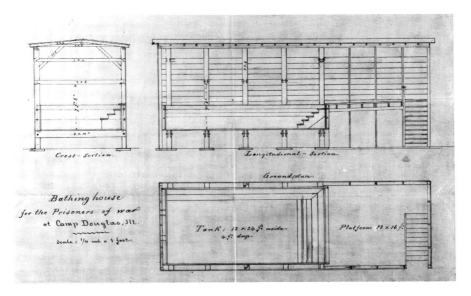

Bath and wash house, circa 1864. It could hold about 100 men at a time (courtesy National Archives).

The sinks were operating efficiently with the six-inch water pipes, according to Copley. Water was conducted to the prison from a reservoir at the lakefront. "A sewer conveyed the filth from the sinks to the outside of the prison walls, the water being conveyed by hydrants into the sewers to wash off the filth from the prison. Wash-houses were conveniently located on different parts of the prison grounds. These were supplied with hydrants, which conveyed the water to the inside, and also with tubs, buckets and soap, but minus towels."[13] Burke described it as a busy place.

"We found the house already very much crowded and about three inches of water all over the floor. The troughs that the tubs set in were full of tubs, so we sat our tub on the floor and got hot water from one of the eight large two-lb. boilers and went to work on our bag of duds. I counted a hundred tubs all in use. After we had given our clothes one rubbing we put them in one of the boilers and boiled them. By this time it was late in the evening. We had washed 29 pieces."[14]

Prisoners who failed to keep clean found themselves on trial before their peers, Copley recorded. "The sentence of the court, after the jury found him guilty as charged, would be that he be taken by the sheriff to the wash house, there stripped, and two men thoroughly scrub him with soap and rags, until the skin was red. One dose of this was sufficient; it never had to be repeated upon the same person. He was then compelled to wash his clothing. Scarcity of clothing shielded no one from the pains and penalties of the wash house. The accused had to pay the court costs, all of which could be settled up and paid with thirds of bread or chews of tobacco. If the party was too poor to pay the costs, the court would remit all except the penalty. All the property a man owned was on record in his own name, and not hid behind his wife; hence we all knew the exact amount of property owned by each man in the barrack."[15]

The alternative was to turn the accused over to the garrison for punishment, which the prisoners were reluctant to do. Many thefts involved food. In one case, the accused admitted stealing flour from a fellow prisoner and agreed to submit his punishment to "a fair trial."[16] A jury of 12 from his and other barracks was sworn in, witnesses were called, and a prosecutor and defense counsel argued for an hour each. "A large crowd was collected, but perfect silence was maintained, and things went on in the same manner as a regular court." A. W. Cockrell prosecuted the case and John Waller sat as judge. John Curd was sheriff, and William McConally represented the defendant.

The jury ordered one side of the defendant's head shaved, and his name, company, and regiment placed on the bulletin board as a thief. John Curd cut the man's hair short on one side. He submitted with dignity, and would leave Camp Douglas with more than one scar. In 1862, Kilpatrick had felt called-upon to carry out summary punishment by himself when Golden broke into the kitchen. That was no longer acceptable. Not all prisoners submitted willingly to the criminal justice system in the square. The following year, when two prisoners were convicted of stealing and selling a blanket, one of them threatened revenge against the "sheriff" who was about to whip him pursuant to the sentence of the court.[17] This caused the strap to be laid on even harder.

Camp Douglas had an established routine by the fall of 1864. The bulletin board near the gate in Prison Square carried many advertisements, notices, and news items. Perhaps the most important person in camp was the bugler. He entered the square twice a day to wake them at 6:30 a.m. and at 8 p.m. to retire them to bunks. The prisoners never saw him, and he was the subject of great curiosity.

Prisoners were notified when money was received for them at headquarters, and they could draw a purchase voucher for the sutler. Sending mail was a now serious problem for the prisoners because of the large population, and they had to stand in line all day to see the censor. The Yankee sergeant delivered incoming mail at roll call or it could be picked up at the sutler. There was also a "dead letter" office in the square. The postal service continued to be sacred, and no prisoner ever claimed that his mail was withheld or not sent as punishment for any offense, no matter how serious. Friday of each week was wash day, and inspection was at Sunday morning roll call. However, prisoners could wash on any other day they wished. Some went into the laundry business, charging two to five cents per garment. Apparently these entrepreneurs escaped the business tax at camp. Prisoners without a change of clothing had to wash shirts in the morning and pants in the afternoon.[18]

Garrison troops left camp regularly to patrol the city. They also camped outside the fence as they had under Colonel Tucker, and a door was built in the west fence of Prison Square for easy access. Guards on the fence stood 50 to 100 hundred feet apart and were relieved every two hours. While walking their beat at night they had to call out regularly to the officer of the guard so that he knew they were awake.[19] Guards were armed with a Springfield rifle, a bayonet, and a pistol.

Copley found that the prisoners formed "rings and cliques," when he arrived in December, 1864. He associated mostly with three comrades in his company. A major concern was protecting their few valuables from thieving guards, especially "Old Billy Hell." Bread still came from outside the prison. Sunday was a special meal because the prisoners could draw two ounces of bacon. Most of their tableware was improvised from tin cans and pieces of wood. The men ate twice a day. At 8:00 a.m. they had one-third of a loaf of bread and a small bit of meat boiled into "a dish rag" in the Farmer's boilers. Coffee was eliminated before Copley arrived, and cost one dollar per pound at the sulter. Dinner was at 1:00 p.m., consisting of bread and beef water or soup.[20]

Tobacco was as valuable as thirds of bread, or one-third of a loaf. It was craved as much as food, Copley wrote. "Camp Douglas was one place where no living prisoner was ever caught by any other prisoner taking a chew of tobacco." Smoking tobacco was 60 cents to $1.50 per pound at the sutler, and chewing tobacco an astronomical $3.00 per pound.[21] Those who could afford it often shared. An oyster can served as a cooking pot and sold for a third of bread or three chews of tobacco.

Some prisoners claimed that deaths from freezing occurred during the winter of 1864-65. P. H. Prince charged: "Often our fellow prisoners were found frozen dead in their bunks in the morning."[22] No one else claims that this happened "often," and Prince, writing 43 years later, did not say that he witnessed it. He became the only survivor of a group of 39 men from his Company sent to Camp Douglas on November 23, 1864. Twenty-three died within two weeks of smallpox and pneumonia, and 15 more perished before the surrender. Prince claimed that inadequate food and clothing caused the mortality. Three of his four brothers and 14 uncles and first cousins died in the war on the Confederate side.

Burke recorded that "A man froze to death in barrack 28 last night [December 8, 1864]." This carries more weight, although Burke did not live in barrack 28 and did not claim personal knowledge. Even Copley admitted that "during extreme cold weather the guards would detail two prisoners to each stove to keep the fires burning all night. This kept the barracks very comfortable and warm."[23] On the other hand, the guard in Burke's quarters threatened to shoot prisoners "if caught putting coal in the stove after taps." Treatment of the men varied from barrack to barrack depending upon the guard. However, Burke also wrote that during severe cold on December 8, 1864, "a man was allowed at each stove along with a bucket of water."

The truth about deaths from freezing cannot be established with certainty, but it is very likely that cold temperatures in barracks finished off sick prisoners who should have been in the hospital had there been room for them. That Chicago winter was devastating. In November, 1864, the death toll was 217, another 323 died in December, 308 in January, 1865, and 243 more answered the long roll in February.[24] This loss of 1,091 lives in only four months was the heaviest for any like period in the camp's history, and equaled the deaths at Andersonville from February to May, 1864.

The arctic weather led to additional suffering. "Another [punishment] was to make the men pull down their pants and sit, with nothing under them, on the snow and frozen ground. I have known men to be kept sitting until you could see their prints for some days afterward in the snow and ice. When they got weary of this, they commenced whipping, making the men lay on a barrel, and using their belts, which had a leaden clasp with sharp edge, the belt would often gather wind so as to turn the clasp edgeways; every lick inflicted thus cut entirely through the skin."[25]

A prisoner swore that when the men who were being punished this way attempted to sit on their coat tails they were "cruelly kicked in the back by the guards and forced to sit longer on the barebones." Prisoners were forced to stand in the snow for hours without moving, and guards checked footprints to see if any had moved. Copley wrote that those who did received 40 to 100 lashes, but this is exaggerated.[26] Some prisoners who arrived in the bitter cold weather lost toes, fingers, and ears. A former prisoner remembered well one poor fellow: "His feet had been frozen while in Camp Douglas, necessitating their amputation. He improvised two wooden pegs as substitutes for feet and hobbled around surprisingly well."[27]

Prisoners could not talk after 8 p.m. Conversation was a means of survival in a Civil War prison.[28] There is no information about when the rule went into effect or by whose order. Burke first mentioned it in July, 1864. Its purpose was to prevent escape plans from being hatched.

Punishment was harsh for breaking silence during these hours, Burke related. "When the men see a Yankee coming they give the alarm consisting of hist, hist, which can be heard on all sides." The patrols were maniacal in enforcing the rule, and it was a losing game for both sides. Everyone was threatened with punishment when the patrol heard someone talking. Burke recalled one incident when the guard "ordered all of us to get up but before we got our clothing on two of the guilty men owned up and we were ordered back to bed again, and the guard marched the men off to ride the wooden mule." All was still for a short time, but the men soon began talking again. "We saw the light of a large fire on the west side of camp in Chicago. The night was cool and rainy. I did not rest well."[29]

Harsh treatment also extended to relatives who came to visit. The lasting hostility of M. J. Bradley toward the North may have resulted from an incident in December, 1864. His wife, step-child, and the sister of a fellow prisoner arrived at Camp Douglas, but were not allowed in. Fortunately, a kindly clerk intervened, but the women were required to take the oath of allegiance, and the visit was limited to 20 minutes in the presence of guards and officers. "The following memorandum is attached to the oath demanded of my wife: —The above named Mollie J. Bradley, has blue eyes, auburn hair, is 26 years old, and is five feet four inches high."[30]

Prisoners came in steadily, amounting to 7,670 arrivals in 1864, with only 510 hospital beds available. A staggering 1,547 sick were in barracks. This averaged 25 patients in each building, and they were mostly dying of dysentery or diarrhea. Burke was critical of the Confederate doctors: "All of our Doctors deserve censure for their neglect of duty for some time past."[31]

The patrols in the square had absolute authority and General Sweet seldom entered. Copley did not object to the strict sanitary regulations, but claimed that prisoners were still hung by the thumbs. Specific guards were responsible for much of the brutality.

Copley named Red O'Hara as one of them. "He was a large man whose oily skin appeared to be infected with vermin." Little Red was another guard. "His eyes were of a steel-gray color, giving to his countenance a cold and hard expression; the mouth large and filled with a set of unsightly and disgusting teeth; it was a perfect harbinger of filth, the stench emitted therefrom when it opened, would permeate the atmosphere for a distance of several feet." Billy McDermott, known as Old Billy Hell, was also unforgettable. "Two small squint eyes which resembled those of a hog; his mouth large, but kept somewhat in the background by a pair of large, thick lips; a short neck, which appeared to be swallowed up by the shoulders; the knees were perfect strangers to each other." Prairie Bull [McCurley] was probably the most infamous of the four. "His hideous features, coupled with a demoniacal expression, revolted every living thing near him. He carried the expression of a demon wherever he went."[32]

Copley's anger had not cooled after 18 years as seen in his later account. "They were the unsightly, hideous, midnight ghouls in human shape, who prowled over the prison square after night to find some frivolous excuse to exercise their assumed authority. They were the ghastly and hungry hyenas digging into the prison barracks for little trivial violations of some foolish and insignificant rule of their own manufacture, and of which the prisoners knew nothing until marched out for punishment."[33] Copley's report is true, based upon what many other prisoners said.

Former prisoner J. W. Cook was also angry years after the war. "A Texas comrade in the April Veteran asks if any Camp Douglas prisoner remembers Prairie Bull and Billy Hell! My recollections of them are more vivid than pleasant. They were inside guards, but called themselves inspectors."[34]

Prairie Bull kept J. W. Cook on the mule one frigid night until he was frostbitten, and then threatened more punishment. "I backed off entirely out of reach of that dreaded club," Cook wrote. "Thousands of men will remember Bull, many of whom have answered the long roll, brought on by exposure just to satisfy his spleen."

P. H. Prince was almost killed by Bull because he left his barrack early for first chance at the wash house. "I heard the Prairie Bull, whose voice I knew well, swear at me an awful oath, and at the same time he shot at me, the ball passing through the top of the tub that my hand was on. I knew it meant death if I did not get away so I jumped to the door of Barrack 13, and he sent another ball at the door facing me, and then followed me with cursing."[35]

Prince hid in No. 13 and escaped. Prairie Bull, frustrated and enraged, drove 200 men outside without their clothes. "The snow was from one to two feet deep and the thermometer twenty below zero, and the wind blew as only it can blow off of Lake Michigan," Prince recalled. Many were marched off to ride the mule.[36] Prince gave no date for this episode, but his responsibility lends credence to the story.

Copley charged Prairie Bull with shooting a prisoner in his barrack who was sick and hardly able to walk, but had started for the hydrant at night. Copley often retold events that occurred before he arrived and which had become prison lore. M. Berry blamed the 1st Michigan Sharpshooters. "I remember when one of them shot a poor, sick Confederate who had gone out of his quarters and was scarcely able to stand alone." Prisoners going to the sink at night had to leave their clothing in the barracks or pay the fatal consequences. Prairie Bull supposedly killed another prisoner who accidentally tripped him as he was being beaten.[37] No dates were given for these alleged shootings, and there is no record of any investigations. Prisoners did not say whether these were eye-witness accounts or hearsay, but their bitterness suggests that these stories had some basis in fact.

Burke claimed that the most hated guard in the camp was not Prairie Bull but O'Hara. "He is always on the alert, watching for a chance to shoot somebody. I often hear it whispered through the ranks, 'lookout here comes Old Red.' He bayoneted several of the men, and we have no particular love for him." Burke was petrified when he spilled some water on the floor, and quickly dried it before he was punished.[38]

Simultaneously, R. T. Bean formed a warm relationship with a guard of almost 50 years of age, who had enlisted to avoid a mortgage foreclosure on his property. The guard's wife refused to make biscuits, which he loved, and at which Bean excelled. Soon Bean was furnishing the flour, which the sutler now sold illegally, and the guard brought the butter. They had many a good meal after that. The guard also made a chair for Mr. Bean, who became the only prisoner in the square to have one.[39]

O'Hara was jailed in Chicago for an unknown reason and was gone for five months in 1864. Then he was back at his old job. "On September 16, 1864 Old Red broke up religious meetings in barracks 13 and 25, and said that if he caught any more singing and praying in the barracks he would put them in irons. Some of the men saw Capt. Sponable about it, and he told them that the guard had no orders to break up such meetings, but that he left such things to the guards and if they chose to break them up he would not interfere."[40] This explains why the guards at Camp Douglas never had to account for their actions.

One prisoner charged that O'Hara shot and killed a prisoner in the 64th North Carolina for laughing when O'Hara slipped and fell on some ice. This may be true, because there were prisoners from this regiment at camp then. Paradoxically, Some Southern Unionists petitioned Washington to release the 64th as a pro-Union regiment.[41]

Another guard who did not endear himself to the prisoners was "Old Socks;" described as tall, raw-boned, long-legged, hump-shouldered, and green-looking. He earned his name while punishing two prisoners when he answered, "I'll sock ye!" to one man's plea for time to don his socks. The following month "Old Socks" was beating prisoners because they crowded around the stove on a cold December day. It was this type of pettiness that angered the men. A prisoner's precious food and container were destroyed for cooking on the barrack stove, and the prisoner was marched out for punishment.[42] This made the Confederates bitter against their fellows who switched sides or took the oath.

Copley's barrack was taken over to house these recruits. They usually came with two guards to retrieve their belongings and move to "Loyal Row." Sometimes it was necessary for the guards to draw and cock their pistols because of the outrage by former comrades.

The sutler had re-opened after the "barrel of sugar escape" and the theft of some money. He now employed two civilian clerks, and two "half-loyal rebel clerks," Burke laughed. The prisoners could cheat them because the clerks did not know the "high prices." Some prisoners went into business for themselves after being prohibited from soliciting orders for the sutler. They purchased supplies from him at a discount and peddled their wares in the barracks for Federal money, only.[43] It really was the old system, and Sweet put a stop to it.

General Sweet found that dealing with General Wessells, the new Commissary General of Prisoners, was easier than approaching Hoffman. The money was allowed without any bickering when Sweet requested permission to spend $1,028 on the smallpox hospital, for enlarging the building and enclosing it with a board fence.[44]

Reports of suffering by prisoners on both sides led to an astonishing incident of the war. The enemies agreed to furnish their own men in prison camps with clothing, blankets, and provisions.[45] Confederate General William Beall, a prisoner of war, was given a parole of honor by the North to bring Southern cotton to New York where he could sell it to raise the money needed by the South for its part of the deal. A notice to this effect was posted at Camp Douglas on December 12, 1864.[46] In keeping with the code of chivalry, Beall promised not to reveal to his government what he learned as he traveled in the North on business, and to return to prison when the pact ended.

The financial arrangements were unusual for warring nations. Sale of Confederate cotton in New York pumped Federal dollars into the Confederacy at a time when the Confederate dollar was collapsing. It meant jobs for Southern industrial workers, profits for agriculture, and generated hard cash for the Confederate war machine. Another irony was that many of the Southern providers used slave labor.

Prisoners were directed to establish committees at Camp Douglas and decide their needs. Barracks elected delegates who then selected four men to receive the supplies. The chairman of the group was A. W. Cockrell, who appeared to have found his calling at Camp Douglas. The promise of supplies, including food, came at an opportune time at Camp Douglas because the rations were several days behind, and according to rumor there would be another food reduction. There was no official intention to reduce rations. Briggs had complained to Sweet earlier that the meat allotment was insufficient for winter, and that one blanket per man was not enough. There was no explanation for the late rations.[47]

General Sweet's administration was as severe as ever. Guards on the fence and patrols on the ground fired at prisoners gathering snow near the dead-line because the hydrants were frozen. Nearly naked bodies of small-pox victims were being hauled out of barracks "like a dead horse or dog."[48] Copley's bunk-mate had smallpox for two weeks before he was removed. Miraculously, Copley never contracted any illness and attributed this to clean habits and the cold bath he took at the wash house every morning.

One night a prisoner bolted into the street toward the lights, shouting, "There's Jesus! I see his light!" He tore a lamp from the fence and ran with it shouting "Glory! Glory! I have got Jesus." A bullet smashed the lamp from his hand, but he was unharmed. The guards caught him at the gate and brought him back to his barrack. Red O'Hara punished prisoners who grumbled about the rations, and mail was restricted to five or six lines per letter. Postal service remained above the conflict, however. It made no difference when a Camp Douglas prisoner mistakenly directed a letter to Flag of Truce, New Orleans, on December 15, 1864. The efficient Federal Post Office sent the letter to the correct Flag of Truce at City Point, Virginia, rather than return it to the sender.[49]

The Camp Douglas Prisoners' Relief Committee working for General Beall issued its report to him on December 16, stating their needs. It had counted "163 1st Sgts., 508 Sgts., 406 Cpls., 32 Citizens, 9,107 Pvts., Total: 10,216." However, members were unaware that over 3,000 more prisoners were coming. The committee expressed an unwillingness to share the Confederate bounty with those who were openly deserters, those who took the oath, or who worked for the garrison. Naturally, Sweet would not allow this report to be sent. "The prisoners will determine what supplies to apply for, precisely as they are instructed, and in the same order make a table and sign the same!" Sweet ordered. "Dissertations on the duty of rebels to remain as such, and matters relating to other than such supplies will not be forwarded!"[50]

Briggs again notified Sweet on December 18 that bedding and food were insufficient for the winter weather. The situation worsened when prisoners arrived on December 23 from the fighting at Nashville, some so frostbitten that they had to be brought from the train by ambulance. A total of 3,341 prisoners arrived late in December, 1864, raising the prison population to its highest point ever: 12,082. This caused the doctors to vaccinate regularly in barracks. Those who wished to renew their smallpox vaccination could do so. So many new prisoners were ill that fires were allowed all day in barracks due to the lack of hospital space. Coal boxes at the barracks were too small, and the work hands built a coal house 25 feet wide by 50 feet long on the east side of the square.[51]

Burke had problems because funds did not arrive for his Christmas dinner, but he was able to borrow generously. The new prisoners overflowed his barrack, with three men crowded into a bunk made for two. This must have caused a good deal of tension. Burke described how "All of the bottom bunks and some of the middle and top bunks had to double up three to the bunk." The new prisoners had a good deal of "new issue" Confederate currency worth one cent Federal, and a prisoner exchange was not forthcoming. Naturally, the new prisoners were promptly named the "New Issue," and they chased the blues by singing "The Girl I Left Behind Me." Two more favorites were "Massa's in the Cold Cold Ground," and "Old Uncle Ned."[52]

Burke cooked a magnificent meal for Pa and friends on Christmas Day, with many ingredients purchased illegally at the army sutler.[53] This must have put a dent in his bank account, with flour at $20 per barrel and butter 80 cents per pound. Men were still cooking on the coal stoves in spite of severe punishments. The one who made the fire in the morning had first go at cooking his breakfast on it.

Briggs issued his last report on Christmas Day, 1864. As usual there were many sick in barracks, but smallpox was steadily decreasing. He was concerned about new arrivals. "The prisoners received during the last week are poorly clad; many of them are nearly barefoot and destitute of blankets," Briggs complained.[54] His reports would be published in the "Official Records of the War of the Rebellion," and studied long after he had disappeared into history. They undoubtedly had some effect, and resulted in constant improvement of conditions. Briggs spoke up conscientiously for the prisoners. This was more remarkable, since his reputation was no doubt "sullied" by the mass tunnel escape in December, 1863, while he was captain of the guard that night.

A Federal inspection was scheduled for the last day of the year. The sutler removed illegal items from his shelves, and the guard called "Smiler" made the men straighten up their quarters. Smiler had earned the name by his murderous nature. Ticks were folded back on the bunks, and blankets folded "nicely on top of the ticks." Anything hanging up was taken down and folded into the bunks. Utensils "such as tin stew pots, plates, cups, etc.

had to be scoured anew and taken to the kitchen." The barrack detail went to work and cleaned thoroughly. They said goodby to 1864, "Long to be remembered by the prisoners now at Camp Douglas."[55]

The year was probably most remembered for its shortage of food, the cruelty of the guards, and rampant disease. Surprisingly, the number of illnesses suffered by the prisoners was about the same that they experienced serving in the army.[56] However, their fatality rate at Camp Douglas was 10% higher. This was attributed to depression, monotony, the savage winters, inadequate clothing, and lack of hospital space. The new hospital received high praise in medical reports for 1864, while doctors criticized the presence of scurvy. Major improvements in 1864 were six-inch water lines and the introduction of the wash house.

About 2,235 prisoners had lost their lives since the prison opened according to the Official Records. This may be 967 short of the true figure at the time, based on *Tribune* reports. Persistent inspections by the various bureaus, doctors, and Lieutenant Briggs had resulted in repairs to barracks and better medical care. Regardless, food, bedding, clothing, and hospital space could not keep up with the collapsing Confederacy. Forty-one prisoners had escaped since Sweet's reorganization of the square in June, a significant number. Seventeen of these occurred in October, 1864, so it is likely that more prisoners escaped in the incident of October 28 than was revealed.

Improvements to Prison Square in 1864 were reputed to be $61,000 and $80,000 more for new buildings, which is questionable. On September 17, 1864, Hoffman had complained about the estimate of $600 per new barrack, including a kitchen.[57] Two prison camps could have been built for $141,000, with enough money remaining to supply sewers and water for downtown Chicago. Either the figures were wrong or contractors were reaping a windfall. One historian claimed that "the daily expenses of camp, aside from the officers' and soldiers' pay were $8,540." At the end of February, 1862, the expense had been $2,000 per day. The prison population was triple the size in 1864, so the figure of $8,540 may be accurate when inflation is added.

The prisoner's chapel was torn down in 1864, and the lumber was used to repair barracks. Later it was discovered that the chapel was exempt from appropriation. This led Reverend Tuttle to campaign for construction of a new chapel that held 600 people. Prisoners built it with money from the prison fund. The government contributed the value of the lumber it had used. Hoffman objected to this reimbursement.[58]

General Sweet experienced some of Colonel Tucker's troubles at the end of 1864, when "a small number of vicious men" created disciplinary problems on the street cars and in town. Some soldiers from the garrison broke into the Chicago Driving Park to commit vandalism. Few cases of bribery occurred at this time, although one guard sold civilian clothing to three prisoners who had used a ladder to get away on Christmas Day, 1864. They stayed at the luxurious Sherman House in Chicago. Dogs were running loose in camp somehow, and Sweet threatened to shoot them.[59]

In spite of the brutality and hardship there was a well-developed social life among the prisoners by the end of 1864, including arts, crafts, entertainment, and gambling. Card playing was as prevalent as religion. Reverend Tuttle claimed that "there were many stabbings among those who were continually gambling."[60] Copley described how some prisoners gambled their rations and became "mere skeletons and living shadows."

One gambler had set up a faro table in 1862 and amassed a fortune of $150,000 in Confederate currency, worth about $10,000 in Federal money at the time. The game of checkers was a favorite time-killer as well. Flying kites was popular, also jumping, foot races, ball games, and playing marbles. The garrison enjoyed watching the kites soar away, not knowing that the sly prisoners were posting letters out of camp. The ruse was soon discovered when none of the kites returned.[61] A heavy snowfall was the signal for day-long warfare.

Morgan's men began publishing a hand-written newspaper on March 21, 1864 called the "Prisoner Vidette." A copy has survived. Lappens' factory advertised "Pipes, Pipes, Pipes, by the wholesale and retail, Block 17, three doors west of the south east corner. Give him a call you [will] not be other than satisfied." Another ad read: "Soldiers Friend. Boyd's Plus Ointment' The cry rings throughout the land, Peace, Peace, Boyd's Pills, No Humbug." The paper reported that John Curd was preparing a variety show with trick animals.[62] Like A. W. Cockrell, Curd had found his niche at Camp Douglas.

While mail was censored, this paper apparently was not. An unsigned editorial made a strong statement on the issue of loyalty: "Because we have declined to publish articles discussing the different questions of the day, we would not have our readers infer that we are loyal. The word loyal expresses nothing the citizen of Dixie owes to his country; it is a damning proof of tyranny, conceit and presuming impudence; and those who use the word, in the affairs of our government, never shall have my confidence as long as our Republican form of government is not proved a fallacy, in theory and in practice."

The writer apparently felt that patriotism was a matter of choice, not duty, and he was not too keen on democracy, either. The *Vidette* was first published by Morgan's command in Tennessee on August 15, 1862, and then

then continued as a journal in various prisons such as Fort Delaware and Camp Douglas. Printed editions of the *Vidette* are considered the most interesting of the Confederate soldier newspapers.[63]

Many prisoners were fine craftsmen. John F. Clarer of the 2nd Kentucky Cavalry was a silversmith with his own room fitted up as a workshop. He produced rings, breast pins, and hat ornaments inlaid with gold, silver, and pearl. There were about 30 ring-makers in camp. These sold from 50 cents to $10. Mechanics of all kinds manufactured furniture, buggies for the officers, and one buggy for Reverend Tuttle.[64]

Burke developed a passion for writing and disliked being interrupted. He also became known in camp as a fine chef. A literary club existed, and books were available through Reverend Tuttle, who still thought that, except for some of Morgan's men, "there are as many men at Camp Douglas who cannot read nor write as there are in the whole State of Illinois."[65]

Many barracks had a story-teller or humorist. The most memorable of these was a ventriloquist, famous since the beginning of the war. He had seen much action with the 42nd Tennessee Infantry and was called "Pig" because of his small size. At Camp Douglas, guards heard chickens squalling in their pockets and under their caps in the winter of 1864.[66] They forced Pig to stop, and he suddenly disappeared. He had taken the oath.

Most barracks were infested with rumor-mongers who whipped up false hopes and anxieties. The most cruel rumor was that 10 prisoners would be shot for the alleged shooting of Union prisoners in the South. Practical jokers were also running loose without a collar and sometimes went too far. As a prisoner prepared to escape through a tunnel, one joker wrote the word "Secesh" on the back of his jacket with chalk or soap.[67]

Each barrack also had a "reader" who was selected to read aloud from banned newspapers. The main qualification, besides reading skills, was a loud clear voice. Pickets were placed outside to watch for patrols, while readers reported what the prisoners wished to hear.[68]

Captured musicians kept their instruments under the code of chivalry. They gave concerts, and soloists or quartets often played in the barracks. Burke described how "A reb string band consisting of two violins, two guitars, and a flute in the next room furnished good music from dark till bed time." The men danced with each other and paid for the music with thirds of bread or a chew of tobacco.[69] The "ladies" wore hats, and Copley said there was no fear of being "churched" for dancing.

Theater was in great demand as when black prisoners planned to stage a minstrel show in barracks, and 400 patrons tried to enter. Their manager was John Curd. Admission was 15 cents Federal or three dollars Confederate, but patrols closed the show because of overcrowding. They could have earned perhaps $30 in Federal money, almost three months' pay for a Yankee soldier. In addition, the Confederate dollars were good for postage or in case of exchange. The troupe did stage the show in Burke's kitchen the following week; admission was 25 cents in sutler's checks. Another diversion was going to Garrison Square in the morning and watching the guard mount at nine o'clock. It was a colorful spectacle preceding the relief of the guards on duty. There was much saluting, barking of orders, dressing the lines, and exercise in the manual of arms, all of which the prisoners observed with a critical eye.[70]

The science of photography fascinated the men, and having a picture taken and sent home was their main contact with loved ones. Daniel F. Brandon, the camp photographer, was probably closer to the prisoners than any other Northerner at camp except the doctors, perhaps. After the prisoners were confined to Prison Square he moved his studio in with them, but was ordered out by Hoffman. Brandon had started a photo studio opposite the camp when it opened in 1861, and was operating a second one in Garrison Square by 1862. He came to Chicago from Pennsylvania before the war, and was married with one or two small children.[71]

The best monotony-breaker at camp was to watch a female visitor come through the camp or to look at one on the fence. There was intense excitement on April 10, 1864, when two women escorted by an officer walked though the square. One of them kissed a prisoner to everyone's great delight, except possibly the officer's. The prisoners responded by clearing her path with the battle cry known to both armies: "Give way to the right and left—let the artillery pass!" A woman standing on the parapet took a liking to a prisoner named Derbis and sent him a basket of provisions and a bouquet. The monotony of prison life cannot be discounted, however. A guard sympathized with the prisoners "in their weary moving about, simply killing time."[72]

Other visitors were also welcome diversions. Twelve Indian chiefs stopped in on their way to Washington. They were "tall and portly and dressed out and out in full Indian costume," according to Copley. General Joseph Hooker visited the square by dashing in on horseback with a fine escort and dashing out again. The prisoners had expected a speech and were disappointed. Governors Morton of Indiana and Ogelsby of Illinois came in a fine carriage after the surrender. Morton spoke to the prisoners about having them released and restored to their citizenship. They were deeply moved, and would have voted for him to be President.[73]

However, the prisoners did not enjoy the insensitive gapers who climbed to the observatory on the east side of Cottage Grove to stare at them. A businessman built it for this purpose. The tower was next to the

Cottage Grove Hotel, which was diagonally across from the camp at 31st Street, one block north of the camp gate. Many drawings of the camp were done from this vantage point. M. J. Bradley reflected the disgust felt by the prisoners: "They could look down on and inspect us as objects of curiosity, as they would wild beasts in a menagerie. And I suppose it was well, for some of the visitors who crowded that platform had never in all their lives seen a gentleman, and the sight was one well worth the money."[74]

Summertime was especially irritating, when a Sunday outing was to take the horse cars to the observatory. "Because of these never-failing Sunday crowds" summer gardens opened in the area to serve the public. The trip from downtown took an hour. This morbid curiosity caused a similar tower to be built at Elmira. There the entrance fee was 15 cents. In Chicago it was 10 cents. Life as a prisoner of war was degrading, and these towers added their own heartache. The tower at Elmira was a wooden, free-standing structure, and stood about 25 feet tall and 10 feet wide, with a lower and upper deck enclosed by railings. The Camp Douglas tower was also described as 25 feet high.[75]

Federal inspectors failed to arrive on New Year's Day, 1865, and Burke cooked another magnificent dinner for his friends and Pa. His casualness is astounding in the midst of so much death and suffering. One explanation is the financial security he enjoyed due to the money sent by his Yankee relatives in Ohio. He would be 23 years of age in three weeks.

The new year opened in Camp Douglas fashion: "At dusk a new prisoner was shot in the mouth for going under his barrack (No. 30) to the sick men's tub. The detail had failed to set the tub out in the street when the retiring bugle sounded, and the prisoner not knowing that he was liable to be shot for going under the barrack after dark. This is a bad beginning for the first night of a new year."[76]

NOTES TO CHAPTER 15

[1] O R Ser.II-Vol.VII, 1104-05; Burke, 10 Nov. 1864.

[2] O R Ser.II-Vol.VII, 1104-05.

[3] O R Ser.II-Vol.VII, 1134-36; E. B; Long, Camp Douglas: "A Hellish Den," 94.

[4] Burke, 9-20 Nov. 1864.

[5] O R Ser.II-Vol.VII, 1117. General Wessells is noted for the loss of Plymouth, North Carolina to the Confederates on 18 April 1864, including the capture of his entire garrison. *Battles and Leaders of the Civil War* 4:107.

[6] Burke, 21, 22 Nov. 1864.

[7] Kelly, 107.

[8] Burke, 24 Nov. 1864.

[9] Burke, 30 Nov. 1864.

[10] O R Ser.II-Vol.VII, 1177-78.

[11] *Battles and Leaders of the Civil War* IV: 440-64; John M. Copley, *A Sketch of the Battle of Franklin, Tennessee, with Reminiscences of Camp Douglas* (Austin: E. Von Boeckman, 1893) 76-77. Copley was only fifteen years old when he enlisted in Co. B, 49th Tennessee Infantry in 1861, but was absent at Fort Donelson due to illness; otherwise this would have been his second visit to Camp Douglas.

[12] Copley, 88.

[13] Copley, 88. The sewer lines ran from north to south at the east end of Prison Square.

[14] Burke. 6 Dec. 1864.

[15] Copley, 160-61.

[16] Burke, 29 Nov. 1864.

[17] Burke, 1 Feb. 1865.

[18] Copley, 159-60.

[19] Copley, 98-99.

[20] Burke, 3 Jan. 1865; Copley, 120-28.

[21] Burke, 3 Jan. 1865.

[22] P. H. Prince, "Hardship in Camp Douglas," *Confederate Veteran* 15 (Dec. 1907) : 565-66. He arrived on 23 Nov. 1864.

[23] Copley, 144.

[24] O R Ser.II-Vol.VII, 986-1003.

[25] T. D. Henry, *Southern Historical Society Papers* I:278.

[26] Sergeant. T.B. Clore in Cornelius Hite's, "Man's Inhumanity to Man" *Confederate Veteran* 32 (Jun. 1924): 218; Copley, 135.

[27] J. A. Templeton, "Prison Reminiscences," *Confederate Veteran* 34 (May, 1926): 196-97. Mr. Templeton was a prisoner from 4 October 1863 to 4 May 1865, and was in the dungeon once for attempting to dig a tunnel.

[28] Sorenson, The Civil War Prisoners of War System, 33.

[29] Burke, 31 Oct., 3 Nov. 1864. Burke saw the flames from a glue factory fire in Bridgeport, twelve blocks west of camp.

[30] Griffen Frost's Camp and Prison Journal, 278.

[31] Medical and Surgical History, 49; Burke, 26 Jul. 1864.

[32] Copley, 109. Prairie Bull was also known as Bull McCurley; J. W. Cook, "Villainous Inspectors at Camp Douglas." *Confederate Veteran* 16 (Aug. 1908):406.

[33] Copley, 103-10.

[34] *Confederate Veteran* 16:406.

[35] Prince, *Confederate Veteran* 15:565. He was one of four brothers, three of whom were killed in Confederate service, and was the sole survivor of forty men in his unit sent to Camp Douglas on 23 November 1864. He blames the deaths on smallpox, pneumonia and lack of warm clothing.

[36] Prince, 565.

[37] J. M. Berry, *Confederate Veteran* 11:37-38. The 1st Michigan left camp in March 1864; J. W. Cook, *Confederate Veteran,* 16:406.

[38] Burke, 3 Apr.; 3 Dec. 1864.

[39] R. T. Bean, *Confederate Veteran* 22:310.

[40] Burke, 16 Sept. 1864.

[41] R. T. Bean, "Seventeen Months in Camp Douglas," *Confederate Veteran* 22 (July, 1914): 310; O R Ser.III-Vol.IV, 1037.

[42] Burke, 9 Dec. 1864; Copley, 143.

[43] Burke, 22 Nov., 8 Dec. 1864.

[44] O R Ser.II-Vol.VII, 1257.

[45] O R Ser.II-Vol.VII, 1199-1200.

[46] O R Ser.II-Vol.VII, 1207; Burke, 12 Dec. 1864; *Hesseltine,* 208.

[47] Also on the committee were Joseph D. Hunt, Thomas J. and Chambers, W. T. Brantly; O R Ser.II-Vol.VII, 1187-88.

[48] Burke, 16 Dec. 1864.

[49] Burke, 15 Dec. 1864; Karlen, 930.

[50] Burke, 19 Dec. 1864.

[51] Burke, 23, 26 Dec. 1864.

[52] Burke, 8, 23 Dec. 1864.

[53] *Burke's "Bill of Fare," Christmas, 1864.*

> *Boiled Beef*
> *Biscuit with short[en]ing Molasses*
> *Tea, sugar, Chip beef*
> *Potatoes , butter, Cheese*
> *Soft Bread, Salt, pepper & vinegar*
> *Delicacies*
> *Prune Pie Tarts*
> *Apple , Ginger cake*
> *Onion, Spice*
> *Potato, Apples*
> *Vinegar*

[54] O R Ser.II-Vol.VII, 1275.

[55] Burke, 31 Dec. 1864.

[56] The Medical and Surgical History of the War of the Rebellion, vol. I, Part III:45.

[57] Andreas, *History of Chicago*, 2:303; O R Ser.II-Vol.VII, 834-35.

[58] R. G. 393, NA; Camp Douglas Letter Book, 282, 462, CHS; R. G. 92.

[59] R. G. 393, v. 244:134; R. D. Rugeley, "Escape from Camp Douglas," *Confederate Veteran* 9 (Jan. 1901):30; R.G. 393, v. 244:128.

[60] Tuttle, *History of Camp Douglas*, 16.

[61] Ill. Adj. General's Report, 1:127; "Dear Emma." John L. Williams to his niece, 18 July 1862, LOC ms. Division; *Chicago Tribune*, 7 Mar. 1864.

[62] Chicago Public Library, Special Collections.

[63] Bell I. Wiley, "Soldier Newspapers of the Civil War," *Civil War Times* 4 (Jul. 1977):27.

[64] Burke, 28 Mar. 1864; Tuttle, *History of Camp Douglas*, 17.

[65] Tuttle, 8.

[66] Copley, 180.

[67] Burke, 9 Jan., 27 Mar. 1864.

[68] Burke, 2 Feb. 1865.

[69] Burke, 21 Apr. 1864; Copley, 172-73.

[70] Burke, 5 Oct. 1863; Currey, *Chicago: Its History and Its Builders*, I:135.

[71] R. G. 393, v. 234:362; Halpin & Bailey's Chicago City Directory, 1862-63; Census, 1870.

[72] Burke, 10 Apr. 1864; Currey, 2:135.

[73] Copley, 184.

[74] M. J. Bradley, Frost's *Camp and Prison Journal*, 276.

[75] Frederick Francis Cook, *Bygone Days in Chicago* (Chicago: A. C. McClurg & Co., 1910) 38-39; John Kaufhold, "The Elmira Observatory," *Civil War Times* 4 (Jul. 1977):31, 33; J. T. Lowry, "Experience as a Prisoner of War."

[76] Burke, 1 Jan. 1865.

16.

WINDING DOWN THE WAR

Camp Douglas was well organized in terms of security by 1865. However, Captain Shurly reported to General Sweet on January 8 that "the quantity of food is barely sufficient to sustain life in the Chicago climate."[1] Shurly urged an increase in rations, and recommended removing restrictions on sale of vegetables by the sutler. "This would save the government money spent on medicines," he pointed out. Like other inspectors, he was critical of the Farmer's boilers. Hoffman was the only person who insisted on them. The dead-line was moved farther into the square, and prisoners could no longer stroll between it and the barracks on pain of being shot.[2] They were now restricted to the streets between the barracks.

M. J. Bradley recalled an incident that still disturbed his sleep. "A man who had just come into the prison, being very thirsty, and the water having been shut off from us, as had frequently been the case, seeing some snow lying near the fence, on the ground, attempted to pick up some and eat it, when he was shot by the guard without any warning whatever, and he fell near that infernal dead-line."[3] Many prisoners, including Burke, confirm that this was a frequent occurrence.

Sergeant T. B. Clore wrote: "These brutal guards would in the dead hours of the night, while walking around the prison, deliberately fire at random into the barracks, where the men were sleeping, just out of pure devilment. So common did this become that many built defenses against these midnight assaults."[4]

J. S. Rosamond confirmed the story. "Many a minnie ball went crashing through our barracks at night at some real or imaginary noise. It was dangerous even to indulge in a snore."[5]

A spent bullet struck Copley in his bunk, and he claimed that guards opened fire if more than two prisoners congregated on the street. He overstated the situation. There was no limit to numbers in a group until February 11, 1865. After that, the prisoners could gather in groups of not more than five.[6] The idea was to prevent a concentrated attack on the fence.

Writing 63 years later, a former prisoner claimed that his cousin was shot in the back while entering a barrack one day, and the guard was promoted. Guards were usually promoted only for shooting escapees, but there may be something to the story. The records show that his cousin, John P. Hutchings, 3rd Kentucky Cavalry, died at camp on October 7, 1863. The following year Burke reported that "Lt. Proseus fired at a man who was standing in the door of his barrack, but missed him."[7] There were two investigations into shootings by guards from the 8th and 15th V.R.C.

On January 12, 1865, Sweet ordered a commission of garrison officers to probe an incident that had occurred on January 7. The commission learned that Private David Tolman, 15th V.R.C., fired at a prisoner who stepped across the dead-line. His ball passed into Ward H [Barrack 41] in Prison Square and wounded two patients. They concluded that Tolman fired too high because of his position on the fence, "but would recommend that the sentinels be instructed to carefully fire low under such circumstances, so as not to injure others who are innocent of any offense." What offense? The guard had fired when a patient crossed the dead-line to retrieve clothing blown from a window in Ward H.[8]

"Smiler" Redmond, the guard in Burke's quarters, committed an equally atrocious crime the next day, January 13. Prisoners were supposed to use the sink assigned to their barrack. For some reason a prisoner was walking towards the wrong sink, and Smiler shot him. The bullet shattered the man's right ankle and lodged in his left foot.[9] There is no record of any inquiry, as Stanton had ordered, although Smiler probably would have been commended, anyway.

Only two days later, the patrol was savagely beating and kicking a prisoner for allegedly taking bones from the garbage barrel. When the prisoner grabbed the foot of one Yank in self-defense, another shot him in the side. The victim was not taken to the hospital. "He was visited by Captain Hastings [Joshua H. Hastings, Co. B, 15th V.R.C] who consoled him by telling him that if his wound did not kill him he would, for he must behave as a prisoner of war and not strike at his men."[10] Meanwhile, the hatred of their fellow prisoners had its effect on the hired hands. A fight exploded in their barracks on January 17, with nine men suffering wounds from knives and other weapons. Several wounds were serious.[11]

Burke had a serious matter to contend with when a total of $15, worth about $1,500 Confederate, was missing from his bank account at headquarters. He saw Captain W. H. Bushell, who had been in charge of prisoners' funds since Colonel Mulligan left, and "thru whose hands all money letters pass after they are examined." Reverend Tuttle claimed that Bushell "has been faithful to the last degree," which showed that Tuttle did not know what was going on under the surface. Burke received no satisfaction from the "faithful" Bushell.[12]

Captain Sponable reported that he had sufficient clothing and bedding for the prisoners, except Hood's men.[13] "Water—a great plenty; same as used in the City of Chicago." The shocking part of this report is that 125 prisoners had died in the past two weeks. About 11,699 prisoners were present at this time, and barracks must have been jammed with the sick.

A large requisition of clothing and blankets was approved by Sweet on January 13, 1865.[14] He called for 8,000 blankets, 2,000 coats or jackets, 3,000 pairs of trousers, 5,000 shirts, 10,000 drawers, 12,000 pairs of stockings, and 3,000 pairs of shoes. This was besides the clothing and blankets received through General Beall.

Union forces captured Fort Fisher, the main importing depot of the Confederacy, on January 15, making it difficult for the South to sustain its troops. Another commission met at Camp Douglas on January 24 to investigate a shooting on the night of January 20. Private Newell Sanford shot William A. Chance, Company A, 33rd Alabama, "who was at the time committing a nuisance (urinating) in a street of said square."[15] Private Sanford was exonerated. Chance died of his wound and is buried in Chicago.

Prisoners could again take the oath, or the "dog" as some called it. Burke and his friends would yell "another state's gone out!" and sing Yankee Doodle. The oath-takers were moved to another part of the camp, probably White Oak Square. On January 29, Sponable reported the death of 85 more prisoners. The situation was approaching that of 1863, when charges of extermination were leveled by Northern doctors. Yet the camp was in the best condition it would ever be in, with sufficient blankets and clothing for the prisoners. The death rate was a steady 8% of the prison population. With almost eight prisoners dying each day, there would be another 1,000 dead before long. It came close to that in the end. Ironically, Sponable claimed that "General health of prisoners—good."[16]

Fortunately for the prisoners, the Cartel was restarting, and a general exchange was to commence on February 1, 1865. Shurly reported an immense saving of $2,969.75 by reducing the bread ration for December, 1864.[17] Burke cooked another lavish dinner on January 24 to celebrate his 23rd birthday. He used a pound of butter and a pound of sugar to make dumplings, boiled beef, bean soup, bread, and delicacies such as vinegar pie. At the same time he noted that "there are a great many who wash clothes for something to eat." He had leftover bread from his dinner to pay for washing, and made a good hash on the coal stove while Henry White stood watch for patrols. Chicago's winter kept the extra rations well refrigerated.

By the end January, 1865, Prison Square contained 64 barracks, but four were used for convalescents. They were 90 feet long by 24 feet wide, and 12 feet to the rafters. The kitchen was 20 feet by 24 feet, and the sleeping dormitory 70 feet by 24 feet.[18] The additional barracks may have

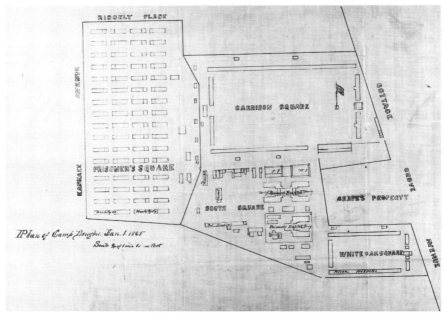

Plan of camp, January 1, 1865. Prison Square is filled. Note the hospitals and chapel in South Square and another hospital on the south side of White Oak Square (courtesy the National Archives).

eased overcrowding, as the medical inspector at this time found only 165 men in "several barracks," which was normal capacity.

Cruelty became worse as the war staggered on. The guards invented a new game called the "circus," and forced prisoners to climb onto barrack rafters and perform tricks. A prisoner was punished this way on January 30, 1865 for sitting by the stove after midnight and smoking. Another was caught spitting on the floor and was made to replace the first one. "Soon after all had quieted down a prisoner in the barrack by the name of [omitted by author], an Alabamian was caught stealing bread from the kitchen which caused a little disturbance."[19] He received 22 lashes with a strap while laid across a barrel with his pants down, "making him beg considerably."

Guards went on a drunken rampage on January 31 in the worst incident ever recorded by Burke. "Some 200 men in barrack No. 5 were driven into the cold night and made to stand on one foot. Several were hung from the second bunk by their feet, and in this position they were whipped with belts by the guards just as a negro would be whipped or worse. All of the men in one whole barrack was made to stand out awhile and then bare themselves and sit on the snow and ice till they melted through to the ground. There were 10 or 12 men whipped altogether in the same manner as those in number 5."[20]

Finally the guards came across one husky prisoner who refused to be whipped and "said he would die defending himself." The guards debated whether to kill him or call off the party. They decided to turn in. Adding to the misery was the overcrowding again, with 200 men in barrack No. 5 alone.

A prisoners' committee informed the authorities about the brutality. No reply was made, and some thought of attacking the fence. This incident caused about 40 or 50 men to take the oath against their conscience in the hope of leaving. The war continued unabated at Camp Douglas. "There has been seven men shot for various trivial offenses this month," Burke noted. The respected U. S. Sanitary Commission confirmed the harsh treatment.[21]

The guards dreamed up a new game which was sure to cause more tension. There were four spit boxes in each barrack. When the patrol caught a man missing the box he had to clean it until he caught someone else spitting on the floor. If that person refused to take his turn at the box, then the first man either reported him to the patrol or continued to clean it. Neither option was pleasant. The last man on the box had to take up his position next to it every morning at roll call.[22]

Only 162 prisoners were released in January. It is likely that these were the sick finally being exchanged under General Butler's plan. This left 11,711 prisoners as the collapse of the Confederacy became imminent. By now the prisoners had given up hope of receiving anything from General Beall, and letters from home urged them to take the oath of allegiance because exchange seemed unlikely. Mr. Nightingale, the sutler, illegally sold "Plantation Bitters," which helped to some extent. This old "reliable remedy" was guaranteed to cure most of the diseases ravaging the camp, and it did succeed in making the men merry.

They needed it because a new mule was in place in Prison Square by January 18, which was 15 feet high and 12 feet long. "It looks like a big trestle, and is about two inches wide on top, rather too sharp to ride comfortably," Burke quipped.[23] Some prisoners who rode it reported that they could see over the fence.

General Sweet gave the prisoners' committee working for General Beall a parole of honor on February 2, 1865 to go to Chicago and investigate the missing supplies.[24] The committee probably made extensive use of the telegraph downtown and checked with the many railroads in person to verify that the goods were not bottled-up somewhere. Some freight clerks were surprised, no doubt, to find four prisoners from Camp Douglas casually dropping in to see about their consignment. The committee then returned to camp in accordance with the code of chivalry, probably on the street car which stopped opposite the gate on Cottage Grove.

Apparently they had succeeded in their mission, because substantial supplies from Beall, but no food, soon reached Camp Douglas. Seven deliveries were received from February 20 to March 14, 1865, consisting of 6,709 blankets, 2,204 pairs of drawers, 4,080 pairs of pants, 4,368 jackets, 5,320 shirts, 200 pantaloons, 5,120 pairs of shoes, 2,600 pairs of socks, and 411 boxes of tobacco.[25] However, a dispute arose because Beall had sent the jackets and pants in Confederate gray, and General Halleck canceled the agreement. The North realized belatedly that the sale of Southern cotton in New York enabled the Confederacy to re-equip prisoners who might be exchanged if the Cartel were resumed. General Beall returned to prison under the code of chivalry. There was no explanation for his failure to ship food to Camp Douglas.

General Sweet began offering prisoners the oath instead of exchange on February 6, so they knew something was up. Burke was proud when only five Kentucky men asked for the oath, while 109 wished to be exchanged. The February report from Camp Douglas told the old dreary story, with 308 men dying that month. On February 12, Sweet complained to Hoffman that "Probably one-third of the prisoners who did not wish to be exchanged would take the oath if they could be assured of immediate release." Reverend Tuttle was already on the lecture circuit with "Three Years Among the Rebel Prisoners."[26]

Sweet planned to make room in the hospital by sending out patients who opted for exchange, and he also clamped down on the prisoners by making it difficult to leave the barracks. Men were punished for being absent from their quarters, but this was still a long way off from locked cell blocks. He probably intended to isolate "die-hards" who were preventing others from taking the oath. Some men were losing faith in ever going back, Burke admitted, "altho the papers say it is a general exchange."[27] On February 13, about 500 men were processed for return to the Confederate army, the largest such group since April, 1863. First they needed to sign their parole in three places at the express office in the square.

Burke's parole probably read: "I, the undersigned Curtis R. Burke, a private of the Fourteenth Regiment of Ky. Cav. Vols., do solemnly swear that I will not bear arms against the United States of America or give any information, or do any military duty whatsoever until regularly exchanged as a prisoner of war. Description: Height, 5 ft. 8 in.; Hair, Auburn; Eyes, gray; Complexion, dark. [signed] Curtis R. Burke."

Prisoners who signed for exchange were moved into special barracks and stripped of their overcoats and blankets despite the cold trip ahead. It was General Grant who suggested that blankets should be taken away. Hoffman returned as sole Commissary General of Prisoners about this time, and resumed his office in Washington. He had mellowed somehow, and was against taking blankets from the prisoners, something he had always insisted upon. The rapidly aging widower planned to cash in his chips for an "I Do," and start a new life with a new love. The responsibility for taking away both coats and blankets in the frigid weather was probably General Sweet's. At the same time, Stanton lifted the ban on the sutler selling vegetables.[28] It was too late. The January and February death toll had reached 551.

Eight of the kitchens cooked five days' rations for their departing comrades, consisting of boiled beef and crackers. On February 17, Sweet called out the entire square at once and requested those who wished to take the oath "to step to the front." Only 14 men from five states did so. "They took their baggage and were moved over to the oath barracks in another part of the camp by themselves," Burke noted.[29] These men had the audacity to come back to Prison Square for their evening meal, but the loyal prisoners had already eaten their share. About 1,500 prisoners left on exchange in February, but Burke sadly conceded that 1,400 wanted to take the oath.

Hoffman's response regarding releases exasperated General Sweet. "Arrangements will be made at the proper time for those who publicly decline the offer of exchange!" Hoffman snapped. Sweet feared that this foot-dragging would leave the prisoners no choice but to be exchanged. Their chance of survival in the field was better than at camp, given the high mortality. "When will that proper time be?" Sweet demanded of Hoffman.[30] It would make him look bad if everyone preferred to go to the war front.

The *Tribune* claimed that out of 10,248 prisoners remaining at camp on February 18, there was 8,000 who did not wish to be exchanged. However, when a squad of 500 started processing out on February 20, Burke saw them as "a fine looking set of men."[31] He was called out for exchange on February 23. Henry White received 20 dollars from home, and "we commenced living well again," Burke said with satisfaction, although guards were drunk that night and abusing prisoners.

Burke purchased note paper from the sutler, "as I suspect paper might be scarce in Dixie." Although the camp was in a state of tumult, "The tailors, shoemakers, ring makers, toothpick makers, and washmen still do a very good business."[32] He began the process of leaving camp on February

27, and used all his sutler's checks. It is significant that he did not give them to Pa. Burke left his blanket "rather than give them a chance to take it from me." The men could carry nothing except a change of underclothing and their personal belongings. The Confederate army was facing a major supply problem when they returned.

A Yankee soldier tagged their blankets and clothing with the name and unit of the owner under the pretense that they were being shipped separately. "Some of the boys comically ordered their blankets, etc. checked to the Spotswood, American, and other Richmond hotels," Burke chuckled. Meanwhile, the war went on at Camp Douglas, with guards beating, kicking, and slapping prisoners. Many whispered of vengeance.[33] Two men, desperate to leave, tried to steal into Burke's squad. They were caught and made to wear the barrel. Pa received permission to see his son before the group was marched into Garrison Square and taken in charge by their guard regiment, the 48th Missouri Infantry, who were mostly rebel deserters. Pa did not wish to be exchanged. Life was comfortable in the Masonic barrack.

The prisoners marched a half-mile to the train. The road back was uncertain as the defenses around Richmond began to crumble, but the prisoners thought about the place they were leaving. "We did not get to see much of the City," Burke regretted, "altho I would have liked very much to have passed through it as we were in sight of it for so long."[34] Burke and Henry White found that they were riding in "third class cars," and took the one behind the locomotive, which almost cost them their hard-won lives. Their train collided with another one just 72 miles out of Chicago.

The engine tender smashed through the front of the car throwing water over everyone. Seats were torn out of the floor with the backs broken. One guard and several railroad workers were injured, and the engineer of the other train was killed. Burke was pinned to his seat by the force of the impact, but was not hurt. The men had to remain in the car all night, with water pouring out of the tender, until they were rescued. They did not arrive in Richmond until March 10. Burke was venomous when he saw black Union soldiers near the city. He found to his dismay that his Company B was not even known to Confederate authorities. It made no difference. Everyone received a 30-day furlough with vague and impossible orders to report to various commands as far away as Tennessee and North Carolina after their leave expired.[35]

Hoffman sent word on March 1 that "guerrillas will not be forwarded until further orders, nor any who are bad characters." A group of 1,492 prisoners signed their parole and left in March. Nothing went well for this batch. They missed the exchange at City Point, Virginia, and Lee surren dered before another one could be arranged.[36] They were stranded, and the North would not furnish transportation for them because of their loyalty to the Confederacy. One of Morgan's men had to walk home to Kentucky, not an easy trek through the devastated South.

On March 3, Hoffman ordered Colonel Sweet to release all civilians "whose homes are within the rebel lines who are not awaiting trial on grave charges." This meant that the Conspiracy suspects at Camp Douglas remained in custody. Exchange was suddenly halted that same day without explanation.[37] It is possible that the South could no longer deliver Union prisoners to City Point due to the devastation.

A curious incident occurred on March 3, when 500 prisoners from Camp Douglas arrived at City Point, and 200 of them changed their minds about exchange. Apparently they were discouraged by bleak stories from Confederate deserters entering the Union lines. They were returned to Camp Douglas. The road back had come full circle.[38]

This was not the first time that prisoners had returned to Camp Douglas voluntarily. Two escapees came back during the terrible freeze of January 1864, and requested shelter. Two others returned to camp after taking the oath of allegiance. One was a Cherokee Indian who found he had a language problem in Chicago. The other, a private in a Tennessee regiment, decided "to stay where he felt most at home."[39]

Brigadier-General Hoffman became a Major-General on March 13, 1865.[40] He had come a long way from the dusty lieutenant trudging down the road to Mexico City, or the captain who had pursued Indians across the wastes of Nebraska. Like General Sweet, he saw his opportunity in the Civil War and made the most of it.

On March 15, Sweet reported the third killing of a prisoner by another since the prison opened. Samuel Turner of the 1st Tennessee Infantry stabbed a man to death. Turner had previously stabbed two other prisoners. Sweet described him as "a desperate man," but had failed to remove him from the prison population.[41] His indifference had cost a man his life. Hoffman ordered Sweet to deliver Turner to the Confederate exchange agent along with witnesses to the killing and a full report on the case. The trial of William Kilpatrick in 1862 would not be repeated in Turner's case. It was the South's problem now, but Turner probably escaped punishment. The Confederacy also lay mortally wounded.

Hoffman continued to deny permission for Sweet to pay detectives with prison funds. Sweet appealed to the Adjutant General of the army on March 29, 1865 for "leave to disburse $3,000 from the prison fund to pay detective salaries and expenses incurred in the Camp Douglas Conspiracy."[42]

Washington apparently had some doubts about the matter, because the answer was no.[43]

Few of the remaining prisoners would opt for exchange according to the *Tribune*, and 9,266 remained at the end of March. However, 99 more did leave for the front before the surrender in April.[44] John M. Copley was never called for exchange. Perhaps he had not signed for it. He did not say. Copley went to work at the prison hospital in May, and was still in camp late in June because hospital workers were required to remain. Those who did not wish to be exchanged continued on as prisoners of war. Only 73 new prisoners arrived in 1865.

General Sweet did not forget the Conspiracy, and arrested a citizen in Chicago for "disloyalty" on April 3, 1865, and jailed him at Camp Douglas.[45] He wielded more power over the city than any other person in its history.

Suddenly, the cataclysmic struggle was almost over. Lee surrendered on April 9, leaving Joseph E. Johnson's army in North Carolina as the remaining threat. General Sweet treated the matter as finished; so did many Confederates. Soon, 10 companies of infantry in the Union army were filled by enlistments among the prisoners at Camp Douglas "to join in the Indian frontier warfare." There were still some victories to be won. These enlistments did not include another 2,000 Camp Douglas prisoners who had joined the Union army and navy during the war.[46]

Sweet ordered 100 cannons to be fired on April 12, which meant that he had received many more big guns since the Conspiracy. He mounted the flagpole platform in Garrison Square and spoke "of the death of the now dying rebellion and the glorious future which now lay ahead for the nation when the white winged messenger of peace shall reign gloriously."[47] He forgot about the Indians. It was from this platform that Parson Brownlow told the prisoners three years before that they were the "dupes of designing leaders." Reverend Tuttle got in a few short words, and the garrison sang "John Brown's Body."

The murder of President Lincoln on April 14 ruined the celebration. On the morning after the assassination General Sweet attempted to lower the flag in Garrison Square to half-mast, but the lanyard came off the pulley. A Union soldier fell to his death attempting to free it, and no one else from the garrison would volunteer. Legend describes "a ragged Georgia boy" climbing the pole as thousands watched, "and in a few seconds fixed the rope; then, waving his old Confederate hat three times about his head, threw it at the crowd below. A mighty cheer went up as he started on his descent. The prisoners caught it up, and for the first and only time a Rebel yell was heard in a Northern prison."[48]

Supposedly, he was carried to headquarters by Federal soldiers and given his freedom and a reward. There are too many mentions of such an incident in Camp Douglas literature for something like this not to have happened. On the other hand, P. H. Prince charged that there was retaliation against the prisoners because of Lincoln's assassination. Writing in 1907, Prince described how an Irish prisoner was beaten and bayoneted to death when he applauded the news of Lincoln's death.[49] Prince conceded that he was in the hospital when this allegedly happened, "but the boys told me about it when I was returned to the barracks." No one else mentioned such an incident. Prince claimed that he was devoted to the Irishman for saving him from a beating, but gave no name or unit for the alleged victim, so the story remains only a "might have been."

However, retaliation continued at camp long after Confederate armies in the field were paroled. On April 23, 1865, five prisoners were made to point for grub for a half hour "with the tip end of their four fingers to the ground." They suffered the painful and exhausting punishment for talking after Taps. Some hope arrived a few days later when Hoffman ordered 1,800 prisoners shipped to New Orleans via Cairo.[50] The old exchange route of 1862 had been re-established, but unlike in 1862, these prisoners were on the road back to a defeated nation.

Sweet still had problems with money demands from his detectives. "As a last resort," he appealed on April 25 to Major H. L. Burnett, the prosecutor in the Conspiracy trials, to obtain payment for his operatives.[51] He had made Burnett a famous man, and detective O'Keefe was demanding $716.82. This was more than a Union private's pay for the entire war. If anyone believed in the conspiracy, it should have been Burnett. There was no response.

Two days later Hoffman demanded a report from Sweet about whether he had reimbursed the prison fund $531.36 for unauthorized payments to detectives. It is not likely that Sweet had done so. The following month, he applied to Hoffman for $358.20 to pay another agent, and a request for $38.46 to an unnamed prisoner who was probably an informer. Four days later, on May 17, he went back to Burnett, confessing that he had paid out $1,614.37 to detectives from the prison fund without authority.[52]

When Sweet's chief "agent provocateur," Winslow Ayer, demanded more money for his testimony at the trial, Sweet exploded and denounced him for failure to give "information at the time of the maturing of the plot to attack Camp Douglas."[53] In truth he was blaming him for lack of imagination.

Transportation order from Camp Douglas to Shelby County, North Carolina. Issued to Alfred Biggenstaff on June 15, 1865 (courtesy North Carolina State Archives).

A historic order was received at Camp Douglas on May 8, 1865. All prisoners were to be released, except those above the rank of colonel. It provided for transportation home upon taking the oath of allegiance.[54] Careful records were to be kept of each prisoner as to name, place of residence, and the date and place of capture. In other words, Sweet was to verify the prison rolls. The prisoners numbered 6,107 at this time, and they began leaving at the rate of 500 per week.

Incredibly, prison mail was still censored. A begging letter from a prisoner dated May 9 to New Hampshire bears the approval stamp, "By order of B. J. Sweet."[55] It is difficult to imagine what Sweet wished to suppress, unless it was news about the mortality at camp, as deaths climbed toward 800.

However, General Sweet continued to protect the city and the nation from treason, and ordered the arrest of the H. H. Forsyth family in Chicago "for hanging a picture of John Wilkes Booth in their house." The Camp Douglas patrol did not find such a picture on May 10. Mr. Forsyth, "an old resident of Kentucky," was too ill to travel, so his two daughters were arrested. This was without the warrants required by the 4th Amendment to the now restored U.S. Constitution. The women denied the charges, and Sweet released them after a "wholesome lecture."[56] He then sent the patrol back to arrest their father.

Prisoners received a visit from some distinguished people on May 12 who were celebrating the formal opening of the new chapel in Garrison Square. It had been under construction since September, 1864.[57] This was a homecoming for Dwight L. Moody, who talked about the origin of religious services for the prisoners in 1862. Reverend Tuttle also spoke, and declared that the building would be open to all Christian denominations and clergymen from the Christian Commission. No one dreamed that the chapel only had about four months to live.

The "great clearing off" did not come until June, when 4,090 prisoners left camp.[58] It is not likely that everyone took the oath. A few may have preferred to walk, or wait for money from home. Only one prisoner escaped in 1865, and the death toll reached 867.

All guards were withdrawn on July 5, 1865, and the war finally ended at Camp Douglas, three months after Appomattox.[59] Sixteen sick prisoners remained in the post hospital. The name of the first prisoner to enter the camp is unknown, because the original records were lost under Colonel Mulligan. Who was the last prisoner out the gate is also speculative, but on the blank side of the final prison roll is hastily scrawled, "Henry Harrison, 64th Va."

NOTES TO CHAPTER 16

[1] O R Ser II–Vol. VIII, 44.

[2] Copley, 82.

[3] Frost, *Camp and Prison Journal*, 273.

[4] *Confederate Veteran* 32 (Jun. 1924):218.

[5] *Confederate Veteran* 16 (Aug. 1908):421.

[6] Copley, 143; Burke, 11 Feb. 1865.

[7] J. A. Yeager, "A Boy With Morgan," *Confederate Veteran* 34 (Aug. 1926): 294; *Confederate Soldiers, Sailors and Civilians who Died at Camp Douglas*; Burke, 3 Jun. 1864.

[8] O R Ser.II-Vol.VIII, 66-67; Burke, 6 Jan. 1865.

[9] Burke, 13 Jan. 1865.

[10] Burke, 15 Jan. 1865.

[11] Burke, 17 Jan. 1865.

[12] Burke, 13 Jan. 1865; Tuttle, 20.

[13] O R Ser.II-Vol.VIII, 76.

[14] O R Ser.II-Vol.VII, 66.

[15] *Battles and Leaders of the Civil War*, 4:642-43; O R Ser.II-Vol.VII, 115-16.

[16] Burke, 27 Jan. 1865; O R Ser.II-Vol.VIII, 144-45.

[17] R. G. 393, V. 245:120.

[18] Medical and Surgical History, 49.

[19] Burke, *Indiana Magazine of History, Vol 65* (Dec., 1969) 134. Entries for the year 1865 are in Vol. 65.

[20] Burke, 31 Jan. 1865.

[21] Burke, 31 Jan. 1865; O R Ser.II-Vol.VIII, 337-51.

[22] Burke, 9 Feb. 1865.

[23] Burke, 12, 18 Jan. 1865.

[24] Burke, 2 Feb. 1865.

[25] Confederate Prisoners of War, R. G. 109, Roll 58.

[26] O R Ser.II-Vol.VIII, 210; *Chicago Tribune*, 16 Jan. 1865.

[27] Burke, 11 Feb. 1865.

[28] Burke, 20 Feb. 1865; O R Ser.II-Vol,VIII, 227, 257, 289; Kelly, 119.

[29] Burke, 13, 17 Feb. 1865.

[30] O R Ser.II-Vol.VIII, 219, 220.

[31] *Chicago Tribune,* 18 Feb. 1865.

[32] Burke, 20, 26 Feb. 1865.

[33] Burke, 2 Mar. 1865. These were favorite hotels in Richmond for those who could afford them.

[34] Burke, 2 Mar. 1865.

[35] Burke, 11 Mar. 1865.

[36] O R Ser.II-Vol.VIII, 322; *Pardon and Amnesty under Lincoln and Johnson,* 157.

[37] R. G. 393. v. 241:227; O R Ser.II-Vol.VIII, 360.

[38] Goodspeed, *History of Cook County,* 1:495.

[39] Kelly, "Camp Douglas," 131; Illinois Adj. General Report, 1:127.

[40] *Brevet Brigadier Generals in Blue,* 288.

[41] O R Ser.II-Vol.VIII, 401.

[42]. R. G. 323, v. 235:263.% Wa

[43] R.G. 323, v. 235:263.

[44] O R Ser.II-Vol.VIII, 1001.

[45] *Chicago Tribune,* 3 Apr. 1865, reporting the rearrest of a suspect in the conspiracy.

[46] *Chicago Tribune,* 12 Apr. 1865; Goodspeed, I:495-96.

[47] *Chicago Tribune,* 12 Apr. 1865.

[48] J. N. Hunter, "Courage of a Georgian in Camp Douglas," *Confederate Veteran* 15 (Sep. 1907): 389.

[49] *Confederate Veteran* 15:566.

[50] J. S. Rosamond, "In Camp Douglas in 1865," *Confederate Veteran* 16 (Aug. 1908):421. Mr. Rosamond took the oath two weeks later and left the camp on 8 May 1865; O R Ser.II-Vol.VIII, 514.

[51] R. G. 393, v. 235:312.

[52] R. G. 393, v. 241:317; v. 235:344; v. 235:352.

[53] R.G. 393, v. 235:359.

[54] O R Ser.II-Vol.VIII, 538.

[55] Karlen, "Postal History of Camp Douglas." 960.

[56] R. G. 393, v. 235:393; *Chicago Tribune,* 12 May 1865; R.G. 393, v. 240:389.

[57] *Chicago Tribune,* 13 May 1865.

[58] O R Ser.II-Vol.VIII, 1002.

[59] O R Ser.II-Vol.VIII, 700-01.

17.

WHY THEY FOUGHT—AN END TO CHIVALRY

Most prisoners were open about why they went to war. Race and slavery definitely played a part. The destitute Arkansas Post prisoners of early 1863 were highly critical of white officers who would lead black troops. "But you have no business to make soldiers of niggers," they argued.[1] Curtis R. Burke wrote that "most of the prisoners would rather remain a year longer than be exchanged for negroes." Racist comments in his journal are common.

M. J. Bradley referred to blacks as "african demons." Many prisoners said they were fighting for "Southern Rights," meaning white supremacy. Camp Douglas records show that some enlisted men did own slaves. Three sergeants in the 7th Texas Infantry each had one at Fort Donelson. On June 20, 1862, a private wrote home from Camp Douglas that he expected the servants "to do their duty until I return."[2] Private John C. Lester, 3rd Tennessee Infantry, a Fort Donelson prisoner, was one of six founders of the Klu Klux Klan at Pulaski, Tennessee, in December, 1865.[3]

Confederates were no different from Union soldiers in opposing political and economic equality with the black race. It would have been difficult to find a white recruit at Camp Douglas or elsewhere who was fighting for social justice. Their letters and diaries spoke about making war on the rebellion, not on slavery. Private Tebbets of the 45th Illinois Infantry, who was killed in action at Shiloh, joined up "to save the best form of government." Slavery was not an issue for most of the Union army.

A black regiment was recruited at Camp Douglas in December, 1863, but it never guarded prisoners. This did happen at Point Lookout, Maryland, where one Confederate complained that "Today the negroes are again on guard and are very insolent." No prisoner at Camp Douglas ever described a white guard as "insolent." There was a black civilian employee at camp whom the Fort Donelson prisoners considered "insolent." This led a member of the 3rd Tennessee to assault him one day.[4]

Race and slavery aside, the most devoted Confederates at Camp Douglas were alienated long ago from the government in Washington, and fought to expel the North from what they considered their native land. William Micajah Barrow of the 4th Louisiana Infantry, for example, saw the struggle "as a second war of independence for the South," and gave his valuable life to maintain Southern institutions. Years after the war, a former

Confederate officer boasted about braving death by refusing to walk under the former U. S. flag as he entered Camp Douglas. Other prisoners found no precise reason for enlisting. One told De Land candidly that he joined for the 50-dollar bonus to pay off his debts. Some said they were drunk when they signed up. Henry Morton Stanley supposedly enlisted to please the father of a young lady with whom he was infatuated.[5]

Camp Douglas was no stranger to other minorities besides the black prisoners of war. Five women and a child were there in 1862, and in 1863 the Arkansas Post prisoners included "Mexicans, Spaniards, quadroons, octoroons, and full blooded contraband; half-blood and full blood Cherokee Indians."

There were a few famous names at Camp Douglas, discounting Henry M. Stanley. Bates Washington, directly connected to George Washington, was a prisoner. Sam Houston, Jr. of Texas, whose father opposed secession to the extent that he lost the Texas governor's office, was held at Camp Douglas. The governor of Kentucky's son, the nephew of the last Southerner to resign from Congress, and sons of Southern judges and politicians saw the inside of the stockade.[6]

Not all prisoners went home. Some refused repatriation to stay in Chicago, and citizens complained that they were taking the jobs of Union veterans who had not yet been mustered out of service.[7] "No true hearted man would give preference to a rebel," the *Tribune* muttered. However, the paper saw no harm "if by working the repentant rebel becomes a useful member of society which he probably never has been previously."

DATA ON THE 700 DAYS.[8]
AUGUST 1863 TO AUGUST 1865

Arrived 13,887
Sick 6,349
Died 2,349
Escaped. 245

The Official Records claim 26,781 Confederates passed through Camp Douglas. In 1862: 8,962; in 1863: January to April, 3,932; from August 1863 to the end of the war: 13,887. The army reduced the figure to 26,060.[9] Perhaps there was a duplication of names.

Ironically, the Camp Douglas prison rolls became important to some ex-prisoners and their survivors who applied to the former Confederate states for pensions. Many released prisoners from Camp Douglas probably did not receive military discharge papers because the Confederate army was already disbanded. Some belonged to units whose muster in rolls were not sent to Richmond. Consequently, there was no record of them except at Camp Douglas. Burke's Company B, 14th Kentucky, is an example of a unit that was unknown in Richmond. Worse, Henry White, Burke's friend in Company B, was using a false name at camp, as were many others, to confuse the authorities. This proved costly. On one page of the Confederate Veteran there are two ads seeking to establish military records through former prisoners at Camp Douglas.[10] Apparently, the alleged veterans did not appear on the prison rolls, and other proof of military service was lacking.

The postwar "Medical and Surgical History of the War of the Rebellion" casts doubt on the Official Records regarding sickness at camp.[11] For example, there were 23,037 cases of sickness in 1864 according to the study. This is more than three times the number shown in the Official Records for the entire 700 days at Camp Douglas; August, 1863 to August, 1865. A major reason for the discrepancy is that the camp was not reporting to Washington the number of prisoners sick in barracks. Only 407 prisoners were listed as sick in December, 1864, while the medical study shows 577 in hospitals and 1,547 sick in barracks.

TABLE 5
CASES AND CLASSES OF DISEASE AND DEATH
CAMP DOUGLAS PRISON DEPOT
FEBRUARY 1862 TO JUNE 1865.[12]

Cases of Specified Diseases/Deaths:
Fevers, such as smallpox, malaria 15,938/1,407
Diarrhea and Dysentery 13,455/698
Anemia. 585/4
Consumption .... 259 /113
Rheumatism 3,212/37
Scurvy. 3,745/39
Bronchitis. 1,628/27
Pneumonia and Pleurisy 4,655/1,296
Wounds, Injuries, Unspec. Diseases 1,279/80
Other Diseases. 25,332/308
Totals: 70,088/4,009

The study does not explain "wounds and injuries," and whether they occurred at camp or in the field. Unspecified diseases may mean those that could not be diagnosed, as well as 25,000 "Other Diseases," that were unknown. The saddest figures relate to the scurvy victims. This was a non-communicable disease, and one for which prevention and cure was known.

A prisoner suffered at least two illnesses on average while at Camp Douglas, and some as many as three, according to figures. Highest mortality among the fevers was smallpox at 823, accounting for 20.5 % of the deaths, a staggering amount. A medical investigator speculated that this resulted from lack of vaccination by the South. "The eruption was reported as having broken out on some of the prisoners within a day or two after their arrival at the depot," he argued.[13] In addition, the vaccinations at camp caused terrible ulcers because of the Confederates' poor condition, including the scurvy they brought with them. The study showed that earlier in the war the Confederate soldier received a full ration in the army and scurvy was rare. Later, fresh beef and vegetables diminished considerably, and scurvy set in. This must have happened earlier than thought, as scurvy appeared among the prisoners in 1862 under Colonel Tucker.

The study theorized that "the hardships and exposures entailed on the men by the military events that ended in their capture were the main causes of the disease and mortality with which they were afflicted during their subsequent confinement." Doctors stressed that diseases were carried by the foul air in and around the barracks. Modern medicine would probably agree that the overcrowding helped spread communicable diseases.

The number of deaths at Camp Douglas from disease and other causes remains uncertain. The official tally by the Medical and Surgical History is 4,039. This is 15%, almost one out of seven prisoners. Elmira was worse with a 24% death rate, and 2,937 out of 10,178 prisoners died in one year.

OTHER MORTALITY FIGURES FOR CAMP DOUGLAS:

1862—*Chicago Tribune*. 976
1863—Official Records 721
1864—Official Records 1,231
1865—Official Records 867
TOTAL
3,795

The worst year for Camp Douglas was 1865, because of the enormous mortality in only six months, when the camp was well-established. While smallpox was down in 1865, the weakened prisoners were falling like tenpins from other diseases. Camp Douglas has undisputed first place in mortality among Northern prisons, although eventually it was no longer the largest prison depot.

Point Lookout, Maryland, where James T. Mackey died, received 32,140 prisoners through November 30, 1864, and 1,532 died. From then until the end of June, when the camp closed, 20,124 more arrived and 1,428 died.[14] Its total of 52,264 prisoners was double that of Camp Douglas; yet, only 2,960 perished there as compared to over 4,000 in Chicago.

Therefore, the theory about hardship causing prisoner mortality does not hold true, since Point Lookout was also a death camp. Perhaps more prisoners died at Camp Douglas because of its proximity to Chicago and its lethal water supply; there was also no control of milk production in the Chicago area. Vendors simply transferred milk from their diseased cows to the camp, and the organism responsible for diphtheria "grows freely in milk."[15] Kentuckians had the right idea in preferring to drink "something more in keeping with the needs of a grown-up individual."

The Official Records did not compile escapes before July, 1862. Camp Douglas rolls list 77 escapes, although this figure is unreliable due to poor record keeping by Colonel Mulligan.[16] From July 1862, to the end of the war, the Records list an additional 319 escapes. About 425 escapes would be more accurate, with about 275 recaptured.

Camp Douglas never approached the status of a maximum-security prison. The constant assaults on the fence prove that, and it was not unusual for prisoners to climb it with a ladder. Burke recorded eight such attempts, most of them successful. The *Confederate Veteran* describes three more, one of them successful. In the mass escape of July 23, 1862, about 20 prisoners went over the fence using ladders. Escape plans of the Supreme Council of Seven were feasible only because of access to the fence. The absence of secure cell blocks permitted prisoners to slip out during the constant repairs and modifications, and corrupt contractors "lent" their crude hand-written passes to the prisoners for copying.[17]

There was no barrier to separate visitors, who often wore an extra suit of civilian clothing to be left in barracks. Inspectors at the express office did not always detect money and other contraband hidden in packages or clothing. Reverend Tuttle remembered two young women placing a package in the supply wagon that he was riding to camp. He investigated and found a "fine blue uniform coat," which he confiscated. Later, he saw the women visiting Polk Johnson, a prisoner and son of the Postmaster General under two presidents of the former United States.[18] Tuttle probably foiled a delightful escape.

The Martial Law Decree of July, 1862 was not properly enforced, and it appears that Mrs. Walsh, the wife of John Walsh, the Conspiracy defendant, took a small daughter to play near the camp and slip in money and letters to prisoners. This would not have been possible near a maximum-security prison. The former State prison at Alton, Illinois, was designed for maximum security and registered only 114 escapes during the three and one-half years that it held Confederates.[19]

Only a comparative few attempted to escape out of the many thousands who went through Camp Douglas. Curtis R. Burke only thought about it. Many tried because they felt little hope of survival as a long-term prisoner. Others saw it as a personal challenge. Some did it out of devotion to the Cause. The risk was evident, although most escapes were without injury.

Bribery was rare under Sweet, which increased the risk of an escape attempt. There are no compiled figures of those killed and wounded in escaping between 1862 and 1865, but it may be close to 25 dead and 45 wounded. This would not include the shooting of at least a 20 others who were not escaping. The prison rolls do not show the cause of death, except for those who were buried in the smallpox cemetery.

Escapes are the least important of the Camp Douglas stories from a practical standpoint. True, they are chronicles of human will, the exploits of men who dared to challenge their fate. However, the rate of escapes was only about 1.5%, with many recaptured. The War Department recognized this, and never invested in sufficient guards or effective weapons. There was no pressure to do so, because escaping prisoners did not harm civilians or damage private property. Had this occurred, the barracks would probably have been turned into locked cell blocks.

The sewer system was the most important development, and was still operating on June 4, 1878, serving the community which replaced Camp Douglas.[20] The prisoner's work survived until 1900, with few people knowing how the sewer came to be there. The camp sometimes witnessed the best as well as the worst parts of human nature and conduct, as shown by the five women who hid among the prisoners rather than leave family and friends. Ada Sweet adored her father, the commanding officer, but she could not betray the prisoner she found in her basement.

The story of primitive medicine at camp can be told by examining medical records preserved in the National Archives. Patients' medical histories were carefully kept on a prescribed form called "Medical Descriptive List," showing diagnosis, treatment, and surgery, if any. Too often it reads, "The patient died." Surgeons performed many autopsies to learn more about diseases sweeping the camp.

The running-water toilets in the new prison hospital were state-of-the-art. In other prisons, an old fashioned dry sink inside the hospital building fouled the air. Bright high ceilings in spacious wards must also have helped the sick prisoners who were able to enter the hospital.

The Camp Douglas Conspiracy story is controversial even today. Characters such as Shanks, Grenfell, Mrs. Morris, Hines, John Walsh, and General Sweet and his detectives and spies would be difficult for a novelist to imagine. Ironically, Chicago panicked because it forgot that when soldiers threatened or harmed civilians the criminals wore blue, not gray.

The war did not end for General Sweet after the prisoners left. Hoffman was chewing him out on July 20, 1865 "due to serious errors" in his hospital accounts. The following month Sweet received another blast from Hoffman for failure to send the roll of prisoners transferred to the post hospital.[21]

One prisoner remained, the University of Chicago. It suffered severe sanitary problems with crude sinks and requested permission to connect to the camp's sewer system. Captain Shurly granted permission on July 29, 1865 according to an engineering plan submitted by the University.[22]

Camp Douglas became a great mustering-out depot, and processed 28 Illinois regiments out of the army. At least 20 regiments from various other states also received discharges at camp through the end of August, 1865. There was talk of keeping it as a permanent installation.[23] The water supply was sufficient, including separate fire hydrants. Medical buildings and the smallpox facility were well established, and the camp was linked to railroads and public transportation. Nevertheless, some people wanted it closed. It was in the way of commercial, industrial, and real estate interests. John Wentworth, a powerful Chicago politician, wrote to Secretary of War Stanton on August 22, 1865: "It is feared that an effort will be made to retain a portion of Camp Douglas to oblige a few officers. Our people want no camps nor garrisons here. Camp D is in a thickly settled portion of our city, near our college, churches, etc., etc."[24]

Disposing of the camp was much easier than building it. On August 2, 1865, General Hoffman ordered that "all the buildings, fencing, etc., were to be sold or otherwise disposed of." Ads in the *Tribune* put everything up for sale, including horses, mules, carts, buildings, and equipment. The camp was gone by the end of November, 1865. The size of the prison fund after the liquidation of the camp was $181,739.96.[25]

While Prison Square contained more buildings, the most valuable property was Garrison and Hospital Squares.

Prison Square contained the drug store, sutler's store, surgeon's office and dispensary, express office, and tool shop, the "Four of Diamonds" dungeon, and the patrol office near the gate. There may have been nine

Number of Buildings/Dimensions[26]

Headquarters	1/80x40
officers quarters	66 rooms
offices	14/2x12
garrison barracks with kitchens	40/85x24
general hospital, 4 wings	1/100x80
post hospital	1/28x204
prison hospital, two wingseach	1/100x28
smallpox hospital, 2 wingseach	1/204x40
quartermaster warehouse	1/60x100
commissary warehouse	1/40x100
ordinance warehouse	1/20x60
prison barracks, Prison Square	64/24x90
garrison guard house	1/20x40
wash house	1/24x66
guard house&court martial hall	1/24x50
post church	1/30x75
water pipes/feet	3,600
sewerage/feet	5,000

water hydrants in the square by the close of the war. The location of structures in Garrison Square is not certain. Stables were inside the main gate, and could feed and house 44 horses. Included were sheds to cover 300 tons of coal, and 800 cords of wood. A bakery equipped with water pipes could bake for 11,000 men. The quartermaster warehouse held equipment for a force of 15,000. The commissary warehouse was capable of storing ten days' rations for 20,000 troops, and a butcher shop could do the same for meat.[27]

Other service structures were a jail to hold 60 men, a carpenter shop for 33 carpenters, a glazer, blacksmith, horseshoer, and tool shop. A power tool consisted of a four-horsepower engine operating a crosscut and rip saw. There were nine latrines which could hold 30 men each, 12 water hydrants, and three fire plugs.[28]

Hospitals are shown on the final plan of January 1, 1865. South Square contained the prison and garrison hospitals plus the chapel and commissary store. The hospital location was sometimes called Hospital Square. According to Dr. Coolidge's inspection, there was a "strong oak fence" around the prison hospital.

Four wards in each wing of the hospital were "well lighted and ventilated by cold-air shafts opening in the floor."[29] It also had air shafts in the walls, with openings near the ceiling and floors. The wards on the second floor of each wing were also well lighted and vented. Ceilings measured 12 feet high throughout. The doctor described the prison hospital in White

Oak Square as a single barrack ward for skin diseases, measuring 80 by 20 feet with 30 beds.

A dispute arose earlier about ownership of the private structures built by businesspeople and the YMCA. Three sutler stores served the garrison, and one stood in Prison Square. There was also an eating saloon, barbershop, newsroom or stand, a photo studio, and chapel. In April, 1864, sutler McBride was denied permission to remove his building from camp on the basis that it belonged to the Government.[30]

Colonel Tucker told Orme, who then told Hoffman, that only the chapel did not belong to the Government. All other private structures became Federal property. Unfortunately, Tucker had neglected to put this in writing, or inform the tradesmen of this rule, so there were some hard feelings and substantial financial losses. In addition, the Government had no intention of returning the YMCA chapel when the camp closed.

General Sweet resigned from the army on September 19, 1865. He was succeeded for a short time by Captain Shurly as commanding officer. The last commander was Captain E. C. Phetteplace, who replaced Shurly around October 1, 1865.[31] The Captain had personally arrested Grenfell in the raid of November 7, 1864 on Grenfell's hotel. Legend has it that Grenfell moved toward his gun, but Phetteplace was too fast for him. Perhaps this is why he had the honor of presiding over a ghostly camp filled with the murmuring of so much pain and death. A grim reminder of the camp was the smallpox cemetery next to the University on Douglas property, holding 655 Confederates and 12 Federal soldiers. The army planned to move them by the end of 1865.

General Meigs received a dramatic telegram from Chicago at 2 p.m. on March 20, 1866: "The ground comprising Camp Douglas was surrendered to Mufflin & Loomis & T. Porter Jany 1st, to Douglas Estate Jany 5th, to H. Graves Jany 8th. The last buildings were sold on the 24th of December. L. H. Pierce Lt. Col. U. S. Q. M."[32]

The Mufflin-Loomis-Porter group were investors who had purchased the Old Fair Grounds west of camp before the war.[33] The property saw heavy use by the army, but it is not known whether they ever received rent from Washington. The smallpox cemetery was already gone from the Douglas estate according to the telegram. However, the story of that cemetery was not over, and history had not yet closed the books on Camp Douglas. It never has.

The chapel continued an unbroken record of bad luck when the War Department sold it to a businessman hostile to religion, instead of donating it to Reverend Tuttle's Saint Mark's Parish as promised. Its new owner harshly rejected Tuttle's pleas for the building. The chapel bell was saved, possibly by Henry Graves. It was cast partly from coins contributed by the prisoners, the garrison, and congregations in the city; even by the Chicago Reform School. The bell was finally donated to the Chicago Historical Society, where it rests today.[34] It had tolled joyously at Union victories and mournfully for President Lincoln. It may also have tolled for prisoners and soldiers whose lives had gone at Camp Douglas.

A desk that held the prisoners' records, a prisoner's song, and the burial records kept by a Captain Charles Goodman are also at the Historical Society. These, along with the *Prisoner Vidette* at the Chicago Public Library, are the only known relics of Camp Douglas. However, the life of the great camp did not go completely out. In 1941 some decrepit tenements in the area were identified as former garrison barracks.[35]

Henry Graves had not been paid for use of his land inside the stockade. In 1863 a commission had decided to allow Graves "$225 per month or $2700 per year."[36] Colonel Potter reduced the award to $1,200 per year, which Graves rejected.

Estimates of the cost to build and repair Camp Douglas vary widely because no records have survived. One figure is $400,000. General Hoffman reported expenditures of $208,230.91 from 1862 to 1865, not counting the cost of maintaining the garrison. The damage caused by the parolees came to about $15,000. De Land spent about $30,000. The new hospital and sewer system totaled about $15,000. Sweet alone allegedly spent $375,000 on barracks, fences, sewers, and new buildings.[37] General Hoffman was probably the most accurate, without counting the original cost to build the camp in 1861.

The constant change of command was only one barrier to improving conditions. General Ammen, an experienced administrator, concentrated on security because Camp Douglas was not designed as a prison. In addition, commanders such as Mulligan, Cameron, and De Land believed that their primary mission was to fight the war. Stanton did not perceive, as did Hoffman, that prison administration was a science which required special training and experience. Moreover, demands for economy and the policy of retaliation were detrimental to the prisoners.

Reports of starvation at Camp Douglas have to be discounted if they meant that men starved to death. It is true that rations were more adequate in 1862 than in the following years. William M. Barrow was getting fat, and James T. Mackey did not suggest that food was a problem. It appears that the worst year for rations was 1864. Curtis R. Burke described hunger, but not starvation. A reasonable argument can be made, however, that hunger becomes starvation when rats are eaten. John M. Copley charged that "the majority of the prisoners used the most rigid and strict economy in taking care of their rations, but with that were continually hungry."[38]

Camp Douglas revealed much about the attitudes and perceptions of the North and South toward each other. General Sweet's frightening invention that the Conspiracy of 1864 included an attack on Chicago was successful because the people wished to believe it. He could turn criminals like Prairie Bull, O'Hara, and others loose in Prison Square because none of the inspectors, including General Hoffman, objected.

Camp Douglas is often compared to Andersonville. It was a death camp, but totally unlike Andersonville. The difference is significant in terms of social behavior. The prisoners could maintain many of their social customs at Camp Douglas. One example was the practice of convening a court and trying wrongdoers the way it was done in the South. Other examples are the camp newspaper, the craft workers, the artisans, and the musicians who played on. Copley's remark, about not being "churched" for dancing, shows that he related his camp experience to life at home. Southern-style cooking was possible until the stoves were removed in 1864.

Burke mentioned that except for card playing, the visiting in barracks was just like at home. The most successful escapes and near-misses were carried out by men who knew each other, and tunneling was possible because of their cooperation and division of labor. All the religion the prisoners needed came from ministers and priests in the area. Superb mail service and express delivery were available. While Hoffman and Stanton continuously interfered with the sutlers, the stores helped alleviate some hardship.

Having pictures taken at the photo studio enabled the men to maintain visual contact with loved ones. There was a bank to hold their money, a modern hospital, if one was lucky enough to find a bed, flush toilets, and a wash house. Fussy prisoners who could afford it went to the barber shop, and surgeons made house calls. Knowing that the garrison would enforce the law was a deterrent to crime. Three Chicago newspapers kept the prisoners aware of what was going on in the world.

Regiments and companies were often formed locally in the South, just as they were in the North, and elections for non-commissioned officers took place often at camp. Pa was involved in one. By maintaining their military organization the prisoners also preserved a useful social structure. Curtis R. Burke would probably have died from his severe illnesses but for the strong support of friends and Pa.

The location at Chicago benefited prisoners to a great extent despite the cold climate. Relief committees, medicine, and supplies were nearby, and the services of many surgeons were available from the medical com-

Andersonville, circa 1865 (courtesy USAMHI)

Picture of Andersonville taken from the stockade, circa 1865. Note the primitive sinks in the foreground (courtesy MCMOLL/USAMHI).

munity in the city. Prison contractors could buy fresh meat at local packing houses, and building materials were easily obtained.

The camp was subject to scrutiny by journalists and many independent inspectors because of easy access to Chicago by rail and water. Continuous monitoring by the Surgeon General's office, various departments of the army, and civilian doctors from Chicago was not difficult. A modern sewer system became possible because of nearby Lake Michigan. This caused conditions to improve steadily, and enabled the prisoners to pursue social activities. By comparison, conditions at Andersonville worsened with time.

In 1865, Major Henry Wirz, the commander of Andersonville, was tried and executed by the Federal government for war crimes. It appears that he, too, was a victim of the death camp. Wirz did not receive the money or materials to build a suitable prison, and the South had no William Hoffman. The site in the desolate swamps of southwest Georgia was the worst possible location for a prison. It was not easily accessible for essentials such as food, building materials, medical care, inspectors, and religion, as was Camp Douglas.[39]

Andersonville was a festering sore, a giant maggot that swallowed men without malice. Union prisoners lacked every support they knew before, which made social cohesion impossible. There were simply no facilities to carry on the activities they knew in civilian life or in the army. In addition, the South was unable to enforce the law in that remote location. Consequently, there were no patrols in the stockade, enabling gangs of criminals to rule.

Camp Douglas prisoners felt that they were entitled to fair treatment, adequate food, shelter, clothing, and medical care. Most of the bitterness after the war was caused by cruelty. Despite serious management efforts to improve living conditions, prisoners were beaten, tortured, and shot, sometimes for no possible reason. Dr. Clark expressed disgust at White Oak dungeon, but he did not recommend closing it. Soon officers saw nothing wrong in killing a prisoner for urinating in the street.

The gain from selling rations poured substantial wealth into the prison fund, which was often misused. Funds from all camps totaled $1,845,125.99 at the end of the war.[40] Spies and detectives were rewarded with this money at Camp Douglas, and it paid bungling contractors for installing inadequate water pipes. Others reaped double profits in building the new prison hospital.

The presence of smallpox in November, 1862 should have closed the camp, and there was never an adequate smallpox hospital after the number of cases increased sharply in 1863 and 1864. Infectious patients were often returned to barracks for lack of space.

Those in power on both sides of the war regarded prisoners as pawns. Confederates at Camp Douglas suffered retaliation for matters beyond their control, such as Andersonville. Withholding antiscorbutic is the worst example of retaliation, and while they were fed with one hand their rations were sold with the other. The South shared blame because it helped to kill the Cartel for long periods with shortsighted racial policies. The *Richmond Inquirer* snarled that if the North used black troops, "none will be taken prisoner: our troops understand what to do in such cases!" When a Confederate general wished to restart the Cartel in the Spring of 1864, except "recaptured slaves," Richmond replied that it would not tolerate any exchange of blacks. Another 1,339 prisoners died at Camp Douglas alone from then until the Cartel restarted in February, 1865, and Confederates were dying in 21 other Federal prisons during this period. Meanwhile, the bureaucrats in Richmond were going to church on Sundays with their nicely starched families.[41]

Survivors of Camp Douglas could not understand the institutionalized cruelty, and attributed it to a "mean Yankee nature." J. S. Rosamond did not believe that the guards had ever been to the war. "Veterans would have treated prisoners like brothers," he thought.[42] He was wrong. Many of the guards had seen action. Mr. Rosamond did not realize that he had become a casualty of modern warfare. The war continued at Camp Douglas, with the enemy subdued by any means. That is why Colonel De Land hung men by their thumbs, Colonel Strong started the use of forced labor, Colonel Sweet would not interfere with sadistic guards, and medical inspectors said nothing about the brutality.

Chivalry was only a dream that was passing, like a beautiful summer slipping into Autumn, but this time never to return. While the prisoners languished in Chicago, the nature of the conflict had changed. On November 15, 1864, General Sherman cut loose from Atlanta to bring total war home to the South. He was too late. It had already happened at Camp Douglas.

Statistics aside, the prisoners themselves must always return as the center of interest. Most had spent the best years of their youth in this alien and deadly environment, and the remainder of their lives would be overshadowed by memories of the camp. The personalities and strength of thousands of Confederates had been forged at Camp Douglas. For many others, weaknesses which they never imagined came to the surface. Reverend Tuttle said about them that "the selfish principal generally predominates." He was right in some cases and wrong in many others. Men created friendships there which lasted until they answered the long roll.

The war was over for most of the prisoners when they passed through the gate on Cottage Grove. When they left, they had to create new lives, new dreams, and new hopes, because they could not pick up the threads of old ones. Those who returned to the South saw that the social, political, and economic orders had been swept away. Many prisoners found the road back too difficult and started new lives elsewhere. In either case, they were forced to redefine their place in society. How they responded had to be influenced in large part by their Camp Douglas experience.

Some Final Words:

T. M. Page: "The survivors of that imprisonment ought to arrange for a general meeting in some Confederate reunion, for no body of men was ever more tried in any ordeal which tests human nature and proves it creditable to mankind."

J. S. Rosamond: "If there are any of those yankees alive who guarded Camp Douglas in 1865, if I were in their shoes, I would not tell that I was one of them."

B. R. Froman: "Who can say that the sudden escape of these twenty-one thousand prisoners, and their addition to the Confederate army would not have altered the result of the civil war, and the destiny of the country."

T. D. Henry: "Think of a man's mind being racked by all these punishments, for the innocent suffered as well as the guilty, and as frequently, when no one was to blame, were all punished; and it is almost a miracle that anyone should have remained there twenty months without losing their reason."

M. J. Bradley: "Thank God, there are enough pure whole-souled Christians remaining in the world to keep the churches in existence. This subject is so revolting and its recollections so sickening that I can pursue it no further-others must contribute their mite as I have done to the memory of the nineteen months of torment endured by myself and others at Camp Douglas. It brings such a crowd of horrors to my mind that I can scarcely realize its truthfulness; although I personally witnessed all, and more than I have stated. Oh, horror of horrors! sooner than undergo their repetition, gladly would I rush upon the bayonet, or force my way to the cannon's mouth. Yea, I would welcome death as a relief."

R. T. Bean: "I wondered what caused all of this fearful mortality. Before me I saw the headstones of five thousand six hundred Confederates whose lives went out in prison. Was it starvation, neglect, and cruelty? God alone knows."

Four Confederate brothers, circa 1920. Two were at Camp Douglas (from Confederate Veteran*).*

J.A. Templeton, 10th Texas Cavl, circa 1912. At Camp Douglas for 19 months. Author of Prison Reminisences *(from* Confederate Veteran, May, 1926*).*

Some old Confederates from Camp Douglas, circa 1920 (from Confederate Veteran)

Curtis R. Burke: "As we marched out the gate into the open country the boys had to give vent to their feeling, by giving three ringing cheers, singing Dixie."

Sergeant T. B. Clore: "Did Wirtz, the commandant of Andersonville prison, ever do anything as inhumanly brutal as was inflicted on Confederate prisoners in Camp Douglas and other Federal prisons, and which was paralleled only by the brutal Germans in the World War?"

E. D. Blakemore: They might very well have given us more to eat, as I did not have a square meal for twenty-one months, and if some of those in authority at that time will come to see me I will show them what they might have given me for dinner. But it was war times and we will have to do what we can to forget its hardships and its brutalities. If some of my old comrades should happen to see this I shall be glad for them to remember me kindly."[43]

John M. Copley: "I, J. M. Copley, of the County of Dickson, State of Tennessee, do solemnly swear that I Will support, protect and defend the Constitution and Government of the United States against all enemies, whether domestic or foreign; that I will bear true faith, allegiance and loyalty to the same, any ordinance, resolution or laws of any State, convention or legislature to the contrary notwithstanding; and further, that I will faithfully perform all the duties required of me by the laws of the United States; and I take this oath freely and voluntarily, without any mental reservation or evasion whatever.

NOTES TO CHAPTER 17

[1] *Chicago Tribune,* 4 Feb. 1863.

[2] Frost *Camp and Prison Journal,* 266; Wiley, "The Common Soldier of the Civil War," 19; R. G. 109, Roll 56; "Dear Ma." G. A. Pope to Mrs. L. J. Pope.

[3] Pulaski *Citizen,* 20 Jan. 1876, 8 May 1890, 12 Dec. 1901. Courtesy of Gilbert D. Dickey.

[4] The 29th Regiment, U. S. Colored Troops, Report of the Adj. Gen., v. 8:777; "In Vinculis: A Prisoner of War," *Confederate Veteran* 23:26.J. T. Lowry, "Experience as a Prisoner of War," ms. Duke University

[5] R.G. 393, v. 234:82; *Autobiography of Henry Morton Stanley,* 166; William H. Harder, memoir.

[6] Tuttle, *History of Camp Douglas,* 19, 21.

[7] *Chicago Tribune,* 19 May 1865.

[8] O R Ser.II-Vol.VIII, 986-1003.

[9] *Medical and Surgical Study,* 63.

[10] *Confederate Veteran* 23 (Apr. 1915):188.

[11] *Medical and Surgical History of the War of the Rebellion* III, I:49.

[12] *Medical and Surgical History,* v. I:46.

[13] *Medical and Surgical History,* 67.

[14] O R Ser.II-Vol.VII, 1243; Vol.VIII, 999-1003.

[15] *Black's Medical Dictionary,*199.

[16] Confederate Prisoners of War, R. G. 109, Roll 56.

[17] Burke, 27 Feb. 1864; 17 Jun. 1864; M. L. Vessey, "Camp Douglas in 1862," *Confederate Veteran* 38 (Mar. 1930):300.

[18] Tuttle, 11-12.

[19] R. G. 393, v. 243:186; O R Ser.II-Vol.VIII, 987-1003.

[20] Bross, *History of Camp Douglas,* 164.

[21] R. G. 393, v. 241:358, 380.

[22] Minutes of the Executive Committee of the Board of Trustees, 11 June 1864, The Old University of Chicago Records; Box 2, Folder 7.

[23] Story, "History of Camp Douglas," 112; *Chicago Tribune,* 10 July 1865.

[24] National Archives, R. G. 92.

[25] O R Ser.II-Vol.VIII, 714; *Chicago Tribune,* 3 Oct. 1865; Kelly, 109.

[26] Illinois Adj. Gen. Report, Vol. 1:121-22.

[27] Kelly, 79, 82.

[28] Kelly, 83.

[29] Medical and Surgical History, 49.

[30] Kelly, 86; R. G. 393, v. 234:282.

[31] R.G. 393, v. 233; Karlen, "Postal History of Camp Douglas," 822.

[32] *Chicago Tribune,* 4 Dec. 1865; R. G. 92.

[33] *Chicago Title & Trust Co., Pre-fire Records,* Book 340: 192-95.

[34] R.G. 92; Camp Douglas newspaper file, CHS; Camp Douglas, Inventory No. 1919.33, CHS.

[35] Camp Douglas Newspaper File, Chicago Historical Society.

[36] National Archives, R. G. 92.

[37] Story, 115; R.G. 249, William Hoffman Papers; Colbert, *Chicago Historical and Statistical Sketch,* II:95, Tuttle, 15, *Chicago Tribune,* 28 Jan. 1863, Kelly, 107.

[38] Copley, 166.

[39] Hesseltine, 140, 243; Kubalanza, "A comparative Study," 53.

[40] O R Ser.III-Vol.V, 147.

[41] Mark W. Sorensen, "The Civil War Prisoner of War System," 24, 25; O R Ser.II-Vol.VII, 995-1000; Burke, 12 Mar. 1865, attending church in Richmond. "The ladies and citizens were generally dressed fine."

[42] J. S. Rosamond, *Confederate Veteran* 16:421.

[43] Miss Mamie Yeary, *Reminiscences of the Boys in Gray, 1861-1865* (Dallas: Smith & Lamar, 1912), 88.

18.

AFTERMATH: LOST IN CHICAGO
EPILOGUE

The treatment of the Confederate dead is a shameful episode in the history of Camp Douglas. No provision was made for a cemetery when the prisoners arrived in 1862, although there was sufficient ground near the camp. A post-war investigation was required to find out what happened to over 4,000 dead. By then it was too late, and a struggle to rescue the remains lasted into the next century.

This is in sharp contrast to other Northern prisons whose reputations were just as unsavory. Burials were under the supervision of the general commanding the post at Fort Delaware. Coffins were tagged, and headboards carefully marked.[1] The treatment of the Camp Douglas prisoners did not remotely resemble such care.

Most of the Camp Douglas dead, about 3,384, went to Chicago's City Cemetery.[2] In addition, 655 smallpox cases were buried across from camp on the Douglas estate beginning August 13, 1864. There could not have been a worse burial site than City Cemetery, and the pauper's section, called "Potter's Field," was worse than the rest of the place.

It was located six miles north of camp, where the playing field in the southeast corner of Lincoln Park is today, at North Avenue and Lake Shore Drive.[3] This was the edge of Lake Michigan during the war, and the playing field was sand. Many prisoner remains are probably still there.

City Cemetery was a wet land. Graves contained water even in the dry season. Potter's Field was to have closed in 1857. "Nor is this the worst of the case," the *Tribune* reported on February 16, 1863. "What is called the Potter's Field, where these 640 rebel corpses are buried at the public charge, are interred, is on the very lowest land, and on the immediate borders of the slough where the lake water constantly ebbs and flows." The graves were described as shallow, "almost on the very surface." Many remains were missing if only 640 graves could be seen. The *Tribune* had reported 980 dead at Camp Douglas in 1862.[4] Only 24 bodies were returned home by families, so 956 dead should have been counted. Somehow, 316 bodies were unaccounted for.

The situation became much worse, considering a report by the Superintendent of Public Works in Chicago for the period January 1, 1862 to April 1, 1863. "There have been buried in the public grounds during the time specified, 2,218 persons, exclusive of the rebel prisoners, which were 615 in number," the city official wrote.[5] It appears that many dead from early 1863 had also vanished. Official Records list 387 deaths at Camp Douglas between January 1 and April 1, 1863. No bodies were sent home during this time. Adding 387 to approximately 980 deaths in 1862, the Superintendent should have found 1,343 graves, deducting the 24 removed home in 1862.

It seems that in the period from February, 1862 to April, 1863 about 728 Confederates were missing. That is not the worst of it. If 700 died in early 1863, as the *Tribune* and some historians of the period believed, then the Superintendent should have found 1,656 graves. Various explanations were put forward for this discrepancy. The bodies were being washed into the lake, according to the *Tribune,* toward the water intake crib only one mile south. The cemetery was also a favorite hunting ground for grave robbers.[6] Another likely explanation is that dead were dumped into unmarked mass graves and soon lost in the swampy soil.

Colonel L. H. Pierce of the Quartermaster General's office began investigating the situation at City Cemetery around December 1, 1865, on orders from Washington.[7] Pierce found that the Confederate remains were further endangered because of a court decision that the city did not own the cemetery ground. He also learned that a Chicago undertaker named C. H. Jordan had a verbal contract with Captain Potter at Camp Douglas "for burying all soldiers who died at camp at $4.75 per body." This included the "removing and interring the body and furnishing the coffin."

Jordan told Pierce that about 4,050 prisoners died. They were all at City Cemetery, except the 655 smallpox victims and approximately 400 dead shipped home to family and friends. C. H. Jordan had been a prominent undertaker in the city for many years.[8] He came there in 1854 as sales manager for a casket manufacturer and started his undertaking business. It was only necessary to call oneself an undertaker to become one. Jordan continued in the business long after the war, and buried most of the Chicago's rich and famous citizens in the best cemeteries.

However, Jordan thought that a pauper's grave was good enough for the prisoners, and he proceeded to purchase burial tickets for Potter's Field from the City Clerk. It is not certain how much he paid. The *Tribune* said $1.50, but the City Attorney claimed it was only one dollar. A ticket in the National Archives reads "One Dollar and Fifty Cents for an adult internment in the Chicago Cemetery."[9] Jordan probably received a 50-cent discount for the pauper's section.

It was not possible that for one dollar the cemetery could furnish a separate grave for each body, make a headboard, and keep records of the location and identity of the graves. It was not logical economically and not likely because these were Confederates. Neither Jordan, the sexton at the cemetery, nor the City Clerk even deemed it necessary for anyone to file reports of these burials as required by law.[10]

Colonel Pierce discovered that "on presenting this ticket at the Cemetery the Cemetery authorities took the body and buried it in the Potter's Field." He described the burial ground as "simply a sand waste over which the sand is continuously drifting. Some of the graves are now on sand ridges which are shifting positions daily," he observed. "In a short time the only traces of the graves can be procured from the fence I shall erect, unless yearly care is taken to remove the sand." The Public Works report had also noted that "the east fence of the cemetery was there to protect Potter's Field, but was rotting away and almost covered by drifted sand."

Legally, the Confederate dead were not paupers. The army paid Jordan $4.75 per body for burial. Based on post-war costs of removing these bodies, the allowance was adequate to include a decent coffin and a proper grave in a good cemetery. This gave Jordan a fair profit of one dollar per body. In spite of this, he furnished rude pine boxes at little cost, and after paying the city only one dollar for the burials, his profit tripled. The Camp Douglas beef scandal was penny-ante by comparison.

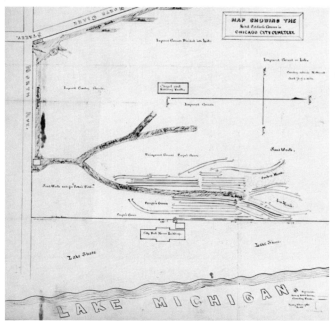

Quartermaster drawing of City Cemetery, April 1, 1866, showing the pauper's graves in sand and marshes [shaded area] (courtesy National Archives).

C. H. Jordan, cira 1876 (courtesy Chicago Historical Society)

The Reverend Edmund B. Tuttle wrote: "Each grave is marked; but sand which is continually being thrown up by the waves will soon cover them, to sleep on till the morning of the Resurrection." Reverend Tuttle did not indicate in his "History of Camp Douglas" that he attended any burials at City Cemetery, and while the camp abounded with other preachers and ministers, there is no report that any attended the dead prisoners. The City Attorney informed Pierce coldly that Chicago "claims the right to again bury on the same ground in eight to ten years (when these bodies will probably be decomposed) should the ground be wanted."

Unidentified infantry near Camp Douglas with C.H. Jordan's hearse passing in left foreground (courtesy USAMHI).

Colonel Pierce reported to General Meigs that he found only 2,968 names of prisoners at City Cemetery.[11] "It is stated that from Feby. 1862 till all the secesh had left here, nearly all of the Medical Colleges in the Northwest were supplied by bodies stolen from the rebel dead buried in the cemetery, and the appearance of some of the graves gives evidence of the truth of this statement."

Cemetery needs at Camp Douglas were comparable to the notorious prison at Elmira, New York. There the commanding officer leased an excellent plot in the Elmira City Cemetery. A prison detail prepared bodies for burial and marked the coffins. The sexton received $2.50 to bury each body in a separate grave, keep the records, and make the headboard. Every grave can be identified today. A man came up from Alabama in 1905 to take his father home, but was so pleased with the Confederate cemetery that he decided to let him rest there.[12]

In Chicago the situation was so desperate that Colonel Pierce recommended removing the remains to Rosehill Cemetery, eight miles northwest of the city. He could purchase an acre there for from $500 to $600 to hold 2,000 dead. Meigs, still concerned with economy, rejected the idea. He ordered the ground at City Cemetery enclosed, "and that yearly care be taken to remove the sand which may have drifted over the graves."[13] The City Attorney had already told Pierce that the army could not put up fences.

Nothing was done, and the severe deterioration and loss of Confederate bodies continued. This brought an urgent report the following year from General C. H. Hoyt, a new Quartermaster officer in charge of the investigation. He had identified only 1,402 graves at City Cemetery on December 1, 1866. "Very little care seems to have been taken in the interment of the bodies; they are crowded together, and in some cases the numbers are confused," he warned.[14] Close to 2,000 bodies were now unaccounted for.

The situation became more critical when Chicago Mayor J. B. Rice informed the army that all bodies must be removed because the cemetery was going to close. The Confederate dead were scattered in two cemeteries at the time, City and Oak Woods, located five miles south of the former camp. Some 655 prisoners from the smallpox cemetery at Camp Douglas had been removed to Oak Woods in December, 1865, by an unknown contractor.[15] This operation was also incredibly botched.

The Oak Woods superintendent told Hoyt "that among the bodies removed were those of twelve U. S. soldiers — That none of the Headboards on the graves at the old Cemetery at Camp Douglas were removed with the bodies, but were thrown aside." The Secretary of Oak Woods "endeavored at the time to procure the necessary information to perfect the records of the Cemetery, but was unable to do so." Consequently, Oak Woods had no names for these Confederate and Union soldiers. Hoyt confirmed that "deceased U. S. soldiers and the Rebel Prisoners of War appear to have been mixed promiscuously and sent by the wagon load from Camp Douglas without care or order."[16] Bodies could not be separated by uniform because these had been burned beforehand at the smallpox hospital.

Meanwhile, the army was doing nothing about removing the Confederate remains from City Cemetery. The Chicago Common Council sent an urgent letter to Hoyt on December 17, 1866. He was informed that the government had not provided a burial ground for the prisoners, and "that the City Government consented to their interment in said Cemetery." It appears that the City of Chicago was unaware that the Federal Government had made adequate provision for proper burials.

Meigs finally gave permission on January 14, 1867 to remove the Confederate remains from City Cemetery. General Bingham, a third Quartermaster officer, reported on February 26, 1867 that Rosehill Cemetery refused to allow any Confederate dead inside the cemetery, but "It might procure a lot outside."[17]

Bingham added that "Oak Woods Cemetery submitted a plan to inter at $2.00 for each grave and that the burials will be made at $1.00 each making the total cost of ground and burial $3.00 each. This does not include the cost of disinterring and removing the bodies from the city to the Oakwood Cemetery. Informal proposals have been received for doing this at $2.50 and $2.00 each." City Cemetery put the number of removals at 3,000. "I have no means of ascertaining whether or not fraud has been practiced in thus increasing the numbers from 1,402 to 3,000," Bingham claimed. The truth is that Bingham did not care. He could easily have ordered a squad of soldiers into Potter's Field to verify the numbers. City Cemetery assured a lone inspector sent by Bingham that only 40 bodies were missing, and these had been sent home. That ended the matter.[18]

The Government had purchased two acres at Oak Woods in a swampy marsh as bad as City Cemetery, which became known as the "Confederate Mound." The 655 prisoners and 12 Federal soldiers from the smallpox cemetery were already there in a mass grave. Adjoining trenches with numbered spaces were planned for the remains coming from City Cemetery "so that each body shall occupy an exact width of two feet and then by reference to the register a ready and certain mode will be provided for finding the location of each body."[19]

Bingham was referred to Joseph W. Ernst, Sexton of City Cemetery. He could move the bodies to Oak Woods and furnish new coffins if required at two dollars and fifty cents for each body. "Mr. Ernst would be a suitable man as he made the interments and knows the locations of the bodies," Bingham advised. "I do not think the price is too high." The trip was eleven miles by land. The price was not too high compared to what C. H. Jordan had received. Mr. Ernst was familiar with the Confederate burials because he worked there at the time, and he was in charge of exhuming all remains as City Cemetery prepared to close.[20]

There was no discussion about removing the dead to the former Confederacy. Cost of shipping may have been a factor, although a free plot was probably available in the South. Oak Woods could have become the largest Confederate burial site outside of the South, but subsequent events make it impossible to learn the number buried there. General Bingham reported on May 1, 1867 that the removal to Oak Woods had been completed. Mr. Ernst had not been given the contract, however. M. O'Sullivan was awarded the job at $1.98 for each body disinterred and removed." The price was supposed to include coffins.[21]

M. O'Sullivan had been a civilian storekeeper at the Federal Quartermaster warehouse in Chicago during the war. He became a Chicago alderman for the central business district in 1867, replacing James J. O'Sullivan, who had resigned. James J. was a lawyer and had also served as City Attorney.[22] M. O'Sullivan may have obtained the contract through his connections at the Quartermaster Department. Another possiblity is that James J. was the City Attorney who had consulted with the army about the burials at City Cemetery.

C. H. Jordan listed the sale by him of "15 Reb coffins plus nails to Alderman James J. O'Sullivan" on April 20, 1867 for $44.50, an extortionate price.[23] A "Reb coffin" meant a crude pine box which cost under one dollar. Neither of the O'Sullivans had the experience, equipment, nor trained employees to make a coffin, much less accomplish the removals from City Cemetery.

James J. O'Sullivan was in a nasty scrape in August, 1864 on an attempted rape charge.[24] He claimed that it was a frame-up to force him to get the complainant's mother out of jail. Several affidavits regarding the woman's "utter worthlessness" were presented to the grand jury, and the male panel refused to indict O'Sullivan. The *Tribune* was happy that the Common Council had not been disgraced. "There are black sheep enough on its roll already," the paper admitted.

The O'Sullivans' bid of $1.98 was woefully inadequate based on what they had to pay Jordan for coffins, and the pair probably failed to consider the cost of transportation. The remains could have been taken south by boat and then west by land, or loaded on the Illinois Central, which ran near Oak Woods. There is no information on what they did, but many remains were probably abandoned.

Like Jack's fabled Bean Stalk, the number of bodies at City Cemetery grew to 3,384. An eyewitness claimed that "that in some of the rude coffins no bodies were found, showing that the nimble grafters had imposed on Uncle Sam by getting paid for burying empty boxes." A reporter confirmed "in many instances the coffins were found to be empty."[25] He described Potter's Field as "a deep ravine, which is a great portion of the time covered by water." The reporter mentioned that the headboards had no names, but numbers were recorded with the name in cemetery records. "When a coffin is exhumed, it is immediately ticketed with the number of the headboard."

Interment at Oak Woods began on April 13, 1867, and lasted through April 30. Unfortunately, there was no certification by Oak Woods as to the number of coffins received or that it counted or inspected the remains. The cemetery simply buried whatever the O'Sullivans brought in and numbered the grave markers at Oak Woods according to City Cemetery records. These records cannot be verified because no Confederate burials were recorded with the City Clerk.[26]

The army failed to supervise, inspect, or validate the removals. History had been blindfolded, and there is no way of knowing how many Confederates, or which ones, are at Oak Woods. Cost of removals was $6,700.32, based on 3,384 bodies. Oak Woods received $10,152. Add approximately $14,250 paid to C. H. Jordan during the war and the total was $31,102 at a time when the dollar meant something. There is nothing to show for it. Only one grave marker is currently visible, and it appears that no religious services were conducted at Oak Woods.

Captain Charles Goodman kept a burial register at Camp Douglas beginning in May, 1864, entitled "Report of Interments made at Chicago and Camp Douglas."[27] The *Tribune* often mentioned Goodman as supervising repairs at camp. He divided the dead into "White, Black, Loyal, and Disloyal." Confederates were listed as "disloyal." Civilian prisoners were "bushwhackers" or "guerrillas." Union dead show in the "loyal" column. He listed 1,733 Confederate burials from August, 1864 thru July, 1865, and 26 civilians. Twelve of these civilians were suspects arrested by Sweet in the Conspiracy of 1864. The Official Records show 1,737 Confederates dying during this period, so his register is accurate. He did not show if interment was at City or the smallpox cemetery. From May, 1864 through July, 1865, he recorded 183 Union soldiers having died at Camp Douglas. Some of these were there for discharge.

Comrades of a deceased prisoner were allowed to telegraph his home if it was within the Union lines. Family or friends could contact Mr. Jordan and pay to have the remains sent home for burial. There are many entries in the prison rolls as, "In the vault of C. H. Jordan." At least 143 bodies were shipped to Kentucky by Jordan, according to official records, and two bodies went to Cincinnati. However, Jordan told the army that he had sent 400 dead to their families, which lends further uncertainty about the number who died at Camp Douglas.[28] Bodies of the less fortunate were stored by Jordan in the morgue at City Cemetery when the ground was frozen. Their identity was soon lost in this place. The victim in the kitchen murder case of 1862 had to be found with help from prisoners who had known him.

Only two Confederates who died at Camp Douglas escaped the calamity of a pauper's grave at City Cemetery without going home. Symbolically, one was Jewish and one was Catholic. "Theodore Hirsch, Pvt., Holmes Light Battery, Louisiana Artillery," died December 12, 1864, and was removed to Chicago Jewish Cemetery, an excellent section of City Cemetery.[29] When Jewish Cemetery closed around 1872 to make way for Lincoln Park, Hirsch found a safe haven at the Hebrew Benevolent Society Cemetery in Chicago.[30] However, his grave is now lost due to a fire in the cemetery office that destroyed some of his records in 1911. The other soldier, James Lyons, Pvt., Co. H, 15th Tennessee Infantry, died January 27, 1865, and was removed to Calvary Cemetery in Evanston, Illinois. Calvary has no record of receiving the body.

The ordeal of the Confederate dead continued long after Camp Douglas was gone. On January 25, 1882, E. R. P. Shurly, the former adjutant at Camp Douglas, still residing in Chicago, reported to Washington that "Recently the remains of Union and Confederate soldiers have been exhumed in the vicinity of Camp Douglas. In 1864-65 the small pox hospital was located near there and about 150 bodies who died in that place were buried there."[31] Shurly was wrong about the number of dead by a wide margin. Regardless, the army contractor had not only botched the removals from the smallpox cemetery in 1865, but had left many bodies there as well.

The army ordered another inquiry, and the Chief Quartermaster in Chicago reported on February 17, 1882 that "These graves are on the site of the burying ground used for those who died of smallpox at Camp Douglas. The bodies dug up are supposed to be those of prisoners. There are signs of more on the premises and the owner says unless some steps are taken for their removal he will take them up himself and bury them."[32]

On May 3, 1882, the Quartermaster informed Washington that "Thirteen bodies have been dug up and removed to the Soldiers' Lot at Oakland

[Oak Woods] Cemetery, at a cost of $7.00." Oak Woods has no record of any Confederate burials in 1882, but the "Soldiers Lot" was the Confederate Mound, and there is no reason to doubt that the 13 were buried as reported.

In 1885, the Confederate Mound was threatened by plans to put a public street through the plot. Nothing came of it except a report that 4,039 Confederates and 12 Union soldiers were buried there.[33] Oak Woods allegedly received 3,384 remains from City; add the 655 from the smallpox cemetery, including the 13 bodies found in 1882, and the total is 4,039.

In August 1887 the Ex-Confederate Soldiers Association of Chicago petitioned Congress to place a monument at Oak Woods. It is unlikely that permission would have been given, except a crisis developed. The place began to look like the Potter's Field at City Cemetery. Complaints caused the Quartermaster's office to repeat its investigations of 1865-67. This would be the fourth time that the Government had to step in.

On September 1, 1890, General Bingham reported that "Many of the graves are sunken and many of the corner stakes are missing. There are evidences that one of the sections has been used as a road way. The ground around these lots has been raised and improved which gives them the sunken appearance." Illinois Congressman Frank Lawler immediately notified the Confederate Association that it had permission to repair and improve the lot, "provided that no part of the expense therefore be made a charge against the United States."[34] Keep in mind that the government owned the plot then, and still does today.

The monument was built in the center of the tract, now sunk far below the level of the surrounding area. It was made of Georgia granite and completed in 1893 at a cost of $10,000. Still owed was $2,000. Of the $8,000 paid, $7,500 came from sympathizers in Chicago and other parts of the North. Not everyone in Chicago was pleased. The monument was opposed by some Union veterans who said it would be "a seeming attempt to eulogize a bad and dead cause."[35]

Nevertheless, about 100,000 persons attended on Memorial Day, 1895 when the monument was dedicated. It was a chance to see President Grover Cleveland, who had avoided the draft during the war by hiring a substitute for about $300 to go in his place. Louisiana sent a magnolia tree. The planting was done by five year-old Jimmy Pope, a descendant of President Tyler, in soil sent up from Mississippi battlegrounds. Assisting was the United Daughters of the Confederacy, Sons of Confederate Veterans, and the Oak Woods Board of Directors.[36] The tree died in the next Chicago winter, and the Confederate plot continued to deteriorate. Nothing was done by the Confederate Association to repair or improve the ground as it was supposed to do, and the weight of the monument probably contributed to further sinking of the swampy land.

Within five years the remains, including the 12 or more Union dead, were on the verge of extinction. All were under weeds and water draining in from the surrounding area. This brought on the fifth inquiry since the war. Only Congress with Federal money could save the remains from final destruction. On May 20, 1899, Oak Woods notified Congress that the solution was to take down the monument, fill the two acres to the level of the rest of the cemetery without removing the dead, and to reset the monument on top.[37] This was done by 1902 with a $3,850 appropriation plus $250 per annum for perpetual care.

Oak Woods covered the burial trenches with about six feet of earth to bring the sunken plot up to ground level. Prior to this, the trenches formed an oval field extending 150 feet to the east and west of the monument and 250 feet to the north and south of it. There were wide walkways between the trenches, which had small stone markers with numbers on them. The numbers could be cross-referenced to names in the Confederate Register at Oak Woods. Visitors to the site do not realize that they are walking over a hidden cemetery. Even the 12 Federal headstones in front of the monument at Oak Woods are only symbolic, since these remains are also lost in the burial trenches.

Confederate monument, Oak Woods Cemetery, January, 1991.

Today, only one marker is visible at the eastern edge of the lot. A headstone reading "James W. Leak, 1st Alabama Infantry, February 10, 1865" stands on the marker which indicates the boundary of the burial trenches below. City Cemetery records were wrong. His name was Joseph W. Leak, and he died on February 11.[38]

It is unlikely that the government will have to intervene again to save the remains. The army inspects the plot yearly to verify that perpetual care is being maintained. The finishing touches were added in 1912 when the monument's base was reinforced with granite and 16 bronze tablets were added bearing the names of 4,234 dead.

Epilogue

Reverend E. B. Tuttle: A benefactor donated a lot for him to build a chapel near the former camp, at 36th Street and Cottage Grove. This became St. Marks Episcopal Church, and it was still active in 1919 when the building was sold to a black congregation. Allan J. Fuller, the former Adjutant General, who became a judge on the Illinois Supreme Court, was a member of St. Marks. Former prisoners wrote to Tuttle asking about job opportunities in Chicago. He abandoned his successful parish in 1867 and returned to the army. He then quit the army to become an expatriate in Europe. Later, he returned to his roots in New York and wrote an Illinois history. The former chaplain died in New York in 1881 at age 65.

Curtis R. Burke: He and Henry White explored Richmond and traveled to Abbeville, South Carolina on their furlough. Burke was in Danville, Virginia when Lee surrendered, and he witnessed the flight of the Confederate government with the arrival of President Davis. The Confederate Commissary was issuing rations as late as May 2, and Burke even drew 32 dollars in silver. He and Henry still had hopes of reaching Texas to carry on the fight. On May 24, they learned that it was truly over, with armed Federal troops firmly in control of all railroads and waterways. Burke had no intention of returning to Ohio, and made his way toward Kentucky. In Memphis, his proposal of marriage to a childhood sweetheart, was cruelly rejected. "Another Lost Cause!" he lamented. Alone now, he could not find work and took the oath of allegiance for a steamboat ticket to Cincinnati. Burke never again mentioned his father, but learned from his brother that Pa had been released from Camp Douglas and was with their mother near Medina, Ohio. Pa had decided that he could live in the North after all.

Lexington painting houses at $1.25 per day, and hurriedly reclaimed a valise that he had left as security for a hotel bill. To his great relief he found that his Confederate uniform was "all safe."

Henry Graves: He continued to live at Cottage Grove. The War Department settled his rent claim and the city paved a street in former Garrison Square, naming it "Graves Place." He became wealthy and drove a fine team of horses along beautiful Grand Boulevard, formerly Kankakee Avenue, the western border of Prison Square, now called Martin Luther King Drive. In 1907 he was dying of old age at 86, and the homestead looked as it did during the war. Both he and the historic building were gone by 1909.

The University of Chicago: It built a theological seminary in 1869 on the former smallpox cemetery. By 1882 the University was bankrupt, killed off by the war, extravagant building schemes, and inadequate financing. It was revived in 1892 with massive funding from John D. Rockefeller, and began laying the foundations for a world-class institution three miles south of its Civil War site. Atomic fusion was born on campus a half century later.

The City of Chicago: When fire leveled the city in 1871, many refugees sought shelter among the empty graves in City Cemetery. Post war Chicago was a city of the poor who had less protection against the savage winters than the prisoners at Camp Douglas. They tore down outhouses and fences for fuel, and as the population grew so did the stench from excrement, sewage, and horses. For them, the flush toilets and wash houses of Camp Douglas were unimaginable. Economic depression was added to the sub-zero cold of the early 1890s, and without public aid programs, the penniless were more imperiled than the Confederates had been. Cholera and typhoid killed thousands who were carted off to a potter's field and lost for one hundred years.

Colonel Joseph H. Tucker: A second son died in the war and the third was considered for West Point. He left Chicago in 1865 and went into business in New York City. Tucker wrote to Reverend Tuttle, but never returned to Chicago. By 1887 he was an invalid and died in New York on October 23, 1894 at age 75. His epitaph reads: "He had never been a military man, just a business man."

General James A. Mulligan: He did not know how to take a backward step. While being carried off the field at Winchester Virginia, he ordered, "Lay me down and save the flag!" His funeral in Chicago was a tumultuous scene in the wartime city, and his monument dominates the western entrance to Calvary Cemetery in Evanston, Illinois.

General Daniel Cameron: His regiment compiled a distinguished record after leaving Camp Douglas. He earned a Division command for his performance at the battle of Knoxville, and fought through the Atlanta campaign to be breveted Brigadier-General. Cameron became active in national politics after the war as a conservative Democrat, and then retired to his farm 17 miles northwest of Chicago. He married a young woman from Scotland and fathered 12 children. The General died at age 51, only 12 years after the war.

General Charles V. De Land: He took his war record to the people of Michigan and was elected to the state legislature. Whatever his failures at Camp Douglas, De Land was one of those combat officers who caused the North to win the war. He held various state offices and was still in government as late as 1895. The General died in 1903 and is buried in Jackson, Michigan.

General William Ward Orme: He resigned from the army due to poor health shortly after leaving Camp Douglas. President Lincoln then appointed him Supervisor of the Treasury Department at Memphis. His illness caused him to leave in November, 1865, and return home to Bloomington, Illinois, where he died on September 13, 1866.

General Benjamin J. Sweet: He is the only Camp Douglas commander who did not win his star on the battlefield. After resigning from the army, he purchased a small farm in Wheaton, Illinois and practiced law. He soon held positions as U. S. Pension Agent in Chicago, Illinois Supervisor of Internal Revenue, and Deputy I.R.S. Commissioner in Washington. The General died suddenly of pneumonia in 1874, aged 41. He was only 33 when he commanded Camp Douglas and leaped into national prominence. He is buried in Rosehill Cemetery in Chicago. The General's reputation was "sullied" in 1876 when U.S. Congressman Hurlbut of Illinois charged that Sweet had bribed a man named George W. Campbell to obtain the Pension Office job. Hurlbut was a member of the Committee on Civil Service Reform and a former Major-General of the Union Army who had commanded the 16th Army Corps. Sweet's powerful political sponsor, Joseph R. Jones, denied that any bribe was paid. He admitted that George W. Campbell and Sweet were the ones considered for the appointment, and that Sweet had agreed to pay George $2,500 yearly to run the pension office while Sweet looked after his law practice. Hurlbut claimed that Sweet paid George the money as a ghost payroller to have Jones sponsor Sweet. The matter was not resolved.

John Walsh: His cartage business in Chicago flourished after the Conspiracy trials, and he even received city contracts to haul mail and clean streets. He never strayed far from the former site of Camp Douglas where he had gained nationwide publicity, and died in his mansion less than two miles away in 1885.

General William Hoffman: He reverted to his rank of Colonel in the regular army in 1865, and commanded posts at St. Louis and Fort Leavenworth. Apparently he found romance at Rock Island, Illinois, where one of his prison camps had been located. Hoffman became a civilian for the first time in his adult life, and married a much younger woman, there upon retiring at age 64. He died on August 12, 1884, of an enlarged prostate, and is buried in Rock Island. A special act of congress raised the widow's pension to $50 per month because of Hoffman's war-time services.

Miss Ada C. Sweet: She never married, but raised her younger brother and two sisters after their mother died in a train accident. She and the General were more like brother and sister than parent and child. Her education had ended at age 14 after three years at the Catholic school in Chicago. Ada became her father's secretary at age 16 when he was appointed U.S. Pension agent in Chicago in 1869. In 1874, President Grant appointed her to that office, an unusual position then for so young a woman. Miss Sweet enjoyed talking about the camp and regretted that all trace of it had disappeared since the landmark University was torn down. Ada's reputation was also "sullied" in the 1876 investigation of the Chicago Pension Office, with Congressman Hurlbut charging that she bribed a man named B. H. Campbell to cause the pension agent in Chicago to resign so that she could have the job. No reply was made, and the matter was not resolved.

Daniel F. Brandon: He gave up photography when the camp closed and opened an artist's studio near downtown Chicago. After four years at Camp Douglas, he could not face the prospect of taking baby pictures and making family albums. Brandon moved away from his house on Cottage Grove in 1867 and directly into the path of the Chicago Fire of 1871. While he and his wife and three children survived, much of his Camp Douglas work did not.

Camp Douglas: The area developed into a fashionable residential district in the 1870s. Cottage Grove was a major business district from 26th to 39th Streets by 1896. Starting in 1900 the area began a sharp decline for the next 52 years and became a notorious slum. Now cleared and redeveloped, the camp site has reappeared. White Oak Square, South Square, and part of Garrison Square are grassy fields; the lawn of a modern apartment building and its parking lot mark the location of the Graves cottage and the entrance to the camp; a child's playground is where the University building stood; automobiles at a nearby shopping center park in the small-pox cemetery; large sections of Prison Square emerge on the east side of King Drive between 31st and 33rd Streets. Like the University, which died and was reborn, the camp is covered with ice and snow again. For the prisoners who are lost in Chicago, the winters never end. For those who reached Oak Woods, Camp Douglas is eternal.

NOTES TO CHAPTER 18

[1] O R Ser. II–Vol. VI, 525.

[2] R. G. 92, Cemeterial Files, Box 141.

[3] I. J. Bryan, *History of Lincoln Park* (Chicago: The Commissioners, 1899); Chicago Park District, ms., "Historical Register of the Twenty-Two Superseded Park Districts" (1941) 132; Chas. Shober & Co., Chicago, *Guide Map to Chicago* (1868) shows "Rebel Graves" near the shore line 150 yards north of North Avenue and State Streets.

[4] *Chicago Tribune* 11 Dec. 1862; 16 Feb. 1863.

[5] "Report of the Superintendent of Cemetery Grounds and Public Parks" (10 April, 1863) 70, Chicago Historical Society.

[6] National Archives. R. G. 92, Cemeterial Files, Box 141.

[7] Cemeterial Files, Box 141.

[8] Andreas, *History of Chicago* 2:450

[9] R. G. 92, box 141.

[10] Common Council Proceedings, 1861-65, Illinois Regional Archives Depository, Northeastern University.

[11] The Quartermaster count of bodies sent home was 143 soldiers and 39 civilians. *Confederate Soldiers Sailors and Civilians Who Died at Camp Douglas.*

[12] Clay W. Holmes, *The Elmira Prison Camp* (New York: G. Putnam's Sons, 1912), 130, 134.

[13] Cemeterial file, box 141.

[14] R. G. 92, box 141.

[15] Cemeterial Files, Box 141.

[16] Box 141.

[17] Box 141.

[18] Box 141.

[19] 56th Congress, 1st Session, House of Representatives, Report No. 1077. "Confederate Mound in Oak Woods Cemetery, Chicago, Ill.," (17 April 1900): 2. Each section consisted of five burial trenches with four walkways, R. G. 92, Cemeterial Files, Box 141.

[20] Cemeterial files, Box 141; Halpin & Bailey's Chicago City Directories, 1861-66; Andreas, *History of Chicago* 2:449.

[21] Cemeterial Files, Box 141.

[22] Halpin & Bailey Directory, 1861-65; Andreas, *History of Chicago,* 2:49-50.

[23] Day Book of Burials, C. H. Jordan. 1866. CHS ms. Coll.

[24] *Chicago Tribune* 16 Sep. 1864.

[25] Chicago Messenger, 16 April 1914, "Interview with Mr. Scharf, Sr." Albert F. Scharf was at Camp Douglas with the 19th Illinois Infantry. He knew Henry Graves and visited him at Cottage Grove. One of his copper pennies went into the bell for the prison chapel, CHS ms. Coll; Chicago Times, 15 Apr. 1867.

[26] Oak Woods Cemetery Archives, Confederate Register, 36-203; Chicago Common Council Proceedings, 1861-65.

[27] Ms. Coll, CHS.

[28] T. M. Page, *Confederate Veteran* 8:63; Confederate Prisoners of War, Roll 58.

[29] There were Jewish prisoners reported at Camp Douglas beginning with Fort Donelson, *The Israelite, A Weekly Periodical,* Cincinnati, Ohio, 28 Feb. 1862; *Confederate Soldiers, Sailors and Civilians Who Died at Camp Douglas.*

[30] Hebrew Benevolent Society Cemetery Records, Register of the Range of Adults, 25. Grave 17. "Theodore Hirsh. Dec. 15 1864 Prisoner of Camp Douglas." The date probably reflects when he was interred at Jewish Cemetery.

[31] National Archives, Office of the Quartermaster General, R. G. 92, Cemeterial Files, Box 41.

[32] R. G. 92, Cemeterial Files, Box 141.

[33] Box 141.

[34] Box 141.

[35] John P. Hickman, "Confederate Monument in Chicago," *Confederate Veteran* 1 (Nov. 1893): 346; Chicago Daily News, 24 Aug. 1968.

[36] Camp Douglas Newspaper file, Chicago Municipal Reference Library; John M. Taylor, "Grover Cleveland and the Rebel Banners," *Civil War Times* 4 (Sep./Oct. 1993):22-24.

Oak Woods Cemetery publication, *Chicago As We Remember Her.* (1951) 18-19.

[37] House of Representatives, Report No. 1077: 2, 4.

[38] Box 141; *Confederate Soldiers, Sailors and Civilians Who Died as Prisoners of War at Camp Douglas.*

BIBLIOGRAPHY

PRIMARY SOURCES

1. Manuscript Materials:
 Baptism Records. St. James Catholic Church, Chicago.
 Chicago Historical Society, Miscellaneous Manuscripts, and Camp Douglas Newspaper File. Original Autograph Letters, Vol. 49.
 Calvary Cemetery Archives, Evanston.
 Chicago Park District.
 City of Chicago Municipal Reference Library
 Hebrew Benevolent Society Archives, Chicago.
 Illinois State Historical Library, Springfield.
 Illinois State Archives, Springfield.
 Illinois Regional Archives Depository, Northeastern Illinois University, Chicago.
 Kentucky State Archives, Louisville.
 Library of Congress.
 Louisiana State University, Baton Rouge.
 Michigan State Archives, Lansing.
 National Archives. Record Groups 92, 109, 249, 393.
 Newberry Library, Chicago.
 Museum of the Confederacy, Richmond.
 Oak Woods Cemetery Archives, Chicago.
 Pre-fire Records. Chicago Title & Trust Co.
 Regenstein Library, University of Chicago.
 Rush-Presbyterian-St. Luke's Medical Center Archives, Chicago.
 Tennessee State Archives, Nashville.
 United States Army Military History Institute.

2. Government Publications:
 Historical Register and Dictionary of the U.S. Army. Government Printing Office, Washington, 1903.
 House of Representatives, Executive Document 50. 39th Congress, 2nd Session. *The Case of George St. Leger Grenfel.*
 House of Representatives, Report No. 1077, 56th Congress 1st Session. *Confederate Mound in Oak Woods Cemetery.*
 National Archives. *Selected Records of the War Department Relating to Confederate Prisoners of War,* Microcopy 598, Record Group 109.

The War of the Rebellion: A Compilation of the Official Records of the Union and Confederate Armies, 70 Vols.,128 *books*. Government Printing Office, Washington, 1901.

The Medical and Surgical History of the War of the Rebellion, 3 Vols. Government Printing Office, Washington, 1888.

3. State Publications:

State of Illinois. Illinois State Historical Library, Report of the Adjutant General, 1861-66. Springfield.

State of Michigan. Michigan State Historical Library, Report of the Adjutant General, *Record of Service of Michigan Volunteers in the Civil War*. Lansing.

4. City of Chicago Publications:

Proceedings of the Common Council, 1861-1865. Illinois Regional Archives Depository.

Reports of the Department of Public Works, 1861-1867. Chicago Historical Society.

5. Newspapers:

Chicago Tribune

Chicago Times.

Chicago Inter-Ocean

Chicago Evening Journal

Chicago Daily News

Chicago Messenger

Chicago Times

Christian Times

Greenville Advocate

The Israelite, Cincinnati, Ohio.

Sunday Record Herald

Ottawa Free Trader

6. Diaries, Letters, Memoirs, Personal Narratives and Recollections:

Barrow, Willie M. Civil War Diary in *Louisiana Historical Quarterly*. Edited by Wendell H. Stephenson and Edwin A. Davis. 17 (1934):436-51, 712-31.

Baxter, Marion F. 20th Miss. Inf. Regt., Diary. Lionel F. Baxter coll., USAMHI.

Bean, R. T. "Seventeen Months in Camp Douglas." *Confederate Veteran* 22 (Jun. 1914):270.

Belknap, Charles W. 125th N.Y. Inf. Regt., Diary. CWTI coll., USAMHI.

Benedict, C. G. *Vermont in the Civil War.* 2 vols. Burlington: The Free Press Assoc., 1888.

Berry, J. M. "Prison Life in Camp Douglas." *Confederate Veteran.* 11 (Apr. 1903):37-38.

Bradley, M. J. "The Horrors of Camp Douglas as related by a prisoner," in Griffin Frost's *Camp and Prison Journal,* Quincy Herald Book and Job Office, Quincy, 1867.

Branch, J. T. "Account of Escapes from Camp Morton." *Confederate Veteran.* 8 (Feb. 1900):71.

Bross, William. "History of Camp Douglas," in *Reminiscences of Chicago During the Civil War.* Mabel McIlvaine, ed. Chicago: Lakeside Press, R. R. Donnelley & Sons, 1914. (First published in "Biographical Sketch of the late Gen. B. J. Sweet." *History of Camp Douglas.* A paper read before the Chicago Historical Society. Chicago: Jansen, McClurg & Co., 1878.

Buckley, James. Co. F. 45th Ill. Inf. Regt. "Dear Niece." Letter dated 19 December 1861 reporting mutiny of the Mechanic Fusileers. Original letter owned by Alan C. Hunt, Springfield, Illinois.

Burke, Curtis R. Civil War Journal in *Indiana Magazine of History.* Edited by Pamela J. Bennett. 65 (Dec., 1969):283- 327; 66 (June, 1970):110-72; (Dec., 1970):318-61; 67 (June, 1971):129-70. Complete journal is in UAMHI.

Calkins, William W. *The History of the 104th Regiment, Illinois Volunteer Infantry, 1862-1865.* Chicago: Donahue & Henneberry, 1895.

Campbell, Andrew Jackson. Civil War Diary. Edited by Jill K. Garrett. Special Collections, Chicago Public Library.

Clore, T. B. in Cornelius Hite's "Man's Inhumanity to Man." *Confederate Veteran.* 32 (Jun. 1924):218.

Coke, James S. *Confederate Veteran.* 14 (Oct. 1906):38

Cook, Frederick Francis. *Bygone Days in Chicago, Recollections of the "Garden City" of the Sixties.* Chicago: A. C. McClurg & Co., 1910.

Cook, J. W. "Villainous Inspectors at Camp Douglas." *Confederate Veteran.* 16 (Aug. 1908):406.

Copley, John M. *A Sketch of the Battle of Franklin, Tenn., With Reminiscences of Camp Douglas.* Austin: E. Von Boeckman, 1893.

De Graff, Nicholay. 115th N. Y. Inf. Regt., Diary. CWTI coll., USAMHI.

Duke, Basil W. *Reminiscences of General Basil W. Duke, C. S. A.* New York: Doubleday, Page & Co., 1911.

Duke, Basil W. *A History of Morgan's Cavalry.* Edited by Cecil F. Holland. Bloomington: Indiana University Press, 1960.

Foute, Samuel L. "Dear Sir." Letter about life as a prisoner of war at Camp Douglas in 1862. Tragg coll., Library of Congress ms. Division.

Froman, B. R. "An Interior View of the Camp Douglas Conspiracy." *Southern Bivouac* 1-No.2 (Oct., 1882):63-69.

Garrett, Jill K. Collection, ca. 1800-1969. Tennessee State Library and Archives, Nashville.

Hankenson, Hazel. "Where Dixie Sleeps Farthest North." *Confederate Veteran.* 33(Aug. 1925):301.

Greble, Edwin. 196th Pennsylvania Inf. Regt., Diary. ms. Div., LOC.

Harris, W. T. *Confederate Veteran.* 33 (Nov. 1925):429.

Harrison, Carter H. *Growing Up With Chicago.* Chicago: Bobs-Merrill Co., 1944.

Henry, T. D. "Treatment of Prisoners During the War." *Southern Historical Society Papers* 1 (Jan.-Jun. 1876):278.

Hickman, John P. "The Confederate Monument in Chicago." *Confederate Veteran.* 1 (Nov. 1893):346.

Hines, Thomas Henry. "The Northwestern Conspiracy." *Southern Bivouac.* New Series II (Jun. 1866-Mar. 1887): 437- 45, 500-10, 567-74.

Hopkins, E. R. "At Fort Donelson." *Confederate Veteran.* 38 (Mar. 1930):85.

Hunter, J. N. "Courage of a Georgian in Camp Douglas." *Confederate Veteran.* 15 (Sep. 1907):389.

Kirk, Edmund [Gilmore, J. R.]. "Three Days at Camp Douglas" in *Our Young Folks* 1 (Apr.-Jun. 1865): 252-60, 291-98, 357- 60.

Lamons, J. T. *Confederate Veteran.* 7(Jan. 1899):28.

Livermore, Mary A. *My Story of the War.* Hartford: A. D. Worthington & Co., 1889.

Lowry, J. T. "Experience as a Prisoner of War." ms. collection, William R. Perkins Library, Duke University.

(First published in *Confederate Veteran* 18 (Jul. 1910):334- 35.

Mackey, James T. Diary. Eleanor S. Brockenbrough Library, Museum of the Confederacy, Richmond.

McNeill, Malcom. Papers. North Carolina State Archives, Raleigh.

Moore, J. J. "Camp Douglas." *Confederate Veteran.* 11 (Jun. 1903):270-71.

Norvell, Otway B. "The Secret Order in Camp Douglas."
Confederate Veteran. 11 (Apr. 1930:168-71.

Page, T. M. "The Prisoner of War." *Confederate Veteran.* 8 (Feb. 1900):64.

Pope, George S. Letters from Camp Douglas, 1862. William R. Perkins Library, Duke University.

Prince, P. H. "Hardship in Camp Douglas." *Confederate Veteran.* 15 (Dec. 1907):565-66.

Robison, John W. Papers, 1861-1863. Tennessee State Library and Archives.

Rosamond, J. S. "In Camp Douglas in 1865." *Confederate Veteran.* 16 (Aug. 1908):421.

Rugeley, J. T. "Escape from Camp Douglas." *Confederate Veteran.* 9(Jan. 1901):30.

Ryan, Milton A. 14th Miss. Inf. Regt. "Experiences of a Confederate Soldier in the Civil War." CWTI coll., USAMHI. Smith, Benjamin T. *Recollections of the Late War, Private Smith's Journal.* Edited by Clyde C. Walton. Chicago: Lakeside Press, R. R. Donnelley & Sons, 1963. (Manuscript is in the Illinois State Historical Library, Springfield).

Stanley, Dorothy, ed. *Autobiography of Sir Henry Morton Stanley.* New York: Houghton Mifflin Co., 1909.

Taylor, Charles E. 20th Miss. Inf. Regt. Diary. (Manuscript is owned by Medford H. Roe, Jr., Mobile Ala.)

Templeton, J. A. "Prison Reminiscences." *Confederate Veteran.* 34 (May, 1926):196-97.

Terrell, Spot F. "A Confederate Private at Fort Donelson." *The American Historical Review.* 31:477-484. New York: Macmillan Co.,1926.

Thompson, Benjamin W. 111th N.Y. Inf. Regt., Diary. CWTI coll. USAMHI.

Tuttle, Rev. E. B. *The History of Camp Douglas; including Official Report of Gen. B. J. Sweet; With Anecdotes Of The Rebel Prisoners.* Chicago: J. R. Walsh & Co., 1865.

Vesey, M. L. "Camp Douglas in 1862." *Confederate Veteran.* 38 (Mar. 1930):299-300.

Williams, John L. "Dear Niece." Letter about life as a prisoner at Camp Douglas in 1862. Library of Congress ms. Division.

Yeager, J. A. "A Boy With Morgan." *Confederate Veteran.* 34 (Aug. 1926):294-98.

Yeary, Mamie., ed. *Reminiscences of the Boys in Gray.* Dallas: Smith & Lamar, 1885.

II

SECONDARY SOURCES

1. Histories:

A. General Accounts.

Battles and Leaders of the Civil War. 4 Vols. New York: Thomas Yoseloff, & Co., 1956.

Johnson, Rossiter. *A History of the War of Secession*. New York: Wessels & Bissell Co., 1910.

Leech, Margaret. *Reveille in Washington, 1860-1865*. New York: Time, Inc., 1962.

Randall, J. G. *The Civil War and Reconstruction*. Chicago: D. C. Heathe & Co., 1937.

B. Illinois Histories.

Cole, Arthur, C. *The Era of the Civil War*, 1848-1870. Vol. 3. Springfield: Illinois Centennial Commission, 1919.

C. Chicago Histories.

Andreas, A. T. *History of Chicago*. 3 Vols. Chicago: A. T. Andreas Co., 1885.

Colbert, Elias A. *Chicago, Historical and Statistical Sketch of the Garden City*. Chicago: P. T. Sherlock, 1868.

Currey, J. Seymour. *Chicago, Its History and Its Builders*. 5 Vols. Chicago: S. J. Clarke Publishing Co., 1912.

Dedmon, Emmet. *Fabulous Chicago*. New York: Random House, 1954.

Gilbert, Paul and Charles Lee Bryson. *Chicago and Its Makers*. Chicago: Felix Mendelsohn, 1929.

Hamilton, Raymond H. *The Epic of Chicago*. Chicago: Willett, Clark & Co, 1910.

Kirkland, Caroline., ed. *Chicago Yesterdays*. Chicago: Doughaday & Co., 1919.

Kirkland, Joseph. *The Story of Chicago*. Chicago: Dibble Publishing Co, 1892.

Kogan, Herman and Lloyd Wendt. *Pictorial History of Chicago*. New York: E. P. Putnam & Co., 1958.

Lewis, Lloyd and Henry Justin Smith. *Chicago, the History of Its Reputation*. New York: Harcourt, Brace & Co., 1929.

Longstreet, Stephen. *Chicago, 1860-1919*. New York: David McKay Co., Inc., 1973

McIlvaine, Mabel, ed. *Reminiscences of Chicago During the Forties and Fifties*. Chicago: The Lakeside Press, R. R. Donnelley & Sons, 1913.

Moses, John and Joseph Kirkland. *The History of Chicago, Illinois*. 2 Vols. Chicago: Munsell & Co., 1895.

Pierce, Bessie Louise. *A History of Chicago*. Chicago: University of Chicago Press, 1940.

"The Chicago Conspiracy." *Atlantic Monthly*. 16 (Jul. 1865): 108-20.D.

D. Histories of Cook County.

Andreas, A. T. *History of Cook County.* 1 Vol. Chicago: A. T. Andreas, Publisher, 1884.

Goodspeed, Weston A. and Daniel D. Healy. *History of Cook County.* 2 Vols. Chicago: Goodspeed Historical Ass'n, 1909.

2. Biographies:

Biographical Sketches of Leading Men of Chicago. Chicago: Wilson & St. Clair, 1868.

Cullum, General George W. *Biographical Register of Officers and Graduates of the United States Military Academy at West Point.* New York: James Miller, 1879.

Dictionary of American Biography. American Council of Learned Societies. New York:Scribner & Sons, 1928-33.

Eisenschiml, Otto. *Vermont General, the Unusual War Experiences of Edward Hastings Ripley, 1862-1865.* New York: Devin Adair Co., 1960.

Flynn, John J. *Hand Book of Chicago Biography.* 1893

Hall, Richard. *Stanley, An Adventurer Explored.* Boston: Houghton Mifflin Co., 1975.

Harpel, Charles. Obituary notices, 11 vol. CHS.

History of Medicine and Surgery and Physicians and Surgeons of Chicago. Chicago: Biographical Publishing Corp., 1922.

Hunt, Roger D., and Jack R. Brown. *Brevet Brigadier Generals in Blue.* Gaithersburg: Olde Soldier Books Inc., 1990. *Lifeof Mary Monholland, One of the Pioneer Sisters of the Order of Mercy in the West.* By a Member of the Order. Chicago: J. S. Hyland & Co., 1894.

Moody, William R. *The Life of Dwight L. Moody.* Chicago: Fleming R. Revell Co., 1900.

Temple, Wayne C., *Stephen A. Douglas, Freemason.* Bloomington: The Masonic Book Club, 1982.

Starr, Stephen Z. *Colonel Grenfell's Wars.* Baton Rouge: Louisiana State University Press, 1971.

Warner, Ezra. *Generals in Blue.* Baton Rouge: Louisiana Winslow, Charles S., *Biographical Sketches of Chicagoans.* 10 Vols. Chicago Public Library, 1948.State University Press, 1964.

3. Special Monographs:

Basler, Roy P. ed. *The Collected Works of Abraham Lincoln.* New Brunswick: Rutgers University Press, 1953.

Bonner, Thomas Neville. *Medicine in Chicago, 1850-1950.* Madison: American Research History Center, 1957.

Bryan, I. J. *History of Lincoln Park.* Chicago: The Commissioners, 1899.

Byrne, Frank L. "Prisons Pens of Suffering." *The Images of War.* 4 vols. Garden City: Doubleday & Co., 1983.

Clingman, Lewis B. Jr. "History of Camp Douglas." Master's thesis, De Paul University, 1942.

Dorris, Jonathan T. *Pardon and Amnesty under Lincoln and Johnson.* Westport: Greenwood Press, 1953.

Dyer. Frederick H. *A Compendium of the War of the Rebellion.* 2 vols. Dayton: Morningside Booshop, 1978.

Eppse, Merle R. *The Negro, Too, in American History.* Nashville: National Publication Co., 1943.

Hauser, Philip M., and Evelyn M. Kitagawa. *Local Community Fact Book for Chicago, 1950.* Chicago: Chicago Community Inventory, University of Chicago, 1953.

Hesseltine, William B. *Civil War Prisons: A Study in War Psychology.* Unger, N.Y.: American Classics, 1971. (First published in Ohio State University Press, Columbus, 1930).

Holderith, George L. "James A. Mulligan."
Master's thesis, Notre Dame University, 1932.

Holmes, Clay W. *The Elmira Prison Camp.* New York: G. P. Putnam & Sons, 1912.

Johannsen, Robert W. *Letters of Stephen A. Douglas.* Urbana: University of Illinois Press, 1961.

Johnson, Rossiter. *A History of the War of Secession.* New York: Wessels & Bissell Co., 1910.

Kelly, Dennis. "A History of Camp Douglas Illinois, Union Prison, 1861-1865." Ms, United States Department of the Interior, National Park Service, Southeast Region, 1989.

Klement, Frank L. *Dark Lanterns: Secret Political Societies, Conspiracies, and Treason Trials in the Civil War.* Baton Rouge: Louisiana State University Press, 1984.

Kubalanza, Joan Marie G. "A Comparative Study of Conditions at Two Civil War Prison Camps: Camp Douglas, Chicago, Illinois and Camp Sumpter, Andersonville, Georgia." Master's thesis, De Paul University, 1979.

Lesser, Hedwig F. *Civil War Prisons: A study of the conditions under which they operated.* Montgomery: University of Alabama Press, 1968.

Lindsley, John B. *Military Annals of Tennessee, Confederate.* Nashville: J. M. Lindsley & Co., 1886.

Locke, Rev. Clinton, D.D. "Grace Church." Rush-Presbyterian-St. Lukes's Medical Center Archives, Chicago.

Marshall, John A. *American Bastille: A History of the Illegal Arrests and Imprisonment of American Citizens during the Late Civil War.* New York: Da Capo Press, 1970.

Maxwell, William Quenton. *Lincoln's Fifth Wheel, The Political History of the United States Sanitary Commission.* New York: Longmans, Green & Co., 1956.

Moss, Rev. Lemuel. *Annals of the United States Christian Commission.* Philadelphia: J. B. Lippencott & Co., 1868.

Murdock, Eugene C. *One Million Men: The Civil War Draft in the North.* Madison: State Historical Society of Wisconsin, 1971.

Nolan, Alan T. *The Iron Brigade.* New York: Macmillan Publishing Co., 1961.

Robertson, John. *Michigan in the War.* Lansing: W. S. George & Co., 1882.

Rosenberger, Jesse L. *Through Three Centuries.* Chicago: University of Chicago Press, 1922.

Schreiner, Samuel A. Jr. *The Trials of Mrs. Lincoln.* New York: Donald I. Fine, Inc., 1987.

Sorensen, Mark W. "The Civil War Prisoner of War System." Ms, Illinois State Archives, 1978.

Story, Howard Kenneth. "Camp Douglas, 1861-1865." Master's thesis, Northwestern University, 1942.

Stover, John F. *History of the Illinois Central Railroad.* New York: Macmillan Publishing Co., 1975.

Terrell, W.H.H. *Indiana in the War of the Rebellion.* Indianapolis: 1960.

Wiley, Bell I. *The Life of Johnny Reb.* New York: Bobs- Merrill Co., 1962)

Winters, John D. *The Civil War in Louisiana.* Baton Rouge: Louisiana State University Press, 1963.

Wright, Marcus J. *Tennessee in the War.* New York: Ambrose Lee Publishing Co., 1908.

4. Articles and Essays in Periodicals, Annuals, and Publications of Learned Societies:

Angle, Paul M. "The Story of an Ordinary Man." *Journal of the Illinois State Historical Society.* 33 (Mar. 1940):229- 32.

Baird, Nancy D. "The Yellow Fever Plot." *Civil War Times.* 7 (Nov. 1974): 16-23.

Cabeen, Richard McP. "Camp Douglas and its Prisoner of War Letters." *Seventeenth American Philatelic Congress Year Book.* (1951): 76-100.

Castel, Albert. "Black Jack Logan." *Civil War Times.* 7 (Nov. 1976):4-10, 40-45.

Clark, James R. "The Cost of Capture." *Civil War Times.* 1 (Mar.1992):26-30.

Eisendrath, Joseph L. "Chicago's Camp Douglas, 1861-1865." *Journal of the Illinois State Historical Society.* 55 (Spring 1960):37-63.

Grimsley, Mark. "Ulysses S. Grant." *Civil War Times.* 7 (Feb. 1990):32-34.

Jackson, Luther P. "Free Negroes of Petersburg, Virginia." *The Journal of Negro History.* 12 (Jan. 1927):386-88.

Karlen, Harvey M., "Postal History of Camp Douglas, 1861- 1865." *The American Philatelist,* Journal of the American Philatelic Society. (Sep. 1979: 815-24; (Oct. 1979): 920- 29, 960.

Kaufhold, John. "The Elmira Observatory." *Civil War Times.* 4(Jul. 1977):30-35.

Long, E. B. "Camp Douglas: A Hellish Den." *Chicago History.* 1 (Fall 1970):83-95.

McCaffrey, James. "A Short History of the Civil War Sutler." *Civil War Times.* 4 (Jun. 1985):36-39.

Meketa, Jacqueline. "A Poetic Plea From Prison." *Civil War Times.* 30 (Mar. 1991):28-32.

Priscilla Pearson and Robert D. Hoffsommer, ed. "In Vinculis: A Prisoner of War, Part II," *Civil War Times* 9 (Jan. 1985):26-33.

Robbins, Peggy. "The Greatest Scoundrel." *Civil War Times.* 5 (Nov. 1992):54-57, 89-90.

Sabine, David B. "The Fifth Wheel." *Civil War Times.* 2 (May. 1980):14-23.

Taylor, John M. "Grover Cleveland and the Rebel Banners." *Civil War Times.* 4 (Sep./Oct. 1993):22-24.

Todd, Gary T. "An Invalid Corps." *Civil War Times.* 8 (Dec. 1985):10-19.

Wesley, Charles W. "Negroes in the Confederate Army." *The Journal of Negro History.* 4 (Jul. 1919):239-53.

Wiley, Bell I. "The Common Soldier of the Civil War." *Civil War Times.* 4 (Jul. 1973). "Soldier Newspapers of the Civil War." *Civil War Times.* 4 (Jul. 1977):20-29.

5. Miscellaneous:

Black's Medical Dictionary. Edited by C. W. A. Havard. 39th Edition. Totowa: Barnes & Noble, 1987.2

Confederate Soldiers, Sailors and Civilians Who Died As Prisoners of War at Camp Douglas, Chicago, Ill., 1862-1865. Kalamazoo: Edgar Gray Publications.

Halpin & Bailey's Chicago Street Directories, 1861-1867.

LIST OF ILLUSTRATIONS

INDEX

CHRONOLOGY OF EVENTS
1861
12 Apr......Fort Sumter fired upon.

15 Apr......Large war meetings in Chicago.

3 Jun.......Death of Senator Stephen A. Douglas.

30 Sep......Camp Douglas opens for recruiting and training.

7 Oct.......Col. William Hoffman named to manage U.S. prisons.

1 Nov.......First barracks are completed at Camp Douglas.

18 Dec......Troops mutiny.

1862.
16 Feb......Fort Donelson falls to Union army.

20 Feb......Prisoners from Donelson arrive at Camp Douglas.

21 Feb......Col. Joseph H. Tucker takes command of Camp.

24 Feb......Mayor of Chicago warns that city is in danger.

25 Feb......Rebel officers and their slaves leave Camp Douglas.

26 Feb......Col. Tucker replaced by Col. James A. Mulligan.

6-7 Apr......Battle of Shiloh.

10 Apr......Island No. 10 captured by the Union army.

16 Apr......Prisoners arrive from Shiloh and Island No. 10.

21 Apr......Prison population reaches 8,962.

25 Apr......Mass escapes foiled by Col. Mulligan.

19 May......Chicago investigates sanitary conditions at camp.

14 Jun......Col. Mulligan replaced by Col. Daniel Cameron.

19 Jun......Col. Cameron replaced by Col. Tucker.

30 Jun......U.S. Sanitary Commission condemns Camp Douglas.

8 Jul.......Martial law is declared around camp.

9 Jul.......Mulligan accused of mismanagement.

15 Jul......Five women and a child found among the prisoners.

23 Jul......Prisoners launch general escape attempt.

4 Aug.......Col. Tucker arrests former mayor for aiding escapes.

12 Aug......Charges filed against Col. Mulligan.

28 Aug......Col. Tucker ordered to ship prisoners for exchange.

27 Sep......Camp emptied of prisoners.

28 Sep......Paroled Union prisoners arrive under General Tyler.

30 Sep......Gen. Tyler relieves Tucker of command.

1 Oct.......Parolees mutiny and burn barracks and fences.

11 Nov......Smallpox strikes Camp Douglas.

23 Oct......Tyler calls in the regular army to end mutiny.

13 Dec......Tyler replaced by Col. Cameron.

27 Dec......Camp emptied of most parolees.

30 Dec......Col. Cameron irelieved of command.

1863.
1 Jan.......Col. Tucker resigns from army.

5 Jan.......Battle of Stones's River, Tennessee.

6 Jan.......Brig. Gen. Joseph Ammen commands Camp Douglas.

11 Jan......Battle of Arkansas Post.

30 Jan......Prisoners at camp number 3,800 from recent battles.

31 Mar......Smallpox epidemic rages at camp.

7 Apr.......Infected prisoners sent to Baltimore for exchange.

13 Apr......General Ammen replaced by Col. Cameron.

19 Apr......Col. Cameron replaced by Capt. John C. Phillips.

4 May.......Camp emptied of prisoners.

12 May......Captain J. S. Putnam commands Camp Douglas.

17 Aug......Morgan's Raiders arrive, including black prisoners.

18 Aug......Col. Charles V. De Land named commandant.

22 Oct......Daring escape made by Morgan's men.

6 Nov.......Running water toilets begin operating.

16 Nov......Retaliation against prisoners begins.

3 Dec.......100 prisoners escape through tunnel.

16 Dec......Gen. William W. Orme commands District and Post.

19 Dec......Orme investigates food contractors.

30 Dec......Blizzard and sub-zero cold strike camp.

1864.
1 Jan.......Orme moves to release black prisoners of war.

3 Jan.......Orme places new restrictions on prisoners.

18 Jan......Prison population reaches 5,616.

28 Jan......New prison square is established.

16 Feb......Col. Hoffman requests court martial for De Land.

19 Feb......Remaining black prisoners released.

1 Mar......De Land is replaced by Col. James C. Strong.

2 May.......Orme resigns. Col. Benjamin J. Sweet appointed.

1 Jun.......Prisoner's Square rearranged to prevent escapes.

11 Jun......Confederate agents plan attack on Camp Douglas.

1 Jul.......Sweet ordered to take personal charge at camp.

4 Jul.......Attack on camp postponed to 20 July.

20 Jul......Attack postponed to 29 August.

10 Aug......Sutler barred from selling food to prisoners.

15 Aug..... Smallpox cemetery opens across from camp.

18 Aug......Hoffman orders prisoners' cooking stoves removed.

28 Aug......Alleged conspiracy to attack Camp collapses.

28 Sep......Sweet warns that escaping prisoners will be shot.

8 Oct.......Prison count is 7,402.

31 Oct......Mass escape thwarted. Ten prisoners wounded.

6 Nov.......Col Sweet begins arresting "conspirators."

5 Dec.......Remnants of Hood's army crowd into Camp.

31 Dec......Number of prisoners rises to 12,082.

1865.
12 Jan......Inquiry ordered into shooting of prisoners.

31 Jan......Guards go on drunken rampage.

1 Feb.......11,711 prisoners in camp.

13 Feb......First prisoner exchange since April 1863 begins.

5 Jul.......Only 30 prisoners remain, and guards withdrawn.

29 Jul......University of Chicago connects to camp sewers.

2 Aug.......All property and buildings at camp ordered sold.

29 Sep......General Sweet resigns.

8 Dec.......U.S. begins search for over 4,000 dead prisoners.

24 Dec......Last buildings sold at camp.

1866.
8 Jan.......Last of Camp Douglas land returned to owners.

2 Mar.......Camp Douglas officially ceases to exist.

27 Apr......Prisoners' remains found in pauper's graves.

1 Dec.......Only 1,402 graves identified.

1867.
13 Apr......Begin removal of Confederate dead to Oak Woods.

1882.
25 Jan......Some prisoner remains found near former camp.

1895.
30 May.....Ex-Confederates dedicate monument at Oak Woods.

1899.
20 May......Confederate graves disappearing into swamp.

1903.
Oak Woods receives Federal grant to save the burial plot.

1992.
Furor in Chicago over proposed landmark status for the monument.